MW01092273

FOUNDATIONAL CONCEPTS IN NEUROSCIENCE

A Brain–Mind Odyssey

The Norton Series on Interpersonal Neurobiology

Louis Cozolino, PhD, Series Editor

Allan N. Schore, PhD, Series Editor, 2007–2014

Daniel J. Siegel, MD, Founding Editor

The field of mental health is in a tremendously exciting period of growth and conceptual reorganization. Independent findings from a variety of scientific endeavors are converging in an interdisciplinary view of the mind and mental well-being. An interpersonal neurobiology of human development enables us to understand that the structure and function of the mind and brain are shaped by experiences, especially those involving emotional relationships.

The Norton Series on Interpersonal Neurobiology provides cutting-edge, multidisciplinary views that further our understanding of the complex neurobiology of the human mind. By drawing on a wide range of traditionally independent fields of research—such as neurobiology, genetics, memory, attachment, complex systems, anthropology, and evolutionary psychology—these texts offer mental health professionals a review and synthesis of scientific findings often inaccessible to clinicians. The books advance our understanding of human experience by finding the unity of knowledge, or consilience, that emerges with the translation of findings from numerous domains of study into a common language and conceptual framework. The series integrates the best of modern science with the healing art of psychotherapy.

A NORTON PROFESSIONAL BOOK

Dedicated to My Teachers

Contents

List of Figures

Preface: From Molecules to Consciousness

Neuroscience—the science of brain and behavior—is one of the most exciting fields in the landscape of contemporary science. Its rapid growth over the last several decades has spawned many discoveries and a large number of popular books. Contemporary news is filled with stories about the brain, brain chemistry, and behavior. Photos and drawings of brains and nerve cells grace the pages of newspapers and magazines. Neuroplasticity—the capacity of neural connections to change and reorganize—has become a buzzword. The notion that your mind can change your brain is pervasive.

We read that drugs used to treat mental conditions such as depression, anxiety, and psychosis are among the best-selling pharmaceuticals in history. Ads for these drugs depict neurons and neurotransmitter molecules. One hears that brain science is being used increasingly in the courtroom—that brain structure and functional activity are used in arguing for guilt or innocence in accusations of criminal behavior. It is said that advertising agencies are spending millions of dollars to study the neural activity in people's brains when they look at ads or use products. What is going on with all of this? How are we to understand fact from fiction?

My intention in this book is to provide the backstory—a description of how nervous systems work and how the workings of our nervous system relate to our mind and our behavior. My description is concise yet thorough, rigorous yet easy to follow (and, I hope, fun to read).

For more than twenty years I have taught a class on introductory neuroscience at the University of California, Berkeley. Hundreds of students take this class every year. Many are freshmen in their first year of college. Some are seniors just before graduation. Students having every sort of disciplinary interest take the class—biological and physical sciences, social sciences, engineering, economics, business, arts, and humanities. Some come to the class already having a passion for science. Others are afraid of science and sometimes have particularly strong aversive reactions to chemistry. Occasionally a few high school students or a few graduate students take the class. And there are generally a few retired professionals and other folks from the Berkeley community sitting in on lectures.

My aim as instructor is to provide a comprehensive overview of brain structure and function—beginning with atoms and molecules, building up to membranes and cells, progressing to neurons, neural circuits, and sensory organs, and then on to perception, memory, language, emotion, sleep, and dreams. A theme throughout the semester is the mystery of how mental experience (which is all we ever truly are able to know) is related to the workings of our brain and body—the deep mystery of mind and consciousness.

That class is the framework for this book. As such, the book is comprehensive enough to use as a text in an introductory course on neuroscience. It gives quite a bit of detail about the structure and function—largely at the molecular and cellular levels—of the human nervous system. Most of the material in this book is basic enough that it will not readily be outdated. Textbooks that endeavor to keep up with the very latest developments need to be rewritten and updated frequently. An instructor using this book for a class can always keep things current by supplementing with additional material drawn from contemporary neuroscience research. This book provides the foundation.

I have taught this subject not only in university classrooms but also in a variety of continuing-education workshop settings for interested individuals of all kinds. I have taught various components of this material in workshops held in the unique setting of the Esalen Institute on the California coast, and I have been privileged to teach neuroscience to Tibetan Buddhist monks and nuns in India as part of a science-education program initiated by the Dalai Lama. In all these diverse settings, this approach to the subject—exacting yet affable—has been well received.

Not just for use in the classroom, this book is also meant for *anyone* interested in learning about how the brain works. It is for those of you who wish to understand just where that news article on brain scans is coming from, or how to appreciate a story about antidepressant drugs. I develop everything as much as possible from the ground up, so that no specific technical background is required to read this book. For those not familiar with molecular structure diagrams, I hope you will quickly come to appreciate their simplicity, beauty, and utility. My intention is to make even the most complex material easy and fun to understand, at least in its essential features.

A goal is for readers to come away with some intuition about how the brain works, to appreciate the beauty and power of molecular and cellular explanations, and at the same time to appreciate that the unfathomable complexity of living systems places substantial limits on any sort of seemingly simple explanation. This last point is frequently forgotten.

Contemporary physical, chemical, and biological sciences have enjoyed awesome success over the last several centuries in accounting for a great deal of what we observe. From the farthest reaches of the universe, billions of light years away, to the inner structure of atomic nuclei, physical theories provide a stunningly powerful and coherent explanatory framework. Living systems, even with their extraordinary complexity, appear to be falling nicely within this remarkable explanatory framework. However, scientific understanding of the human mind—and how our capacity for conscious awareness relates not only to the brain but also to everything else we believe we know about the physical universe—is considered to be among the greatest mysteries in modern science, perhaps *the* greatest mystery. It is my hope that this book will provide the foundation from which to more deeply appreciate this awesome subject.

FOUNDATIONAL CONCEPTS IN NEUROSCIENCE

A Brain–Mind Odyssey

CHAPTER 1

Origins

Early in the winter of 1994, a trio of speleologists made an amazing find: a limestone cavern in the south of France containing some of the most spectacular examples of prehistoric art ever seen. The charcoal, ochre, and carved wall paintings of Chauvet Cave date from more than thirty thousand years ago and are among the oldest currently known examples of Paleolithic cave art. Before its modern discovery in December 1994, it is likely no one had entered this cave for more than twenty thousand years.

A number of other caves in this region of southwestern Europe are also filled with wall paintings dating from ten thousand or more years ago. Often these drawings are deep inside the caves, far removed from the entrances and completely impervious to light from outside—places of deep darkness. The Paleolithic humans who made these drawings carried torches and stone lamps and built small fires to illuminate their artistic undertakings. It is also likely, given the opportunity afforded by these nether regions so isolated from outside light, that these ancient humans used the darkness as an aid to inner exploration.

In darkness is the absence of the compelling visual stimuli that fill so much of our daily lives. Without these distractions, darkness can become a catalyst to enter the inner recesses of the mind, to wander in the richness of internal mental experience. In contemporary preindustrial societies, great value is often placed on the capacity to explore the inner world of the mind. Some individuals are said to be particularly skilled in accessing states of mind that are sources of knowledge and power, which may then be used in the service of others in the community. These folks are the shamans, the healers in their communities, who are believed by some to communicate with animals, plants, and other elements of nature in ways not explicable within the worldview of contemporary science. Much of modern society has lost connection with these traditions, considering them ill-informed and primitive, inconsistent with the latest science-based knowledge about our world. Nonetheless, shamans are respected members of societies all over the world, and have been throughout recorded history.

Animals are the prominent images in these cave paintings (Fig. 1.1): individual beasts, groups of animals, even figures that appear to be fusions of animal and human forms. Because present-day shamans often speak of connecting with ani-

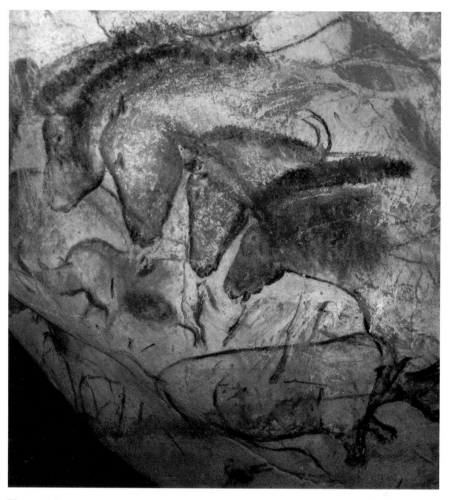

Figure 1.1. Masterpiece of Paleolithic art: four horses and other animals, drawn in charcoal on the wall of Chauvet Cave.

mals as sources of knowledge and power, it has been proposed that at least some of these ancient cave paintings may represent shamanic connections between the ancient humans and the local animals. Moreover, contemporary shamans sometimes use darkness, including the darkness of caves, as an aid to their shamanic journeying. Caves have an otherworldly quality about them—evoking magic, archetypal descent into an underworld, weirdness, and connection to other realms. Of course, we don't know what the cave painters of thirty thousand years ago were experiencing—what they may have been thinking and feeling as they made their drawings. But given the sophistication of their drawings, it is reasonable to hypothesize that these folks had internal mental worlds of significant complexity.

How far back in time does the human experience go? The plains of eastern Africa are where most of the oldest fossils of human ancestors have been found. These great savannas are believed to be a principal site of ancient human evolution. A dramatic depiction of this is in the opening scenes of Stanley Kubrick's (1928–1999) acclaimed 1968 film *2001: A Space Odyssey*.

Picture this: Africa, perhaps four million years ago—zebra, antelope, pigs, and cats roam the savanna foraging food, attacking and being attacked. We are introduced to early hominins, the name given to the group of primates that includes modern humans and the ancestors of modern humans going back perhaps five million years. These protohumans are shown quietly gathering food, socially interacting in various ways, living with some fear of attack by predator animals like big cats, comforted by companionship with one another. The hominins are social creatures, living together in small groups or tribes. We witness an encounter of one tribe with another over the use of a watering hole. The encounter is not friendly; there is much screaming, jumping around, and gesticulating. Finally one of the tribes backs down and departs. Although the encounter is not friendly, it stops short of violence.

Eventually there comes a discovery by one of these hominin characters that bones can be used as tools. A femur (thigh) bone from a dead animal is found to make an excellent tool with which to bash things. As such, it is useful as a weapon to aid in the hunting and killing of animals for food. It is a dramatic discovery. And then, there is another intense scene where the same two groups of hominins encounter one another again at the watering hole. As before, the encounter entails much yelping and jumping around and gesticulating. However, things are different now, in that one of the tribes, but not the other, has made the discovery that bones can be weapons. In the midst of yelling and posturing, one of the hominins whacks his adversary on the head. Yikes! Then his compatriots jump into the act, brandishing their bone weapons and repeatedly striking the downed creature. Clearly the poor fellow has been killed. The scene is depicted as possibly the first time in human history that a hominin willfully and intentionally kills a conspecific. It is portrayed with dramatic intensity and depicted as a powerful moment in the history of human evolution, as it may well have been—even if little or no evidence exists that such things actually happened!

What has been pieced together of ancient human evolution comes largely from the study of fossils discovered in eastern and southern Africa. The oldest fossils considered to be in the category of direct human ancestor are generally thought to be in the range of five to six million years old. Hominin fossils have been classified into three primary groups, or genera: *Ardipithecus*, *Australopithecus*, and *Homo*. A number of different species names have been introduced over the years. A few are listed here, in order of those that lived longest ago to those of more recent eras:

Ardipithecus ramidus	~4.4 million years ago
Australopithecus afarensis	~3 to 4 million years ago
Australopithecus africanus	~2 to 3 million years ago
Australopithecus robustus	~1 to 2.5 million years ago
Homo habilis	~1.4 to 2.3 million years ago
Homo erectus	~200,000 to 1.9 million years ago
Homo neanderthalensis	~30,000 to 300,000 years ago
Homo sapiens	~200,000 years ago to now

Only the last in this list, *Homo sapiens*—our own species—is alive today. All others have vanished. These dates are approximate and subject to alteration as more is discovered from the fossil and archeological record. Even the names may change. The field of hominin paleontology is dynamic, and much presumably still lies out there, buried, waiting to be uncovered and interpreted.

Examination of the fossil fragments of ancient skulls allows us to estimate the brain sizes of these early hominins:

Ardipithecus ramidus	~350 cubic centimeters (cc)
Australopithecus africanus	~500 cc
Homo habilis	~650 cc
Homo erectus	~1200 cc
Homo neanderthalensis	~1400 cc
Homo sapiens	~1400 cc

There has been a substantial increase in the size of the brain over the several million years of hominin evolution. Part of this increase can be attributed to an increase in the size of the body; the typical *Homo sapiens* is larger than the typical *Australopithecus*, and larger animals tend to have larger brains. However, there is more to this bigger brain than increased body size. It appears that the size of the hominin brain expanded rapidly during the last two million years of our evolutionary history. Accompanying the expansion of the brain has been the development of ever more sophisticated behaviors: tool use, nuanced social interaction, language, mathematical skill, complex problem-solving abilities, and a capacity to construct elaborate explanatory frameworks to aid in understanding our world.

This book is about our brain and its connection with our behavior. One of those connections is our capacity to kill our fellow humans, something that was portrayed in very primordial form in *2001: A Space Odyssey* and something that is very much a major issue in the modern world. The ability to create and deploy powerful weapons, a result of our sophisticated intelligence and ability to understand the world through physical and mathematical reasoning, has formed a deadly marriage with our primal capacity for fear and violence.

Fortunately, we also have other capacities, notably a tremendous capability for kindness, trust, love, and compassion. The consistency of the European Paleolithic cave paintings over a period of more than twenty thousand years (from thirty thousand to ten thousand years ago), suggests that stable, perhaps relatively peaceful cultures existed for thousands of years. Martin Luther King (1929–1968), in receiving the Nobel Peace Prize in 1964, said in his acceptance speech: "I refuse to accept the cynical notion that nation after nation must spiral down a militaristic stairway. . . . I believe that unarmed truth and unconditional love will have the final word in reality." John Lennon (1940–1980) and *The Beatles* put it simply: "All you need is love." We honor at least some individuals who speak this way. And contemporary research in the biology and psychology of emotion demonstrates that the human capacity for compassion and kindness is strong—perhaps the strongest and most natural of our behavioral tendencies.

In *2001: A Space Odyssey*, when the ancient protohuman has accomplished the deed of killing another ancient protohuman and thus secured the dominance of that particular tribe at that particular moment, he (or she) yells in victory and throws the femur-bone weapon high into the air. The camera catches it turning end over end, flying upward against a blue sky. When it reaches the top of its arc and begins to fall back down to Earth again, the spiraling bone becomes a spiraling space station, in orbit around planet Earth millions of years in the future. The year is presumably around 2001, still decades into the future at the time the film was made.

Later in the film a spaceship with a crew of astronauts leaves Earth on an interplanetary mission to the vicinity of Jupiter. Because it takes a great deal of time to travel from Earth to Jupiter, most of the crew is asleep in a state of cryogenic hibernation or suspended animation. Two members of the crew remain awake to oversee the operation of the spaceship, but most of the ship's operation is under the control of a computer called HAL. Everything appears very tranquil.

Then, when one of the two nonhibernating crew is outside the spaceship making repairs on an antenna, HAL initiates actions that result in the astronaut's lifeline being severed, and he drifts off into space. The other nonhibernating astronaut, named David Bowman, then exits the ship in a pod to attempt a rescue of his comrade, or at least recover his body. At this point, HAL shuts off the life support for the crew who are asleep in suspended animation. They all quickly die in their sleep. When astronaut Bowman attempts to reenter the spaceship, HAL locks him out and will not let him in. A conversation takes place over the radio during which the astronaut first instructs, and then orders, HAL to let him back into the ship. HAL responds: "I'm sorry, Dave, I'm afraid I can't do that." Then: "This mission is too important to allow you to jeopardize it." Then, finally: "This conversation is over." In the movie, HAL certainly appears to be operating as if it has intentions, reasoning, and even emotions. My question is this: does HAL have a mind?

To even begin to answer this, it is essential to first decide what we mean by *mind*. Mind is not so solid a thing to define as is bone, cell, or molecule. For the purpose of initiating discussion, I will adopt the following definition of *mind*: the collection of mental experiences. By mental experiences I mean our subjective (first-person, internal) experiences, including our thoughts, feelings, perceptions (visual, auditory, olfactory, gustatory, tactile), mental images, and sense of self.

The term *consciousness* is often also used in this context. By *consciousness* I will mean the capacity to be aware. Aware of what? We are aware of our mental experiences—our thoughts, feelings, and perceptions. Because to have a mind is to have mental experiences, and to have consciousness is to be aware of these mental experiences, these definitions of *mind* and *consciousness* are very closely related. As a result, one often finds the two terms used interchangeably.

What would it mean to have thoughts and feelings without awareness? This may happen, for example, in dreaming during sleep. Our dreams are filled with thoughts, feelings, and other mental phenomena—although we are seemingly not aware of this at the time of dreaming. We may become aware—when we awaken and remember a dream, or in states of lucid dreaming—but often we are not aware. (There is the additional complication of the possibility that we are aware during dreaming but we simply don't remember being aware. Clearly, the issue of awareness is subtle. We return to this in later chapters.)

Another example would be the Freudian unconscious, Sigmund Freud's (1856–1939) concept of how cognitive content out of our awareness may nonetheless have substantial impact on our behavior. However, precisely because this content is mental, it has the potential to enter awareness. This is the task in psychoanalysis: bringing unconscious things related to one's behavior into consciousness, into awareness, where they can be subjected to analysis and become amenable to change.

In any case, to have mind or consciousness by these definitions is to have an experience of what it is like to *be* a particular person, or animal, or organism, or—who's to say at this point?—thing. Thus, to ask whether HAL has a mind (by this definition) is to ask whether HAL has an experience of what it is like to be HAL. For if HAL has mental states like thoughts, feelings, and perceptions, then HAL, through its experience of those mental states, would have an experience of being HAL. A key feature here is that consciousness and mental experience are irreducibly subjective phenomena.

So, what do you think about HAL? Does HAL have a mind?

It is clear that HAL is behaving as if it might have subjective mental states of experience. But, really, who's to say? HAL may even say that it is experiencing feelings, but how can we know this? HAL may execute sophisticated intentional behaviors, but we have no way of knowing if this is accompanied by mental experience.

What are the conditions for mental experience to take place? This is an unanswered question in science. We know the human capacity for mental experience is related to the functioning of our brain and nervous system. There is a lot of evidence for this, and some is discussed in this book. However, does this mean that something akin to a brain and nervous system is necessary for mental experience, for mind? Most neurobiologists, psychologists, cognitive scientists, and philosophers believe that this must be the case, that there cannot be mind without something like a brain. Nevertheless, the fact that brain and mind are intimately related does not prove that mind is solely a product of brain and nervous system physiology and nothing more. This brings us face-to-face with perhaps the greatest question in all of science, and a longtime subject of great debate—what has been called the *mind-body problem*: what is the relationship between our mental experience and the physiology of our body and brain? I maintain that this question contains within it the most profound questions we can ponder: Who are we? What is our relation to everything else we believe we know and understand about physical reality? Indeed, what is the nature of reality?

Thank you, HAL.

CHAPTER **2**

Nervous Systems and Brains

Who are we? How are we related to everything else we believe we know and understand about the universe? What modern science brings to these age-old questions are a powerfully successful explanatory framework and a technical capacity to conduct physical and chemical investigations of living organisms. William James (1842–1910), a pioneer in the modern scientific study of mind, wrote in his classic 1890 book *The Principles of Psychology*:

> If the nervous communication be cut off between the brain and other parts, the experiences of those other parts are non-existent for the mind. The eye is blind, the ear deaf, the hand insensible and motionless. And conversely, if the brain be injured, consciousness is abolished or altered, even although every other organ in the body be ready to play its normal part.

Damage to the brain is known to be associated with specific changes in mental functioning. Wherever mental experience is coming from, the brain is clearly involved.

Figuring out how brains and nervous systems work has become one of the most exciting arenas of contemporary science. The nervous system is a network within the body that functions to manipulate external and internal information. It is specialized for rapid communication of signals throughout the body, and the brain is considered to be the locus of central control in the nervous system. Animals presumably have nervous systems to facilitate movement through the world. Collection and analysis of sensory information and coordination with the mechanisms of movement are needed to safely accomplish the task of moving around in an environment that is often challenging and sometimes unpredictable. Plants and fungi, the other kingdoms of multicellular organisms, do not move around in the fashion of animals and have evolved other, nonneural ways to flourish.

The human brain (together with the brains of a few other mammals) is perhaps the most complex structure known. This complexity is embodied in its makeup, consisting of several hundreds of billions of cells interconnected by hundreds of trillions of connections. Each of these connections is a locus of signal transfer between cells, so at all times there are vast networks of cells intercommunicating in some manner. The complexity of these networks of intercellular communication is staggering.

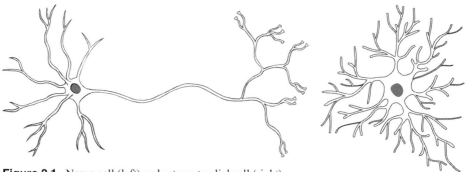

Figure 2.1. Nerve cell (left) and astrocyte glial cell (right).

Brains are made up of two general classes of cells: neurons and glia (Fig. 2.1). It is currently estimated that there are around a hundred billion (10^{11}) nerve cells (neurons) in the human brain and at least that number of glial cells (glia). The cellular units of signal transmission are generally considered to be the neurons, although it is now appreciated that many glia, especially the astrocyte glia, are also directly involved in signaling.

Animal nervous systems have been undergoing evolutionary refinement for hundreds of millions of years, and millions of years were required for the complexity of the human brain to develop among the primates. How far back in animal evolution do nervous systems go? Sponges are ancient animals, believed to have come on the scene more than half a billion years ago. As far as is presently known, sponges do not contain nerve cells or any sort of nervous system. Hydra are tiny (usually smaller than an inch) aquatic animals that have a very simple nervous system—a loosely connected network of a small number of cells, allowing for simple signal communication throughout their body. The jellyfish, distant cousins of hydra, also possess relatively simple neural networks (Fig. 2.2).

Figure 2.2. Compass jellyfish, *Chrysaora hysoscella*, from the spectacular 1904 book *Kunstformen der Natur* (*Artforms of Nature*) by Ernst Haeckel.

Figure 2.3. Planarian nervous system.

The tiny nematode or roundworm *Caenorhabditis elegans* is an animal that has, since the 1970s, been widely studied by biologists interested in molecular, cellular, and developmental biology. It is small (about 1 millimeter [1 mm] in length) and somewhat transparent and has a relatively simple organismal structure, at least for an animal that is able to manifest some degree of behavioral sophistication. Behaviors of *C. elegans* include navigation through the soil environment in which they live using olfactory and thermal cues. The nervous system of *C. elegans* is pretty simple; there are only 302 neurons, and the location, connectivity, and developmental history of each and every one of them have been determined by researchers. That is, the complete wiring diagram of the *C. elegans* nervous system is known.

A bit larger (typically several millimeters long), and quite a bit more complex in structure than nematodes, are the planaria, flatworms found in both aquatic and terrestrial environments. The planarian nervous system contains an extended network of interconnected neurons, together with two clusters of neurons at the head end of the worm (Fig. 2.3). Some neurobiologists consider these clusters to represent a primitive brain.

Insects clearly have complex brains. They also execute complex behaviors. The tiny fruit fly *Drosophila* has been extensively studied by biologists for more than a century and has been a focus of neurobiological research for several decades now. Its brain is less than 0.5 mm in width and contains around 150,000 neurons.

Many hundreds of millions of years of evolutionary variation and selection have formed the backstory for the brains of contemporary vertebrate animals—fish, amphibians, reptiles, birds, and mammals. The basic structure of all vertebrate animal brains is similar and can be represented as shown in Figure 2.4. The vertebrate brain develops in the embryo when a tubular structure (the neural tube) folds in and then closes off and expands at one end (on the left side in the diagram in Fig. 2.4). The interior spaces of the tube will become the ventricles (fluid-filled internal spaces) in the mature brain.

If we examine the external structure of brains from various vertebrate animals, we observe general similarities. The embryonic forebrain, midbrain, and hindbrain regions expand in the mature brain to contain millions of cells organized into distinct anatomical structures. The forebrain is dominated by the cerebrum, the midbrain by the optic tectum, and the hindbrain by the medulla and the cerebellum. As one moves from the evolutionarily older fish, amphibians, and reptiles to the evolu-

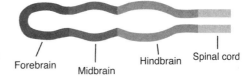

Figure 2.4. Basic plan of the vertebrate brain.

Forebrain   Midbrain   Hindbrain   Spinal cord

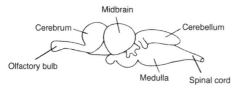
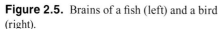
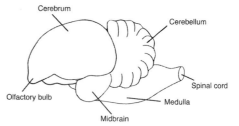

Figure 2.5. Brains of a fish (left) and a bird (right).

tionarily more recent birds and mammals, the size of the cerebrum increases relative to the rest of the brain (see Figs. 2.5 and 2.6).

In many mammalian brains, a distinctive feature may be observed in the structure of the cerebrum: rather than being smooth, the cerebrum often has bumps and grooves. The bumps and grooves are called *gyri* (singular: *gyrus*) and *sulci* (singular: *sulcus*), respectively, and are a consequence of the cerebrum in many mammals being a highly folded structure. While mice, rats, and squirrels do not exhibit this cerebral folding, capybaras (the world's largest rodents), as well as dogs, cats, and primates, all have folding of the outer layer of the cerebrum. This outer layer is called the cerebral cortex (*cortex* in Latin means bark, or outer layer).

In the human brain, the cerebral cortex is actually a sheet of neural tissue, around 3 millimeters thick (about 1/8 inch), with its thickness varying from region to region. The sheet is highly folded so that its large size can fit inside the skull. If the cerebral cortex could be carefully removed from the human brain, unfolded and laid flat, it would be about the size of a small newspaper opened up, around 2.5 square feet.

Figure 2.7 shows two views of the human brain: dorsal (top) and lateral (side). Many gyri and sulci are visible. Some prominent features are indicated. Among these are the four lobes of the cerebral cortex: frontal, parietal, occipital, and temporal. There are actually eight lobes, four in the right hemisphere and four in the left hemisphere.

There are several prominent landmark grooves: the central sulcus separates the frontal lobe from the parietal lobe, the lateral fissure separates the temporal lobe from the frontal and parietal lobes, and the very prominent longitudinal fissure divides the right and left cerebral hemispheres. The boundary between the occipital lobe and the temporal and parietal lobes is not so clear at the gross anatomical level. Figure 2.8 gives two more views of the human brain: ventral (bottom or underside)

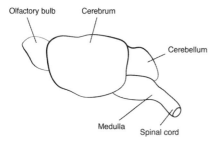

Figure 2.6. Brain of a mouse (a mammal); the cerebrum has covered over the midbrain (compare with Fig. 2.5).

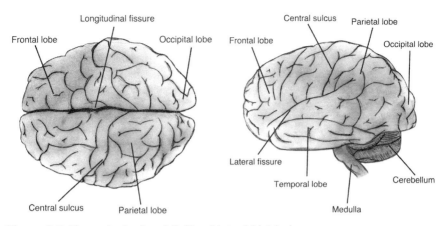

Figure 2.7. Human brain: dorsal (left) and lateral (right) views.

and medial (inside, revealed by cutting the brain in half down the middle, along the longitudinal fissure). Cranial nerves are described in Chapter 7. The corpus callosum is a bundle of approximately 200 million nerve fibers connecting the right and left cerebral hemispheres. The diencephalon, a structure located between the base of the cerebral cortex and the midbrain, consists largely of the thalamus and hypothalamus. The medulla, pons, and midbrain are collectively called the brainstem. Some definitions of the human brainstem also include all or part of the diencephalon. And some definitions include the cerebellum.

Some of the most beautiful drawings ever produced of human anatomy were published in 1543, in a classic book by Andreas Vesalius (1514–1564), a physician who lived and taught in Italy. His book was called *De Humani Corporis Fabrica*, which translates as *On the Fabric of the Human Body*, and was spectacularly illustrated by one or more professional artists who had carefully witnessed Vesalius's dissections of human bodies.

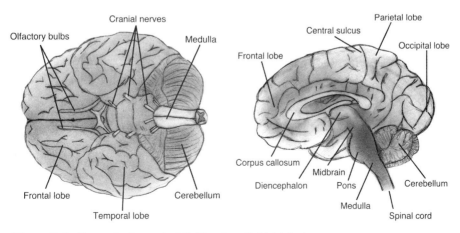

Figure 2.8. Human brain: ventral (left) and medial (right) views.

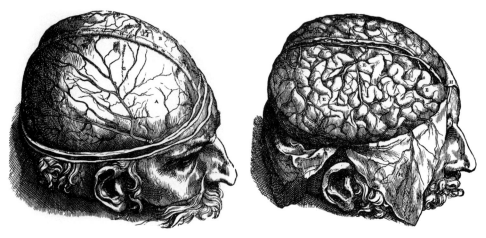

Figure 2.9. Open human skull with dura intact (left) and with dura peeled back (right), from Andreas Vesalius's *De Humani Corporis Fabrica* (1543).

If the hard protection of the bony skull is removed (Fig. 2.9, left), one sees covering the brain a skin-like sheet of tissue called the *dura mater*, from the Latin words meaning "hard or tough mother." This can be peeled away (Fig. 2.9, right) to reveal another, much more delicate layer of tissue covering the brain—the *arachnoid*, from the Latin meaning "like a spider web." Beneath the arachnoid tissue and closest to the brain is a third delicate layer called the *pia mater*, Latin for "soft or tender mother." Between the arachnoid and pia layers is the subarachnoid space. This space contains the cerebrospinal fluid, a liquid that cushions the brain inside the skull and transports soluble substances throughout the central nervous system. The dura, arachnoid, and pia are collectively called the *meninges*. If the meninges becomes inflamed as a result of infection or other process, this condition is called *meningitis*, an extremely serious occurrence because of its close proximity to the brain.

Vesalius, as well as other early anatomists, noted that the brain was highly interconnected via fiber pathways to the entire body (Fig. 2.10). There were fibers connecting the brain with the sensory organs: the eyes, ears, nose, and tongue. There were fibers connecting the brain with the heart, and lungs, and digestive system. And there were fibers connecting the spinal cord—which was contiguous with the brain—with muscles throughout the body. It seemed likely that extensive communication of some sort was taking place between the brain and all parts of the body.

One of the early thinkers on signaling in the nervous system was René Descartes (1596–1650). Born in France and living much of his adult life in the Netherlands, he was a key figure in the history of Western philosophy and science. Descartes was interested in how the human body worked, how we are able to perceive the world, and how the actions of the body are related to the subjective mental experiences of mind. Among his early writings, when he was in his thirties, were essays on the world (*Le Monde*) and on man (*L'Homme*). These were published only after he had died. Some say he was worried about publication in part because these essays addressed big questions about the nature of reality, perception, and mind. Descartes

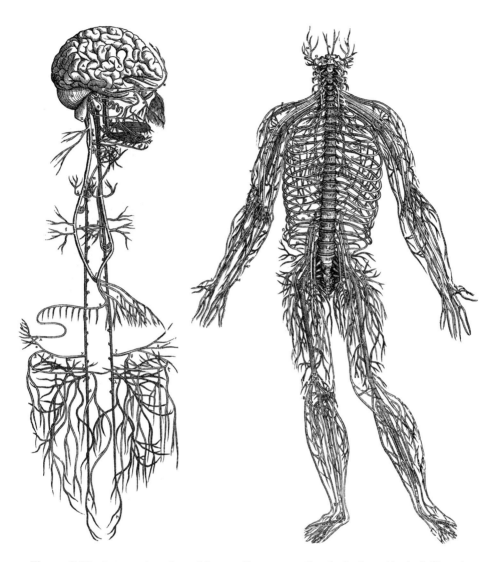

Figure 2.10. Autonomic and cranial nerve fibers connecting the brain and body (left), and nerve fibers connecting the spinal cord and the body (right), from Andreas Vesalius's *De Humani Corporis Fabrica* (1543).

was aware that at the very time he was writing his pieces (the 1630s), elsewhere on the European continent Galileo Galilei (1564–1642) was being tried and sentenced by the Catholic Inquisition for heresy as a result of his writings on related topics of grand scope.

Descartes's *Treatise on Man* was published, posthumously, initially as an imperfect Latin translation in 1662 and then in the definitive French edition in 1664: *L'Homme de René Descartes*. The publication very nearly never happened. Descartes died in 1650 in Stockholm, and his personal effects, including the manuscript for *L'Homme*, were aboard a boat that sank en route from Sweden to Paris. Fortu-

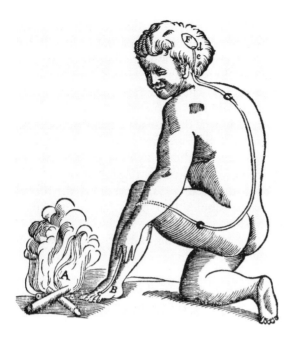

Figure 2.11. Person reacting to fire, from *L'Homme de René Descartes* (1664).

nately, this accident occurred along the Seine River, not in the open seas, and the manuscript was recovered intact.

Figure 2.11 shows a drawing from *L'Homme* illustrating a person reacting to fire. When the person's foot gets close to the fire, a signal is sent from the foot to the head. From the head another signal goes back to the foot and generates movement, causing the person to pull away from the fire. We execute behaviors like this all the time. Descartes was trying to understand how this happens. In the 1600s, one idea was that this type of action was driven by fluid pressure of some kind, perhaps liquid or air. The fluid is heated by the fire, resulting in increased pressure that forces it through channels up to the head and then back again.

Descartes was very interested in trying to understand perception—how is it we are able to sense the world, and how is it that physical sensations lead to mental experiences? His *Treatise on Man* contains drawings illustrating dissections of the eye and speculations about the connections between the eye and the brain (Fig. 2.12).

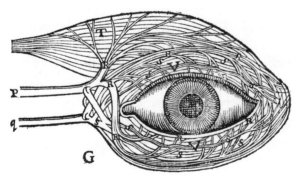

Figure 2.12. Dissection of muscles surrounding the eyeball, from *L'Homme de René Descartes* (1664).

It seemed that light is captured optically by the eye and that signals must somehow be transmitted to the brain (Fig. 2.13). But then what? How can the physical sensations of light lead to our mental experience of the world—to visual perception? Four centuries later, this is still an outstanding question.

It is now appreciated that signaling in the nervous system is fundamentally electrical in nature—electrical meaning involving the movement of charged particles. That process is described in detail in Chapter 5. In Descartes's time, descriptions of electricity were only just beginning to enter the realm of scientific discourse. The word *electricity* was introduced into the English lexicon during the 1600s, its origin being the Greek word for amber—*elektron*—the fossilized tree resin known for its properties of attraction: rub a piece of amber with a cloth, and the amber will attract light materials, such as hair or small pieces of paper.

By the 1700s, a number of scientific luminaries were researching and writing

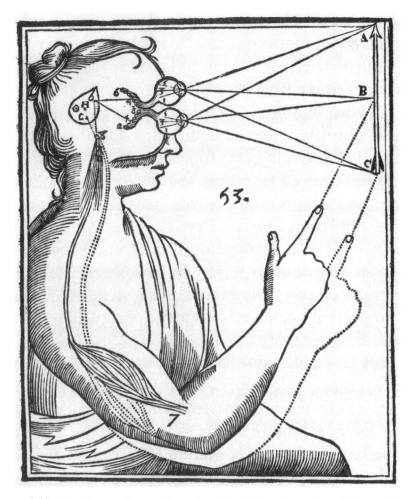

Figure 2.13. Visual perception and the action of pointing a finger, from *L'Homme de René Descartes* (1664).

about electrical phenomena. Benjamin Franklin (1706–1790) conducted many experiments with electricity, including, some have said, flying a kite during a thunderstorm (circa 1752). Electricity was very much in the air.

In the late 1700s, the Italian physician Luigi Galvani (1737–1798) studied the effects of electrical stimulation on animal muscles. He found that legs severed from dead frogs could twitch when electrically stimulated and hypothesized that muscles move as a result of internal electrical forces that can be triggered by external electrical stimulation (see Fig. 2.14). Galvani published his experimental results and speculations with the Bologna Academy and Institute of Sciences and Arts in 1791. His essay was written in Latin and is called *De viribus electricitatis in motu musculari, commentarius.* This translates into English as "Commentary on the effects of electricity on muscular motion."

Galvani's nephew, Giovanni Aldini (1762–1834), continued his uncle's work and contributed to increased public attention to connections between electricity and life. Around the same time, another Italian, Alessandro Volta (1745–1827), invented the first battery. Later, near the end of the 1800s, the unit of electric potential difference, the volt, would be named after him.

In the mid-nineteenth century, Scottish physicist James Clerk Maxwell (1831–1879), building on the work of Hans Christian Oersted (1777–1851), André Ampère (1775–1836), Michael Faraday (1791–1867), and others, derived a set of elegant mathematical relations that provided a unified description of electricity and magnetism. Even light could now be understood as a propagating wave of electromagnetic energy. Electricity was getting really big, and increasingly central to all of physics.

As electricity became more a focus of experimental investigation, Galvani's suggestion that neural signaling was electrical in nature continued to catch on. Around 1850, the German physician and physicist Hermann von Helmhotz (1821–1894) measured the speed of an electrical signal moving along a nerve fiber, finding it to be about 100 kilometers per hour in the preparation of frog leg muscle he used. He later obtained a similar speed for nerve conduction in humans. A few years later, Walt Whitman (1819–1892) wrote a famous poetic line: "I sing the body electric."

What are nerve fibers? Nerve cells have a basic construction and biochemistry very similar to all cells for all of life on Earth. There are chromosomes containing genetic information, coded into the molecular structure of DNA. There are structures involved in the synthesis of proteins and their transport to desired locations within the cell. There are structures dedicated to the generation of cellular energy. All this is enclosed by a cell membrane, the structure that forms the boundary of the cell. Within the cell there is also elaborate molecular scaffolding, composed of protein polymers called microfilaments and microtubules. Far from being a bag of disorganized fluid protoplasm, a living cell is a highly ordered system of vast complexity.

Nerve cells are further characterized as having additional parts—dendrites and axons—specialized for the communication of signals from one cell to another (see Fig. 2.15). What we have been calling nerve fibers—the thread-like structures connecting the brain with various parts of the body, and observed by Vesalius and Descartes in their dissections—consist mainly of bundles of axons.

Microscopic analyses of the brain revealed it to consist of densely packed neu-

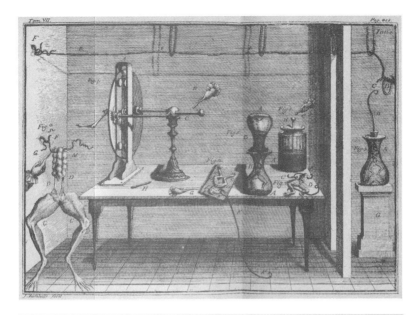

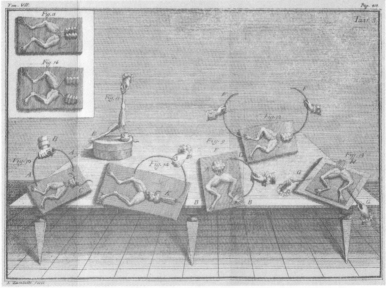

Figure 2.14. Two figures from Galvani's 1791 publication, depicting experimental devices and arrangements, together with dissected frog legs.

rons and glial cells. The elaborate interconnectivity of nerve cells in the brain was gorgeously illustrated in the drawings of two great pioneers of neuroscience, Camillo Golgi (1843–1926) and Santiago Ramón y Cajal (1852–1934), working in their respective countries of Italy and Spain at the end of the nineteenth and beginning of the twentieth centuries (Fig. 2.16). Golgi and Ramón y Cajal spent thousands of

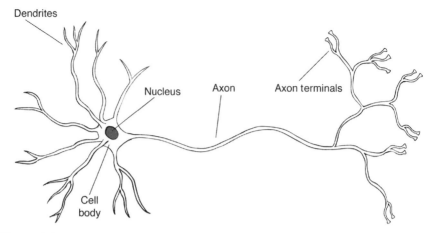

Figure 2.15. Nerve cell, with axon and dendrites.

hours looking at slices of brain tissue under microscopes and drawing in exquisite detail what they saw. Both were using a technique for staining neurons developed by Golgi in 1873.

While working as a physician in a large psychiatric asylum administering to more than five hundred patients, Golgi, in his "spare time," developed his famous

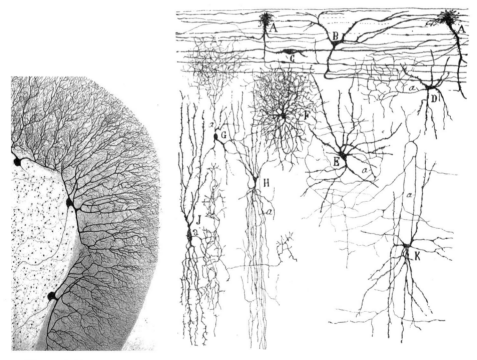

Figure 2.16. Human cerebellar neurons drawn by Golgi (left) and neurons from human cerebral cortex drawn by Ramón y Cajal (right).

stain. He called it *la reazione nera*—the black reaction. It made neurons, together with all their dendrites and axons, eminently visible under the microscope. Here is the recipe, in brief, of his technique:

| potassium dichromate (K_2CrO_4) (a red crystalline salt) (marinate neural tissue in H_2O solution of K_2CrO_4) | $+$ | silver nitrate $(AgNO_3)$ (a white crystalline salt) (continue the marination in H_2O solution of $AgNO_3$) | $=$ | silver chromate (Ag_2CrO_4) (a dark crystal) forms and collects in neurons |

The dark crystals of silver chromate stain the neurons completely, rendering even very minute structures exquisitely visible. (In some variations of the procedure, glial cells are also stained.) If every neuron in a small piece of brain tissue was stained in this way, the result would be a glob of dark-colored mess, so densely packed with silver chromate that it would be useless to look at in hopes of seeing individual cells. But the most amazing thing about the Golgi stain is that it is woefully inefficient, only about 1 percent of neurons are stained! These 1 percent are stained really well, and the remaining 99 percent aren't stained at all. Neuroscientists have been using Golgi's staining method for more than a century, and yet it is still not known why only some neurons are stained. They appear to be a kind of random subset of the neurons present. Perhaps it has something to do with being recently active, or inactive, or something else about the recent state of the cell's physiology. Such little mysteries are sweet!

And so, by the beginning of the twentieth century, here was the broad scenario: brains and nervous systems were understood as highly sophisticated networks for connecting sensory information with movement, having evolved in the animal kingdom to facilitate survival while moving around in complex and challenging environments. Signaling in the nervous system was electrical in nature—meaning that it involved the movement of charged particles. These charged particles were likely to be atomic in nature. The brain was appreciated as being somehow central to the functioning of the mind—mental experience and consciousness. Developments in the sciences of physics and chemistry made it increasingly attractive to try to understand the phenomena of life at as microscopic a level as possible—that of cells and molecules. There were many mysteries, many questions—but the future of the life sciences looked bright.

> Nerve currents sparkle.
> A trillion nodes resonate.
> The mind engages.

CHAPTER **3**

Chemistry and Life

To understand how nerve cells work—how they generate signals and pass information from one cell to another—it is essential to introduce a few basic concepts of chemistry. This subject, at least at the level of basic concepts, is not difficult to understand, is fun, and provides a remarkably useful structure for describing matter in general and living matter in particular. In contemporary science, *chemistry*, the word and the discipline, is derived from an older word and discipline, *alchemy*. And alchemy, some say, comes from the Arabic *al kamia*, ancient name for Egypt: black-earth land—fertile land of the Nile River delta—rich, creative, transformative.

Chemistry is the scientific endeavor concerned with the nature of matter and its transformations. Matter is described in terms of fundamental constituents—the *chemical elements*, understood as *atoms* that are themselves composed of protons, neutrons, and electrons—and chemistry investigates the conditions of how these elemental constituents (atoms) interact to form larger entities called *molecules*. As with chemistry, alchemy was also concerned with the nature and transformation of matter and was involved with processes like extraction, conversion, fermentation, distillation, and so forth.

Among the alchemists of old were metalworkers who "magically" extracted metals from rock, and physicians who prepared extracts and essences from plants for healing the body and mind. Some alchemists sought the Philosopher's Stone, a legendary substance said to facilitate transformation of common metals such as iron and lead into precious metals such as gold and silver. But some say this is only part of the alchemical story, perhaps even the lesser part. More importantly, there was also an esoteric or occult aspect of alchemy that was concerned with investigation of the psyche, and with transformation of one's self and the human psychological condition—a kind of psychotherapy or vision quest. In this context the Philosopher's Stone is understood as a vehicle for self-transformation—the method by which the alchemical practitioner achieves an integrated wholeness.

Throughout the seventeenth and eighteenth centuries in Europe alchemy was gradually redefined as chemistry, a science of matter devoid of psyche. Robert Boyle (1627–1691) and Isaac Newton (1642–1727) considered themselves alchemists, and both sought the Philosopher's Stone. But Boyle and Newton also made central contributions to a new conception of the cosmos, one that sought to describe nature independent of any references to mind or magic.

By the end of the 1700s the transition was nearly complete. Antoine Lavoisier (1743–1794) and Joseph Priestley (1733–1804), for example, occupied themselves not with the Philosopher's Stone but with such things as discovering oxygen and investigating its roles in combustion and respiration. Priestley published works on electricity, carbonated water, and gases. And in 1789 Lavoisier published what some consider the first modern text on chemistry—*Traité Élémentaire de Chimie*—translated into English the next year as *Elements of Chemistry in a New Systematic Order, Containing All the Modern Discoveries*. In his writing, Lavoisier developed chemical nomenclature still in use today and set forth what he believed to be a comprehensive listing of all the chemical elements known in his time.

Life was not easy for these pioneers of modern chemistry. Priestley's primary vocation was as an educator and minister. He was a dissenter from the Church of England and a supporter of the American and French Revolutions. In 1791, his home and laboratory in Birmingham, England, were destroyed by a riotous mob, and he fled with his family first to London and then, in 1794 to America, where he lived the final decade of his life in rural Pennsylvania. Lavoisier's fate was far worse. Because of his history of involvement with an institution that collected taxes for the French crown, he was arrested during the French Revolution and executed by guillotine in 1794 at the age of fifty. Later, the new French government is said to have apologized to Lavoisier's family.

Flash forward to 1869: Russian chemist Dmitri Mendeleev (1834–1907) puts forth a way of organizing the known chemical elements into what we now call the *periodic table*. The periodic table of the chemical elements qualifies as one of the great achievements of the human intellect, representing a large amount of information in a very compact form. From gaps in his organizational scheme, Mendeleev predicted the existence of several not-yet-discovered chemical elements. Three of these elements, discovered later, are now called gallium, germanium, and scandium. Figure 3.1 shows the basic form of the modern periodic table of the chemical elements.

1 H																	2 He
3 Li	4 Be											5 B	6 C	7 N	8 O	9 F	10 Ne
11 Na	12 Mg											13 Al	14 Si	15 P	16 S	17 Cl	18 Ar
19 K	20 Ca	21 Sc	22 Ti	23 V	24 Cr	25 Mn	26 Fe	27 Co	28 Ni	29 Cu	30 Zn	31 Ga	32 Ge	33 As	34 Se	35 Br	36 Kr
37 Rb	38 Sr	39 Y	40 Zr	41 Nb	42 Mo	43 Tc	44 Ru	45 Rh	46 Pd	47 Ag	48 Cd	49 In	50 Sn	51 Sb	52 Te	53 I	54 Xe
55 Cs	56 Ba	57-71	72 Hf	73 Ta	74 W	75 Re	76 Os	77 Ir	78 Pt	79 Au	80 Hg	81 Tl	82 Pb	83 Bi	84 Po	85 At	86 Rn
87 Fr	88 Ra	89-103	104 Rf	105 Db	106 Sg	107 Bh	108 Hs	109 Mt	110 Ds	111 Rg	112 Cn	113 Uut	114 Fl	115 Uup	116 Lv	117 Uus	118 Uuo

57 La	58 Ce	59 Pr	60 Nd	61 Pm	62 Sm	63 Eu	64 Gd	65 Tb	66 Dy	67 Ho	68 Er	69 Tm	70 Yb	71 Lu
89 Ac	90 Th	91 Pa	92 U	93 Np	94 Pu	95 Am	96 Cm	97 Bk	98 Cf	99 Es	100 Fm	101 Md	102 No	103 Lr

Figure 3.1. Periodic table of chemical elements.

In the periodic table, the chemical elements are represented by one- or two-letter abbreviations (or three letters for some of the heavy elements that have not yet received permanent names): H for hydrogen, He for helium, Li for lithium, C for carbon, N for nitrogen, O for oxygen, Na for sodium, Mg for magnesium, P for phosphorus, S for sulfur, Cl for chlorine, K for potassium, Ca for calcium, Fe for iron, U for uranium, Bk for berkelium, and so forth. The identity of an element is determined by the number of protons (a type of positively charged subatomic particle) within its nucleus; this number is indicated on the periodic table along with the element's abbreviated name.

What are the chemical elements that make up living matter? Life on Earth is based on carbon, meaning that carbon is the primary structural atom for building the large molecules making up living organisms. However, carbon is not the most numerous atom in living organisms, because most living things are composed primarily of water. A molecule of water is made of two atoms of hydrogen and one atom of oxygen: H_2O. A typical living human body is composed of approximately 65 percent water. The elemental abundances in a living human body, by weight, would look something like this, with oxygen being in first place because of all the water:

oxygen ~ 65%
carbon ~ 18.5%
hydrogen ~ 9.5%
nitrogen ~ 3.2%
calcium ~ 1.5%
phosphorus ~ 1.0%
potassium ~ 0.4%
sulfur ~ 0.3%
sodium ~ 0.2%
chlorine ~ 0.2%

These are the top ten chemical elements (with abundance represented as percentage of body weight) that make up a living human body and, indeed, that make up most living organisms on Earth. Ten other elements are also present and essential for healthy human life—magnesium, manganese, iron, cobalt, nickel, copper, zinc, selenium, molybdenum, and iodine—but these are found in much smaller amounts than the top ten.

If we represent the list of elements in terms of numbers of atoms (rather than percent weight) present in a living human body, then hydrogen would be number one, because there are vastly more hydrogen atoms than any other type of atom in a living organism. If we were to remove all the water and dry out the body, it would first of all no longer be living, because water is, as far as we know, essential for life. However, with all those H_2O molecules gone, carbon would assume first place in the list of elemental abundances represented as percent (dry) body weight. Hydrogen would still be in first place if we are counting atoms, as there are more hydrogen atoms than there are carbon atoms in the molecules that make up organisms.

Wet weight or dry weight, the top five most abundant elements in the human body, by weight or by number, would be, in some order: carbon, hydrogen, oxygen, nitrogen, and calcium. And the other five members of the top ten are phosphorus, potassium, sulfur, sodium, and chlorine. These are the atoms of life, as we know it. It is interesting to speculate as to what other forms of life might be possible. Life without water? Silicon as a structural element, replacing carbon? Life as an integrated circuit, or a vast network of integrated circuits?

When discussing an atom, it is generally assumed that the atom is in a state of neutral electric charge, with the positive charge of the atomic nucleus balanced by the negative charge (equal in magnitude and opposite in sign) of electrons in orbital clouds surrounding the nucleus. *Ions* are charged atoms, formed when atoms either gain or lose one or more electrons; ions thus have either net negative or net positive charge. One of the beautiful things about the periodic table of chemical elements is that an atom's position on the table tells us whether it is likely to give up electrons and become a positively charged ion (called a *cation*) or take on electrons and become a negatively charged ion (called an *anion*). Elements on the far left side of table will easily give up electrons and become cations (sodium, potassium, and calcium, for example), whereas elements on the far right side (except for the last column) will tend to take on electrons and become anions (chlorine, for example).

Elements in the rightmost column of the table have outer orbitals that are completely filled with electrons and tend to neither gain nor lose electrons. Because chemical interactions between elemental atoms depend on the gaining, losing, or sharing of electrons, these rightmost column elements are not interested in interacting or reacting with anything; they form a collection of unreactive gaseous elements called the noble or inert gases. Because of their lack of reactivity, they are not involved in any known way as part of the life process.

The importance of water for life as we know it cannot be overemphasized. Water is the canvas upon which life is painted, the landscape or stage upon which the molecular drama of life is played out. Water is an example of a molecule—a stable configuration of atoms held together in a particular geometric shape by the sharing of electrons between atoms.

$$\text{water} = H_2O = H\text{--}O\text{--}H$$

This sharing of electrons between atoms is called a *covalent chemical bond*. In water, each hydrogen atom contributes one electron and the oxygen atom contributes two electrons for mutual sharing. The shared electrons constitute a sort of glue that holds the atoms together.

The molecules from which living organisms are built and the molecules that interact with living organisms are often more complex than the simple water molecule. Here is one such molecule, a relatively small one, though substantially larger than water. This is a depiction of the molecular structure of the fluoxetine molecule, a substance synthesized by chemists and marketed as a treatment for the mood disorder called depression (see Chapter 21). In the United States, fluoxetine is associated with the brand name

Fluoxetine

Prozac. It is drawn here in a diagrammatic way that has been developed in organic chemistry to represent molecules. This is a diagrammatic language that may look mysterious and obscure when you don't know the rules (as any language would), but it is actually pretty easy to understand once you know a few rules.

Let's talk about these rules. First, molecules produced by life (*organic* molecules, organic from organism) are composed largely of carbon and hydrogen and may contain dozens or hundreds or thousands of atoms. While the most abundant atom in an organic molecule is usually hydrogen, carbon atoms form the scaffold that defines the overall shape of the molecule. Hydrogen, though numerous, has only a single electron to share and so can form only one chemical bond at a time. It has no possibility of forming the scaffold for a molecule and can only be stuck around the edges. Carbon, however, has four electrons available for sharing, and each carbon atom can form four bonds and be covalently joined to up to four other atoms. This allows carbon to form the structural framework for molecules that can become very large. Oxygen has two electrons to share and so can form two bonds. Nitrogen has three electrons to share and thus is able to form three bonds. Largely from these four elements—carbon, hydrogen, oxygen, and nitrogen—are built the basic structures of an enormous number of biologically interesting molecules.

To understand the diagrammatic rules for molecular structure, let's start simple. Consider a molecule that is a bit more complex than water, but not too much so—a small organic molecule composed of two carbon atoms, one oxygen atom, and six hydrogen atoms joined together by chemical bonds. This is the molecule ethyl alcohol, or ethanol, the primary psychoactive component of alcoholic beverages such

$$H-\overset{\overset{\displaystyle H}{|}}{C}-\overset{\overset{\displaystyle H}{|}}{C}-O-H$$

Ethyl alcohol

as beer, wine, and distilled liquor. In this drawing of the chemical structure of ethanol, carbon is represented by C, oxygen by O, and hydrogen by H. Covalent chemical bonds, the sharing of electrons between atoms, are represented by lines connecting the atoms. One sees that each carbon has four chemical bonds, reflecting four electrons to share; each hydrogen has one chemical bond, and the oxygen has two chemical bonds. The particular molecular shape produced by this geometric arrangement of atoms confers upon ethanol its peculiar properties.

Here are some other relatively simple organic molecules—relatively simple in that they are built from linear chains of carbon and hydrogen, and nothing else. Organic molecules composed solely of carbon and hydrogen are called *hydrocarbons*.

Methane   *Ethane*   *Propane*

Hexane   *Octane*

The simplest combination of carbon and hydrogen consists of a single carbon atom bonded to four hydrogen atoms. This molecule is called methane. It is a gas that is combustible (burnable) in the presence of oxygen. In fact, it is so-called natural gas, obtained from fossil fuel deposits in the earth and shipped into our homes by pipeline to be burned in stoves and furnaces. The combination of two carbons and six hydrogens is called ethane; it is also a combustible gas. Three carbons and eight hydrogens make up propane, also a combustible gas that easily liquefies under pressure and thus can be more easily stored and transported in tanks. Four carbon atoms and ten hydrogen atoms form butane, an even more easily liquefied combustible gas. Five carbons make pentane and six carbons make hexane, both combustible liquids. Seven carbons make heptane and eight carbons make octane, also both combustible liquids. As the number of carbons grows larger, the liquids develop an oily consistency and get progressively thicker. When the number of carbon atoms reaches twenty or more, the resulting substance is a waxy solid.

These molecules are fossils—molecular remnants originating with living organisms millions of years, or hundreds of millions of years, ago. Geological processes have transformed the once living material into hydrocarbons. Crude oil—petroleum (Latin *petra* = rock, *oleum* = oil)—is composed of a mixture of all these molecules and many more. Petroleum refineries separate crude oil into its molecular components, making them available to be used as fuels and other materials in the modern industrial world. All these molecules are combustible—that is, in the presence of oxygen they can burn and release energy as the covalent bonds connecting the carbons and hydrogens are broken. Fossil fuel. Complete combustion will break all of the carbon–carbon and carbon–hydrogen bonds and convert the hydrocarbon into a mixture of carbon dioxide (CO_2) and water.

Carbon, as well as some other atoms, also has the capacity to participate in bonds with other atoms in which it shares more than one electron. For example, in the ethylene molecule each carbon contributes two (rather than one) electrons to the carbon–carbon bond, forming what is called a *double bond*, drawn with a double line connecting the atoms.

Ethylene

The most widespread commercial use of ethylene is to make polyethylene plastics by linking many ethylene molecules together in very long chains (*polymers*) of various shapes. Ethylene is also produced by plants and used as a signaling molecule—a plant hormone.

The arrangement of carbons in a hydrocarbon molecule is not always linear. The chains of carbons may be branched, such as in this branched octane molecule.

Branched octane

The chain of carbons may even fold back upon itself to form a closed ring. Here is an example of that, the cyclohexane molecule. Note that in all cases each carbon atom still forms four covalent chemical bonds and each hydrogen atom forms one covalent bond.

There is another cyclic arrangement of six carbons that occurs commonly in nature. The benzene molecule contains six carbons in a ring structure together with six hydrogens (rather than twelve hydrogens, as in cyclohexane). The existence of such a combination of six carbons and six hydrogens

Cyclohexane

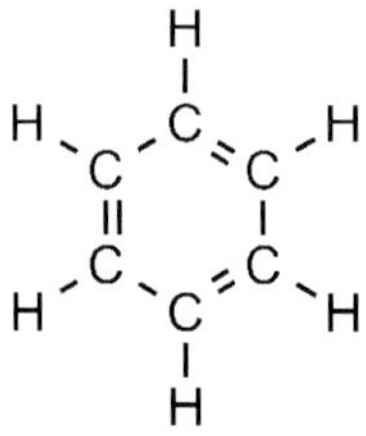

Benzene

was puzzling until Friedrich Kekulé (1829–1896) suggested a novel structure in 1865 for benzene.

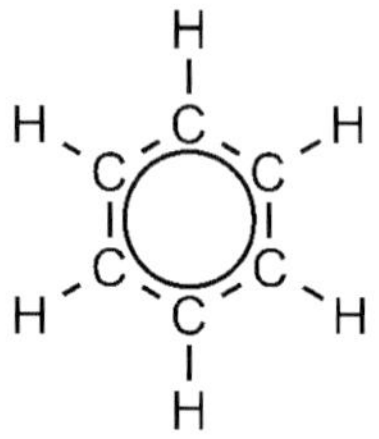

It is now appreciated that, rather than an alteration of single and double bonds, all the carbon–carbon bonds in benzene are equivalent and are sort of intermediate between single and double bonds in strength. The shared electrons are best described as exist-

Benzene

ing in molecular orbitals that encompass the entire ring structure. To represent this, the structural diagram for benzene is sometimes drawn with a circle inside the hexagon of carbons. While benzene itself does not occur in living organisms (it is a highly toxic and combustible liquid), the ring structure of benzene does occur widely as part of larger structures of many biological molecules. Let's look at several of these that have relevance to the human nervous system.

Here are two famous molecules found in the brain, the neurotransmitters dopamine and serotonin.

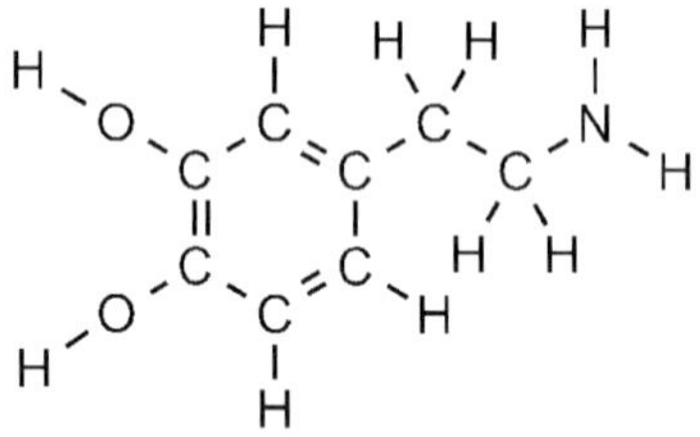

Dopamine

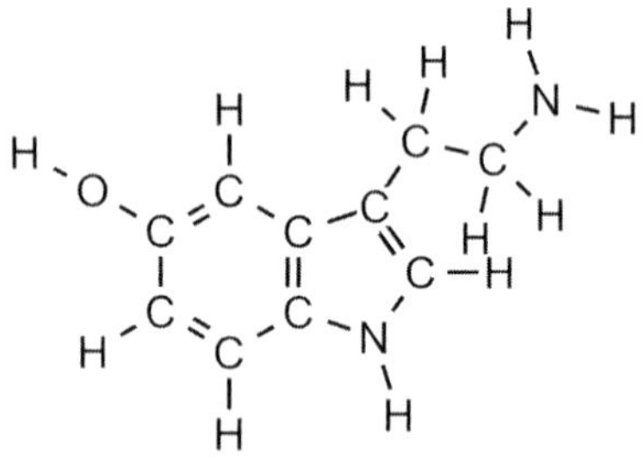

Serotonin

While not the most abundant neurotransmitters in the human brain, these two molecules are perhaps the best known of the neurotransmitters, due to their frequent mention in the news media. If you were to randomly stop people on the street and ask them to name a neurotransmitter, if they had any idea at all as to what you were asking, they would likely answer with the name of one of these two molecules.

Notice that within the diagrams for these molecules the benzene-ring structure occurs. Also notice that each of these molecules consists of a bunch of carbon atoms, several nitrogen and oxygen atoms, and a bunch of hydrogen atoms around the periphery of the molecule, all joined by chemical bonds so that a particular geometric shape results. Thus, these molecules are appreciated to be just a bunch of atoms (mostly carbon and hydrogen) connected together by the sharing of electrons (covalent chemical bonds) to form a particular geometric shape. It is their unique shapes that determine the properties of particular molecules within, say, the human nervous system.

If you spend time drawing a few molecular structures like those of dopamine and serotonin, you very quickly appreciate that mostly what you are doing is drawing lots of Cs (representing carbon atoms) and Hs (representing hydrogen atoms). There may be a few other atoms, like the several oxygen and nitrogen atoms in dopamine and serotonin, but mostly there are Cs and Hs, lots and lots of Cs and Hs. There can be so many Cs and Hs that it becomes difficult to notice the most important things about the molecule, such as the overall shape and what kinds of other atoms are part of the structure. Thus, chemists have developed a shorthand language for depicting the structures of organic molecules. In this shorthand language, the structures of dopamine and serotonin look like this:

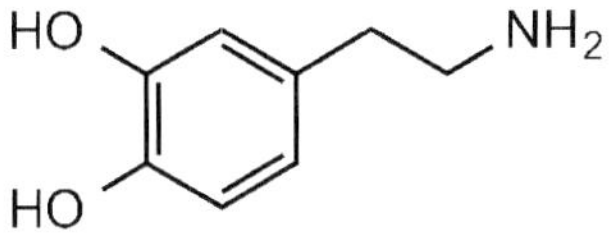

Dopamine

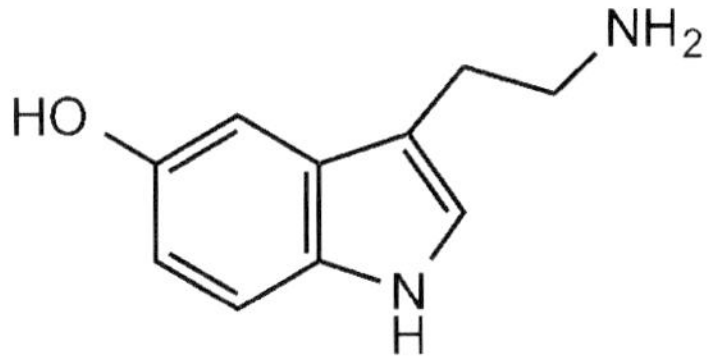

Serotonin

Here we are simply not drawing the Cs and most of the Hs. We are drawing only the bonds connecting the various atoms together.

So now, at last, we can articulate the rules for drawing and interpreting molecular structure diagrams. Covalent bonds are drawn as lines. If there is no letter explicitly shown at the end of a line, then it is assumed there is a carbon atom in that location. Thus, each line (bond) has a carbon atom at either end, unless another atom is explicitly drawn. Atoms other than carbon are indicated: N for nitrogen, O for oxygen, P for phosphorus, F for fluorine, and so forth. What about the hydrogen atoms? Because we know that carbon forms four bonds, any bonds not shown explicitly are assumed to be with hydrogen, enough hydrogens so that the total number of bonds per carbon equals four. Hydrogen atoms forming bonds with other elements (such as nitrogen and oxygen) are explicitly drawn in.

That's it for the basic rules. Really pretty simple!

One of the things we can easily do with this shorthand notation for molecular structure is compare similarities in shape between molecules. For example, one can see that these molecules—dopamine and norepinephrine, which are neurotransmitters; amphetamine, methamphetamine, and ephedrine, which are psychoactive drugs; and phenylalanine, an amino acid—all share a basic similarity of shape, something about their gestalt, or form.

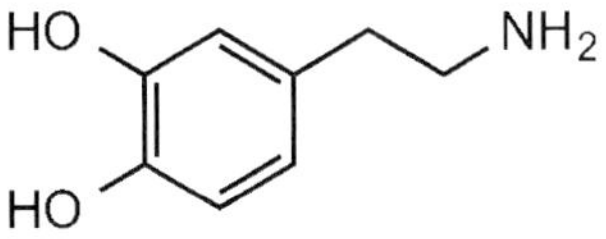

Dopamine

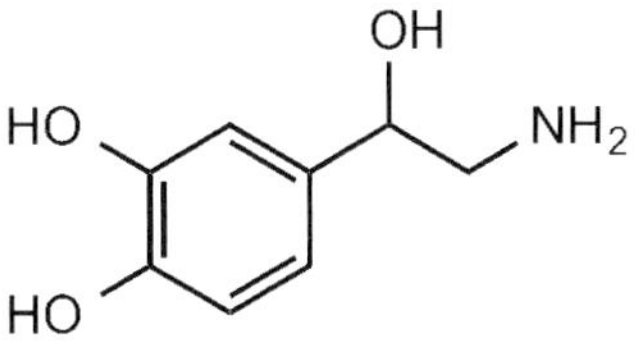

Norepinephrine

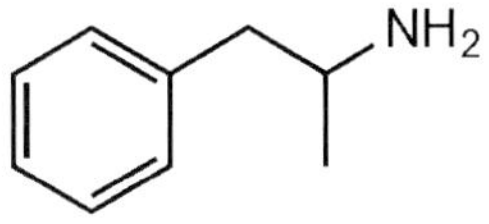

Amphetamine

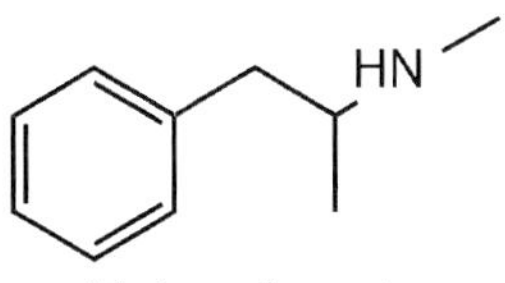

Methamphetamine

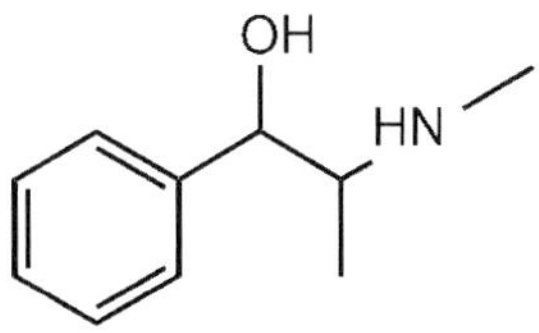

Ephedrine

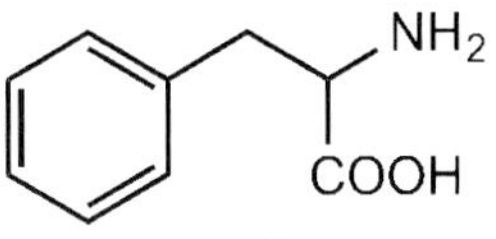

Phenylalanine

In fact, they can all be chemically converted from one to another in straightforward ways, given the right conditions. And because of their similar molecular shapes, there are connections between what these molecules do in living organisms.

The three molecules below—tryptophan, an amino acid; serotonin, a neurotransmitter; and psilocin, a psychoactive molecule from *Psilocybe* mushrooms—all look somewhat similar to one another and different from the molecules pictured above.

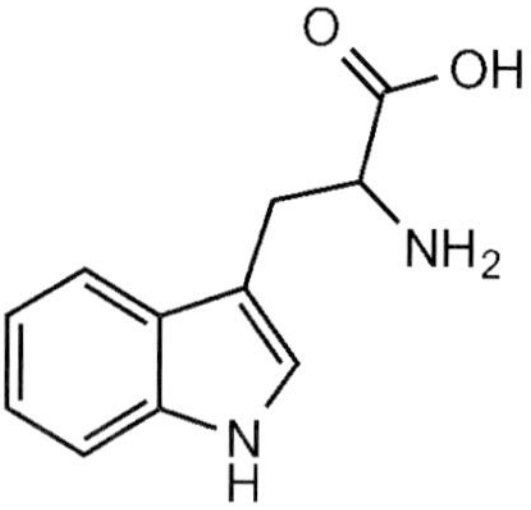

Tryptophan

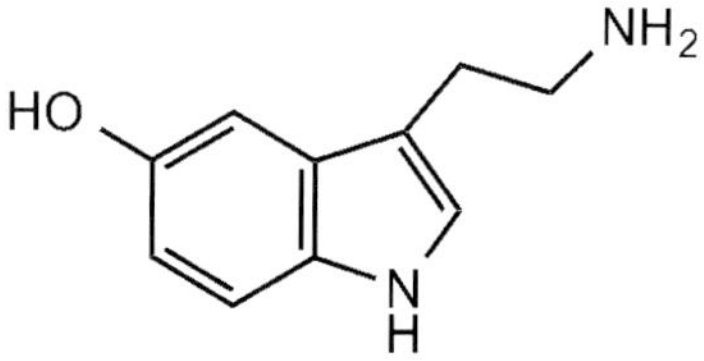

Serotonin

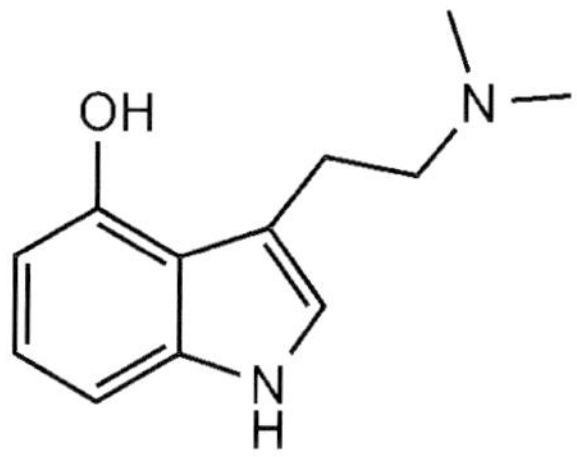

Psilocin

Finally, here is another famous molecule—caffeine.

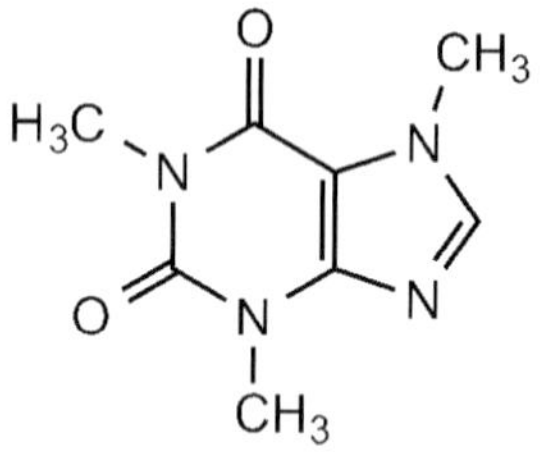

Caffeine

One sees that it, too, is simply a combination of rings of carbon and nitrogen atoms, together with a couple of oxygen atoms, but with a distinctly different shape compared with the other molecules drawn above. Again, these differences in shape determine the different functions these molecules have in living organisms.

Returning to water, a key reason that water is so important in living systems is that it is so very effective at dissolving things. Why is this so? The answer lies in a property of water known as *polarity*. In the water molecule (H_2O), the hydrogen atoms, being from the left side of the periodic table, are prone to giving up their electron and becoming positively charged. The oxygen, being from the right side of the periodic table, is prone to picking up electrons and becoming negatively charged. The result of these tendencies is that when the electrons forming the covalent bonds in water are distributed in the molecular orbitals describing the bonds, they essentially spend more time in the vicinity of the oxygen and less time in the vicinity of the hydrogens. So the oxygen atom in water becomes slightly negatively charged and the hydrogen atoms in water become slightly positively charged. This is what is meant by polarity. *Polar* means separation, and in this case there is a separation of charge between different parts of the water molecule. Water is a polar molecule.

Water's polarity causes the molecules to loosely stick to one another, a phenomenon called *hydrogen bonding*—the slightly negative oxygen atom of one water molecule is attracted to the slightly positive hydrogen atom of another. (Opposite electric charges are attracted to one another.) This results in a matrix of water molecules held together in a loose way by hydrogen bonds, depicted here as dashed lines.

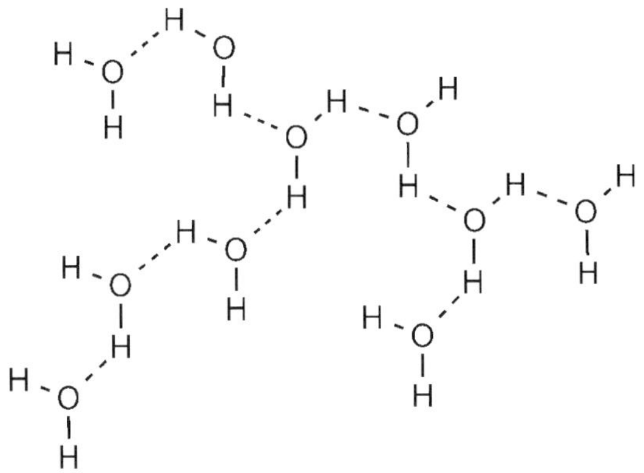

Water, with hydrogen bonds

Hydrogen bonding is *noncovalent*—it does not involve sharing of electrons. The water molecules are able to easily slip and slide past one another, producing the wateriness of liquid water. When water is heated the energy of the heat causes the molecules to jitter and shake more vigorously. At the boiling point, the jittering becomes vigorous enough to overcome the hydrogen bonding between water molecules, and the H_2O molecules escape as gaseous water—steam. Cool the water, and the molecular vibration lessens until, at the freezing point, the water molecules lock into a rigid matrix interconnected by hydrogen bonds—ice. The slight expansion of water when it freezes is due to the rigid matrix of hydrogen bonds taking slightly more space than when the molecules of water can slip and slide past one another in their liquid state.

The polarity of water also accounts for water's amazing ability to dissolve many things, including ions. This can be illustrated by considering what is called table salt, sodium chloride (NaCl). A sodium atom (Na), being from the left side of the periodic table, very readily gives up an electron to form a positively charged sodium cation (Na^+). A chlorine atom, being from the right side of the periodic table, will very readily take on an electron to form a negatively charged chloride anion (Cl^-). Crystalline table salt, sodium chloride, can be described as an array of alternating sodium and chloride ions, held together by the electrical attraction of their respective positive and negative charges. In the absence of water, NaCl is an extremely stable structure. However, introduce even a small amount of water and the NaCl will begin to dissolve, that is, fall apart into the water.

This illustrates water's extraordinary ability to dissolve ions. Because the charged ions are attracted to the opposite-charged portions of the polar water molecule, water molecules can slip into the otherwise very stable matrix of sodium and chloride forming the salt crystal. As the salt crystal dissolves, the cations and anions become surrounded with polar water molecules, attracted to the ionic charges. A saltwater solution is formed. Water is very effective at dissolving all kinds of atoms and molecules that have a net electrical charge (such as ions) or, indeed, any polar molecule, because the positive and negative separation of charge in a polar molecule will be attracted to the positive and negative separation of charge in the water molecule.

This allows us to introduce a very important concept into our description of solubility. Water, a polar molecule, dissolves (or loves to hang out with) other things that have polarity or charge. We call things that like to hang out with water *hydrophilic* (Greek *hydro* = water, *philos* = loving). Hydrophilic substances like to be around water, and water likes to be around them. At the other extreme of solubility in water, consider the hydrocarbons. These molecules consist only of carbons and hydrogens linked by covalent bonds. When electrons are shared among carbon and hydrogen atoms, the electrons are essentially equally likely to be found in proximity to either type of atom. Thus, there is no significant polarity, or separation of charge, in a hydrocarbon molecule and so nothing with which a water molecule can form a hydrogen bond. Thus, hydrocarbons don't dissolve in water. This is illustrated by the well-known adage that oil and water don't mix. Substances such as hydrocarbons that don't dissolve in water—that don't like to hang out with water—are called *hydrophobic* (Greek *phobos* = fearing). Hydrophilic things like to hang out with other hydrophilic things, and hydrophobic things like to hang out with other hydrophobic things.

Okay, so where is all this chemistry stuff taking us? Let's return to the cell. Cells are the fundamental organizational units for all known living organisms. There are some characteristics shared by all cells, from bacterial cells to cells in the human brain. Among these shared features are a boundary membrane (composed of phospholipid bilayer), genetic material (composed of nucleic acids), ribosomal structures (for protein synthesis), protein receptors, pumps, and channels within the cell membrane, and so on. The component materials, the building blocks of a cell, are molecules, and the machinery of life, that which characterizes a cell as living rather than nonliving, is understood to be the chemical processes taking place within. Some of the molecules from which cells are constructed are quite large, consisting of thousands of atoms held together by covalent bonds. Below four fundamental types of biological molecules are described: lipids, proteins, carbohydrates, and nucleic acids.

The fats or lipids (Greek *lipos* = fat) are medium-size molecules composed primarily of carbon and hydrogen atoms in long chains, generally sixteen to twenty-four carbon atoms long. Often there are a few oxygen atoms at one end of the chain of carbons. The roles of these molecules within cells are diverse and include energy storage (lots of energy is contained in the carbon–carbon and carbon–hydrogen bonds within the molecule), signaling within and between cells, precursor molecules the cell uses to make certain neurotransmitters and hormones, and formation of membranes enclosing cells and its interior structures.

A *fatty acid* is a kind of lipid molecule consisting of a hydrocarbon chain with a *carboxylic acid group* (–COOH) at one end. Palmitic acid is a sixteen-carbon fatty acid. It is called a *saturated* fatty acid because all the carbons are fully bonded with

Palmitic acid

hydrogen atoms; there are no double bonds. Palmitic acid is very common in plants and animals. It draws its name from palm trees and is a major component in palm oils.

Another example of a lipid molecule is oleic acid, an eighteen-carbon fatty acid.

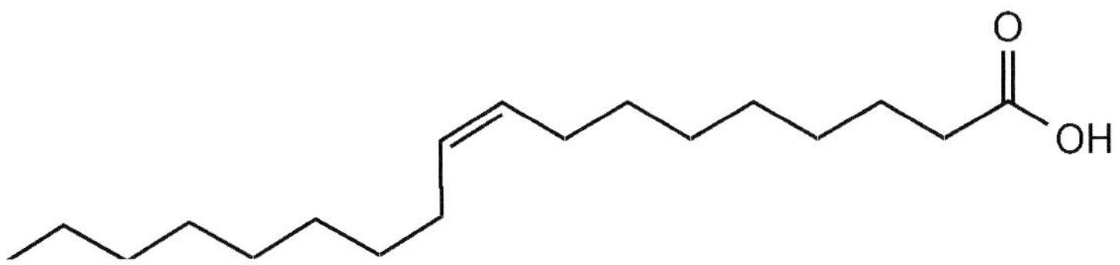

Oleic acid

Its name comes from *oleum*, Latin for "oil." The chemical composition of olive oil is more than 50 percent oleic acid. Oleic acid contains one double bond, and thus is an *unsaturated* (monounsaturated) fatty acid. The double bond is located nine carbons in from the end of the hydrocarbon chain, a so-called omega-9 fatty acid.

Because lipids are composed primarily of carbon and hydrogen atoms, they are largely hydrophobic in nature, preferring the company of other lipids rather than that of water. *Lipophilic* (lipid loving) is synonymous with hydrophobic. And conversely, *lipophobic* (lipid fearing) means the same as hydrophilic. Oil and water don't mix.

Of great importance in living organisms are the *phospholipids*. These lipids are composed of two carbon–hydrogen chains (each chain generally sixteen to twenty-four carbons in length), joined together at one end by a group of atoms containing, in addition to the ubiquitous carbons and hydrogens, atoms of oxygen, phosphorus, and perhaps nitrogen. These latter atoms form bonds having polarity and sometimes even electric charge. Thus, phospholipids have a highly hydrophilic portion (the polar or electrically charged phosphorus-containing "head group") and a highly hydrophobic portion (the two long nonpolar hydrocarbon chains, or "tail groups").

Among the most abundant phospholipids in the cells of animals and plants are the phosphatidylcholines, an example of which is shown here:

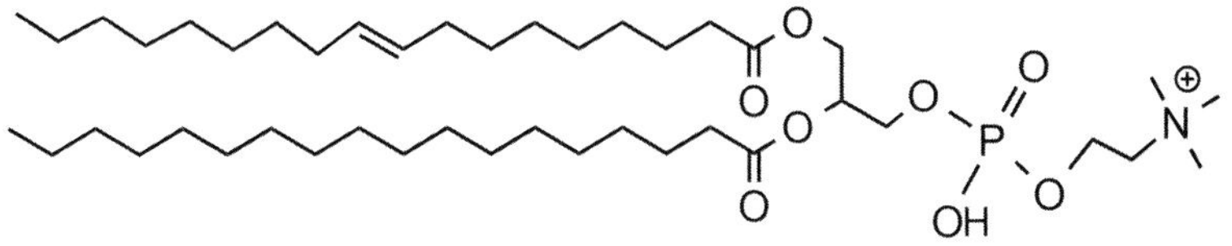

Phosphatidylcholine

The two hydrocarbon lipid tails, here both eighteen carbons long, may be of varying lengths. The head group contains a phosphorus atom, multiple oxygen atoms, and a nitrogen atom that carries a positive charge. The positive charge comes from an electron deficit arising from the nitrogen having four bonds with other atoms, rather than its customary three. This configuration is called a *quaternary amine.*

The peculiar structure of phospholipids, with their distinct hydrophilic and hydrophobic portions, gives rise to a remarkable phenomenon when these lipids are present in an aqueous (water) environment. When surrounded by water, phospholipids will cluster together such that the hydrophobic/lipophilic tail groups associate

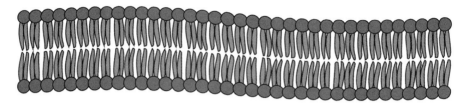

Figure 3.2. Diagram of phospholipid bilayer: the head groups, represented as small circles, are to the outside of the bilayer, and the hydrocarbon tails are inside. There would be water above and below the bilayer.

with one another and the hydrophilic/lipophobic head groups associate with one another. Moreover, the hydrophilic head groups want to be in contact with the water environment and the hydrophobic tail groups want to be protected from contact with the water environment. To accomplish this, they form a double layer of phospholipid molecules (Fig. 3.2): the hydrophilic head groups form the exterior surfaces (in contact with one another and in contact with the water environment), and the hydrophobic tail groups are inside the layers (in contact with one another and shielded from contact with the water environment by the hydrophilic heads).

Phospholipid bilayers form sheets in three dimensions that can fold to form enclosed surfaces separating two aqueous environments, such as the inside and outside of a cell. Indeed, phospholipid bilayers constitute the membranes forming the boundary layers around all cells for all of life on Earth. The cell membranes of bacteria, of plants, of mushrooms, and of brain neurons all have the same fundamental structure: a bilayer of phospholipid molecules. It is one of the most beautiful and elegant structures in the known universe!

These phospholipid bilayer membranes are very tiny structures, with thicknesses of only about 5 nanometers (5×10^{-9} meters, or five billionths of a meter). The phospholipid bilayer membranes of cells contain a diversity of protein molecules that serve a variety of functions vital to cells. In nerve cells, among the various membrane proteins are ion channels, ion pumps, neurotransmitter receptors, and neurotransmitter reuptake transporters. In an actual biological membrane, the density of membrane proteins can be quite high, and the proteins will have a variety of wild and crazy shapes (Fig. 3.3).

The molecules that make up a phospholipid bilayer are constantly jiggling as a result of thermal vibration, and there can be quite a lot of mobility of the proteins and other molecules within a biological membrane. In many ways, these membranes are more like fluids in their properties than they are like solids.

This brings us to the next category of biological molecule: proteins. Proteins are large molecules built from *amino acids* linked into long chains by covalent chemical bonds, called *peptide bonds*. So, first, what is an amino acid? In organic chemistry, an amino acid is a molecule that contains both an *amine group* ($-NH_2$) and a carboxylic acid group ($-COOH$). The amino acids used as protein building blocks by all life on Earth are characterized by having amine and acid groups linked to the same carbon atom; these are termed alpha-amino acids.

$$NH_2$$
$$R - \overset{|}{\underset{|}{C}} - COOH$$
$$H$$

Alpha-amino
acid

Figure 3.3. Phospholipid bilayer forming a biological membrane. Membrane proteins are here depicted as amorphous, potato-like structures. In actuality, proteins have a great deal of internal structure.

Here R represents a portion of the molecule containing other atoms. Different amino acids are characterized by having different R groups. The simplest amino acid has R = H. This amino acid is called glycine. The next simplest has R = –CH_3. This is alanine. Another amino acid, called phenylalanine, has an R group consisting of a carbon attached to a benzene ring. Life on Earth uses twenty different amino acids (characterized by twenty different R groups) as the molecular building blocks of proteins.

Here is a representation of two amino acid molecules, with all the atoms drawn out explicitly:

Amino acids

The R groups, R_1 and R_2, may be the same or different. If amino acid molecules are simply mixed together in water and shaken up, nothing happens—they do not spontaneously join together to form chains. However, in the appropriate environment inside living cells, amino acids can join together with peptide bonds to form a chain of amino acids called a *polypeptide*.

Here is the molecular structure diagram of how two amino acids can join together into a dipeptide by the formation of a covalent bond between them. This joining does not happen spontaneously but only under specific catalytic conditions found within the ribosomes of cells. Ribosomes are structures inside cells that are built from proteins and nucleic acids. They are the sites of protein synthesis within

Amino acids forming a dipeptide

cells, with enzymatic activity of the ribosome facilitating, or catalyzing, the formation of covalent bonds between amino acids. The diagram above shows that an –H and an –OH are removed in the formation of a peptide bond. They will produce one molecule of water, H_2O, which floats away. You can also see that the two ends of the resulting polypeptide structure have an amine group and an acid group available to form additional peptide bonds. Thus, it is possible to form very long chains of amino acids, covalently linked by peptide bonds. Ribosomes provide the conditions for this to take place.

When a bunch of amino acids link together to form a polypeptide chain, they fold around and form a shape. Similar to water flowing downhill, the polypeptide chain folds in such a way so as to arrive at a lowest-energy configuration, determined by the myriad attractions and repulsions among the component atoms. Thus, the chain of amino acids develops a unique three-dimensional shape, and it is this shape that will help determine how it functions in the cell. Any chain of amino acids is called a polypeptide; if it is more than about forty amino acids long, then it is called a protein. The threshold number for defining when a polypeptide becomes a protein is somewhat arbitrary. Some might say thirty, some fifty.

Figure 3.4 is a diagram of a small protein called myoglobin. It is a chain of 153 amino acids that binds, stores, and transports oxygen molecules within animal muscles. In this drawing, myoglobin is depicted as a ribbonlike structure representing the polypeptide chain and overall shape of its folding. The chain of amino acids spontaneously folds into a stable configuration characterized by an energy minimum. The result is a unique three-dimensional structure for the protein. In addition to its 153 covalently linked amino acids, myoglobin contains a component called heme (not shown in this diagram), a planar molecule embedded within the protein's structure that functions to bind a molecule of oxygen. The diameter of myoglobin is only about two nanometers; even though proteins are considered relatively large molecules, they are still very tiny indeed.

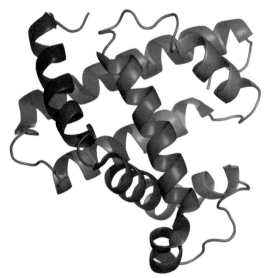

Figure 3.4. Myoglobin molecule.

In describing proteins, several descriptive levels of structure have been defined. What is called the *primary structure* of the protein is the linear sequence of amino acids forming the protein—a list of the component amino acids in the order they occur in the polypeptide chain.

The *secondary structure* describes the interactions of nearby amino acids to produce patterns of local folding within the protein. Nearby amino acids may interact with one another via hydrogen bonding and other sorts of electrical attraction and repulsion. This may give rise to distinct varieties of local folding within the protein. The most famous example of protein secondary structure is the alpha helix, first described by the great chemist Linus Pauling (1901–1994). In Figure 3.4, alpha helices are represented by twisted sections of ribbon.

The *tertiary structure* is the overall shape of the entire protein molecule, created by all the electrical and geometric properties of the constituent amino acids guiding the folding of the chain of amino acids into a unique three-dimensional form.

Many functional proteins in living organisms are composed of a complex of more than one polypeptide subunit, with each subunit generally consisting of hundreds of amino acids. Such an arrangement is termed the *quaternary structure* of the protein. For example, hemoglobin—which binds and transports oxygen in our blood—is composed of four polypeptide subunits. And ionotropic receptors for the neurotransmitter GABA (see Chapter 6) are composed of five subunit polypeptides.

Our third category of biological molecule is that of carbohydrates. The name comes from a conjunction of carbon (*carbo*) and water (*hydrate*), and carbohydrates are built from atoms of carbon, hydrogen, and oxygen, covalently joined to form molecules. Some carbohydrates are small molecules, such as the sugars glucose, fructose, and ribose.

Glucose *Fructose* *Ribose*

And some carbohydrates are enormous molecules, such as glycogen, starches, and cellulose. Starches consist of polymers of hundreds or thousands of glucose molecules linked by covalent bonds into very long chains. As with the fats, substantial amounts of energy are stored in chemical bonds joining the carbon, hydrogen, and oxygen atoms, and carbohydrates serve as sources of fuel for living organisms.

The fourth and final category of biological molecule to be introduced here is that of the nucleic acids, represented by DNA (deoxyribonucleic acid) and RNA (ribonucleic acid). DNA and RNA are by far the largest molecules in living organisms, containing many thousands, even millions, of atoms and serving as the repositories for the information required for constructing a living cell—the genetic or hereditary information. The DNA double helix is composed of two very long chains of four component *nucleotides*—adenine (A), cytosine (C), guanine (G), and thymine (T)

—coupled with deoxyribose sugars and phosphate (phosphorus and oxygen) groups. Each long chain is held together by covalent bonds between the sugars and phosphates. The two chains wind around one another in a helical form and are held together by noncovalent hydrogen bonds between nucleotides. Adenine forms hydrogen bonds with thymine, and guanine forms hydrogen bonds with cytosine.

The discovery of the double-helical structure of DNA and its ramifications is one of the great sagas of twentieth-century science. The field of molecular biology and the modern biotechnology industry were among the offspring of this discovery. Also, among the ramifications, I believe, was the strengthening of confidence that the known chemistry of atoms and molecules will be able to account for all the phenomena of life, including even that of mind and consciousness.

So, let the tale be told . . .

> Molecules and cells,
> atoms play their varied roles.
> Theater of life!

CHAPTER **4**

Genes and the History of Molecular Biology

The molecular building materials for life are the biological molecules discussed in Chapter 3: lipids, proteins, carbohydrates, and nucleic acids. The same twenty amino acids are used by all life on Earth to construct proteins, and the structures and functions of proteins are similar all the way from single-celled bacteria to animals composed of trillions of cells. Genetic information is stored in nucleic acid molecules (DNA and RNA) according to the same universal code, used by viruses, bacteria, and human brain cells. The elucidation of the mechanism of information storage, readout, and replication in living organisms is one of the great tales in the history of science. Now, for some of the backstory.

Observant humans have appreciated for thousands of years that characteristics of organisms are carried through from one generation to another in systematic ways. Selective breeding of animals gave rise to domesticated pets (dogs and cats), cattle, and horses. Selective breeding of plants produced cereal grains for brewing beer and making bread; fruits and vegetables of many different shapes, sizes, colors, and flavors; and cannabis for fiber and medicine. In the mid-1800s Charles Darwin (1809–1882) introduced revolutionary new thinking into biology by proposing that all life is deeply related—having developed over vast expanses of time from common origins—and the great diversity of living organisms can be understood as resulting from processes of variation and selection.

Darwinian evolution posits that there must be some underlying source of variation—something that is capable of changing—producing variant organisms that can be selected by natural (or domestic) processes. This variation is associated with how information is stored and passed on from one generation to the next in living organisms. Gregor Mendel (1822–1884), a Catholic Augustinian friar and eventual abbot of his monastery, had a deep interest in scientific approaches to understanding the world. Although he studied astronomy and meteorology and taught physics at his monastery, Mendel is known today for his experiments on inheritance in plants. In his monastery's garden, he investigated inheritance in pea plants, observing that various traits of pea plants (such as shape and texture of the seed, color of the seed, color and shape of the pea pod, color of the flower, and size of the plant) parceled out in an orderly fashion during breeding from one generation to the next. This led to the idea that information needed to build an organism is packaged into units associated with specific traits. Though Darwin and Mendel were contemporaries, they apparently did not know of one another's work. And although Darwin's ideas achieved widespread dissemination both during his lifetime and after, Mendel's discoveries were relatively obscure, not widely known during his lifetime, and not appreciated by the scientific community until several decades after his death.

Thus, it came to be believed that inheritance involved fundamental units or packets of information. The scientific study of inheritance acquired the name *genetics* (Greek *genesis* = origin, birth), and the fundamental unit of heredity came to be called a *gene*. The words *genetics* and *gene* appear to have been first used in the early years of the twentieth century. Although genes were somehow associated with traits exhibited by organisms (such as the color and shape of peas), at that point the notion of a gene was essentially an abstract concept. What the connection might be between genes and the physical properties of cells was, in the early years of the twentieth century, completely obscure.

Meanwhile, a revolution was brewing in the physical description of nature. Interestingly, only a few years earlier, at the end of the nineteenth century, prominent physicists were saying that no new major discoveries would be needed to achieve a complete description of nature—so many things had been observed, so many regularities discovered, and so many beautiful mathematical frameworks developed by which to describe observations and predict new phenomena that to some it appeared that the physical description of nature had achieved a kind of closure and completeness.

Then, along came Albert Einstein (1879–1955), who with his special and general theories of relativity radically changed the physical description of space and time, as well as notions of mass and energy. Space, time, matter, and energy were seen as interconnected and malleable in ways previously unimagined. The dust hadn't settled from the Einstein relativistic revolution when another, perhaps even greater one took place. From groundwork laid by Max Planck (1858–1947) in 1900 and by Einstein in 1905, a large group of physicists in the 1920s found that in order to successfully describe the observed properties of atoms and molecules, it was necessary to develop an entirely new physical description of matter and energy. This new description would eclipse that of Isaac Newton, one that had stood the test of time for more than two centuries. This new physics is called *quantum mechanics*.

Quantum mechanics represents a radically different description of what might be called physical reality. In pre-quantum (so-called classical) physics, the objects of analysis and the properties of physical systems are conceived as having an existence independent of observation. The properties of matter and energy are inherent qualities of the universe that may be fathomed by our observations but are not in any way dependent upon observations. In quantum physics, interaction is crucial to defining the properties of a system. In part, this stems from the fact that atomic and molecular systems are so small that the act of observation necessarily perturbs the system in unexpected ways, changing its properties. However, it goes beyond this in complicated ways, with the interaction we humans have as observers seemingly playing a new and critical role in defining the properties of systems being measured, a concept completely unanticipated in classical physics.

Figure 4.1 shows the crème de la crème of early twentieth-century physicists at a conference in Belgium in 1927. Front and center in the photo is Albert Einstein. To Einstein's right are Hendrik Lorentz, Marie Curie (the only person in the group to have received two Nobel Prizes), and Max Planck. The folks in the rows behind Einstein include Erwin Schrödinger, Wolfgang Pauli, Werner Heisenberg, Paul Dirac, Louis de Broglie, Max Born, and Niels Bohr. They had come together to discuss the rapid developments in the new physics of quantum mechanics.

Niels Bohr (1885–1962) was one of the most influential physicists in the development of quantum mechanics; some say he was second only to Einstein in his impact on twentieth-century physics. Both Bohr and Einstein were deeply interested in what physics can say about the nature of reality. Einstein maintained that there is an underlying physical reality to the universe that exists independent of any observation and that the job of physics is to describe, as best as possible, this reality. Bohr, taking the lessons of quantum mechanics to heart, maintained that acts of observation place fundamental limits on what we are able to know about the universe, and this will necessarily limit the capacity of any physical theory to describe what kind of reality might exist independent of our observations. Bohr and Einstein engaged in many dialogues related to these deep, foundational issues in physics and challenged one another with thought experiments.

In August 1932 there was a conference in Bohr's home city of Copenhagen, Denmark, of clinicians interested in the application of light to treat skin conditions—the International Congress on Light Therapy. Because Niels Bohr was the most famous scientist in town, the congress extended an invitation to him to give a keynote lec-

Figure 4.1. Solvay Conference, Brussels, Belgium, 1927.

ture at the meeting. Bohr accepted the invitation to speak and proceeded to use the occasion to think deeply about the physical description of living organisms in new and unprecedented ways.

In 1932 very little was known about the molecular components of living organisms, and pretty much nothing was known about the physical basis of heredity and the nature of the gene. In his lecture, Bohr speculated that in order to study the structure and function of living organisms at the subcellular level, it would be necessary to probe the cell with measuring instruments, and that such probing actions would necessarily perturb and disrupt the molecular components of the cell in profound ways. Such disturbances could include robbing the life from (that is, killing) the very living organism one was wishing to study in order to get at the physical basis of life. In Bohr's words:

> We should doubtless kill an animal if we tried to carry the investigation of its organs so far that we could describe the role played by single atoms in vital functions. . . . And the idea suggests itself that the minimal freedom we must allow the organism in this respect is just large enough to permit it, so to say, to hide its ultimate secrets from us.

The comparable situation in physics would be the measurement of properties of atoms and molecules, where the measurement process necessarily perturbs and changes the phenomena being measured. Classical physics was inadequate to describe the results obtained when measurements were made on atoms, and an entirely new mathematical-physical framework, quantum mechanics, had to be developed. The consequence was one of the most exciting things that had ever taken place in the history of science.

Thus, Bohr goes on to say, perhaps an analogous scenario might play out in biology: that in trying to elucidate the submicroscopic molecular processes that determine life, limits would be encountered that could not be negotiated using the currently known frameworks of chemistry and physics. An expansion of our description of nature might be required to describe life at the molecular level, just as an expansion of our description of nature was required to describe the structure and properties of atoms. It could turn out to be a very exciting time for biology, just as it had very recently been for physics!

In the audience at Bohr's lecture was Max Delbrück (1906–1981), a young theoretical physicist from Berlin who had been spending time at Bohr's Copenhagen institute since the previous year. Bohr's notion that one might encounter fundamental impasses in attempting to understand life in physical terms fascinated Delbrück and inspired him to begin to think about how to investigate the molecular infrastructure of living organisms.

Figure 4.2 shows physicists at a gathering in Bohr's institute in 1933. In the front row, left to right, are Niels Bohr, Paul Dirac, Werner Heisenberg, Paul Ehrenfest, Max Delbrück, and Lise Meitner. Between 1932 and 1937 Delbrück worked as an assistant to Lise Meitner (1878–1968) in Berlin, applying concepts and methods from mathematical physics to the investigation of radioactive decay and what would by 1939 be appreciated as atomic fission. On the side, he began learning about biology.

In 1935, Delbrück collaborated with a geneticist and a radiation experimentalist to publish his first work in biology, a technical monograph titled, in English transla-

Figure 4.2. Niels Bohr Institute, Copenhagen, Denmark, 1933.

tion, "On the nature of gene mutation and gene structure." In this paper, Delbrück and his collaborators proposed that genes were likely to be large molecules, the atomic configurations of which could be rearranged when impacted by high-energy electromagnetic radiation, such as x-rays. Although the publication remained relatively obscure, the authors distributed copies around and about, and one eventually landed on the desk of Erwin Schrödinger (1887–1961), one of the principal architects of quantum mechanics.

In 1944 Schrödinger published a little book called *What Is Life?*, dealing with deep questions concerning the molecular basis of life and drawing attention to Delbrück's idea that genes are likely to be large molecules. Schrödinger was particularly impressed with the notion that pursuing the investigation of life at the most fundamental molecular and atomic levels might lead to the discovery of new physical laws. In Schrödinger's words:

> From Delbrück's general picture of the hereditary substance it emerges that living matter, while not eluding the "laws of physics" as established to date, is likely to involve "other laws of physics" hitherto unknown, which, however, once they have been revealed, will form just as integral a part of this science as the former.

What is Life?—its author one of the best-known scientists of the time—attracted a wide readership, especially among physicists. Additionally, after World War II many physicists, having spent the war years doing weapons-related work, were receptive to tackling problems in a completely new and refreshing domain of inquiry. A significant number of physicists, after being inspired by *What is Life?*, became interested in researching the physical basis of life. Some of them became key figures in the early years of the discipline that would come to be called molecular biology.

Meanwhile, in 1937, Delbrück had left Germany for the United States on a fellowship to study genetics. There he had encountered the idea of using a species of bacteria, *Escherichia coli*, and viruses (called bacteriophages) that infect the bacteria, as a way to investigate the physical properties of heredity. Just as there are viruses that infect people—like the flu, common cold, hepatitis, and HIV—there are viruses that specifically infect certain bacteria. Indeed, a substantial percentage of the biomass on Earth consists of bacteria and bacteriophage viruses. They are everywhere.

Viruses lie at the definitional boundary of life. They contain the genetic information (genes) needed to build copies of themselves but not the machinery, so they must commandeer (infect) an appropriate host organism to carry out the process. Being small and presumably relatively simple particles that contain genes, Delbrück felt they would be ideal subjects for the study of the physical basis of heredity. He described his first encounter with bacteriophages like this:

> I was absolutely overwhelmed that there were such very simple procedures with which you could visualize individual virus particles; I mean you could put them on a plate with a lawn of bacteria, and the next morning every virus particle would have eaten a macroscopic one-millimeter hole in the lawn. You could hold up the plate and count the plaques. This seemed to me just beyond my wildest dreams of doing simple experiments on something like atoms in biology.

Soon World War II was consuming Europe, and Delbrück remained in the United States, settling in Nashville, Tennessee, where he taught physics at Vanderbilt University and conducted research with *E. coli* and bacteriophages.

A bacteriophage virus was known to be composed only of proteins and nucleic acids (DNA or RNA). In animal and plant cells, chromosomes appeared to be the locus of genetic information, and chromosomes were also composed of proteins and nucleic acids. Thus, if genes are molecules, it must be the case that they consist of either proteins or nucleic acids. In the early 1940s, given these choices, it was generally assumed that genes must be made of proteins. After all, proteins are hundreds of amino acids in length, and each of these amino acids may be one of twenty different types. This allows for enormous variability and complexity among proteins, the kind of complexity that surely would be needed to encode the vast amount of information required to build an organism. In contrast, nucleic acids were known to be composed of only four different kinds of units—adenine, thymine, guanine, and cytosine in the case of DNA—and thus were presumably far less able to code complex information. Some folks even referred to DNA as a "stupid substance." Whatever genes were, they must surely be made of protein—so everyone believed.

Then, in 1944, Oswald Avery (1877–1955) of the Rockefeller Institute in New York described experiments with pneumococcal bacteria demonstrating that DNA can carry genetic information from one cell to another. The work of Avery and colleagues was published in the *Journal of Experimental Medicine*; their report concluded by stating that "the evidence presented supports the belief that a nucleic acid of the deoxyribose type is the fundamental unit of the transforming principle." However, their work failed to convince others interested in the physical basis of heredity that genes were composed of DNA. It's not that Avery's work was thought to be wrong or sloppy science. It's just that because DNA was too "stupid" a molecule to carry genetic information—genes simply could not be made of DNA. Thus, Avery's work was essentially ignored. In addition, *E. coli* and bacteriophages had become the system of choice for the mainstream researchers in the field, and those researchers tended not to take too seriously work conducted with other organisms.

Although Avery's work was published in 1944 and essentially ignored, after a few more years went by there was more willingness to entertain the possibility that genes might be made of DNA. In was only in 1952, however, that an experiment conducted by Alfred Hershey (1908–1997) and Martha Chase (1927–2003) convinced the scientific community that DNA, and not protein, was indeed the carrier of genetic information. Hershey and Chase were members of the mainstream community of bacteriophage researchers and used *E. coli* bacteria and bacteriophages in their demonstration (Fig. 4.3). And their experiment is one of great elegance and simplicity.

Hershey and Chase used a bacterial virus called phage T2. They grew T2 on two different media: one containing radioactive sulfur atoms and another containing radioactive phosphorus atoms. Two of the twenty amino acids, cysteine and methionine, contain sulfur. Thus, most proteins contain sulfur, whereas DNA does not contain any sulfur atoms. Conversely, DNA contains phosphorus atoms and proteins do not. Thus, phages grown with radioactive sulfur would have radioactive protein, and phages grown with radioactive phosphorus would have radioactive DNA.

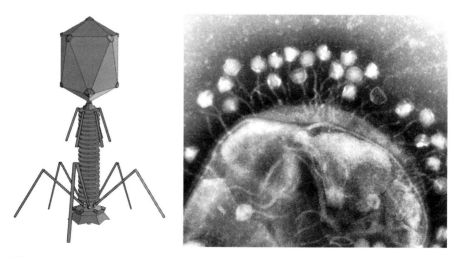

Figure 4.3. Drawing of a bacteriophage virus (left) and electron micrograph of bacteriophages attached to a bacterial cell during the infection process (right). The size of a bacteriophage virus is approximately 0.1 micrometer (100 nanometers), too small to be seen with light microscopy. The outside shell of the bacteriophage is made of protein, and its "head" portion has a strand of DNA packed inside.

Hershey and Chase then allowed the phages to infect *E. coli* bacteria, a process that can be accomplished in a liquid nutrient solution. In such an infection, a phage T2 attaches to the surface of a bacterium (Fig. 4.3, right). Less than thirty minutes later the bacterial cell bursts open, and several hundred newly formed phage particles are released. The phage that originally attached to the bacterial cell has presumably injected its genes into the bacterium, commandeered the cell's metabolic machinery, and produced copies of itself. However, in their experiment, Hershey and Chase did not allow the infection process to go to completion. They allowed phage particles to attach to the bacteria and let a few minutes elapse so that the infection process could commence—time for the phage genes to be introduced into the bacteria. Then, they agitated the cells just enough to dislodge the virus particles from the surface of the bacteria but not enough to break open the bacterial cells. The resulting solution would contain *E. coli* bacterial cells (with viral genes inside) and whatever remained of the T2 bacteriophage particles after their genes had been transferred to the bacteria. Because bacterial cells and virus particles are very different in their sizes and masses, and because they are all suspended in a liquid solution, it is possible to separate them by rapid spinning in a device called a centrifuge. Spinning in a centrifuge causes the larger, heavier bacteria to settle into a pellet at the bottom of the tube, while the smaller, lighter virus particles remain in the supernatant (the liquid at the top of the tube).

Here's what they found: Infection with phages containing radioactive sulfur led to the finding that the radioactivity remained in the supernatant and thus stayed with the original phages after the infection. Infection with phages containing radioactive phosphorus led to the radioactivity being in the pellet, and thus it must have been transferred to the bacteria during the infection. The interpretation is simple and straightforward: it is viral DNA (containing phosphorus) and not viral protein (containing sulfur) that is transferred from virus to bacteria during infection. Whatever genes are, they are made of DNA! Eight years after Avery's seminal publication, there was now another independent demonstration that everyone accepted and believed.

Several scientists at the time were already investigating the molecular structure of DNA, and the results of the Hershey–Chase experiment made the question of DNA's structure all the more interesting. Among those investigators were Rosalind Franklin (1920–1958) and Maurice Wilkins (1916–2004) in London, Francis Crick (1916–2004) and James Watson (born 1928) in Cambridge, England, and Linus Pauling at Caltech in Pasadena, California. Within a year, in early 1953, Crick and Watson proposed their famous double-helical structure for the DNA molecule. They published their structure in a one-page paper in the journal *Nature* in April 1953 and suggested that the genetic material was composed of two long strands of DNA, deoxyribonucleic acid. Each strand consists of a sequence of nucleotide bases, adenine (A), thymine (T), guanine (G), and cytosine (C), joined by covalent bonds to a very long backbone of sugar molecules (deoxyribose) and phosphates (phosphorus–oxygen groups). The two strands wrap around one another, forming a double helix, and are held together by hydrogen bonds (dashed lines) between the nucleotides—adenine to thymine, and guanine to cytosine.

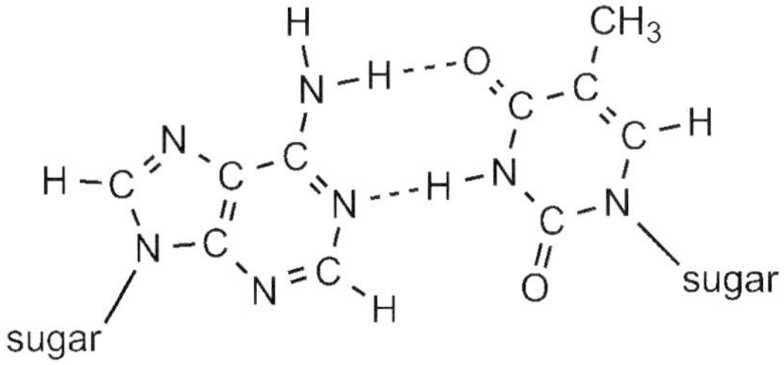

Adenine   *Thymine*

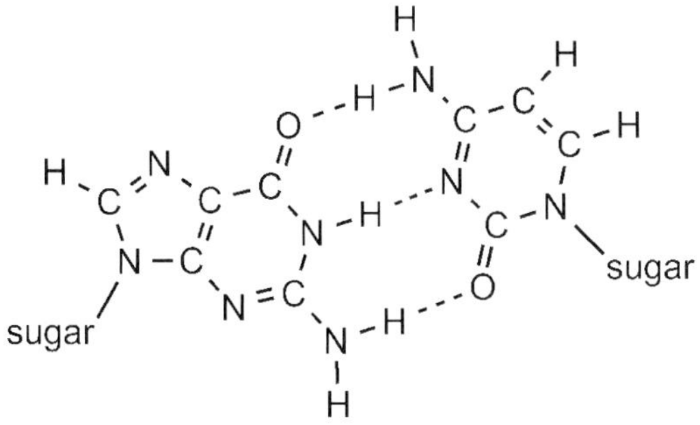

Guanine   *Cytosine*

Watson and Crick's brief paper turned out to be one of the most impactful publications in the history of science and was *the* major event in founding the field of what is now called molecular biology. They concluded their paper with the following sentence, sometimes considered one of the great understatements in the history of biology: "It has not escaped our notice that the specific pairing we have postulated immediately suggests a possible copying mechanism for the genetic material." In other words: Oh, by the way, we have solved how genetic information is encoded in cells and passed on from one generation to the next—the molecular basis of the gene and the physical basis for inheritance. The details still needed to be worked out, but the basic scheme was now understood.

It would take another few years and the combined efforts of many investigators to work out the details of how genetic information is encoded in DNA and how it is read out and translated into what is needed to build and operate a cell. But Watson and Crick appreciated the explanatory significance of their structure and were confident that the details would be illuminated. And they were right.

The structure of DNA suggested that genetic information is encoded in linear sequences of adenines, thymines, guanines, and cytosines. In the decade after Watson and Crick's publication, exactly how sequences of As, Ts, Cs, and Gs code for sequences of amino acids in proteins was elucidated. Each of the twenty different amino acids used to build the structure of proteins is represented (coded for) by a triplet (sequence of three) of nucleotides in DNA. The relationship between triplet sequences of nucleotides (called *codons*) and corresponding amino acids is called the *genetic code*. Because there are 4 × 4 × 4 = 64 different triplet combinations of four nucleotides (A, C, G, T) and only twenty different amino acids needing to be represented, there is redundancy in the code. That is, each of the amino acids is generally represented by more than one triplet combination of nucleotides. For example, the amino acid phenylalanine is coded for by DNA nucleotide triplets AAA and AAG, and the amino acid glycine is coded for by the triplets CCA, CCG, CCT, and CCC.

The reading out of information from the DNA takes place in the following way (see Fig. 4.4). The DNA double helix unwinds, little bits at a time. In the unwound portion of the helix, one of the two strands is used as a template for the synthesis of a molecule of ribonucleic acid (RNA), composed of a sequence of nucleotides complementary to the sequence in the DNA. Complementary means that where there is a G in DNA, there would be a C in RNA, where there is a C in DNA, there would be a G in RNA, where there is a T in DNA, there would be an A in RNA, and where there is an A in DNA, there would be a T in RNA. However, for structural reasons thymine (T) does not occur in RNA and is replaced by the very similar nucleotide molecule uracil, denoted by U. Thus, the RNA molecule so formed is a copy of the exact genetic information in the DNA, but now represented in a slightly different form. This process is called *gene transcription*, because transcription means to make a copy.

The RNA molecule then moves from the cell nucleus to regions of the cell where synthesis of proteins takes place. Because this RNA carries the genetic message from the DNA to the site of protein synthesis, it is called *messenger RNA*, or mRNA. The synthesis of proteins takes place in structures called *ribosomes*. In the ribosomes molecules of transfer RNA match nucleotide triplets in mRNA with their corresponding amino acids, according to the genetic code. The amino acids are then enzymatically joined into a linear chain by way of peptide bonds—a protein is born.

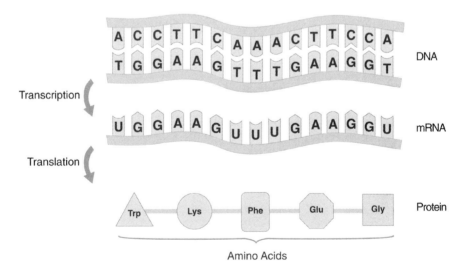

Figure 4.4. Transcription of nucleotide sequence in DNA into a nucleotide sequence in messenger RNA, followed by translation of the mRNA sequence into a sequence of amino acids linked to form a protein. Each amino acid is coded for by a sequence of three nucleotides, called a codon. Amino acids are here represented by three-letter abbreviations: Trp = tryptophan, Lys = lysine, Phe = phenylalanine, Glu = glutamic acid, and Gly = glycine.

This process is called *gene translation*, converting the nucleotide sequence information in the DNA and RNA into a different form—the sequence of amino acids in a protein.

The general form of all these processes and the nature of the genetic code were elucidated through the combined work of many investigators in the decade after the publication of the double helix structure of DNA. And thus was born the discipline of molecular biology and the seeds of what has since become a vast industry of biotechnology. Recall that only a few years earlier it had been thought by some that attempts to uncover the physical basis of life and to explain phenomena such as heredity in terms of physical mechanisms might lead to an impasse and precipitate some kind of revolutionary expansion of the scientific framework—perhaps some sort of "new laws of physics." Delbrück had set to work on physical mechanisms in genetics in part because of his interest in this possibility, as originally articulated by Bohr.

Delbrück, incidentally, had also been inspirational to Watson and Crick's pursuit of DNA's structure. Indeed, when the crucial insights about the double helix had been attained, before their paper to *Nature* had even been written, one of the first people to whom Watson wrote to tell of the discovery was Max Delbrück, who by that time had moved to the biology faculty at Caltech.

At least with respect to the physical basis of heredity, no impasses have been encountered and no expanded scientific framework has been needed. Indeed, quite to the contrary, the description of the structure of DNA, the genetic code, and the processes of gene transcription and translation are sufficiently simple that they are now taught to children in elementary school. As Delbrück put it many years later:

> Nobody, absolutely nobody, until the day of the Watson–Crick structure, had thought that the specificity might be carried in this exceedingly simple way, by a sequence, by a code. This dénouement that came then—that the whole business was like a child's toy that you could buy at the dime store—all built in this wonderful way that you could explain in *Life* magazine so that really a five-year-old can understand what's going on. That there was so simple a trick behind it. This was the greatest surprise for everyone.

And there you have it, in outline at least—a beautiful saga in twentieth-century science. The physical nature of the gene and the subsequent understanding of mutations as nucleotide changes in the DNA sequence provided a mechanism for the generation of variation upon which selection could operate. Darwin's ideas on variation and selection now had a solid physical foundation and could be described in molecular terms.

An important factor here, regarding the topic of this book, is that the dramatic and profound success in explaining, by way of physical mechanism, the previously deeply mysterious problem of heredity has set the stage for thinking that a similar straightforward molecular perspective will serve to explain every problem in biology, including the nature of mind. Whether this will be the case is by no means certain. Nonetheless, let us, for awhile, forge ahead, in that vein.

> Concept so simple,
> beautiful fit in a box.
> Can your mind fit, too?

CHAPTER 5

How Neurons Generate Signals

> It was on a dreary night of November, that I beheld the accomplishment of my toils. With an anxiety that almost amounted to agony, I collected the instruments of life around me, that I might infuse a spark of being into the lifeless thing that lay at my feet. It was already one in the morning; the rain pattered dismally against the panes, and my candle was nearly burnt out, when, by the glimmer of the half-extinguished light, I saw the dull yellow eye of the creature open; it breathed hard, and a convulsive motion agitated its limbs.

So goes the story of how Victor Frankenstein discovered he could use the power of electricity to bring life to the body he had constructed. Mary Wollstonecraft Shelley (1797–1851) began writing her celebrated story of *Frankenstein; or, The Modern Prometheus* in 1816, when she was eighteen years old.

Twenty-five years earlier, Luigi Galvani had described his experiments on electricity and the stimulation of movement in muscles—evoking movement in legs dissected away from the bodies of dead frogs. Electricity could make dead muscles move. Beginning in the first years of the 1800s the word *galvanize* came to mean to charge, excite, animate, exhilarate, arouse, electrify. There was a buzz in the air about electricity.

Our description of the microscopic nature of neural signaling begins with a discussion of the electrical properties of neurons, leading up to how a signal is propagated along an axon. These electrical properties begin with ions. Electricity is the movement of charge; ions are charged particles, and ions abound in living organisms. Calcium, chlorine, potassium, and sodium are among the top ten most abundant chemical elements in the human body. And these elements occur as ions dissolved in the fluids of the body: Ca^{++}, Cl^-, K^+, and Na^+.

Particles in solution are constantly moving as a result of the energy of thermal agitation. The movement is random and tends to cause particles to move apart and distribute uniformly over whatever volume of fluid is available, a process called *diffusion*. Diffusion can be readily observed by putting a spoonful of milk in a cup of tea. The milk spreads out and is soon uniformly distributed through the entire cup of tea. If the tea is hot, the energy of thermal agitation is relatively large and the diffusion process takes place rapidly. If the tea is cold, the lower energy of thermal agitation makes for a noticeably slower diffusion.

The neuronal boundary, like all cell boundaries, is composed of a phospholipid bilayer membrane (described in Chapter 3). An important property of such membranes is that they are impermeable to ions, meaning that ions cannot pass through them. This is because most of the thickness of the bilayer is composed of the phospholipid hydrocarbon chains and is a highly hydrophobic environment. Ions, however, are very hydrophilic and will collect polar water molecules around them. This shell of H_2O molecules prevents ions from penetrating into and through the hydrophobic core of a phospholipid bilayer.

However, the phospholipid bilayer membrane of a nerve cell, like all biological membranes, is studded with protein molecules of various kinds. Some of these proteins are channels that can open and close, allowing specific ions to pass through them and cross the membrane when the channels are open. Figure 5.1 shows a lipid bilayer membrane containing channel proteins that allow Cl^- ions, but not Na^+ ions, to cross the membrane. On the left, sodium and chloride ions are distributed in water, and the channel proteins in the lipid bilayer membrane separating the two compartments are closed. On the right, channel proteins allowing the passage of chloride ions open, and Cl^- flows across the membrane. Given this opportunity, Cl^- will tend to move by diffusion from where it is more concentrated (upper compartment) to where it is less concentrated (lower compartment); diffusion is said to be "down the gradient of concentration." As long as the channels are open, the movement of Cl^- continues until the tendency to equalize concentration is offset by the tendency of the positive charge in the upper compartment to pull the Cl^- back to its side. An equilibrium balancing these two tendencies is rapidly established.

Biological membranes also contain pump or transporter proteins that use energy to move specific ions from one side of the membrane to the other. A very important

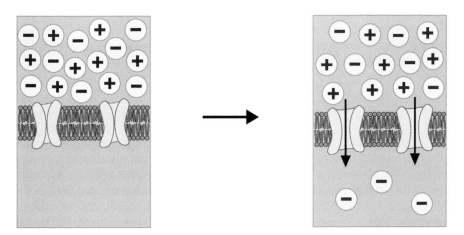

Figure 5.1. Lipid bilayer membrane with channel proteins. Sodium and chloride ions distributed in water cannot pass through the membrane when the channel proteins are closed (left); when they are open, these channel proteins allow chloride ions, but not sodium ions, to cross the membrane (right).

ion-transporter protein found in all neurons is the sodium–potassium or Na/K pump, which moves sodium ions (Na^+) out of the neuron and potassium ions (K^+) into the neuron. This process requires energy because as Na^+ is pumped out, the concentration of Na^+ outside the cell becomes larger than that inside the cell—the Na^+ needs to be "pushed" up its concentration gradient. It's like carrying water uphill—the water tends to flow down, and energy is required to carry it up. Similarly, with potassium ions energy is required to move them into the cell, against their concentration gradient.

The energy to power the Na/K pump comes from adenosine triphosphate (ATP).

Adenosine triphosphate

An ATP molecule consists of an adenine portion (right)—the same molecular structure that is part of DNA and RNA—together with a ribose sugar portion (the carbon–oxygen ring structure, middle) and three phosphate groups linked by covalent phosphorus–oxygen bonds (left). The phosphorus–oxygen bonds store a substantial amount of energy, and when the bonds are broken by specific enzymatic actions within a cell, that energy becomes available to other cellular processes. Life has capitalized on this property of the phosphate bond to store energy—from bacteria to plants to fungi to human brains, phosphate bonds provide a primary currency for moving energy around inside cells and powering all sorts of cellular processes. ATP is a widely used representative of this phosphate-bond energy currency.

For the Na/K pump, one molecule of ATP will power one cycle of the pump, in which three Na^+ ions are pumped out of the cell and two K^+ ions are pumped in. Consider this: a human body at rest needs approximately one kilocalorie per minute to maintain life (what is called a *calorie* in nutrition is actually the energy unit of a kilocalorie in physics). This is called the basal metabolic rate of energy consumption. It varies by body size (larger bodies use more energy) and by age (older people generally use less energy), but one kilocalorie per minute is a good rough approximation. That works out to be about 1440 kilocalories per day. If one moves around, then several hundred more kilocalories are required to power the action of muscles. Within the body, the brain accounts for a large amount of energy consumption, perhaps 25 percent of the total basal consumption, or about 360 kilocalories per day. Of the energy usage by the brain, about 60 percent of it—amounting to about 220 kilocalories per day—goes to run the Na/K pumps. That's quite a lot of energy just to power a single type of protein in the brain. Clearly, Na/K pumps must be doing something pretty important.

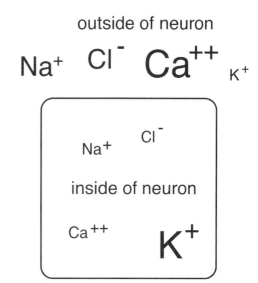

outside of neuron

Na⁺ Cl⁻ Ca⁺⁺ K⁺

Na⁺   Cl⁻

inside of neuron

Ca⁺⁺   K⁺

Figure 5.2. Relative ion concentrations inside and outside a nerve cell, represented by the relative sizes of the chemical symbols of the ions.

The result of all this pumping, pumping, pumping of Na^+ out of the cell and pumping, pumping of K^+ into the cell is that the concentration of Na^+ outside of the cell is greatly increased relative to the inside and the concentration of K^+ inside the cell is greatly increased relative to the outside. Other pumps, channels, and ion-exchanger proteins influence the movement of calcium (Ca^{++}) and chloride (Cl^-) ions across the membrane. Thus, the concentrations of these various ions inside and outside the nerve cell are different, with Na^+, Ca^{++}, and Cl^- more concentrated outside than inside, and K^+ more concentrated inside than outside (Fig. 5.2).

Because ions carry electric charge, the concentration differences result in electric-charge differences between the inside and outside of the cell. If we examine a small region near the outside of the nerve cell membrane and add up all the positive and negative charges there, we arrive at some value for net electric charge. And if we examine a small region near the inside of the nerve cell membrane and add up all the positive and negative charges there, we arrive at some other value for net electric charge. The net electric charge obtained by doing these sums differs between the two sides of the cell membrane. This can be described as a voltage across the cell membrane, where voltage represents the stored potential energy available to do work.

The voltage across the nerve cell membrane can be measured by placing one electrode from a voltmeter inside the cell and a second voltmeter electrode outside the cell. For a human brain cell this will be about 65 millivolts (mV)—65 thousandths of a volt—with the inside of the cell being negative relative to the outside. By convention, this is written as –65 mV and is called the resting membrane potential or resting voltage of the cell—"resting" because the nerve cell is not sending a signal.

AA and AAA batteries have potential differences of approximately 1.5 volts between their positive and negative terminals. These batteries are relatively big chunks of material. It is impressive indeed that a tiny nerve cell has a potential dif-

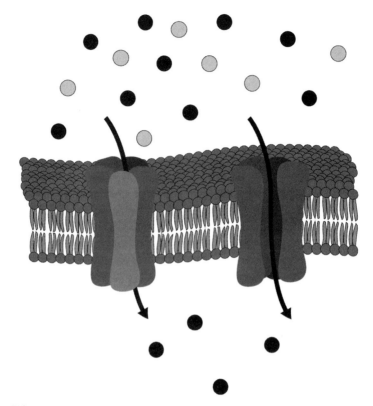

Figure 5.3. Cell membrane with ion-channel proteins.

ference of 65 mV across its cell membrane. The voltage across the membrane is a measure of stored energy that can be used to do work—just as batteries can be used to power lights and radios, the voltage across the neuronal membrane will be used to power the transmission of a signal along the cell's axon. Let's see how.

Present throughout the nerve cell membrane are various ion-channel proteins (Fig. 5.3). These are polypeptides made of hundreds of amino acids folded up into secondary and tertiary structures, with multiple subunits grouped together into quaternary structures, having pores or holes through their interiors of the right size and structure to allow specific kinds of ions to pass through. There are many kinds of ion channels, including Na^+ channels, K^+ channels, Ca^{++} channels, and Cl^- channels. If the channel is open, then specific ions can flow through from one side of the cell membrane to the other.

    Some ion channels are continuously open, and many ion channels open or close depending upon various conditions, such as changes in membrane voltage, the binding of a neurotransmitter molecule, or interaction with various other molecular regulators (phosphorylation, cyclic nucleotides, and so on). Consider this: if an ion-channel protein selective for potassium ions opens, then potassium ions will diffuse through the channel and across the cell membrane from inside the cell (where K^+ is more concentrated) to outside the cell (where K^+ is less concentrated). Because potassium ions are positively charged, this decreases the amount of positive charge inside the cell relative to the outside; that is, the membrane potential (voltage) becomes less positive (more negative) inside relative to outside. If we measure the membrane voltage before, during, and after the transient opening of potassium channels, we would see a change toward a more negative value (Fig. 5.4).

Similarly, if an ion-channel protein selective for chloride ions opens, chloride ions will flow through the channel and across the cell membrane from outside the cell (where Cl⁻ is more concentrated) to inside the cell (where Cl⁻ is less concentrated). Because chloride ions are negatively charged, the amount of negative charge inside the cell increases relative to the outside. Thus, the membrane potential will become more negative, inside relative to outside.

In both the K⁺ and Cl⁻ cases, the membrane potential becomes more negative and the actual magnitude of the membrane voltage becomes larger. Larger magnitude means a greater separation of charge between inside and outside. The term *polarity* is used to describe a separation of charge. The creation of a greater separation of charge across a cell membrane is referred to as a *hyperpolarization*, and opening K⁺ or Cl⁻ channels in a nerve cell at rest produces a hyperpolarizing effect on the cell membrane, as shown by the graph in Figure 5.4.

If an ion-channel protein selective for either sodium or calcium is opened, then Na⁺ or Ca⁺⁺ will flow through the respective channel from outside the cell to inside the cell, in either case making the inside of the cell more positive (less negative) relative to the outside. Thus, if we measure the membrane voltage before, during, and after the transient opening of sodium or calcium channels, we would see a change toward a less negative (more positive) value. This represents a decrease in the magnitude of the charge difference across the membrane and is referred to as a *depolarization* of the cell membrane (Fig. 5.5).

If a voltmeter is used to measure the membrane potential along a portion of an axon, we will generally observe voltage to be in the vicinity of the resting membrane potential (approximately −65 mV), with frequent small deviations above and below the resting potential (small depolarizations and hyperpolarizations). However, when a signal passes along a nerve cell's axon, a striking change in membrane voltage is observed, called an *action potential* (Fig. 5.6). These changes in membrane poten-

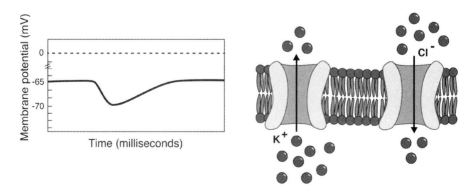

Figure 5.4. Hyperpolarization (left) may result from opening potassium channels or chloride channels (right).

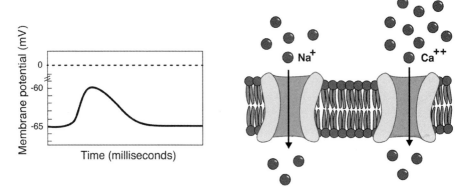

Figure 5.5. Depolarization (left) may result from opening sodium channels or calcium channels (right).

tial are the result of electrically charged particles (ions) moving across the membrane. A flow of electric charge is what defines electricity. Something electrical is happening. Neural signaling is electrical in nature.

What is happening when a signal moves through a neuron? As stated above, when observing the membrane potential in a cell at rest (although a neuron is never really at rest; interesting things are always going on), there may be small deviations of hyperpolarization and depolarization around the resting potential. But nothing really big happens unless a depolarization large enough to reach about –50 mV takes place. When this occurs, things change abruptly and dramatically. The membrane potential very rapidly becomes more and more positive, up to a peak of about +30 mV, at which point it decreases and becomes negative again, all the way back down to where it was at rest. The rapid reversal and then return to resting potential takes place very quickly, in about 1 millisecond, one thousandth of a second!

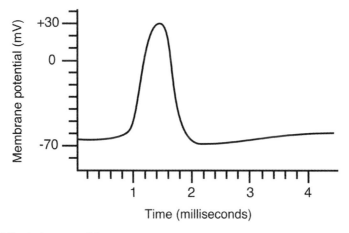

Figure 5.6. Action potential.

Direct measurements of the voltage changes across an axon membrane during an action potential were made by Alan Hodgkin (1914–1998) and Andrew Huxley (1917–2012) and reported in a short paper in the journal *Nature* in 1939. They worked with axons from squids, axons with a diameter large enough (0.5 millimeter) to allow insertion of a small voltmeter electrode within a functioning axon. Working with minimal equipment, Hodgkin and Huxley made a major contribution to modern cellular and molecular neurophysiology.

Shortly after their initial publication, Great Britain was drawn full tilt into World War II and both Hodgkin and Huxley devoted the next several years of their lives to working in war-related activities, such as the development of radar. Six years went by, at which point they picked up right where they left off. After several more years of careful experimental measurements and a lot of clever mathematical reasoning, they were able to propose a comprehensive description of what happens when a neural signal travels along an axon. Their theory predicted the existence of voltage-gated ion channels years before they were discovered.

Among the ion-channel proteins found in nerve cell membranes, two very important kinds, located primarily along the length of the axon, are sodium and potassium channels that open and close depending upon the membrane voltage. These are called *voltage-gated channels*. Voltage-gated Na^+ channels along an axon are closed when the membrane potential is at rest and open when the membrane potential reaches about –50 mV. Thus, if some inflow of positive charge occurs (this happens as a result of signals received from other nerve cells, discussed in Chapter 6) and the depolarization moves the membrane voltage to –50 mV, then Na^+ channels open and Na^+ (which is much more concentrated outside the cell) flows into the cell, bringing with it more positive charge, thereby making the membrane voltage more and more positive. When the voltage reaches +30 mV, the electrical forces tugging on the sodium-channel protein cause the channel to close and the flow of Na^+ into the cell ceases.

There are also voltage-gated K^+ channels in the axonal membrane. These channels are closed when the cell is at rest, and they begin to open as the voltage becomes more positive. By the time the voltage reaches +30 mV and the sodium channels are closing, the voltage-gated potassium channels are rapidly opening and K^+ is flowing out of the cell, carrying positive charge with it. The outflow of K^+ causes the membrane voltage to become less positive (Fig. 5.7). Enough K^+ flows out to return the cell to its resting potential of –65 mV, at which point the potassium channels close and conditions are nearly back to the way things were before the action potential started. Actually, the membrane potential reaches about –70 mV before the voltage-gated K^+ channels fully close, which is followed by a rapid adjustment to the –65 mV resting potential.

An analogy can be made between an action potential and the flushing of a toilet: once the lever is pushed down, water first flows into the waste basin and then flows away, emptying it; then freshwater flows into a storage basin to refill it, resetting the system—the flush runs to completion and returns the system to where it started. Similarly, with an action potential positive charge first flows into the nerve cell (Na^+) and then flows back out (K^+), returning the neuronal membrane potential to its resting value. Na/K pumps then function to reestablish the inside/outside concentration differences.

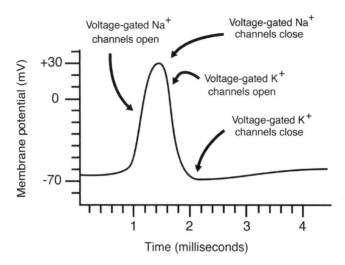

Figure 5.7. Actions of voltage-gated ion channels during an action potential.

To summarize the important concept of a voltage-gated ion channel, the electrical forces across the membrane (measured by the voltage) tug on the amino acids of the channel protein; at certain values of voltage the protein shifts shape and a channel opens. This allows ions of specific size and charge to flow through and across the membrane. Ions will flow from the region where they are more concentrated to the region where they are less concentrated: Na⁺, Ca⁺⁺, and Cl⁻ flow from outside to inside the cell, and K⁺ flows from inside to outside the cell.

Voltage-gated sodium and potassium channels are located along the entire length of a nerve cell axon. This provides a mechanism for the propagation of a nerve impulse or signal along the length of the axon, from the cell body, or *soma*, down to the axon terminal. It works like this: once an action potential gets started and voltage-gated sodium channels open at some location on the axon, sodium ions flow into the axon and make the region inside the axon at that location more positive. The Na⁺ ions rapidly drift away from where they flow in and make the nearby regions more positive. This local depolarization triggers the voltage-gated Na⁺ channels in the adjacent axonal region to open and more Na⁺ flows in. These sodium ions then rapidly drift and make the adjacent region inside the axon more positive causing the voltage-gated Na⁺ channels in that region to open. This process is repeated over and over again along the length of the axon—this is the mechanism by which the action potential moves along the axon. It is analogous to a crowd of thousands of people doing a wave at a sport event.

Once an action potential gets started, it moves all the way to the end of the axon without stopping. No new input of energy is required to power the propagation of the action potential along the axon's length. The energy has already been stored in the form of the membrane voltage and the concentration differences of sodium and potassium, the result of the continuous work of Na/K pumps charging up the "batteries" of the neuron.

To recap: an action potential consists of the sequential opening and closing of voltage-gated sodium and potassium channels, resulting in a rapid depolarization of the membrane, followed by a rapid return to resting membrane potential. Axonal action potentials initiate in the region where the axon emerges from the soma of the cell. This region is called the *axon hillock* or axon initial segment (Fig. 5.8). Here voltage-gated sodium and potassium channels occur in high density. As signals received from other cells (see Chapter 6) result in changes in membrane potential that diffuse through neuron, the first place where voltage-gated channels are encountered in high density is the axon hillock. The channels are triggered to open, an action potential results, and propagation continues without stopping along the entire length of the axon.

The action potential propagates in only one direction along the axon, from the hillock to the terminus. It does not propagate from the hillock into the soma, because there are few voltage-gated Na⁺ channels in that direction. And as it moves along the axon, it does not go backward because of a phenomenon called the *refractory period*: after the voltage-gated sodium and potassium channels are triggered to open and close, they require several milliseconds to return to a state that can be triggered again to open. (Again, there is an analogy with a flushing toilet: after the toilet is flushed, it cannot be flushed again until the system refills.) When Na⁺ comes flowing in, although it drifts in both directions in the interior of the axon from its point of entry, it will trigger sodium channels to open only in the downstream direction. The upstream sodium channels will be in their refractory period and unable to open again for another millisecond or two. This prevents the neural signal from bouncing around in both directions along the axon, which could make for quite a confusing mess.

Now consider this: many nerve cell axons in the human brain and body (and, indeed, in the brains and bodies of all vertebrate animals) are covered along their length by something called *myelin* (Fig. 5.9). Myelin is formed when particular types of glial cells—oligodendrocytes in the brain and Schwann cells in the peripheral nervous system—develop large flattened bodies and wrap around and around the axon (Fig. 5.10). Myelin is largely composed of layers of lipid bilayer membrane. About 70 percent of the dry weight of myelin is lipid. And more than 25 percent of this lipid

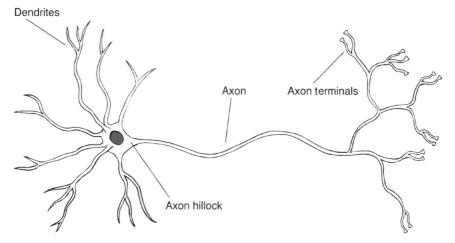

Figure 5.8. Location of the axon hillock.

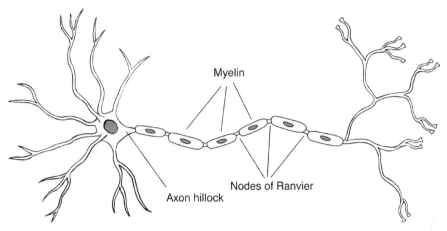

Figure 5.9. Neuron with myelinated axon.

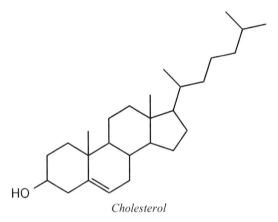

Cholesterol

is cholesterol. Cholesterol is an important component in all lipid bilayer membranes in animals, contributing to the structural integrity and the fluidity of the membranes. The cholesterol molecule orients so that its –OH group is within a hydrophilic edge portion of the bilayer, and the main body of the molecule is within the hydrophobic core of the bilayer.

Several types of protein are also found in myelin. One function of the proteins is to link layers together, so that the myelin doesn't unravel from the axon.

Myelin was first noted by neuroanatomists in the mid-nineteenth century. It was in the 1870s that Louis-Antoine Ranvier (1835–1922) observed that in axons covered with myelin (myelinated axons), the myelin was not continuous along the axon but occurred in sections separated by very small gaps. These gaps were later named the nodes of Ranvier, in honor of their discoverer (see Fig. 5.9).

So what's up with myelin? The generation and propagation of action potentials along an axon depend on the controlled flow of sodium and potassium ions across the membrane via the opening and closing of voltage-gated channels. If the axon is covered with layers and layers of fatty material (myelin), how can ions flow through channels across the membrane? Well, they couldn't—so the action potential couldn't propagate if the axon were completely covered with myelin. The key lies in the nodes of Ranvier. Along a myelinated axon there is a gap or node every few hundred micrometers, and all the voltage-gated channel proteins and Na/K pump proteins that would be distributed along the entire length of an unmyelinated axon are jammed together at the nodes. The density of voltage-gated sodium channels in an

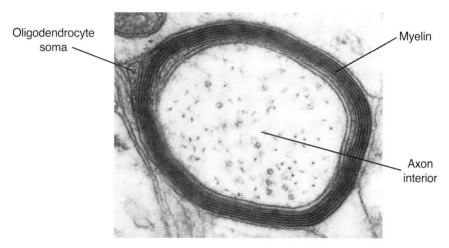

Oligodendrocyte soma

Myelin

Axon interior

Figure 5.10. Electron micrograph of a cross section of a myelinated axon from human cerebral cortex. Note the multiple-layered structure of the myelin. The diameter of the axon interior is approximately 1.3 micrometers, and the thickness of the myelin surrounding the axon is around 200 nanometers. The spots visible in the interior of the axon are microtubules and microfilaments, components of the neuronal cytoskeleton (see Chapter 10).

unmyelinated axon is around a hundred channel proteins per square micrometer of axonal membrane, whereas in a myelinated axon the density of voltage-gated sodium channels at the nodes of Ranvier is more than one hundred times more concentrated—ten thousand channel proteins per square micrometer.

As described earlier, what happens in an unmyelinated axon is this: when voltage-gated sodium channels open and sodium ions come pouring into the axon, the ions drift around inside the axon and depolarize the immediately adjacent region of the membrane, causing the voltage-gated sodium channels there to open and more Na$^+$ to come pouring in and drift around to depolarize the next immediately adjacent region of the axon, and so on. Thus, each small region of the axon initiates a depolarization of the immediately adjacent region, and the action potential propagates along the axon in a more or less continuous way.

In a myelinated axon, when the sodium ions come pouring in through opened voltage-gated sodium channels, the immediately adjacent region of the axon membrane is not available to produce an action potential because it is covered by myelin and ions cannot flow through channels and change the membrane voltage. The next place the impact of the inflow of Na$^+$ ions can be experienced along the axon is at the next node of Ranvier, where again there are voltage-gated Na$^+$ channels that can be triggered to open if the membrane voltage becomes positive enough. Thus, the inflowing charge carried by the Na$^+$ ions moves in the interior of the axon to the next node of Ranvier, the membrane is depolarized there, and the voltage-gated Na$^+$ channels open. In comes more Na$^+$, the impact of which will be felt at the next node of Ranvier as the positive charge moves as a sort of electric current along the length of the axon. This type of propagation of action potential from one node of Ranvier to the next is called *saltatory conduction*, from the Latin word *saltare*, meaning to leap as in a dance. The action potential leaps from one node to the next, dancing its way along the axon!

When sodium ions flow into the axon, what actually happens is the positive charge of the Na^+ pushes against the positive charge of nearby K^+ (a dominant ion within the cell), as positive charges repel one another. The pushed-on K^+ then pushes on whatever K^+ is next to it and so on down the line: little push, little push, little push, little push. Thus, the effect of incoming Na^+ is very rapidly transmitted along the interior of the axon as a sort of current flow of positive charge. In this way, the impact of the incoming positive charge and resulting membrane depolarization is quickly transmitted from one node of Ranvier to the next. This jumping from node to node results in a more rapid movement of action potentials along the axon than in the unmyelinated case, where each small region of the axon impacts the immediately adjacent small region in a slower, more continuous flow.

It is analogous to traveling by a local bus or train, which stops at many intersections or towns to pick up and let off passengers, versus traveling via an express bus or train, which makes many fewer stops—the express is much faster than the local. And the neural signal propagation in a myelinated axon is much faster than in an unmyelinated axon. The speed of an action potential moving along an unmyelinated axon might be several miles per hour (less than 10 meters per second), while the speed in a myelinated axon can be 100 meters per second—more than 200 miles per hour!

The dramatic increase in signaling speed within the nervous system provided by myelin allows for more rapid communication throughout the body, permitting such things as coordinated control of muscles in large animals. Insects don't have myelin, and there are no giant insects in part because it would be difficult to coordinate the synchronous movement of muscles in a large body using more slowly conducting unmyelinated nerves. Faster neuronal signaling also underlies increased computational power and complexity in the brain, related, we believe, to more sophisticated abilities to perceive, think, and feel. All from just wrapping axons with lipids—another amazing innovation of biological evolution!

> Axons and ions,
> dancing neural impulses.
> Here, the puppeteer?

CHAPTER **6**

Synapses, Neurotransmitters, and Receptors

Synapses (Greek *syn* = together, *haptein* = to fasten, join, clasp) are the points of communicative contact between neurons. While most studies of synapses have involved neuron-to-neuron communication, it is now appreciated that synaptic connections also involve glial cells—between neurons and glia and between glia and glia. The word *synapse* was introduced into the lexicon of science in the 1890s. Synapses come in two varieties: electrical and chemical.

An electrical synapse (also called a gap junction) is built from clusters of proteins that form channels in the membranes of two adjacent cells. A single channel is called a *connexon*, and each connexon is made up of several component proteins called *connexins* (Fig. 6.1). An electrical synapse forms when one or more connexon pairs join together, allowing ions to pass directly from one cell to the next. The size of the channel pore is larger than that of the ion channels discussed in Chapter 5, such as those involved in action potentials, and ions of various sizes and charges may all pass through the connexon pore. The pore is even large enough for small molecules like ATP and glucose to pass through. In electrical synapses, ions can flow rapidly from one cell to another, resulting in very fast propagation of membrane potential changes between cells. The signaling mediated by electrical synapses is relatively simple: communication of ion concentration or membrane potential changes from one cell to another, and perhaps the transfer of small molecules having regulatory functions within cells.

The chemical synapse is more complex and provides opportunities for additional kinds of regulation, such as changes in strength, feedback, and varied effects on different target cells. When the term *synapse* is used without further qualification, it generally refers to a chemical synapse. Figure 6.2 shows a diagram of a chemical synapse. A narrow gap, the *synaptic cleft*, separates the presynaptic axon terminal and the postsynaptic cell. The synaptic cleft is very small, around 20 nanometers (nm) in width, and is filled with water and ions. Although this gap is too small to see with a light microscope—an electron microscope is required to visualize it—the space is still considerably larger than the tiny gap separating cells connected by electrical synapses. Cells connected by electrical synapses can be seen as essen-

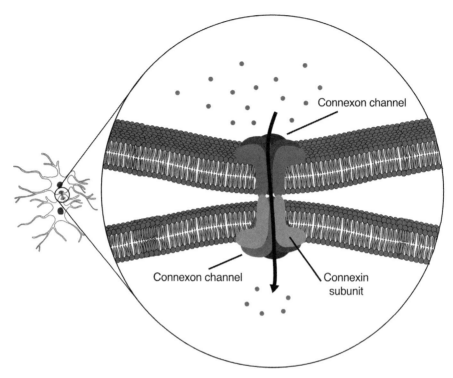

Figure 6.1. Electrical synapse. Connexon channels from two cells join together, forming a pore connecting the cells. Where the two connexons join, the membranes of the two adjacent cells are separated by a gap of about 3 nm. Each connexon channel is formed from six connexin subunit proteins, joined in a doughnut-like fashion with a hole in the center.

tially touching or in direct physical contact, whereas cells connected by chemical synapses are separated by a space that a signal passing from one cell to the next must traverse.

The part of the postsynaptic cell with which the axon is connecting is generally a dendrite, but it could also be the soma or even a part of the axon of the downstream neuron. If the synapse is with a dendrite, then it is often with a dendritic spine, a bulge on a dendrite that increases the surface area available for receiving signals.

Within the axon terminal are numerous small spheres formed of lipid bilayer membrane (Figs. 6.2 and 6.3). These are synaptic storage vesicles, each filled with several thousand neurotransmitter molecules. Specific proteins in the lipid membrane of vesicles function to attach some of the vesicles to other specific proteins in the boundary membrane of the axon terminal. Collectively, these attachment proteins are called the *SNARE complex*, and they result in vesicles being poised to fuse with the boundary membrane of the axon. (SNARE is an abbreviation for the rather unwieldly name soluble *N*-ethylmaleimide-sensitive factor attachment protein receptor.)

What happens when a nerve cell passes a signal along to another neuron at a chemical synapse? Let's begin with an action potential being initiated in the presynaptic neuron (we'll see how initiation happens shortly). The action potential propa-

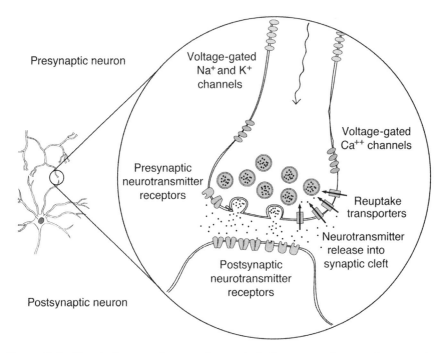

Figure 6.2. Chemical synapse between the terminal of a presynaptic neuron's axon and a dendrite of a postsynaptic neuron.

gates along the length of the axon until it reaches the axon terminal or, in most cases, multiple axon terminals, because generally axons are branched at the ends. When the action potential reaches the end of the axon, the membrane no longer has any voltage-gated sodium and potassium channels. Rather, it has another kind of voltage-gated ion channel, a calcium channel. When the depolarization reaches the axon

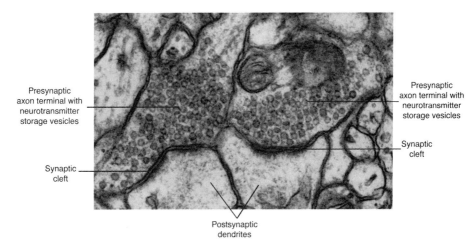

Figure 6.3. Electron micrograph of chemical synapses.

terminal, the changing electrical forces on the voltage-gated calcium channel induce the channel to open, and Ca^{++} ions flow into the cell. The calcium binds to proteins present in the SNARE complex, and a sequence of molecular events results in fusion of the vesicular membrane with the boundary membrane of the axon terminal. The contents of the storage vesicle—the neurotransmitter molecules—then spill into the synaptic cleft. Neurotransmitter release has occurred.

The molecules of neurotransmitter rapidly bounce and bang around in the synaptic cleft, moved by the forces of thermal agitation and diffusion. Very quickly they bump into all sorts of things, including neurotransmitter receptor proteins located in the cell membranes of postsynaptic neurons. If the appropriate neurotransmitter molecule makes contact with the appropriate receptor protein, it sticks, or binds, like a key in a lock. The interaction of the neurotransmitter with its corresponding receptor protein changes the shape of the receptor protein, which passes a signal to the postsynaptic neuron. Neurotransmitter receptor proteins may also be located in the presynaptic membrane of the axon terminal, and thus a signal may be passed from the axon back onto itself, allowing for various kinds of feedback regulation.

No sooner is neurotransmitter released from the axon terminal into the synaptic cleft than processes take place to remove it from the synaptic cleft, to inactivate the signaling. This occurs in one of two ways. One way is via reuptake transporter proteins located in the cell membrane of the axon terminal. When neurotransmitter bangs into its corresponding reuptake transporter protein, it will bind to the transporter and be moved from the exterior of the cell back into the interior, and so out of the synaptic cleft. Most known neurotransmitters are removed from the synaptic cleft by specific reuptake transporter proteins. A second mechanism of inactivation involves an enzyme in the synaptic cleft; this mechanism is used where acetylcholine is the neurotransmitter. An enzyme called acetylcholinesterase rapidly breaks the acetylcholine molecule into two pieces, thereby inactivating it as a functional neurotransmitter.

These processes of inactivation—either reuptake or enzymatic—act very rapidly and efficiently to remove neurotransmitters from the synapse. It is essential that this process be rapid and efficient, because the synapse must be ready to receive another nerve signal, should it occur, and be able to discriminate a new signal from the remnants of a previous signal. It is like having written a bunch of stuff on a blackboard and then needing to erase the board in order to make room to write new stuff. Otherwise, the board would become so cluttered that it would be hard to tell when new information appears.

All this takes place very rapidly, in perhaps 1 millisecond or so.

The concept of chemical neurotransmission was first demonstrated by Otto Loewi (1873–1961) in 1920. And the idea for the experiment demonstrating chemical neurotransmission occurred to him in a dream. Loewi had been investigating neural regulation of the heart in his laboratory when he awoke one night in the spring of 1920 and jotted down some ideas for an experiment on a slip of paper. The next morning he found that he couldn't decipher his scribbles from the night before. However, feeling that some good ideas had occurred to him during sleep, he resolved to attempt to recover them. His intention was successful: the next night he awoke around 3 a.m. with an idea for an experiment. This time, he got up and went to his laboratory to perform the following experiment.

Loewi was studying neural regulation of the heart using a preparation in which the heart from a frog was kept functioning in a jar containing a solution of ions in water. Animal hearts contain their own rhythmic oscillators, and a heart in a jar can maintain a regular rhythm even when not connected to the animal's brain or body. In a living animal, the heart rate is modulated by signals from the brain via the autonomic nervous system. Loewi left some of these autonomic fibers attached to the heart and by stimulating one of them, the vagus nerve, the beating of the heart slowed. This much Loewi had already investigated. The new experimental idea, emerging from his dream, was this . . .

The experiment was set up as described above. After the vagus nerve was electrically stimulated and the beating frog heart exhibited the expected slowing, Lowei collected fluid from the jar containing that frog heart and poured it into another jar containing a second beating frog heart. Lowei then observed that this second frog heart slowed its beating, too, but without any electrical stimulation of its vagus nerve. Loewi's conclusion was that some soluble chemical substance must be released when the vagus nerve is stimulated, and it is this chemical substance that mediates the signal from the vagus nerve to the heart to slow its beating. Chemical neurotransmission!

Loewi called the mystery substance *Vagusstoff*, German for "substance from the vagus" nerve. *Vagusstoff* was later identified to be acetylcholine, the first molecule recognized as a neurotransmitter.

Acetylcholine

Neurotransmitter molecules are contained in the storage vesicles of an axon terminal and are released into the synaptic cleft as a result of an action potential in the presynaptic neuron. After bouncing around in the synaptic cleft, they interact with neurotransmitter receptor proteins found in the membrane of the postsynaptic cell. One major type of neurotransmitter receptor is called an *ionotropic receptor*. These proteins are channel proteins similar in function to voltage-gated ion channels: when the channel is open, ions of a specific kind flow across the cell membrane. But an ionotropic receptor channel is opened not by changes in membrane voltage but, rather, by the binding of a specific neurotransmitter molecule to a particular location on the receptor protein. This causes the receptor protein to shift shape, opening the channel. Another name for an ionotropic receptor is a ligand-gated channel receptor, where the term *ligand* means a small molecule (in this case, the neurotransmitter molecule) that binds to a larger molecule (in this case, the receptor protein) and causes something to happen (in this case, the opening of an ion channel). When an ion channel opens and ions flow across the membrane, either a depolarization or a hyperpolarization results, depending upon which kind of ion the channel allows through.

The most abundant neurotransmitter molecule in the human brain is glutamic acid, or glutamate. Glutamate is also one of the twenty building-block amino acids used to construct proteins for all of life on Earth. As an amino acid component of proteins, glu-

Glutamic acid

O
||
⊖O—C ... NH₃⊕ ... C—O⊖
||
O

Glutamate

tamate was discovered in the mid-nineteenth century as a breakdown product of wheat gluten (Latin *gluten* = glue), from which it received its name. Its neurotransmitter function did not come to light until nearly a century later, in the 1950s and 1960s. In its neutral or nonionized form, this molecule is most correctly called glutamic acid. As a soluble molecule inside the brain, the acid portions of the molecule will give up a positive charge to the solution and become negative, and the amine portion of the molecule will take on a positive charge. This ionized form is properly referred to as glutamate. In many descriptions of neurochemistry, including my own, the terms are used interchangeably, and it is understood that in physiological solution the ionized form prevails.

Glutamate is the primary excitatory neurotransmitter in the human brain. How does glutamate communicate an excitatory signal between neurons? Large numbers of glutamate receptors in the brain are ionotropic receptors that are Ca^{++} and Na^+ channels. Thus, the binding of glutamate to ionotropic glutamate receptors initiates a flow of Ca^{++} or Na^+ from outside the cell (where these ions are higher in concentration) to inside the cell (where these ions are lower in concentration). This produces a change in the membrane voltage such that the inside of the cell becomes more positive, a depolarization. The membrane potential moves away from its value at rest and closer to the threshold for triggering the opening of voltage-gated Na^+ channels and the resulting generation of an action potential and neural signal. This is excitation.

Billions of nerve cells in the brain use glutamate as their neurotransmitter. That is, billions of neurons store glutamate in the storage vesicles in their axon terminals and release it into the synaptic cleft as a result of a nerve impulse propagating along the axon—these are called *glutamatergic* cells. These billions of neurons form trillions of synaptic connections with other neurons. Most, if not all, neurons have glutamate receptors on their cell surfaces, receiving excitatory input from glutamatergic cells.

-ergic: from the Greek *ergon* = work, *-ergic* has come to be used as a suffix for neurotransmitter names, turning them into adjectives. *Glutamatergic* has a more poetic ring to it than *glutamate-releasing, glutamate-binding,* or *glutamate-using.* Thus, we may speak of glutamatergic neurons, glutamatergic receptors, glutamatergic synapses, glutamatergic circuits, glutamatergic drugs, and so forth.

In addition to excitatory input, most if not all neurons will receive inhibitory input. The major inhibitory neurotransmitter in the human brain is the molecule gamma-amino-butyric acid, commonly known as GABA. Large numbers of GABA receptors in the brain are ionotropic receptors that are Cl^- channels. The binding of GABA to ionotropic GABA receptors allows Cl^- to flow from outside the cell (where Cl^- is more highly concentrated) to inside the cell. This produces a change in the membrane voltage such that the inside of the cell becomes more negative, a hyperpolarization. The membrane poten-

O
||
H₂N ... C—OH

GABA

tial moves further away from the threshold for triggering the opening of voltage-gated Na$^+$ channels and the resulting generation of an action potential and neural signal. This is inhibition.

If the membrane voltage is measured in a postsynaptic cell as it receives excitatory input, depolarization of the membrane is observed. This change in membrane potential—most often by way of ionotropic glutamate receptors—is called an excitatory postsynaptic potential, or EPSP. If excitatory signals are received repeatedly in close temporal sequence from an input neuron, or are received from several different input neurons at around the same time, then the depolarizing effects on membrane voltage will be enhanced by the summed effects from the individual EPSPs.

Similarly, if the membrane voltage is measured in a postsynaptic cell as it receives inhibitory input, hyperpolarization of the membrane is observed. This change in membrane potential—most often by way of ionotropic GABA receptors—is called an inhibitory postsynaptic potential, or IPSP. Just as with the summation of EPSPs, if inhibitory signals are received repeatedly in close temporal sequence from an input neuron, or are received from several different input neurons at around the same time, then the hyperpolarizing effects on membrane voltage will be enhanced by the summed effects from the individual IPSPs.

Any actual neuron receives input from dozens, hundreds, or thousands of other neurons. Any given neuron will have many synapses that are excitatory and many that are inhibitory. The excitatory and inhibitory synapses will be located all over the cell, primarily among the dendrites, and also on the body of the cell. Such a neuron then adds up all the EPSPs and all the IPSPs generated as a result of signals received from other nerve cells. When the sum of all the EPSPs and IPSPs is such that the membrane voltage at the location of the axon hillock reaches the threshold voltage for opening voltage-gated sodium channels (approximately –50 mV), then an action potential will be triggered (Fig. 6.4). It is at the axon hillock that voltage-gated Na$^+$ channels occur in high density, and so it is at the hillock that the action potential begins its propagation along the axon.

For synapses located on dendrites, the voltage changes from any EPSPs and IPSPs may have an appreciable distance to move through the interior of the cell by diffusion of electric charge. The greater the distance from the axon hillock, the more the voltage changes will dampen out and decrease in magnitude as they move through the cell. Thus, synapses that are closer to the axon hillock will have greater impact on influencing whether or not the cell receiving the input is triggered to generate action potentials. However, signals in dendrites can propagate, too: voltage-gated Na$^+$ and K$^+$ channels and action potentials, discussed thus far only in the context of signal propagation along axons, can also occur along parts of dendrites. This maintains the effectiveness of signals received in dendrites distant from the axon hillock, by boosting propagation along dendrites to offset their dampening out with distance. A mechanism this good—that is, the action potential—is bound to be used in more ways than one.

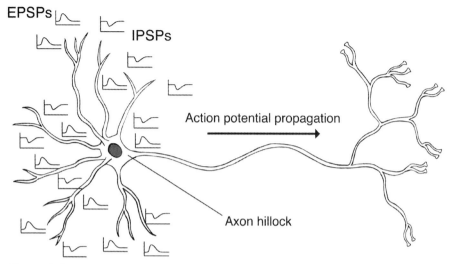

Figure 6.4. Excitatory and inhibitory postsynaptic potentials are generated throughout the dendritic field of a neuron by excitatory and inhibitory signals received from other neurons. The effects of these EPSPs and IPSPs are summed at the axon hillock, where an action potential, when triggered, begins its propagation along the length of the axon.

Neurons are thus continuously doing computation, summing up all the incoming EPSPs and IPSPs. If the voltage at the axon hillock reaches the threshold for opening voltage-gated sodium channels, then a nerve impulse will begin there and propagate along the length of the axon, triggering the release of neurotransmitter when the signal reaches the axon terminal.

To first approximation, we can consider neurons to store and release a single specific type of neurotransmitter. Thus, there are glutamatergic neurons, GABAergic neurons, and so forth. It turns out that some neurons release more than one type of neurotransmitter (neuropeptides; see Chapter 7), but for the moment we will stay with the one neurotransmitter per neuron narrative.

Glutamate and GABA have a close chemical relationship. GABA is made from glutamic acid by the action of an enzyme called glutamic acid decarboxylase (GAD).

Glutamic acid   *GABA*

All cells contain glutamic acid, as it is one of the amino acid building blocks for proteins. However, GAD is present only in GABAergic neurons, where it catalyzes the conversion of glutamic acid to GABA. (An enzyme is a protein that facilitates a particular chemical reaction, in this case chopping off a carboxylic acid group in glutamic acid to form GABA.) The gene coding the GAD enzyme is present in the DNA of all human cells, but only GABAergic neurons transcribe the gene to make a functional enzyme.

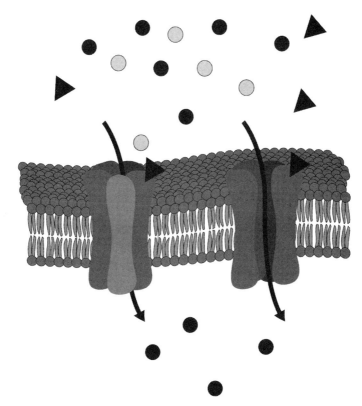

Figure 6.5. Ionotropic receptor. Binding of a neurotransmitter molecule (triangles) to a specific site on the receptor shifts the shape of the protein and opens a channel that allows specific ions to pass through.

To recap: an ionotropic neurotransmitter receptor protein, or ligand-gated receptor, is made of protein that spans the lipid-bilayer cell membrane and has a doughnut-like hole or pore running through its structure (Fig. 6.5). Such receptor proteins are often composed of several (generally four or five) protein subunits arranged to form the channel. The channel or hole is generally closed and opens when a specific neurotransmitter molecule binds to a particular site on the surface of the receptor protein. This binding induces a shift in the shape of the protein, which opens the channel. Depending on the size, shape, and electric charge properties of the channel, different receptors allow different types of ions to cross the membrane. Na^+ or Ca^{++}, which would both flow into a neuron, produce EPSPs. Cl^- flowing in or K^+ flowing out both produce IPSPs.

In addition to the ionotropic type, there is a second major category of neurotransmitter receptor protein, called metabotropic (Greek *metabole* = change, *tropos* = turn toward). Metabotropic receptors affect chemistry inside the cell (*intracellular* chemistry). Binding of a neurotransmitter to a metabotropic receptor does not directly open an ion channel (as ionotropic receptors do) but can cause a variety of different things to happen: ion channels may open or close, enzymes may be activated or inactivated, gene transcription may be turned on or off, and so forth.

After the initial observations of the existence of this kind of receptor, many years of experimental study worked out that intricate sequences of events take place after the binding of neurotransmitter. Here is one summary; consider reading through it as you might a poem on first reading—don't get caught up in the details . . .

The binding of a neurotransmitter molecule to the appropriate location on the extracellular side of the metabotropic receptor protein shifts the shape of the receptor to make its intracellular surface available to bind another protein—called a G-protein—present inside the cell. When the G-protein binds, it changes shape and becomes activated in the following way: a molecule of GDP (guanosine diphosphate) attached to the G-protein comes off and is replaced with a molecule of GTP (guanosine triphosphate, a chemical relative of ATP) taken from the intracellular medium, and the G-protein breaks apart into two subunit proteins. These pieces of G-protein then move around on the inner surface of the cell membrane and bind to other things, resulting in a variety of possible effects. One type of protein to which an activated G-protein (more accurately, a piece of the G-protein, the alpha subunit) might attach is an enzyme called adenylate cyclase. The binding of the G-protein alpha subunit to adenylate cyclase changes the activity of the enzyme, either up or down. This particular enzyme catalyzes the formation of molecules of cyclic-adenosine monophosphate (cAMP, another chemical relative of ATP). cAMP molecules move around inside the cell and interact with various proteins, altering their enzymatic activities. Among the proteins that are activated by the binding of cAMP are members of a class of enzymes called protein kinases. Protein kinases catalyze the attachment of phosphate groups (a process called phosphorylation) to still other (substrate) proteins, changing the activity of these latter proteins as a result. Among the proteins that can be phosphorylated by cAMP-activated protein kinases are various ion-channel proteins. Phosphorylated ion channels may open or close with different kinetics than their nonphosphorylated forms, thus bringing about changes in the membrane potential and thereby moving the cell toward greater or lesser excitability. Also among the proteins that can be phosphorylated by cAMP-activated protein kinases are various transcription factors. These proteins interact with DNA in the cell nucleus and influence the transcription of genes. Transcription factors will promote or inhibit the transcription of specific genes, and their ability to do this will be influenced by whether or not they have been phosphorylated by activated protein kinases. Okay, enough for the moment.

Several important things emerge from this description. Ionotropic receptors do one thing and do it very quickly: neurotransmitter binds, ion channel opens, specific ions flow across the cell membrane, membrane potential changes, and the cell experiences a very rapid change in its state of excitability. Metabotropic receptors have a very different and slower effect: neurotransmitter binds, G-protein attaches and becomes activated, G-protein interacts with adenylate cyclase, intracellular cAMP concentration changes, protein kinase activity changes, channels open or close, genes are turned on or off, and so forth (Fig. 6.6). Compared with effects of ionotropic receptors, the potential effects of metabotropic receptors are far more varied. They will also take longer, because several molecular steps are involved. And the effects will generally be more prolonged.

There is also very likely a substantial amplification of effect. For ionotropic receptors, one neurotransmitter binds to one receptor protein and opens one chan-

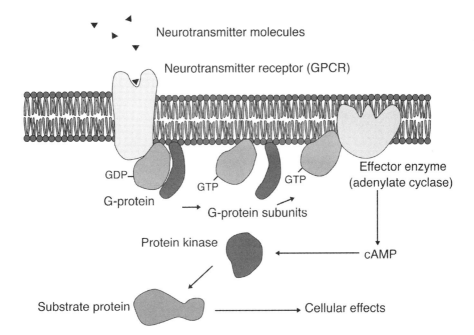

Figure 6.6. An intracellular cascade resulting from activating a G-protein-coupled receptor (GPCR), with adenylate cyclase as the effector enzyme. Substrate proteins are targets of phosphorylation by protein kinases. Examples of substrates are channel proteins (which would be located in the cell membrane) and transcription factor proteins.

nel—end of story. For metabotropic receptors, one neurotransmitter binds to one receptor protein, true, but after that several G-proteins may be activated by sequentially attaching to that receptor. One G-protein interacting with adenylate cyclase may increase or decrease the synthesis of hundreds or thousands of molecules of cAMP inside the cell. This may affect numerous protein kinases and thus numerous ion channels and transcription factors. Thus, the binding of a single neurotransmitter molecule to a single metabotropic receptor may result in many channels being opened or closed and many genes being turned on or off—a big amplification effect.

Here's another thing: depending upon the type of cell, G-proteins can and do interact with other things besides adenylate cyclase. One alternative is guanylate cyclase, the enzyme that catalyzes the synthesis of cGMP, a chemical relative of cAMP that can have similar functions inside a cell. Another is the enzyme phospholipase C, an enzyme that catalyzes the cleavage of a particular phospholipid (phosphatidylinositol) in the cell membrane to form two product molecules, IP_3 (inositol triphosphate) and DAG (diacylglycerol). IP_3 and DAG can act as intracellular signaling molecules, moving about and activating other processes. Thus, these cascades create further diversity and amplification in the effects of metabotropic receptors. The various targets of activated G-proteins are sometimes collectively called *effector enzymes* because they have various effects within the cell. Molecules such as cAMP, cGMP, IP_3 and DAG are sometimes called *intracellular messengers* or *sec-*

ond messengers, with the neurotransmitter being understood as the extracellular or first messenger.

Finally, because G-proteins have been found to be a central feature in all of these scenarios, metabotropic receptors are generally referred to as G-protein-coupled receptors, or GPCRs. These receptors occur widely in the brain as neurotransmitter receptors. And because of their sensitivity and versatility, GPCRs also occur throughout the body playing other roles, several of which are discussed later in this book.

Highlighting again the poetic molecular beauty of all this, here is a sonnet, in Shakespearean form—a lyric poem to the GPCR:

> Neurotransmitter binds, receptor shifts,
> Within the cell G-protein attaches,
> G-protein changes, and we get new gifts,
> Like from GDP, GTP hatches.
>
> Now G-protein transmutes from whole to parts,
> Each subunit starts down a differ'nt road;
> Adenylate cyclase labor surge starts,
> Cyclic AMP now increased or slowed.
>
> Protein kinase attaches phosphate group
> To the neuron's ion channel protein,
> Open channel or closed gives the cell's soup
> The potential to fire or stay serene.
>
> And here, just one subbranch of just one path.
> Think of the prospects—now, you do the math!

And, in closing, a haiku:

> Neurotransmitters,
>   shape shifting, G-proteins, whoosh!
>   Genes, transformation.

CHAPTER 7

Neuroanatomy and Excitability

Glutamate and GABA are the primary excitatory and inhibitory neurotransmitters in the human brain, used as signaling molecules by billions of neurons. Much of their action consists of evoking rapid changes in cell excitability by interacting with ionotropic receptors. In addition, these neurotransmitters also act at G-protein-coupled receptors (GPCRs), producing varied and longer-term effects on cell excitability, structure, and function.

Another neurotransmitter acting on both ionotropic receptors and GPCRs is acetylcholine. Ionotropic acetylcholine receptors (AChRs) are positive ion channels, primarily for Na^+. Thus, when acetylcholine binds to an ionotropic AChR, Na^+ flows from the outside of the cell inward, depolarizing the membrane and increasing the excitability of the postsynaptic cell. Ionotropic AChRs mediate communication between nerves and skeletal muscles in humans and other vertebrate animals. This connection is called the *neuromuscular junction*. Acetylcholine was the first neurotransmitter to be identified, following Otto Loewi's discovery of chemical neurotransmission in his investigation of the slowing of the heartbeat by the vagus nerve. The vagus nerve is part of the brain's connection with the autonomic nervous system, one of the principal divisions of the body's neural network.

What are these divisions? There is the central nervous system (CNS), consisting of the brain and spinal cord. And there is the peripheral nervous system (PNS), which encompasses all other parts of the body's neural networks. The PNS includes the various sensory systems of the head (eyes, ears, nose, tongue) and their connections to the brain; the several types of sensory input from the body's skin—systems responding to touch, temperature, and pain; and all the receptors located within the muscles, tendons, and joints that provide information about muscle tension and body position. Also part of the PNS are the connections from the brain and spinal cord to the muscles throughout the body, allowing for the control of body movements (neuromuscular system).

Another component of the PNS is the *autonomic nervous system*. This system regulates various body organs and internal functions, such as heart rate, blood pressure, respiration, and digestion. Much of this is normally outside our awareness—

things that are largely automatic. The autonomic nervous system is divisible into two complementary components—the sympathetic nervous system and the parasympathetic nervous system. Most of the organs (for example, eyes, heart, lungs, stomach, intestines, bladder, genitals) innervated by the autonomic system receive both sympathetic and parasympathetic input. The regulation of the autonomic nervous system ultimately comes in large part from the brain.

A last component of the PNS is called the *enteric nervous system*. This is an elaborate network of neurons and connections within the gastrointestinal system. It is involved in regulating digestion, moving food through the system, absorbing fluid, secreting hormones, and presumably other things yet unknown. It is sometimes referred to as part of the autonomic nervous system. Although the enteric system has extensive neural interconnections with the CNS, it also appears to operate with a great deal of autonomy, internally regulating its own processes.

Connections between the CNS and the PNS are either by way of the spinal cord or via one of twelve pairs of *cranial nerves*. The cranial nerves enter and exit the brain at several points in the brainstem or, for cranial nerve 1, via the olfactory bulbs. Here are the numbers and names of the cranial nerves, together with something about their connections and functions:

1. Olfactory (nose; smell)
2. Optic (retina of eye; vision)
3. Oculomotor (eye muscles; eye movement, pupil constriction)
4. Trochlear (eye muscles; eye movement)
5. Trigeminal (face; facial sensation and movement)
6. Abducens (eye muscles; eye movement)
7. Facial (face; facial sensation and movement, salivation, lacrimation)
8. Auditory-vestibular (inner ear; hearing and balance)
9. Glossopharyngeal (tongue and pharynx; taste and movement)
10. Vagus (pharynx, larynx, internal organs of chest and abdomen; taste, heart rate, respiration)
11. Accessory (neck muscles; movement)
12. Hypoglossal (tongue; movement, swallowing, speech)

Although it is often convenient to partition the nervous system into different components for ease of description and study, it is essential to appreciate that all these parts are highly interconnected. And beyond this, the nervous system is in intimate interaction with the endocrine system, the cardiovascular system, the immune system, and so forth—other bodily systems that may also be separated out for convenience of study. The body is a highly interconnected whole—an organism, the structure, function, and evolution of which can ultimately be understood only as a holistic system.

Neural fibers of the sympathetic nervous system emerge from the spinal cord and form connections with clusters of nerve cells just outside the spinal cord all along its length. These clusters of cells are called the *sympathetic ganglia*. The word *gan-*

glion (plural *ganglia*) refers to a cluster of nerve cells. Cells in the sympathetic ganglia send fibers out to the various target organs and other structures. Structures in the upper body that make connections with the sympathetic nervous system have ganglia along the upper part of the spinal cord, and structures in the lower body that make connections with the sympathetic system have ganglia along the lower part of the spinal cord.

For the upper and middle body, neural fibers of the parasympathetic nervous system connect with the CNS via cranial nerves 3, 7, and 10. For the lower body (pelvic region), the connections are via the lower end of the spinal cord. These fibers connect with clusters of neurons called the *parasympathetic ganglia*, anatomically located farther from the CNS than are the sympathetic ganglia. Cells in the parasympathetic ganglia send fibers out to the various target organs.

The regulatory actions of the sympathetic and parasympathetic systems have opposite effects; for example, heart rate is speeded by sympathetic input and slowed by parasympathetic input. Both the sympathetic and the parasympathetic systems are active all the time, and the balance of activity between the two systems determines the ultimate effects on the target organ. Thus, in times of stress, when the body may benefit from marshaling resources to respond rapidly to a situation, the sympathetic system is more active, resulting, for example, in increased heart rate and respiration. For this reason, the sympathetic system is sometimes simplistically referred to as the "fight or flight" system, highlighting its role in preparing the body to respond to a crisis. Conversely, in times of rest and recuperation, parasympathetic activity dominates. Several of the prominent effects of sympathetic and parasympathetic activity are listed here:

Sympathetic	Parasympathetic
increases heart rate	decreases heart rate
dilates lung airways	constricts lung airways
dilates pupils of eyes	constricts pupils of eyes
inhibits salivation	stimulates salivation
inhibits bladder from voiding	stimulates bladder to void
decreases intestinal motility	stimulates intestinal motility

The sympathetic and parasympathetic systems use different neurotransmitter molecules. When the sympathetic nerve fibers make connections with target tissues— such as the heart, lungs, intestines, bladder, or iris of the eye—the signaling molecule (neurotransmitter) used at those connections is norepinephrine. For the parasympathetic neural connections with target tissues, acetylcholine is the neurotransmitter. In both cases, the receptors are GPCRs.

Chemical synapses are often sites of action for the effects of drugs upon the nervous system. Here by *drug* I mean a chemical that in small amounts has a significant effect on the functioning of an organism. How might a drug molecule have an effect at a chemical synapse? One possibility is for the drug molecule to bind to a neurotransmitter receptor and either activate the receptor or block it.

There are specific terms to describe these actions of drugs. An *agonist* is a molecule that binds to a neurotransmitter receptor and activates it. Thus, for example, a neurotransmitter is an agonist at its own receptor. An agonist drug molecule would have a shape similar to the natural neurotransmitter for that receptor, so that it can bind to the receptor in a fashion similar to the neurotransmitter. Sometimes the molecular similarity between a neurotransmitter and an agonist is discernible by comparing the respective molecular structure diagrams, but often it is not apparent from such simple diagrams. In the key-and-lock analogy for a neurotransmitter and its receptor, an agonist is like a second type of key that opens the same lock.

An *antagonist* is a molecule that binds to a neurotransmitter receptor and blocks the action of the neurotransmitter at the receptor. Thus, an antagonist might be similar enough to the neurotransmitter to bind to the receptor but not similar enough to activate it—it just sticks there and blocks the binding site so that the neurotransmitter cannot bind and activate the receptor. In the key-and-lock analogy, an antagonist is like a key that fits into the lock but doesn't open it.

One more bit of terminology: any drug or other action that has a stimulating effect on the sympathetic nervous system is termed *sympathomimetic*, from the Greek word *mimesis*, meaning imitation. Drugs that have an activating effect on the sympathetic nervous system are called sympathomimetic drugs. The converse is termed *sympatholytic*, from the Greek *lysis*, to disrupt. Thus, sympatholytic substances decrease the effects of the sympathetic nervous system on its target organs. There are analogous terms that apply to effects on the parasympathetic nervous system—*parasympathomimetic* and *parasympatholytic* substances act to increase or decrease, respectively, the effects of the parasympathetic system on its target organs.

Because the sympathetic and parasympathetic systems are always active and have opposite effects, enhancing the effects of one has essentially the same consequences as decreasing the effects of the other. Thus, a sympathomimetic drug might produce very similar effects on the body as a parasympatholytic substance. And a parasympathomimetic drug might produce effects similar to a sympatholytic one. While their bodily effects might be comparable, the underlying cellular and molecular mechanisms would be different. This may or may not be of consequence, depending upon the exact nature of the systems being affected.

Consider the following example. Muscles in the iris of the eye make connections with the autonomic nervous system, and these connections are used to regulate the size of the pupillary opening. The sympathetic nervous system activates muscles— called radial muscles—that pull the iris back, opening or dilating the pupil (Fig. 7.1).

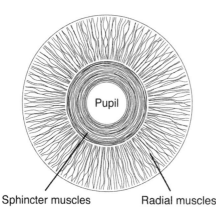

Figure 7.1. Muscles in the iris of the eye. The pupillary opening, through which light passes, is in the center. Sphincter muscles constrict the opening; radial muscles dilate it.

Pupil

Sphincter muscles   Radial muscles

The parasympathetic nervous system activates muscles—called circular sphincter muscles—that pull the iris closed, constricting the size of the pupil. Thus, the pupil of the eye is dilated by either sympathomimetic or parasympatholytic drugs and constricted by either sympatholytic or parasympathomimetic drugs.

For some kinds of eye examinations, the examining clinician may put drops into the eye to dilate the pupil. When drops are put directly into the eye, the target of their action is very close by, and the effects are fully experienced within a few minutes. Dilating the pupil allows the clinician to take a close look inside the eyeball and examine the retina. From our discussion, we conclude that either a sympathomimetic drug or a parasympatholytic drug can be used to accomplish the needed dilation of the pupil. Suppose the clinician applies some drops of a solution containing a sympathomimetic drug. Within minutes the drug enhances activity at the connections of the sympathetic nervous system with the radial muscles of the iris, the muscles contract, and the pupil opens—mission accomplished.

Now the clinician must shine a bright light into the eye in order to see inside the eyeball and examine the retina. However, when the bright light shines on the eye, it triggers a rapid constriction of the pupil to protect the visual system from being overstimulated. This is what happens when you walk outside on a sunny day after having been inside a darkened room, like a movie theater. This light-induced constriction of the pupil is achieved via parasympathetic neural input to the sphincter muscles of the iris. Thus, in order to carry out the eye examination, the clinician must use not a sympathomimetic drug but a parasympatholytic one. Both result in pupil dilation, but only the parasympatholytic drug blocks the muscles that constrict the pupil in response to light.

Historically, in ophthalmology, a drug called atropine was used for this purpose. (More on atropine in Chapter 8.) These days eye doctors often use a combination of two kinds of drops, one containing a parasympatholytic drug and the other containing a sympathomimetic drug, in order to maximize the amount of pupil dilation. A currently used combination is the parasympatholytic drug tropicamide (an antagonist at metabotropic acetylcholine receptors) and the sympathomimetic drug phenylephrine (an agonist at metabotropic norepinephrine receptors).

A similar pharmacologic combination is used for respiratory inhalers used to treat conditions like asthma, chronic obstructive pulmonary disease, and emphysema. Inhalers deliver a vaporized preparation of drug directly into the lungs, so that, as with eye drops for effects on the pupil, the desired site of action is close by. Sympathomimetics dilate the air passages in the lungs, allowing for easier breathing. So also do parasympatholytics. There are inhalers that contain sympathomimetic drugs—the drug albuterol, for example. Albuterol is an agonist at metabotropic receptors for norepinephrine.

Norepinephrine   *Albuterol*

Other inhalers contain parasympatholytic drugs, such as one called ipratropium, an antagonist at metabotropic acetylcholine receptors. There is also an inhaler that contains both albuterol and ipratropium, using the combination to maximize lung airway dilation effects that make breathing easier.

The neurotransmitter acetylcholine (ACh) was discovered following Otto Loewi's investigation of the parasympathetic neural connections with the heart via the vagus nerve. In addition to its signaling actions in the autonomic nervous system and at the neuromuscular junction, ACh is also a neurotransmitter in the brain. ACh receptors of both types—ionotropic and metabotropic—are found in the brain. Unlike glutamate and GABA, molecules that are released by billions of neurons as neurotransmitters, acetylcholine is produced and released by a relatively small number of neurons—perhaps a few hundred thousand—clustered into several regions deep in the brain's interior. These cholinergic neurons, however, send highly branched axons throughout large parts of the brain and thus affect hundreds of millions and perhaps billions of brain neurons (Fig. 7.2).

The molecular precursors to ACh are the molecules acetate (or acetic acid) and choline (part of the head-group component of phosphatidylcholine membrane lipids), both of which are found in abundance throughout the human body. However, only nerve cells that use ACh as a neurotransmitter have the capacity to make ACh from these ubiquitous precursors. The enzyme choline acetyltransferase catalyzes the synthesis of ACh from acetate and choline, and the gene coding for this enzyme is expressed (transcribed and translated) only in cholinergic neurons.

Similarly, only cholinergic neurons express the gene to make acetylcholinester-

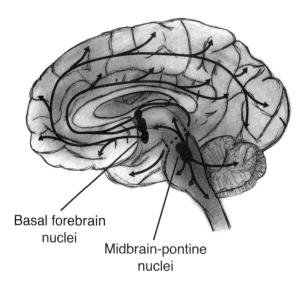

Basal forebrain
nuclei

Midbrain-pontine
nuclei

Figure 7.2. This medial view of the brain labels several clusters of cells known to release acetylcholine as a neurotransmitter. The word *nucleus* here means a cluster of nerve cells having a distinctive morphology. These clusters of cholinergic cells are located beneath the cerebral cortex, at the base of the forebrain (basal forebrain), and in the midbrain and pons of the brainstem. Axons of the neurons in these nuclei innervate large regions of the brain.

ase, the enzyme responsible for the rapid cleavage of ACh back to acetate and choline after its release at axon terminals. ACh is removed from the synaptic cleft by rapid enzymatic degradation rather than by direct reuptake into the axon terminal (as is the case for most other neurotransmitters).

Another group of neurotransmitters in the human brain are the monoamines, so called because they possess an amine (nitrogen-containing) group located at the end of a short chain of carbon atoms. Serotonin, dopamine, norepinephrine, epinephrine, and histamine represent this group of neurotransmitters. Serotonin, also called 5-hydroxytryptamine or 5HT, is biosynthesized in two steps from the amino acid tryptophan.

Tryptophan   *5-hydroxytryptophan*   *Serotonin*

The two steps are catalyzed by the enzymes tryptophan hydroxylase (1st step) and aromatic amino-acid decarboxylase (2nd step). Humans cannot make tryptophan from smaller molecules. It is one of the so-called essential amino acids, because it is necessary to get it from the food we eat. Nine of the twenty building-block amino acids are essential in the adult human diet. Plants can make all the amino acids.

During the 1940s, serotonin was identified as a molecule found in blood and having effects on constriction and dilation of blood vessels. Its name reflects this role: *sero* (blood serum) + *tonin* (vascular muscle tone). Serotonin receptors are located on blood vessels throughout the body. Only later was serotonin found to also be a neurotransmitter in the brain. The serotonergic neurons in the vertebrate animal brain are located in several clusters of cells in the brainstem (Fig. 7.3), collectively called the raphe nuclei (Greek *rhaphe* = seam, suture).

Figure 7.3. The raphe nuclei are located along the midline of the brainstem. Serotonergic axons from the raphe nuclei innervate the entire brain.

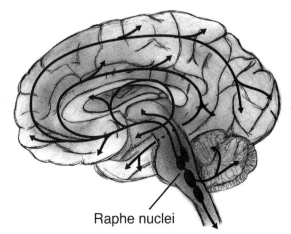

Raphe nuclei

　　　The total number of serotonergic neurons in the human brain may be on the order of only a hundred thousand or so cells, but these neurons likely have an impact on billions of other cells by way of highly branched axons extending throughout the brain.

　　　The monoamine neurotransmitters dopamine, norepinephrine, and epinephrine are made from the (essential) amino acid phenylalanine (Fig. 7.4). Norepinephrine and epinephrine also go by the names noradrenaline and adrenaline, respectively. The different names derive from different root words for "next to the kidney" (Greek *epi* + *nephros*, Latin *ad* + *renal*), the location of the adrenal gland, where these molecules were first identified.

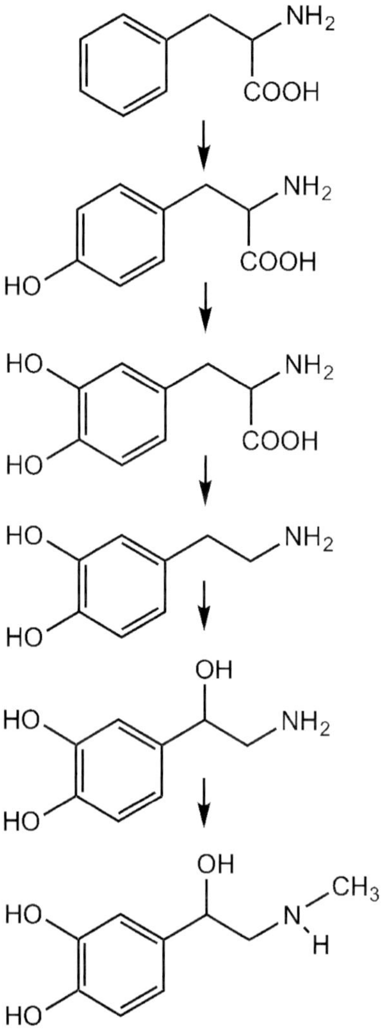

phenylalanine

tyrosine

DOPA

dopamine

norepinephrine

epinephrine

Figure 7.4. Biosynthesis of the monoamine neurotransmitters dopamine, norepinephrine, and epinephrine from the essential amino acid phenylalanine. Specific enzymes catalyze each step in this pathway.

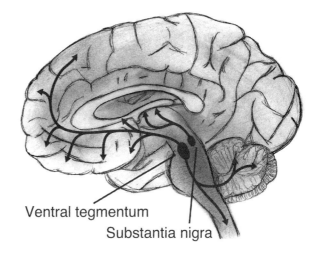

Figure 7.5. Some of the dopaminergic pathways in the brain.

As is the case for acetylcholine and serotonin, the neurotransmitters dopamine, norepinephrine, and epinephrine are associated with clusters of neurons deep in the interior of the brain, with the numbers of neurons in these clusters relatively small, on the order of one hundred thousand cells or so. And as before, the axons from these clusters innervate large regions of the brain, so these neurotransmitters potentially impact billions of other cells in the brain. The dopaminergic brainstem nuclei include the substantia nigra and ventral tegmentum (Fig. 7.5).

Nearly all the norepinephrine-producing (noradrenergic) cells in the brainstem are located in the locus coeruleus, a small nucleus in the pons (Fig. 7.6). The epinephrine-producing neurons are relatively few in number and are also found in the vicinity of the locus coeruleus.

The substantia nigra (Latin *nigra* = dark) and locus coeruleus (Latin *coeruleus*, *caeruleus* = dark blue) are named for the dark color of their cells—the darkness being due to intracellular accumulation of melanin, a polymer with components

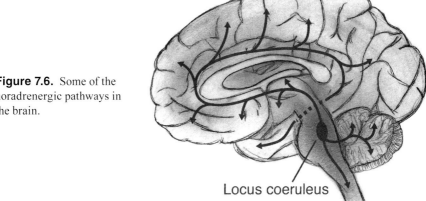

Figure 7.6. Some of the noradrenergic pathways in the brain.

related to dopamine. Melanin (Greek *melas* = black, dark) actually refers to a group of chemically related polymers found in many organisms. Melanin is what gives human hair and skin its color. One function of melanin in the skin is to absorb ultraviolet radiation from sunlight, protecting the body from potential damage. The function of melanin in brain cells (sometimes called neuromelanin) is unknown.

Acetylcholine and the monoamine neurotransmitters share the property of being produced by relatively small numbers of neurons in the interior of the brain that impact the activity of billions of cells throughout the cerebral cortex, cerebellum, and the entire brain. These neurotransmitters are involved in global modulation of alertness and arousal, wakefulness and sleep, attention and memory, and selection and initiation of behavioral actions—many important things.

Another category of neurotransmitter is composed of polypeptides, ranging in length from five to thirty-one amino acids. These peptide neurotransmitters include the opioids, such as the enkephalins, dynorphins, and beta-endorphin—collectively called the endorphins—and a variety of other neuropeptides, such as vasopressin, substance P, somatostatin, oxytocin, orexin, neurotensin, neuropeptide Y, galanin, and cholecystokinin. Interestingly, some of these neuropeptides are coreleased from neurons together with other neurotransmitters. Mostly we do not yet know very much about what they do.

The known neurotransmitters in the human brain may be grouped into several categories. There are amino acid neurotransmitters: glutamate and glycine (alpha-amino acids) and GABA (a gamma-amino acid) constitute the known members of this category. There are neurotransmitters made directly from amino acids by small molecular modifications—serotonin, dopamine, norepinephrine, epinephrine, and histamine represent these. There is acetylcholine. There are polypeptide neurotransmitters, the neuropeptides. And there are several more: adenosine, the endocannabinoids, nitric oxide, and a few others that are known, and no doubt a few others are yet to be identified. The diversity of neurotransmitter molecules allows for nuanced regulation of the networks of interconnected neurons in the brain.

The two major categories of neurotransmitter receptor are the ionotropic and GPCR types. Chapter 6 discussed the actions of glutamate, GABA, and acetylcholine at their associated ionotropic receptors. Glycine also acts as a neurotransmitter at ionotropic receptors. There is one type of serotonin receptor—the $5HT_3$ receptor—that is ionotropic. There are receptors that respond to ATP, ADP, and AMP as neurotransmitters that are ionotropic; these are called purine receptors. Most other known neurotransmitter receptors are GPCRs. There are GPCRs that respond to glutamate, GABA, and acetylcholine. All the known serotonin receptors other than $5HT_3$ are GPCRs. There are GPCR purine receptors. All the known dopamine, norepinephrine, epinephrine, histamine, adenosine, cannabinoid, opioid, and other neuropeptide receptors are GPCRs. Thus, there is enormous diversity of neurotransmitter receptor types, both ionotropic and GPCR—hundreds (minimally) of different receptor types.

The vast interconnectivity of the brain consists in large part of the trillions of glutamatergic and GABAergic chemical synapses, mediating an immense number of rapid excitatory and inhibitory effects. In addition, there is extensive excitatory and inhibitory interconnectivity via electrical synapses. And then there are trillions of chemical synapses modulating neural excitation and inhibition via GPCR effects. All in all, such complex circuitry combining excitation and inhibition provides opportunities for problems to occur if something gets out of whack. Too much excitation and not enough inhibition may, for example, set off a kind of explosive chain reaction of excitation. One manifestation of such runaway excitation is the clinical condition called a seizure (old French *saisir* = to take possession of).

A variety of different things may happen as a result of a seizure, depending upon the region of the brain that is affected. There may be sudden changes in sensory perception, such as visual disturbances or the smell of an unusual odor. There may be rapid and inexplicable emotional or cognitive changes. There are often involuntary muscle movements, and sometimes even complete loss of control over the movement of one's body. Obviously, this could lead to serious consequences if someone has a seizure while, for example, driving a car. Amnesia, or memory loss, frequently accompanies the experience of a seizure. Severe seizures can produce a loss of consciousness and even death. Too much excitation is not a good thing.

Sometimes seizures are associated with particular identifiable causes. A tumor—an abnormal growth of cells in the brain—may disrupt neural circuitry, producing unbalanced excitation. New onset of seizures in an adult is always reason to check for the existence of a brain tumor. Brain infections and high fevers may trigger seizures. Traumatic physical injury to the head, such as from a car or bicycle accident, may disrupt the neural connectivity in such a way that seizures are a result. Drugs that increase brain neuronal excitability (stimulant drugs are discussed in Chapter 9) have the potential to produce seizures. Some drugs that produce the opposite effect of stimulants, inhibiting neural activity in the brain, can also increase the risk for seizures if these drugs are used regularly and then abruptly stopped. Examples of such drugs are alcohol and other sedative-hypnotics, also discussed in Chapter 9.

Most seizures, however, have not been associated with any identified causes. These are called idiopathic seizures. *Idiopathic* is a word widely used in medicine. It means that the condition arises from an obscure or unknown cause. The roots are from the Greek *idios*, meaning personal, private, separate, and *pathos*, meaning suffering.

Idiopathic seizures may appear spontaneously at any point in life, although they most often first appear in childhood. There are genetic and developmental components to idiopathic seizures, although these remain still largely uncharacterized. Certain configurations of neural connectivity arising during the wiring of the brain early in life can apparently increase the risk of occurrence of unbalanced runaway neural excitation, and thus of seizure.

Susceptible persons may develop idiopathic seizures without any precipitating factors. However, these seizures may be triggered in a variety of identified ways. Intense sensory stimuli, especially of a strongly rhythmic nature—such as brightly flashing strobe lights or other flashing visual displays—can set up powerful rhythmic neural activity in sensory regions of the brain that may lead to the explosive runaway activity of a seizure. Other possible triggering factors include sleep deprivation, stress, physical trauma to the head, stimulant drug use, and withdrawal from sedative-hypnotic drugs.

The prevalence of idiopathic seizures is actually quite high. Nearly 1 percent of the population in the United States is believed to suffer from chronic, recurrent seizures, most of which are idiopathic. This corresponds to about three million people in the United States—a large number. The clinical condition of recurring seizures is called epilepsy. Seizure disorders are generally diagnosed when people are young. By the time someone is an adult, if they have a predisposition to seizures, often they know it. This is why something like a seizure-triggering television episode viewed by a very large number of young children might reveal seizure disorders that have not yet emerged.

Seizures are about runaway overexcitation. Thus, a potential treatment would be one that reduces the amount of excitation, or enhances the amount of inhibition, in the brain. A number of available drugs do exactly that, and many are effective medications for the treatment of seizure disorders. In the United States, at present more than a dozen different pharmaceutical drugs are marketed as antiseizure medications. As to the molecular mechanisms of how they work to reduce neuronal excitability, the general themes are interference with voltage-gated sodium, potassium, and calcium channels; facilitation of the inhibitory action of GABA; and reduction of the excitatory action of glutamate. The trick is somehow to blunt excitability enough so that seizures are prevented but not so much that the normal functioning of the brain is impaired—it's a delicate balance.

Most people with seizure disorders find that a regular regimen of one or more of the available antiseizure medications will effectively control their seizures. It is important to do everything possible to prevent seizures from occurring, especially the more severe seizures. First off, severe seizures are life-threatening, either from direct effects on the brain or from the possibility of a fall or other accident while the seizure is happening. Next, whenever a seizure occurs, it is likely that at least some of the underlying neural pathways are reinforced and strengthened, thereby increasing the risk for the occurrence of subsequent seizures. Finally, it is likely that seizures, especially severe ones, result in death of cells in the brain.

How do seizures cause cell death? It turns out that overexcitation of neurons by glutamate is known to be quite a toxic phenomenon. It is called *excitotoxicity*, glutamatergic excitotoxicity, or excitotoxic cell death. The exact mechanisms of toxicity remain unclear, but the general scenario is thought to be something like this: Overexcitation is associated with activation of many ionotropic glutamate receptors that allow large amounts of Ca^{++} into the cell. Calcium ions activate many different enzymes, including proteases (enzymes that break proteins apart), phospholipases (enzymes that break phospholipids apart), and endonucleases (enzymes that break DNA apart). The activity of enzymes such as these is very carefully controlled under most circumstances. However, if large quantities of Ca^{++} enter the cell quickly, the normal regulatory processes may lose their grip, and havoc and damage may result.

Thus, for multiple reasons, seizures are to be avoided. As stated earlier, for most epileptics most of the time, antiseizure medications work. However, a substantial percentage of people having epilepsy (perhaps as many as 30 percent) find their seizures are not adequately controlled by the available medications. Pharmaceutical companies continue to search for new antiseizure medications, hoping to provide relief for those who may have not responded to the drugs currently available.

In some cases of severe and nonresponsive seizure disorders, surgical procedures are carried out to excise small regions of the brain that have been pinpointed as the source, or initiatory foci, of seizures—so-called epileptogenic brain tissue. Of course, such surgeries must be conducted with utmost care and remove no more than the minimal amount of tissue necessary to control the onset of seizures. These surgeries have resulted in some interesting discoveries about the functions of various parts of the human cerebral cortex. We'll return to some of these in later chapters.

> Glutamate, GABA,
>   brilliantly balanced, just so—
>   or a fit may flare.

CHAPTER 8

Poison, Medicine, and Pharmacology

We can think of a *drug* as a chemical that in small amounts has a significant effect on body function. Medicines used to decrease the likelihood of seizures are examples of drugs. Other drugs will, if ingested, increase the likelihood of having a seizure. Tropicamide, a parasympatholytic, and phenylephrine, a sympathomimetic, are drugs used to dilate the pupil of the eye for eye examinations. However, ingest too much of either of these drugs and a heart attack may be the result.

Pharmacology is the scientific study of drugs: their origins, compositions, and effects on the body. The word *pharmacology*—as well as related words like pharmacy, pharmacist, and pharmaceutical—derives from the Greek word *pharmakon*. This is a remarkable term, because it means medicine *and* poison—at the same time. A medicine is a substance used for promoting health or treating disease. Medicines are understood to have beneficial effects on one's state of health. A poison is a dangerous or deadly substance. The ancient Greeks, in formulating *pharmakon*, understood that poisons may be medicines and that medicines are also poisons.

Centuries later this important notion was articulated by the sixteenth-century Swiss physician and alchemist Paracelsus (Fig. 8.1). One of the many things he is known for is his teaching that all substances are poison and that whether something acts as a poison or a medicine may depend on the dose.

Everything is a poison. Even substances essential for human life, such as water and oxygen, are poisons if taken in sufficiently large amounts. And *all* chemical substances that are taken as medicines—that may have beneficial therapeutic effects on the body—are also, and at the same time, poisons. This is a very powerful teaching.

Although everything may be a poison, some things are more poisonous than others. One of the most poisonous substances known is a chemical called tetrodotoxin (TTX). This poison famously occurs in the body of certain varieties of puffer fish (also called blowfish or fugu) that live throughout the world in

Tetrodotoxin

Figure 8.1. Theophrastus Philippus Aureolus Bombastus von Hohenheim, better known as Paracelsus (1493–1541). Engravings from the 1500s: on the left Paracelsus is depicted at around thirty years of age, on the right he is shown shortly before his death.

tropical and semitropical oceans. TTX has also been identified in other animals, including several varieties of salamander or newt, a blue-ringed octopus, and various crabs and starfish. That a weird molecule like TTX is found in a number of unrelated animal species suggests it is not synthesized directly by the animals themselves but, rather, may be the product of a microorganism living inside these various animals. Indeed, TTX is now known to be made by bacteria living symbiotically within the animal species found to possess it. The bacteria get a nice place to reside, with food and shelter provided. And the animals harboring the TTX-making bacteria receive protection—because of TTX's poison qualities—from being eaten by predators.

The shape of TTX promotes its sticking to the outside surface of the voltage-gated sodium channel in such a way that it blocks the pore through which sodium ions pass when the channel opens. This compound is such an effective blocker of voltage-gated Na^+ channels that even a very small amount of it is highly poisonous. Blocking Na^+ channels prevents neurons from sending signals. Numbness occurs because signals from sensory neurons in the skin do not reach the brain. And signals from the brain don't reach the muscles, so the experience after TTX ingestion is one of muscle weakness, difficulty moving, and shortly thereafter paralysis—including the muscles controlling breathing. So, if someone dies from TTX poisoning, as occasionally happens, it is from respiratory paralysis and the resulting suffocation. There is no chemical antidote to TTX poisoning. However, its effect on sodium channels is not permanent. The TTX molecule sticks to a channel only temporarily, eventually falls off, and is washed out of the body. Thus, if a person who has been poisoned with TTX can be mechanically respirated during the period of paralysis—up to several hours—they will survive the ordeal.

Two other interesting things may be noted about the poisonous effects of TTX. First, the heart does not stop beating—the Na^+ channels in the heart are of a suffi-

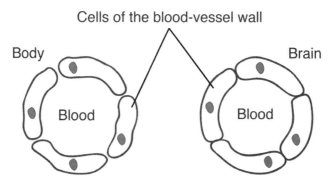

Figure 8.2. Blood vessel cross sections: in the body (left) and in the CNS (right). Note the gaps between the cells on the left and the tight joining of cells on the right.

ciently different molecular type that they are not blocked by TTX. Second, the brain is not affected—the ability of nerve cells in the brain to send signals is not impaired. Why not? Because TTX does not enter the brain! This brings us to the concept of the blood–brain barrier.

The *blood–brain barrier* refers to how the blood vessels are constructed within the central nervous system, or CNS (the brain and spinal cord), to regulate the passage of material from the blood into the brain and vice versa. Blood vessels anywhere in the body have vessel walls that are made of cells (just as all parts of the body are made of cells) packed together just as bricks may be packed together to form the walls of a building. For blood vessels in most of the body, the cells forming the walls of the vessel are not tightly joined together—there are tiny gaps between the cells (Fig. 8.2). Although these gaps are very small, they are large enough for many molecules to pass through. Thus, there is free exchange of molecules between the blood and the tissues of the body. This occurs everywhere in the body, except in the CNS. There, cells forming the walls of the blood vessels are tightly joined together, with no gaps, no pores, no holes between the cells.

What are the implications of this? There must be exchange of molecules between the blood and the tissues of the body. Certain molecules carried by the blood—oxygen, glucose, and essential amino acids, for example—are necessary for cells to function. In all parts of the body outside of the CNS, these molecules and others can readily move between the blood and body tissues through gaps between cells in blood vessel walls. In the CNS there are no such gaps—this is the blood–brain barrier.

There are two ways by which molecules can cross the blood–brain barrier. One is via transporter proteins that shuttle specific molecules across the membranes of the cells forming the blood vessel walls. Such a transporter exists for glucose, the primary energy currency used to move energy throughout the body. (Phosphate bonds, especially ATP, are the primary energy currency inside of cells.) Other transporters are known to move specific amino acids across the blood–brain barrier, and still others move other essential molecules.

The second way in which molecules may cross the blood–brain barrier is by dissolving right through the blood vessel cell walls. The cells that make up the blood vessel walls are bounded, like all cells, with phospholipid bilayer membrane. In order to dissolve into and pass through a lipid bilayer membrane, a molecule must be sufficiently hydrophobic (lipophilic) to comfortably pass through the highly hydrophobic central core of the bilayer. Oxygen and other small gaseous molecules are able to do this. And pretty much all the known drug molecules that have impact on brain function cross the blood–brain barrier because they are lipophilic enough to dissolve right through the cells forming the barrier.

TTX is not sufficiently hydrophobic. It contains many polar oxygen–hydrogen groups that will attract water molecules, which prevents it from entering the hydrophobic interior of a lipid bilayer membrane. Thus, its poison qualities do not impact the functioning of the brain.

How is it that animals containing TTX are not poisoned by it? I have already mentioned that the voltage-gated Na^+ channels of the heart are resistant to the blocking effects of TTX. It turns out that very small changes in the primary structure of the voltage-gated Na^+ channel (as little as changing a single amino acid, if it is the right amino acid) can dramatically reduce its sensitivity to being blocked by TTX. Animals harboring TTX-producing bacteria have variants of the voltage-gated Na^+ channel that are much less affected by TTX. Another place where this phenomenon occurs is in a species of garter snake that eats newts containing TTX. Certain populations of this snake have evolved a variant Na^+ channel that is resistant to TTX, thus allowing these snakes to safely eat the TTX-containing newts.

Other poisons besides TTX bind with voltage-gated sodium channels and block the passage of Na^+ through the pore in the channel protein. Saxitoxin (STX), a molecule found in several species of dinoflagellates, also blocks Na^+ channels in a similar way to TTX and similarly interferes with nervous system function. Dinoflagellates are single-celled marine organisms, part of a diverse group referred to as plankton. Dinoflagellates are consumed by shellfish (such as clams, mussels, and scallops) and humans can be exposed to this poison if they eat shellfish that have accumulated STX. This is especially a problem during dinoflagellate blooms—population explosions of dinoflagellates. (Because these dinoflagellates may have red pigment, the blooms are sometimes called red tides.) Coastal areas are occasionally closed to the collection of shellfish during dinoflagellate blooms to reduce the risk of human exposure to this poison.

Saxitoxin

The medical condition resulting from STX poisoning has been called paralytic shellfish poisoning (PSP), because in humans it would most often result from consuming shellfish containing STX. The symptoms of PSP are like those of TTX poisoning: numbness, muscle weakness, and paralysis, with death, if it occurs, from respiratory paralysis and the resulting suffocation. Whales and other marine animals have been known to die from PSP after consuming sufficient quantities either of dinoflagellates or of other animals that have themselves consumed STX-containing dinoflagellates. PSP is probably a bigger problem for whales and other marine animals than it is for people.

Like TTX, STX is a hydrophilic molecule and does not cross the blood–brain barrier. And as for TTX, the treatment for STX poisoning is artificial respiration until the effects of the poison dissipate as the STX is gradually eliminated from the body.

As with TTX resistance, there are also cases where variation in the structure of the voltage-gated sodium channel will dramatically decrease sensitivity to STX. One compelling example has been studied in a variety of clam living in regions where there are frequent dinoflagellate blooms. The clam has a sodium channel variant that is much less sensitive to the blocking effects of STX. Moreover, it is impressive that this reduced sensitivity results from a single amino acid change in a particular position in the structure of the protein. The amino acid change is from glutamic acid to aspartic acid, two very closely related molecules.

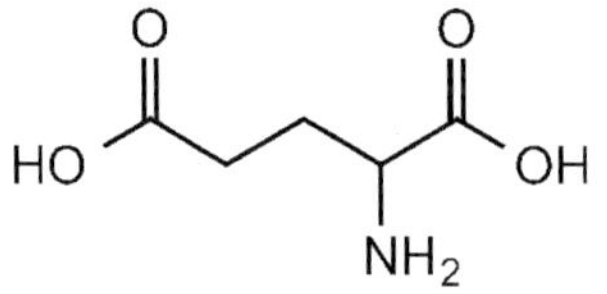

Glutamic acid 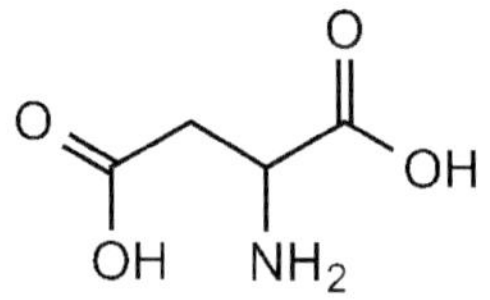   *Aspartic acid*

This highlights the dramatic sensitivity of protein function to very tiny structural changes, if the changes occur in just the right way.

Another example of a poison that works by messing with voltage-gated sodium channel function comes from the secretions found in the skin of certain tropical frogs, such as *Phyllobates terribilis* from the Amazon jungle in South America. A collection of closely related molecules have been identified, called batrachotoxins (BTXs). The molecular structure of the first BTX to be identified is shown here.

Batrachotoxin

Other BTXs are close chemical relatives.

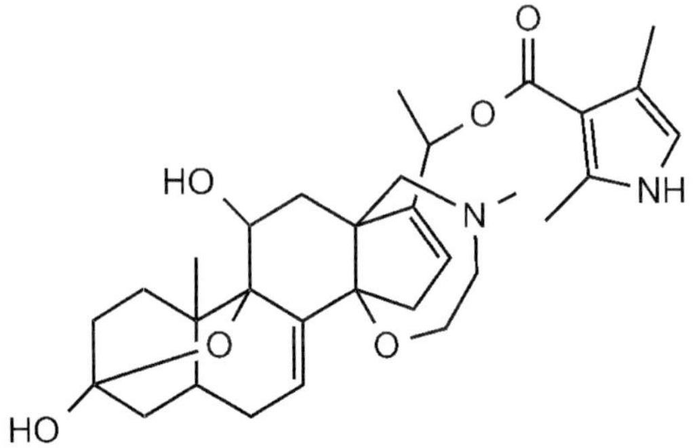

The BTXs interact with voltage-gated sodium channels in a way different from TTX and STX: rather than blocking the pore of the channel and preventing sodium ions from passing through, BTXs interact with the channel protein and prevent it from closing. If the channels are open all the time, Na$^+$ flows through continuously, and action potentials cannot be generated. Nerve signaling does not work, and the same end results as with TTX and STX occur.

The muscle weakening and paralytic properties of BTX-containing frog secretions were discovered long ago by tribal peoples of the Amazonian jungle. Secretions were and still are collected from *Phyllobates* frogs and applied to the tips of arrows and darts used for hunting. Animals hit by such poison-tipped darts quickly become impaired in their ability to move and can be more easily captured.

Another place where BTXs have been identified is in the skin and feathers of the New Guinea pitohui bird. In this case, the bird is known to acquire the BTXs from eating a type of beetle from the genus *Choresine* that contains the toxins. This suggests that the Amazonian frogs may also acquire their BTXs from ingestion of insects. The ultimate source of BTXs in these cases is not presently known—perhaps synthesis by insects, or perhaps symbiotic microorganisms.

Local anesthetics provide yet another example of the effects of altering sodium channels. The word *anesthesia* means "loss of sensation." Two general categories of anesthetics are used in medicine: general and local. General anesthetics are chemicals that produce a global loss of sensation over the entire body. They work by impacting the brain to produce a change in consciousness that affects all perception (see Chapter 9). Local anesthetics are chemicals that produce a loss of sensation locally, that is, only in the region of the body near where they have been applied. They are local because their action is relatively weak. When the chemical drifts around, enters the bloodstream, and reaches other parts of the body, its concentration becomes too low to have any noticeable effect. Local anesthetics are widely used in modern medicine: from dental procedures to knee, elbow, and brain surgeries to childbirth, local anesthetics facilitate the accomplishment of various procedures without pain.

The first local anesthetic chemical to be appreciated by modern medicine was cocaine. It was purified in the mid-nineteenth century from the coca plant, *Erythroxylum coca*, a South America plant used by native peoples of the region for thousands of years for its medicinal and stimulant properties.

In addition to its potent effects on the brain and autonomic nervous system (discussed in Chapter 9), cocaine has a weaker local anesthetic effect. Several synthetic chemicals have been developed that also act as local anesthetics to numb sensation but do not possess the other CNS and autonomic nervous system effects of

Cocaine

cocaine. Such molecules include benzocaine, lidocaine (brand name Xylocaine), and procaine (brand name Novocain).

All these local anesthetic molecules exert their action by binding to voltage-gated sodium channels and disrupting the ability to open and close in a normal voltage-dependent fashion. Unlike TTX and STX, they do not completely block Na^+ channels, but they do interfere enough to significantly alter the generation of action potentials. This results in a reduction in signals from neurons sending sensory information to the brain—the local anesthetic effect.

Let's now return to a discussion of the neurotransmitter acetylcholine (ACh) and its ionotropic and metabotropic receptors. Many years before the protein structures and properties of these receptors were characterized as ionotropic Na^+ channels and G-protein-coupled receptors, it was appreciated that there were two different types of ACh receptor (AChR) that could be characterized as having different pharmacological properties, that is, different agonists and antagonists.

One type of AChR is activated by binding nicotine, a molecule isolated and identified from the tobacco plant, *Nicotiana tabacum.*

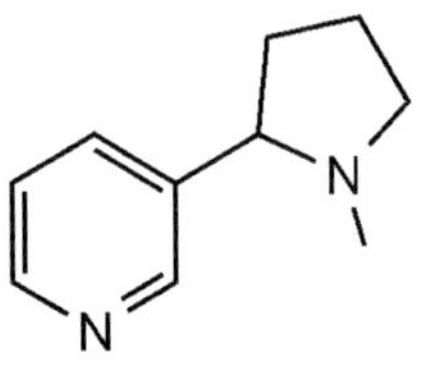

Nicotine

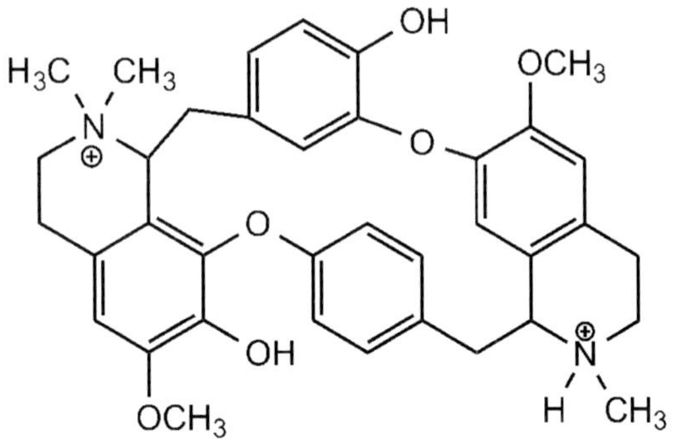

Tubocurarine

The AChR that binds nicotine is blocked (antagonized) by the molecule tubocurarine, identified from a South American curare preparation, a plant extract used as an
arrow-tip poison by native hunters in the Amazonian jungle. A variety of plants are
used to make curare; the plant source of tubocurarine is a woody vine named *Chon-
drodendron tomentosum.* This type of AChR is named the nicotinic AChR (nAChR).
It is the neurotransmitter receptor at the neuromuscular junction. It is also present in
the brain. The nAChR is now recognized as an ionotropic receptor.

Curares are used as arrow-tip poisons because they kill by paralysis, including
stopping respiration. Blocking nAChRs at the neuromuscular junction produces
muscle paralysis. Because it is a large charged molecule (it has two quaternary-
amine nitrogens), tubocurarine is not absorbed through the digestive system. To be
effective as a poison, it must enter the blood directly, via a puncture wound. How the
native peoples of the Amazon jungle, centuries or millennia ago, discovered such a
property of an extract of one among the countless species of plants in the jungle is
an enduring mystery to contemporary science. The shamans of the jungle have their
answer—direct communication with the plants tells how and for what they are to be
used.

The other type of AChR is activated by the molecule muscarine, identified from
and named after the colorful mushroom *Amanita muscaria.*

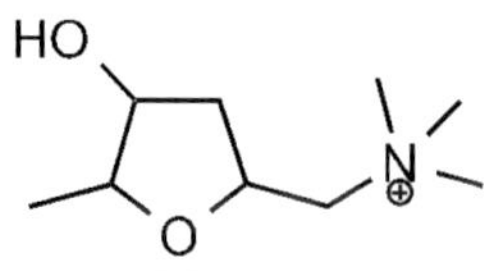

Muscarine

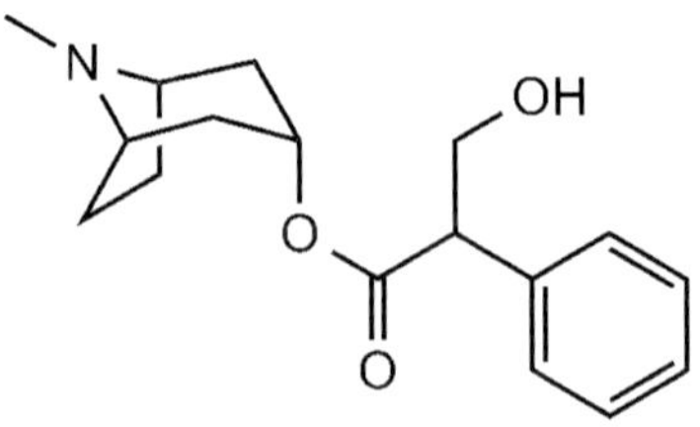

Atropine

Receptors activated by muscarine are antagonized by the molecule atropine, identified from and named after the plant *Atropa belladonna.* This type of AChR is named
the muscarinic AChR (mAChR) and is found in the parasympathetic neural connec-

tions with target organs, as well as in the brain. The mAChR is now recognized as a G-protein-coupled receptor.

The molecular structure diagrams of these drugs remind us that all these chemicals are composed of carbon, nitrogen, oxygen, and hydrogen atoms, hooked together by covalent chemical bonds into specific geometric shapes. The different shapes of the molecules confer upon them their differing pharmacologic properties. Note that tubocurarine and muscarine both have positive charges and will collect water molecules that prevent them from crossing the blood–brain barrier. Nicotine and atropine are hydrophobic molecules that readily cross the blood–brain barrier and have effects on brain neurons.

Drugs that enter the brain and impact brain function may produce effects on mental experience—thoughts, feelings, and perceptions. Such drugs are called psychoactive—they affect the mind or psyche. The study of how psychoactive drugs interact with the brain is called psychopharmacology. More is said about nicotine in Chapter 9; I'll say more about atropine now.

Atropine receives its name from one of the plants in which it is found, *Atropa belladonna*, the deadly nightshade (Fig. 8.3). *Atropa belladonna* has long been known as a highly poisonous plant, used for its deadly effects to poison enemies and, in lower doses, for its medicinal effects. Atropine was first isolated from *Atropa belladonna* around 1831. Being an antagonist at mAChRs, it is a parasympatholytic. As such, it will slow intestinal motility, making it useful as a medicine to treat diarrhea, spastic colon, and other kinds of gastrointestinal problems. Historically, it has also been used to dilate the pupil of the eye, although in contemporary ophthalmology its use has been replaced with shorter-acting mAChR antagonists.

The Latin genus for the plant comes from one of the goddess sisters of Greek myth called the Moirai (plural of Greek *moira* = share, apportion, fate). These sisters are Clotho, who spins the thread of life; Lachesis, who measures out the thread

Figure 8.3. Deadly nightshade, *Atropa belladonna*.

of life; and Atropos, who cuts the thread of life. In English they are called the Fates. Clearly the genus name *Atropa* refers to the poisonous aspects of the plant. The Latin species name, *belladonna*, literally means beautiful (*bella*) woman (*donna*). This is in reference to the pupil dilation effect of the plant. Other things being equal, folks will often judge a person having larger pupils as more attractive. Ladies of yore used extracts of *Atropa belladonna* to dilate their pupils, enhancing their beauty.

In addition to slowing intestinal motility and dilating the pupil of the eye, the other parasympatholytic effects of atropine include increased heart rate, dilation of the lung airways, dry mouth, and difficulty urinating. Collectively, these effects of blocking parasympathetic neural activity are often called anticholinergic effects. In addition, blocking mAChRs at the heart may produce heartbeat irregularities, which can be fatal—hence the deadly poisonous aspect of atropine and its mother plant *Atropa belladonna.*

Atropine crosses the blood–brain barrier and there are many mAChRs in the brain. Thus, atropine has psychoactive effects, and these CNS effects may be very strong. Among these effects are alterations of consciousness that may be dreamy and hallucinatory. A moderate increase in dose often produces disorientation and confusion. This may be accompanied by intense hallucinatory activity—powerful hallucinations in which the intoxicated person loses all capacity to distinguish between what is "real" and what is being hallucinated. Lack of memory (amnesia) is common. The connection between the known neurochemical action of atropine in the brain—antagonist at mAChRs—and these powerful psychoactive effects is completely unknown.

Now take a look at these two molecular structures:

Atropine

Ipratropium

Atropine, as mentioned, crosses the blood–brain barrier, allowing it to trigger pow-erful psychoactive effects. Ipratropium is nearly identical except for a small, but very significant, addition to the molecule. Do you notice what it is?

There is an additional group of atoms attached to the nitrogen—a three-carbon isopropyl group. Attachment of a fourth structure to the nitrogen atom produces a charged quaternary amine. The positive charge collects water molecules around it, turning what was once a largely hydrophobic molecule (atropine) into a hydrophilic one (ipratropium). As a result, ipratropium does not cross the blood–brain barrier. This allows it to be used medically as a parasympatholytic (for example, as a pulmo-nary inhaler) without the additional complication of CNS effects.

The major poison in *Atropa belladonna* is atropine. The plant also contains a

Figure 8.4. Two powerfully poisonous plants: henbane, *Hyosyamus niger* (left), and jimson weed, *Datura stramonium* (right).

smaller amount of a closely related and equally poisonous molecule, scopolamine. Several plants—cousins to *Atropa belladonna* and all members of the Solanaceae, or nightshade, family of plants—contain varying amounts of atropine and scopolamine. These include *Mandragora officinarum* (mandrake), *Hyosyamus niger* (henbane), *Datura* (jimson weed or thorn apple), *Brugmansia* (angel's trumpet), and *Brunfelsia.* All these are known and respected for their poison qualities. Shamans or herbalists who have interest in these plants practice their art with the greatest of care.

Not too many people on the planet are intentionally ingesting nightshade plants containing atropine and scopolamine. However, psychoactive drugs (or their associated plants) are being intentionally ingested by very large numbers of people throughout the world. Which poses a question: what are the most widely used psychoactive drugs in the world? Before turning the page, take a moment to ponder this question and venture a guess. What is number one? Number two? Number three? Number four?

If you said caffeine for number one, you are correct. Caffeine, identified as the principal psychoactive chemical in a variety of plants, is by far the most widely used psychoactive drug in the world. It is found in coffee, tea, cacao (the plant source of chocolate), kola, guarana, yerba mate, and other plants. Easily over half the adult population on the planet consumes caffeine on a regular basis for its psychoactive effects. So caffeine is solidly in first place as the most widely used psychoactive drug in the world. What's next?

The second most widely used psychoactive drug in the world is likely to be ethyl alcohol (ethanol). Certainly it is number two in the United States. While not directly from a plant, ethyl alcohol comes from the transformation of sugars found in plants. The transformation is accomplished by the metabolic action of fermentation carried out by yeast cells. The world's enormously diverse collection of alcoholic beverages is produced from a variety of different plants and may be additionally flavored by an even larger variety of plants containing countless interesting and exotic molecules. All alcoholic beverages contain ethyl alcohol as the primary psychoactive component.

Number three would be nicotine, by virtue of its identification as the principal psychoactive chemical in the tobacco plant. While caffeine and ethanol are consumed via oral ingestion into the digestive system, tobacco is commonly used by burning the dried leaves of the plant and inhaling the smoke, containing vaporized nicotine and other chemicals.

The fourth most widely used psychoactive drug in the world is not one most people correctly guess. It is the areca nut, also known as the betel nut, the seed of the palm tree *Areca catechu* native to India, Southeast Asia, and the southwestern Pacific Oceana region. As with any plant material, there are many, many molecular constituents, and many of these have potential physiological activity. In the areca nut, the molecule arecoline has been identified as the chemical constituent perhaps most responsible for the physiological effects of the nut, a combination of relaxation and mental stimulation.

Arecoline

While the areca nut is not widely known in the Western hemisphere, many millions of people in India, Southeast Asia, and Oceana ingest it on a daily basis for its psychoactive effects. That makes it very likely to be number four.

How about the fifth most widely used psychoactive drug in the world? Most likely it is the cannabis plant (genus *Cannabis*) in its various forms—marijuana and hashish, smoked and orally ingested—or, represented by its primary identified psychoactive chemical component, delta-9-tetrahydrocannabinol (THC). This statement now becomes sketchier, because there is no good worldwide data on the prevalence of cannabis use. Because cannabis is prohibited by law in many countries, determining the prevalence of use is all the more difficult.

The drug molecules discussed above—caffeine, ethanol, nicotine, arecoline, and THC—all come, directly or indirectly (in the case of ethanol), from plants. Importantly, though, plants and chemicals are very different. Chemicals are single, identified substances, which may have specific effects on physiology associated with well-defined molecular interactions. Plants are far more complicated, and we may

Figure 8.5. The tea
plant, *Camellia sinensis*,
native to East Asia.

not even know the half of it. First of all, plants are extraordinary chemical factories. In addition to the hundreds of molecular components shared with many other life forms, they are well known for their ability to create weird molecules of many different kinds. Every plant (and fungus) contains strange molecules, perhaps a handful, perhaps dozens. Some of these weird molecules are known to have drug effects in humans.

Most of the strange molecules found in plants have not been carefully investigated for the physiological effects they may cause. Thus, the effect of any plant, when ingested, will be a complex combination of many things. We may be able to attribute a substantial part of the plant's effect on physiology and behavior to a single molecular entity, but the overall effect will necessarily be more complex (and interesting) than that. Coffee, tea, cacao, yerba mate, guarana and kola all contain caffeine, but all also differ in the effects they have on the human psyche. And one kind of tea may be different in effect from another kind of tea—even though all may contain caffeine and all come from the same species of plant, *Camellia sinensis* (Fig. 8.5).

The history of drugs is mostly a history of ethnobotany, the study of how people— over the course of millennia and continuing to this day—have discovered and used the powers of plants. Long ago it was appreciated that plants have powers and that among those powers are their poisonous and their medicinal properties. These days we understand this in terms of the effects of certain chemical constituents of the plants. The conventional view is that this is the whole story—that it's all in the chemicals.

Maybe . . .

For thousands of years indigenous peoples, who have tended to live much closer to plants than many of us do in the modern world, have always had among them individuals who cultivated deep relationships with the local plants. They were herbalists, curanderos, vegetalistas, wizards, witches, medicine people, shamans. Plants were part of their power source, but more generally these were individuals who had mastered working with the spirits of nature in many forms. They used their skills to help and to heal. They were the original doctors and much of what we now call medicine has developed from their tradition.

The fact that particular plants and particular chemicals can have profound impacts on mental experience highlights the importance of psychopharmacology to the study of the mind–brain relation. Drugs that affect the psyche are powerful probes of how brain physiology is related to consciousness and mind.

> Healing medicine,
> and the dark, deathly poison—
> are one and the same.

CHAPTER 9

Psychoactive Drugs

The British and Dutch East India Companies were the world's first multinational corporations and wielded great power during their heyday—the 1600s to the 1800s. They had the capacity to wage war in the service of their business enterprises. Among their most important commodities were tea, coffee, and spices. During its later years, the British East India Company was also heavily into opium. Psychoactive drugs have been an important factor in the history of human civilization and, more recently, in the history of neuroscience.

Caffeine.   Coffee (*Coffea arabica*, native to northeast Africa), tea (*Camellia sinensis*, native to East Asia), and cacao (*Theobroma cacao*, native to South and Central America), from which chocolate is made, are the three best-known plant sources of caffeine. Other caffeine-containing plants include kola (*Cola acuminata*, native to Africa), guarana (*Paullinia cupana*, native to South America), and yerba mate (*Ilex paraguariensis*, native to South America). The widespread consumption of beverages made from these plants unquestionably makes caffeine (1,3,7-trimethylxanthine) the most widely used psychoactive drug in the world.

Caffeine	*Theophylline*	*Theobromine*

Closely related to caffeine are two other molecules with similar psychoactive effects: theophylline (1,3-dimethylxanthine), found in tea, and theobromine (3,7-dimethylxanthine), found in cacao—a dynamic trio.

Caffeine-containing plants are for the most part consumed by making hot water extracts of the seeds (coffee, guarana) or leaves (tea, yerba mate). Kola nuts are often eaten intact. Cacao seeds are dried and then ground into a paste and combined with sugar to make various forms of chocolate.

In contemporary times, another primary source of caffeine consumption is the large variety of commercially manufactured caffeinated beverages. These began more than a century ago with Coca Cola, introduced in 1886 as a nonalcoholic beverage to stimulate mental function. The caffeine in Coca Cola originally came only from the kola nut, but caffeine content has since been increased beyond what would be obtained from the nut alone by adding additional quantities of the pure chemical. Pepsi Cola appeared a few years later, in 1898. Its caffeine also originally came from the kola nut. A variety of these so-called soft (nonalcoholic) drinks containing caffeine were introduced during the twentieth century. By the beginning of the twenty-first century, caffeine-fortified beverages collectively called "energy drinks" had proliferated via hundreds of brands worldwide. These commercially manufactured sweetened and flavored beverages generally contain more caffeine than traditional soft drinks.

Caffeine is a powerful stimulant drug, acting on the central nervous system (CNS) to increase wakefulness and alertness. In addition, caffeine has stimulant effects on the cardiovascular system, increasing heart rate and blood pressure. Caffeine consumption is pervasive in the modern world and meshes well with the modern lifestyle of extreme production and consumption. Whether or not you yourself are a regular consumer of caffeine, we all live in a highly caffeinated world. So pervasive is caffeine consumption that we have, to large extent, lost touch with what a powerful stimulant it is.

Caffeine's molecular structure is quite similar to the structures of two of the nucleotides of DNA, adenine and guanine. Indeed, plants synthesize caffeine (or theophylline or theobromine) from adenine and guanine precursor molecules. Adenosine is also made from adenine by the attachment of a ribose sugar. Thus, there is a molecular similarity between caffeine and adenosine. It turns out that one of the several roles adenosine plays in the body is as a neurotransmitter. And caffeine acts at adenosine receptors as an antagonist.

Adenosine receptors in the heart mediate a slowing of heart rate, adenosine receptors on blood vessels mediate vasodilation (opening up of the vessels), and adenosine receptors in the brain act to decrease neuronal excitability. Antagonizing these receptors gives rise to caffeine's stimulant effects: increasing heart rate, vasoconstriction contributing to increased blood pressure, and increasing excitability in the central nervous system. This illustrates how the blocking of neural effects that are normally in one direction produces an outcome in the opposite direction. Blocking the normal neuronal inhibitory effect of adenosine produces neuronal excitation, because the usual balance between excitation and inhibition is altered.

Adenosine receptors are G-protein-coupled receptors (GPCRs). Thus, adenosine's effect as an inhibitory neurotransmitter is not a direct effect on opening an ion channel, such as GABA acting at ionotropic GABA receptors. Rather, adenosine's action at adenosine receptors results in activation of G-proteins, which then affect adenylate cyclase, thereby impacting intracellular cAMP concentration, which changes the activity of protein kinases and alters the opening of K^+ channels, leading to a hyperpolarization of the membrane and decreased neuronal excitability. The action of caffeine is to prevent all this from happening, reducing some of the inhibition that would normally be present in the brain, thereby making the neurons more excitable. This is presumably connected with the experience of increased wakefulness and alertness.

Figure 9.1. Tobacco plant,
Nicotiana tabacum.

Nicotine.   Tobacco (*Nicotiana tabacum*, *Nicotiana rustica*, and related species) is
a plant native to the Americas (Fig. 9.1). The genus *Nicotiana* is named after Jean
Nicot (1530–1600), a diplomat who introduced tobacco to the French royal court—
they loved it.

The molecule nicotine was isolated from and named after
the tobacco plant by German chemists around 1828. While
tobacco, being a plant, contains hundreds of different chemicals, a number of which may possess physiological activity,
nicotine is considered the primary psychoactive constituent.
It is generally taken into the body by smoking the dried leaves
of the plant. It may also be absorbed through the nasal mucosa
or oral cavity, if a snuff preparation or chewing tobacco is used.

Nicotine

The major known neurochemical effect of nicotine is to bind as an agonist at
nicotinic acetylcholine receptors (nAChRs). This produces effects in the brain that
presumably are related to the behavioral effects of relaxation, alertness, and focused
attention experienced by users of tobacco. Although there are nAChRs at the neuromuscular junction, they are slightly different in amino acid sequence from the CNS
nAChRs and, as a result, are less sensitive to nicotine binding.

Nicotine is a serious poison. The tobacco plant presumably makes nicotine
because its poison qualities confer some protection against insects and other animals that might munch on its leaves. Insects, too, have nAChRs that can be overstimulated by nicotine. In humans, nicotine poisoning produces disruptions in heart
rhythm, blood pressure, and respiration.

Alcohol and the sedative-hypnotic drugs.   Used in the context of human consumption, *alcohol* refers to the two-carbon ethyl alcohol or ethanol. All organic
alcohols are poisons, but ethanol appears to be the least poisonous to the human
body. Ethanol in alcohol-containing beverages is formed by the metabolic action of
yeast on sugars coming from various plant materials. The yeasts consume the sug-

ars—a biochemical process called fermentation—and excrete ethanol as a waste product. A piece of fruit sitting around will ferment from the action of wild yeasts that settle upon it. And because yeasts are living all over the place, humans probably serendipitously discovered the intoxicating properties of alcohol a very long time ago.

Ethanol is a member of a larger class of drugs known as sedative-hypnotics, so named because in low doses they produce sedative or relaxing effects and in higher doses they produce a hypnotic or sleep-inducing effect. This spectrum of effects for alcohol and other sedative-hypnotics is well known: from the relaxation of mild intoxication, to impaired judgment and coordination, to grossly impaired movement, to loss of consciousness (passing out), to death. Along the way, people may also experience what is called a blackout—loss of memory without loss of consciousness (see Chapter 19).

While ethyl alcohol may be the most ancient and widely used of the sedative-hypnotic drugs, there are many other representatives of this category, mostly from the world of pharmaceuticals—synthetic drugs manufactured and sold for medical use. Among these are the barbiturates, first introduced into medicine in the early twentieth century and for many decades widely prescribed by physicians to treat anxiety and insomnia. Examples—given here with generic, or chemical, names and in some cases trademark brand names used in the United States—include phenobarbital, secobarbital (Seconal), amobarbital (Amytal), pentobarbital (Nembutal), and thiopental (Pentothal). Their use to treat anxiety and insomnia has been largely eclipsed by newer medications, although phenobarbital still sees use as an antiseizure medication, especially in veterinary medicine.

Barbiturates were among the first synthetic drugs (not coming from plants) to be introduced into medicine. A chemical is considered to be a barbiturate if it has a certain type of molecular structure.

Phenobarbital   *Pentobarbital*   *Amobarbital*

The various barbiturates were invented by the pharmaceutical industry by making chemical modifications to molecules that were already on the market, thus creating a new representative of the category that could be independently patented and marketed.

In the 1960s, another group of synthetic sedative-hypnotic drugs was introduced into the pharmaceutical marketplace—the benzodiazepines. Chlordiazepoxide (Librium) appeared in 1960, followed several years later by diazepam (Valium). Both these drugs continue to be widely used and have been joined by many other representatives of the benzodiazepine class, all of which share certain features of chemical structure.

Diazepam   *Lorazepam*   *Alprazolam*

Note that diazepam, lorazepam (Ativan), and alprazolam (Xanax) all appear similar in shape.

Librium and Valium were introduced by the same pharmaceutical company in the 1960s and quickly became, at the time, among the best-selling drugs in history. As was the case with barbiturates, once the first benzodiazepines were introduced, other pharmaceutical companies produced modifications of chemical structure that allowed for independent patenting and sales.

Several other pharmaceutical sedative-hypnotic drugs are sold as pills for medical use, but not all are barbiturates or benzodiazepines. These include the older drugs meprobamate (Miltown) and chloral hydrate and several relatively new drugs used as sleep-inducing (hypnotic) agents: zolpidem (Ambien), zaleplon (Sonata), and eszopiclone (Lunesta).

General anesthetics are another category of sedative-hypnotic used in medicine. Anesthetics induce loss of sensation. As mentioned in Chapter 8, local anesthetics do this by weakly interfering with voltage-gated sodium channels, which alters the propagation of nerve signals locally. General anesthetics are potent sedative-hypnotics administered during surgical procedures. They act in the brain to reduce overall CNS neural activity, producing a loss of consciousness and thus lack of awareness of any sensory experience, including pain. They tend to be easily volatilized liquids that can be delivered to the patient by inhalation, allowing for rapid onset of effects and quick responses to adjustments in dose.

The first general anesthetic to be used in medicine was ethanol: the patient would be given whiskey to drink before surgery was performed. In the mid-nineteenth century, diethyl ether was introduced as a surgical anesthetic; it was more potent than alcohol and more volatile, and thus readily administered by inhalation. Used for more than a century, diethyl ether was replaced in the mid-twentieth century by various other volatile chemicals.

Diethyl ether   *Halothane*   *Sevoflurane*

Most of these new molecules were derived from small hydrocarbons and ethers by replacing one or more of the hydrogen atoms with halogen atoms, such as bromine, chlorine, or fluorine. The first to be introduced was halothane, in the 1950s. Currently used inhalation general anesthetics include desflurane and sevoflurane.

These diverse sedative-hypnotic drugs are all thought to have similar primary neurochemical mechanisms of action in the brain. They all act at ionotropic GABA receptors, facilitating the action of GABA at the receptor. This increases inhibition in the CNS by increasing GABA-induced Cl⁻ flow into cells. This is believed to in some way give rise to relaxing, anxiety-reducing (anxiolytic) effects at low doses, impaired movement and memory storage at higher doses, loss of consciousness at still higher doses, and, at sufficiently high doses, death—too much GABAergic inhibition in the brain shuts things down completely.

Opium and opioids.   The opium poppy, *Papaver somniferum*, has been appreciated for its medicinal properties for thousands of years (Fig. 9.2). It was cultivated by the ancient Sumerians of Mesopotamia (modern-day Iraq) five thousand years ago. They referred to the opium poppy as the "joy plant," suggesting they were well aware of its potential to produce psychoactive effects of relaxation, pain relief, and even euphoria (intense good feeling).

Prominent effects of the opium poppy are its ability to reduce the perception of pain (analgesia), to suppress cough, and to slow the motile muscle action of the intestines, making it useful as a treatment for diarrhea. These medicinal properties of *Papaver somniferum* were long ago found to be concentrated in a resinous secretion obtained by carefully slitting the unripe seed pods. This secretion is called opium (Greek *opos* = plant juice). Opium is good medicine.

Around 1804, Friedrich Wilhelm Sertürner (1783–1841), a young apprentice pharmacist in Germany, made a remarkable discovery. He isolated and purified a chemical substance from opium and demonstrated that the effects of this substance,

Figure 9.2. Opium poppy, *Papaver somniferum.*

when ingested, produced the analgesic, soporific, and euphoric effects of opium, except in a more potent manner. He named this chemical constituent of opium morphine, after Morpheus, the god of dreams in Greek myth.

Sertürner's discovery had profound implications. It was the first time a chemical substance had been isolated from a plant and shown to account for the medicinal properties of the plant. This finding gave birth to a new way of thinking about plant medicines.

Morphine

In the coming years of the nineteenth century, chemists, pretty much all of whom were working in Germany, would seek out and discover the chemical principles associated with the physiological actions of many plants. Caffeine isolated from coffee and tea, nicotine from tobacco, cocaine from coca, atropine from belladonna, and mescaline from peyote are examples of these nineteenth-century discoveries.

By the latter half of the nineteenth century a pharmaceutical industry was emerging. Initially, their business was extraction and purification of chemicals from plants, making them available for medical use. Then semisynthetic substances were introduced; beginning with a plant-derived compound, synthetic chemical modifications were made in an attempt to improve the action or reduce the toxicity. A pioneer in this regard was the Bayer Company in Germany, where morphine was reacted with acetic anhydride to produce diacetylmorphine, and salicylic acid from the willow tree was acetylated to form acetylsalicylic acid. The first product was introduced to the market in 1898 as an analgesic and cough medicine having the brand name Heroin. The second was introduced in 1899 as an analgesic with the brand name Aspirin.

Morphine   *Diacetylmorphine*

Diacetylmorphine was found to be about twice as potent as morphine in its physiological effects in humans. The increased potency is now understood to be due to its more efficient entry into the brain—acetyl groups are less polar than hydroxyl groups, so diacetylmorphine crosses the blood–brain barrier more efficiently than does morphine. Diacetylmorphine was the first of a number of semisynthetic opioids (chemicals having opium-like effects in the body) that were developed. During the twentieth century, a number of chemical derivatives of morphine were synthesized by pharmaceutical companies and marketed under various brand names—for example, hydrocodone (Vicodin), hydromorphone (Dilaudid), and oxycodone (Oxy-Contin, Percodan, Percocet).

In the early years of World War II, German chemists developed the drug methadone, the first instance of a completely synthetic opioid.

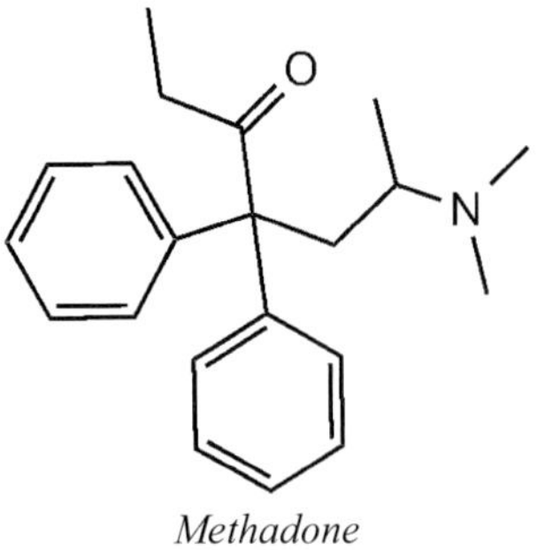

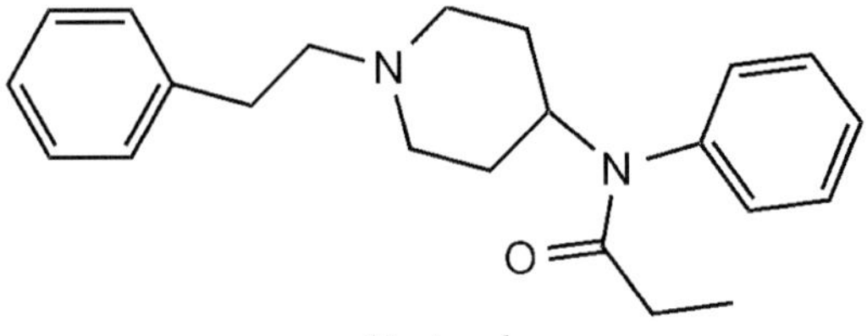

Fentanyl

Methadone

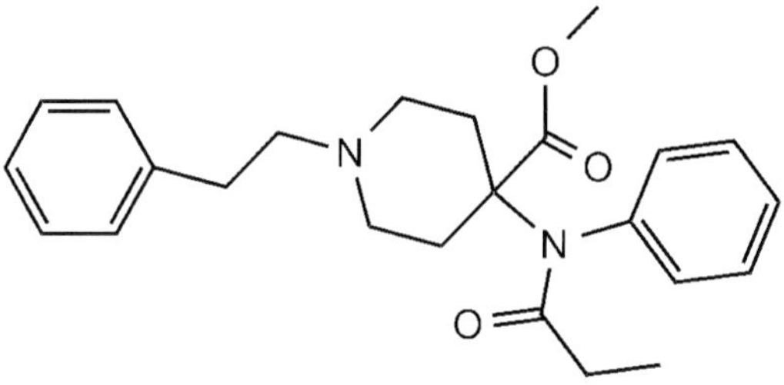

Carfentanil

Another example of a synthetic opioid is fentanyl, which is about 100 times more
potent than morphine and is widely used in human medicine. Certain derivatives of
fentanyl are the most potent opioids known, and among the most potent of any drugs
presently known, naturally occurring or synthetic. The fentanyl derivative carfentanil is approximately 10,000 times more potent than morphine, too strong to be
useful in human medicine. Its brand name, Wildnil, suggests what it is used for—
sedation of large animals, such as elephants.

How do opioids act in the body? Beginning in the early 1970s, protein receptors
were discovered in the brain and in the gut that bind morphine and other opioids.
These opioid receptors were found to exist in several distinct subtypes (now called
mu, delta, and kappa) having different distributions in the brain and body and different pharmacological properties (that is, different agonists and antagonists). All
are now known to be GPCRs.

The discovery of receptors that respond to chemicals found in poppies and produced by the pharmaceutical industry prompted a search for whatever molecules
might be the endogenous (made within the body) neurotransmitter ligands for the
opioid receptors. By the mid-1970s, molecules began to be discovered that were
found in the brain and functioned as agonists at opioid receptors. About a dozen
such molecules have now been identified from animals, collectively called *endorphins*, a word derived from "endogenous" and "morphine." These endogenous
opioid neurotransmitters were the first of a new class of neurotransmitters—the
neuropeptides. The endorphins are chains of amino acids (polypeptides), the short-
est of which are five amino acids in length (leu-enkephalin and met-enkephalin),
and the longest of which is thirty-one amino acids long (beta-endorphin).

Figure 9.3. Coca plant, *Erythroxylum coca.*

Cocaine. *Erythroxylum coca*, native to South America, is another example of a plant that has had a very long relationship with humans for the physiological effects it produces (Fig. 9.3). The chemical cocaine, isolated from the coca plant, was mentioned in Chapter 8 as an example of a local anesthetic. However, more widely known and more powerful than the local anesthetic effects are the stimulant effects of the coca plant, first appreciated by native peoples of northern South America thousands of years ago. The leaves of the coca plant are chewed or used to make a tea, producing increased wakefulness, focused attention, decreased fatigue, and increased stamina.

Some of the effects of coca are similar to those of coffee, tea, and other caffeine-containing plants, but coca also produces a distinctly different experience. Other effects include decreased appetite, increased positive mood, and stimulation of the sympathetic nervous system (increased heart rate, vasoconstriction, opening up of the bronchial airways and nasal passages, dilation of pupils). Coca is also said to have beneficial effects on the digestive system. Native peoples of South America have been using coca leaf for many centuries; to them it is Mama Coca, a plant considered sacred and treated with respect and reverence.

Coca, being a plant, contains hundreds of chemical constituents, and among these there are no doubt several that have significant physiological effects. Around 1860 German chemists isolated the molecule cocaine from the coca plant and identified it as the primary constituent responsible for the stimulant effects of the plant. Cocaine as a purified and very potent chemical substance thus became available for human consumption. Perhaps nowhere is there a better example of how the use of a plant can differ profoundly from the use of a purified chemical constituent of a plant. It is easy to use the coca plant productively and safely. The purified chemical has far more apparent poison qualities and is very prone to dysfunctional patterns of use.

The major identified neurochemical effect of cocaine is the blocking or inhibition of reuptake transporters for the neurotransmitters norepinephrine and dopamine. Interfering with reuptake transport means that these neurotransmitters will be slowed in leaving the synaptic cleft and thus will have a greater effect at the synapse after their release. Thus, cocaine results in excessive activity at all synapses in the nervous system that use norepinephrine or dopamine as a neurotransmitter. Enhanced activity at the noradrenergic and dopaminergic circuitry in the brain produces the CNS stimulant effects of increased wakefulness and alertness, focused attention, decreased appetite, and increased positive mood. The sympathomimetic effects in the autonomic nervous system stem from enhanced activity at noradrenergic synapses in the sympathetic nervous system.

Some of the poisonous qualities of cocaine include overarousal of the CNS, resulting in anxiety, irritability, and impaired judgment. Psychosis can also result. Psychosis is a discombobulation of the perception of what we call reality, characterized by delusions (fixed false beliefs) and/or hallucinations (perceptual experiences that do not seem to be generated by ordinary sensory stimuli, such as hearing or seeing things that are "not there"). Overstimulation of the CNS can also lead to seizures, which can be fatal. Overstimulation of the sympathetic nervous system can produce cardiovascular stress, leading to heart and circulatory system damage. There may also be acute, potentially fatal consequences, such as stroke and heart attack. Finally, another profound poisonous quality of cocaine is its high potential to promote addictive use.

Why does the coca plant make this weird and poisonous molecule, cocaine? The answer may be—as is thought to be the case for caffeine in coffee and tea, and for nicotine in tobacco—that the poison qualities of cocaine confer protection on the plant from being consumed by insects and other leaf-munching predators. Just as cocaine can produce an overstimulation of the human nervous system, it can also produce aversive overstimulation of nervous systems in insects.

Amphetamine-type stimulant drugs. Related to cocaine by their effects on the nervous system and behavioral attributes, although not at all related to cocaine in origin or molecular structure, are amphetamine and several of its chemical relatives.

Amphetamine

Methamphetamine

Methylphenidate

Ephedrine

Cathinone

The structures of these molecules are similar to one another. Amphetamine (commercial brand names include Dexedrine and Adderall), methamphetamine (Desoxyn) and methylphenidate (Ritalin), are synthetic pharmaceutical drugs and, in the case of methamphetamine, illicit street "speed." Ephedrine is present in many plants of the genus *Ephedra*, found worldwide. Cathinone comes from the khat plant,

Catha edulis, native to a region of northeastern Africa, including Ethiopia and Somalia and, across the Red Sea, Yemen.

The primary identified neurochemical action of amphetamine and related molecules is at synapses using norepinephrine or dopamine as neurotransmitter. These drugs interact with reuptake transporters for norepinephrine or dopamine and cause them to become leaky, so that rather than transporting neurotransmitter from the synaptic cleft back into the presynaptic axon terminal after release, neurotransmitter continuously leaks out of the axon terminal and into the synaptic cleft via the transporter. This results, as with cocaine, in overstimulation of neural circuits using norepinephrine or dopamine as neurotransmitter.

Thus, similar stimulant effects on brain function take place, with increased arousal, stamina, and focus of attention. And similar sympathomimetic effects occur: increased heart rate and blood pressure, opening of nasal and bronchial air passages, and pupil dilation. One of the major uses of *Ephedra* among practitioners of plant-based medicine is treatment of asthma. In Chinese medicine, *Ephedra* goes by the name *ma huang*. When synthetic amphetamine was introduced into pharmaceutical medicine in the 1930s, it was initially marketed as a treatment for asthma and other respiratory problems. As with cocaine, the nervous system stimulation produced by amphetamine-type drugs may result in similar serious and potentially lethal adverse effects.

> Drugs like cocaine, amphetamine, opioids, ethyl alcohol, barbiturates, benzo-diazepines, and nicotine all possess substantial risk for addictive use—a high addictive potential. By *addiction* I mean a behavioral syndrome in which one's relationship with the drug becomes dysfunctional. This may include manifestations of loss of control over use, such as excessive use and difficulty in limiting one's use; it may include the experience of adverse effects on one's life, such as negative impacts on function in school, work, and interpersonal relationships; and it may include negative effects on the health of one's body. The interaction of these drugs with the reward-reinforcement neural pathways in the brain is believed to be an important component of the neurobiology of addiction (see Chapter 21).

Psychedelics.   This is perhaps the most interesting group of all known psychoactive substances. Psychedelics produce a variety of complex effects on the brain and mind, including intensified thoughts and feelings and altered sensory perception. Reported effects range from novel and insightful thoughts and feelings, to experiences of awe and profound connection with nature, to anxiety and panic.

To a greater degree than is the case for other psychoactive drugs, the effects of psychedelics on behavior and mental experience are influenced by what is termed "set and setting." *Set* (or mental set) refers to psychological factors such as expectations, memories of prior experiences, mood, and so on. *Setting* refers to the physical environment in which the experience of intoxication takes place—for example, alone, in a social setting with others, therapeutic context with a healer, inside a room, or outside in nature. The effects of any psychoactive drug will be affected by set and setting, but some drugs are more susceptible to set-and-setting effects than others. Thus, caffeine may generally have a small set-and-setting effect, and alcohol an intermediate one, while for the psychedelics the set-and-setting effect is generally very large.

As their properties came under investigation by twentieth-century biomedical science, many of these compounds were initially called psychotomimetics, because it was believed their effects were much like the symptoms of psychosis. This term was eventually eclipsed in favor of hallucinogen, highlighting that effects may include alterations of perception, including hallucinations. In 1956 the psychiatrist Humphry Osmond (1917–2004), in correspondence with the author Aldous Huxley (1894–1963), proposed the word *psychedelic* (Greek *psyche* = mind, *delos* = visible, manifest) to describe the unique effects of these substances on consciousness. Osmond proposed the name in the following ditty, written in a letter to Huxley: "To fathom Hell or soar angelic, just take a pinch of psychedelic." In their plant and fungal forms, and under the guidance of shamans, psychedelics have been used for thousands of years to facilitate states of consciousness conducive to psychological health. This has led to the use of the word *entheogen* (generating god within) to emphasize their ritual use to facilitate mystical-type experiences.

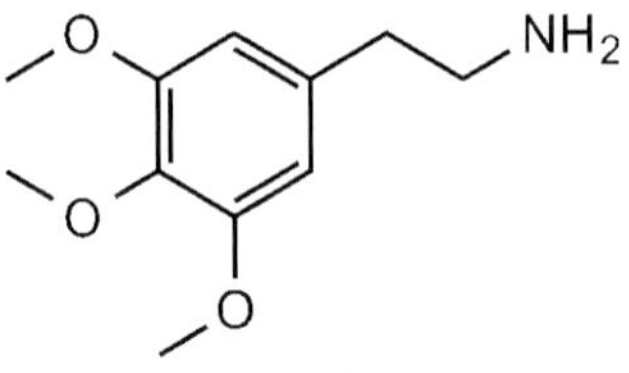

Mescaline

Among the known psychedelically active chemicals are mescaline, lysergic acid diethylamide (LSD), psilocybin, psilocin, and dimethyltryptamine (DMT). Mescaline was identified in 1897 by Arthur Heffter (1859–1925) from peyote (*Lophophora williamsii*), a small cactus growing primarily in Mexico, with a range extending northward into southern Texas.

Heffter, a German pharmacologist, studied the chemical constituents of peyote after it had come to his attention that this cactus was used for its potent psychoactive properties by native peoples of the Americas, consumed in ritual settings under the guidance of shamans. Mescaline was the first psychedelic substance to be chemically identified.

Perhaps the most famous psychedelic chemical is LSD. Its profound psychoactive properties were not known until it was synthesized and tested in 1943 by Albert Hofmann (1906–2008). It is derived from ergotamine, produced by a fungus called *Claviceps purpurea*, also known as ergot. LSD is one of the most potent psychoactive substances known, active in quantities of a few micrograms.

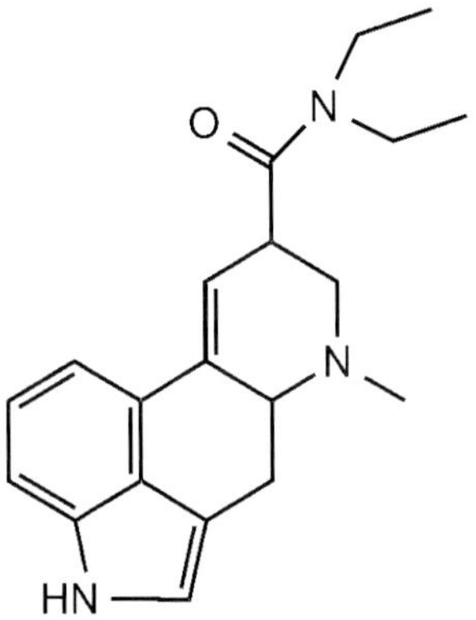

LSD

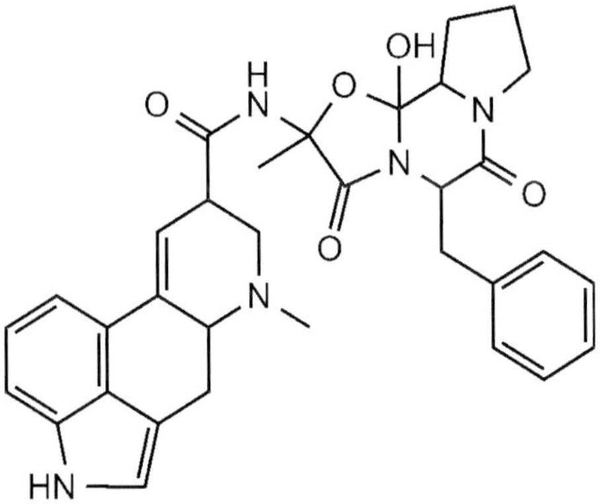

Ergotamine

Albert Hofmann's discovery of LSD's potent and complex effects on the mind was a landmark event in the history of neuroscience. Before the 1940s, the workings of the brain were not conceptualized as being closely associated with chemical signaling. Only a single molecule, acetylcholine, was known to be a neurotransmitter, and this was associated with the peripheral nervous system, not the CNS. The discovery that a few millionths of a gram of a chemical could have profound effects on thinking, feeling, perception, and conscious awareness really made the point that there were powerful chemical connections between brain physiology and mental experience. This may seem obvious now—just like genes being made of DNA might seem obvious—but it was a novel idea not so long ago. When molecular structural similarities were noticed between serotonin and LSD, it was proposed that serotonin might be a brain neurotransmitter and LSD might exert its effects in part by interacting with some kind of serotonergic system in the brain. A new era in neuroscience was emerging.

Psychedelic mushrooms—sometimes referred to as "magic mushrooms"—many of which are members of the genus *Psilocybe*, grow throughout the world. Their shamanic use is known from the Mazatec peoples of southern Mexico, where their ritual use extends back many centuries. However, when the Spanish conquistadors came to Mexico in the 1500s, they brought with them from Europe the Catholic Church and the Roman Inquisition. Rituals using plants and fungi to facilitate access to states of consciousness considered sacred and mystical were condemned by the Inquisition as devil worship, and practitioners of such rituals risked torture and even execution. Thus, the mushroom ceremonies became closely guarded secrets, and the secrecy persisted for four hundred years.

Contemporary society learned about psychedelic mushrooms only in 1957, via an article in *Life* magazine written by R. Gordon Wasson (1898–1986), a New York City bank executive and mushroom scholar. Wasson, together with his physician wife, Valentina, had received knowledge of the ritual use of these mushrooms from Maria Sabina (1894–1985), a Mazatec healer from a small mountain village in southern Mexico. Maria Sabina made a profound decision in choosing to share this ancient secret with outsiders, knowing it would be secret no more and, indeed, would be revealed to a large number of people. Her decision had a tremendous impact on history, as Wasson's magazine article would be one of the major ways by which information concerning the powerful consciousness-altering effects of psychedelics reached a wide audience. After his meeting with Maria Sabina, Wasson connected with Albert Hofmann, and in 1958 Hofmann identified two psychedelically active chemicals from Mexican *Psilocybe* mushrooms. Hofmann named the two chemicals psilocybin and psilocin. Note their similarities in molecular structure to serotonin.

Psilocybin

Psilocin

Serotonin

Another example of a powerful psychedelic molecule is dimethyltryptamine, or DMT. It also looks similar to serotonin, as well as to psilocin. It can be readily synthesized, by enzymes present in many organisms, from the amino acid tryptophan.

DMT   Tryptophan

DMT has been found to occur widely in nature; it has been identified in a large number of different plants and in the human body as well. It is quite possible that it functions as an endogenous neurotransmitter in the animal nervous system.

Several DMT-containing plants are used for their powerful medicinal effects by tribal peoples living in the Amazon jungle of South America. One Amazonian preparation combines a DMT-containing plant (usually *Psychotria viridis*) with another plant—the ayahuasca vine, *Banisteriopsis caapi*—the presence of which potentiates the effects of DMT. The combination of these two plants is cooked up to yield a strong-tasting brew that also goes by the name ayahuasca, as well as other names, such as yage.

A couple of other related psychedelic chemicals identified from plants include lysergic acid amide from the seeds of certain morning glories, and ibogaine from the root of the African plant *Tabernanthe iboga*. These plants also have a history of ritual use in shamanic ceremonies: morning glories in southern Mexico and iboga in western Africa.

The substances thus far discussed are sometimes grouped together as "classical" psychedelics or hallucinogens. Neurochemically, the classical psychedelics have been found to bind as agonists to various serotonin receptor subtypes, especially type 2A serotonin receptors (called $5HT_{2A}$ receptors). Psychedelics also bind to other neurotransmitter receptors, including those for dopamine and norepinephrine. The connection between their neurochemical effects and their profound effects on mental function remains largely obscure.

Other substances also have psychedelic effects, but of a qualitatively very different character from the classical psychedelics. Among these other substances are MDMA (methylenedioxymethamphetamine: street name "ecstasy"), MDA (methylenedioxyamphetamine), salvinorin (from the plant *Salvia divinorum*), the dissociative anesthetic ketamine, and anticholingeric hallucinogens such as atropine and scopolamine. These various molecules have distinctive neurochemical mechanisms that are quite different from those of the classical psychedelics. As with the classical psychedelics, the connection between their known neurochemical actions and their impact on mental function is largely obscure.

The effects of psychedelics can range from ecstatic to terrifying. They may facilitate great psychological healing, but they also may trigger or exacerbate psychological problems. Various sectors of human society have used them, in their plant or mushroom forms, for a very long time for their healing potential. This potential is conferred upon them by the power they have to open the human psyche, with all the risks that may come from delving deeply into the world of the mind. In their use by indigenous shamans, be it Mazatec mushroom ceremonies in Mexico, peyote circles in North America, ayahuasca rituals in the Amazon, or iboga ceremonies in Africa, the experiences are conducted with the utmost care, support, and ritual structure.

When psychedelic drugs were explored as medical psychotherapeutic tools by psychiatrists and other therapists in the 1950s and 1960s, they were found to be of great value. Clinical research during those years focused on the treatment of alcoholism and on psychotherapeutic work addressing death in patients having terminal illnesses. As word of the powerful effects of these drugs reached society at large, the interest of many individuals was piqued. By the late 1960s millions of people were experiencing the effects of the drugs LSD, psilocybin, and mescaline.

When used in less-controlled settings, the effects are more unpredictable and negative reactions are more likely. The powerful effects of these substances proved too much for society to handle. And it certainly did not help that psychedelics during the 1960s became associated with folks, many of college age, advocating for greater political expression and civil rights, and advocating against escalating military involvement in Southeast Asia. And there was also the association of psychedelics with that crazy new music by the Beatles, Jimi Hendrix, and many others. All this served to raise concern and contempt within the power structures of society at the time.

The first laws against LSD in the United States were passed in 1966. By 1971 it was illegal throughout the world, even though most of the world had never heard of it. Concurrently, all clinical research with psychedelics taking place at hospitals and medical centers came to a halt. After years of being off-limits, beginning in the 1990s and continuing to this day, the therapeutic utility of psychedelics is again being investigated by biomedical and clinical scientists. There is ample reason to believe that, when used with therapeutic intent in carefully controlled settings, they can be of extraordinary value. Such great power is worthy of our very highest respect.

Cannabinoids.   Plants of the genus *Cannabis* are believed to have originated in central Asia but now grow everywhere in the world. (The Latin genus name *Cannabis* has been widely adapted as a common name for the plant—thus, cannabis.) Wherever people have gone, cannabis has followed. Some say the cannabis plant may have been in domestic relationship with humans for longer than any other plant—perhaps more than ten thousand years—predating by thousands of years the domestication of cereal grains and other food plants. Cannabis has long been appreciated for its fiber properties, useful for making strong rope and durable cloth, and for its powerful and diverse medicinal and psychological applications: analgesic, muscle relaxant, appetite stimulant, sedative, stimulant, psychedelic-like changer of consciousness. When used to make fiber, cannabis is often referred to as hemp; when used for psychoactive and other medicinal effects, the plant or preparations from it bear many names—marijuana, pot, hash, ganja, and bhang, to name a few.

Cannabis, like any plant, contains hundreds of different kinds of molecules, dozens of which are likely to possess physiological activity in humans. One molecule, delta-9-tetrahydrocannabinol, or THC, has been identified as the major psychoactive chemical constituent of cannabis.

THC was identified from cannabis only in 1964, relatively recently given that so many other psychoactive molecules from plants were identified in the nineteenth century.

Delta-9-tetrahydrocannabinol (THC)

THC is one of about sixty different chemically related molecules found in cannabis. Collectively these molecules are called cannabinoids. They are not known to exist in any other variety of plant. Many of the cannabinoids are undoubtedly physiologically active in varying ways and to varying degrees and contribute to the many medicinally useful effects of cannabis.

After the discovery of THC, another twenty-five years went by before the site of action of THC in the nervous system was revealed. THC is a very hydrophobic molecule and easily sticks to lipids and dissolves into phospholipid bilayer membranes. This prompted speculation that perhaps the primary mechanism of action of THC in the brain involves dissolving into lipid membranes of neurons and somehow disrupting the cell's normal function. However, work during the 1980s suggested that THC interacted with a specific receptor, and by 1990 the cannabinoid (CB) receptor was identified. Like many neurotransmitter receptors, the CB receptor is a GPCR. A surprising piece of the story is that the CB receptor occurs pretty much everywhere in the brain and appears to be the most abundant of all known GPCR receptors in the vertebrate brain.

Just as with the discovery of the opioid receptor nearly twenty years earlier, the discovery of the CB receptor prompted a search for molecules that functioned as its endogenous ligands. Within a couple of years the first was discovered—it was a new molecule, not previously known and written about, and the authors of the research proposed a new name for the molecule: anandamide, from the Sanskrit word *ananda*, meaning bliss.

Anandamide

Anandamide, also know as *N*-arachidonoylethanolamine, is an endogenous agonist of the CB receptor, the first of several molecules to be discovered that appear to function as neurotransmitters at the CB receptor. Another endogenous agonist of the CB receptor is 2-arachidonoylglycerol (2-AG).

2-arachidonoylglycerol (2-AG)

Collectively these molecules are called endocannabinoids, even though chemically they are not cannabinoids—that is, they do not have structures that are directly related to THC. However, the anandamide and 2-AG molecules must bend around in three dimensions to be sufficiently similar in shape to some portion of the THC molecule, so that they all can act as agonists at the same receptor—the interaction of an agonist with a receptor is all about shape, just like a key inserted into a lock.

Because CB receptors and endocannabinoids are widespread in the brain, they no doubt serve important functions. What might these be? As it turns out, CB receptors appear to be largely present on the presynaptic axon terminals of neurons. And the endocannabinoid molecules appear to be synthesized and released from postsynaptic dendrites in response to glutamatergic stimulation. The endocannabinoid then travels across the synaptic cleft to interact with CB receptors on presynaptic axon terminals. The CB receptors may be on the axon terminal of the neuron that originally released the glutamate neurotransmitter, or they may be on axon terminals of other nearby neurons, or they may be on nearby astrocyte glial cells. A key point here is the backward, or *retro*, nature of the signaling. Endocannabinoids are examples of *retrograde* neurotransmitters, molecules that carry signal information in the direction opposite from the way neural signals were generally thought to move.

Retrograde neurotransmission occurs at a very large number of chemical synapses in the brain, probably trillions of synapses. It is thought that retrograde signaling by endocannabinoids is intimately involved in the dynamic tuning of the strengths of synapses—the intensity of the signal transmission from one cell to the next. This tuning of synaptic strength is an aspect of *neuroplasticity*—the capacity of neural circuitry to alter its properties. The English word *plastic* derives from the Greek *plassein*, meaning "to mold or form." Neuroplasticity is a dynamic phenomenon that occurs throughout one's entire life and is believed to underlie, for example, all of learning and memory formation (see Chapter 19). Wiring and rewiring are happening all the time.

> Forward and backward,
> transmitters cross the synapse—
> sculpting connection.

CHAPTER **10**

Neural Development and Neuroplasticity

From the fusion of a female egg and a male sperm comes the development of an animal body with all its grand complexity. This scenario of one cell (the fertilized egg) becoming the trillions of intricately connected and interacting cells of the adult animal has to be among the most mind-boggling phenomena imaginable. How does this happen? Not all that long ago this was a complete enigma. Now, after decades of investigation, some understanding of cellular and molecular processes involved in the orchestration of organismal development is emerging. It begins with information contained in the genes, encoded in the DNA of the body's cells.

Every cell in the human body contains the same genetic material. The human genome consists of forty-six chromosomes: twenty-three inherited from the mother and twenty-three inherited from the father. Chromosomes from the two parents carry similar information—the same genes, although there are often different variants of some of the genes between the parents. The two sex chromosomes—an X from the mother and either an X or a Y from the father—have more differences between them, because they are responsible for sex-specific aspects of structure and function. For humans, twenty-three is called the *haploid* chromosome number and forty-six the *diploid* chromosome number. The haploid number is often used in reference to distinct (counting only the genes from one parent) genetic material.

The twenty-three chromosomes of the haploid human genome contain approximately three billion (3×10^9) nucleotide base pairs: adenines, thymines, guanines, and cytosines. The entire human genome has now been sequenced; every single one of the three billion nucleotide base pairs is known, as well as the precise order in which they occur. (This is also the case for the complete genomes of numerous other organisms.) Of course, there are differences in nucleotide sequence between individuals, and as the technology to sequence DNA becomes more refined, it will become increasingly easier and less expensive to obtain complete DNA sequences for anyone. It is presently estimated that these three billion bases contain genes coding for approximately twenty-one thousand proteins.

Though every cell in a person's body contains the same genetic information, there are many different types of cells doing many different kinds of things. This is

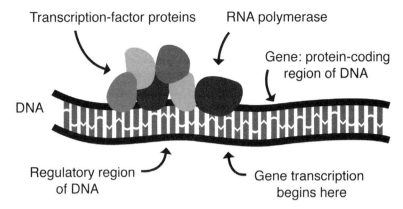

Transcription-factor proteins   RNA polymerase

Gene: protein-coding region of DNA

DNA

Regulatory region of DNA

Gene transcription begins here

Figure 10.1. Transcription factor proteins bind to regulatory regions of DNA and modulate the readout of genes. The enzyme RNA polymerase catalyzes the synthesis of RNA transcripts using DNA as the template.

because the information in the genome is transcribed and translated differently in different cells. Very early in organismal development, only hours (if not sooner) after fertilization of the egg, cell differentiation begins to take place. This is regulated via transcription factors—proteins that bind to regions of the DNA and regulate the readout of genes (Fig. 10.1).

A surprising recent discovery is that while only a small part (<3 percent) of the human genome codes for functional protein, most (>85 percent) of the genome is transcribed into RNAs of various kinds. These RNAs that are not translated into protein appear to be crucially involved in the regulation of gene expression, in ways that are not yet understood. Referencing the famous and mysterious dark matter and dark energy of cosmology, some folks have referred to the >97 percent of the human genome that does not code for functional protein as the dark matter of the DNA. In the 1970s, when these nontranslated sequences first began to be characterized, the phrase "junk DNA" was often used. However, because cells spend a great deal of energy transcribing and manipulating these nontranslated sequences, they are clearly playing important roles and are certainly not junk. Figuring out the roles of this regulatory RNA is one of the most exciting projects of contemporary molecular biology.

After conception, the fertilized egg begins to divide and form multiple cells—embryonic stem cells—with the capacity to continue dividing and to differentiate into any type of cell in the body. Embryonic stem cells in the developing nervous system differentiate into neural progenitor cells, which are on track to become various types of neurons or glia. The formation of nerve cells and glial cells from neural progenitor cells is called *neurogenesis* and *gliogenesis*.

Occurring in tandem with neurogenesis and gliogenesis is cell migration—as they differentiate, cells move around to occupy specific locations. Developing neurons grow out their dendrites and axons and differentiate so as to use one or another particular molecule for neurotransmitter signaling. As the neurons mature they also begin to wire together, forming synapses, a process called *synaptogenesis*. And thus the remarkable symphony that is neuronal development: neurogenesis, gliogenesis, migration, and synaptogenesis—all happening for billions of cells in the growing brain.

Within three weeks of conception in a developing human embryo, a group of cells begins to fold and form a structure called the *neural tube* (Fig. 10.2). The entire central nervous system will develop from this folded piece of tissue as it grows and differentiates.

Human conception to human birth requires approximately nine months of development within the mother's womb. By the third month after conception brain growth really takes off. Convolutions of the cerebral cortex, the gyri and sulci, begin to form during the final two months before birth, reflecting rapid expansion of the density and connectivity of cells in the cerebrum. The expanding volume of the brain is due to the proliferation of neurons and glia from dividing stem cells, as well as the growth and branching of dendrites and axons and the formation of trillions of synaptic connections between cells.

More than a century ago, Santiago Ramón y Cajal examined the cellular morphology of developing neurons and described how axon tips extended and sought out places of connection with other neurons. From his examination of static microscopic images of growing neurons in chicken embryos, Ramón y Cajal hypothesized that the tips of growing axons possessed exquisite mechanisms of sensitivity, motility, and guidance. He writes in his autobiography:

> In my inmost heart, I regard as the best of my work at that time the observations devoted to *neurogeny*, that is to the embryonic development of the nervous system. . . . I had the good fortune to behold for the first time that fantastic ending of the growing

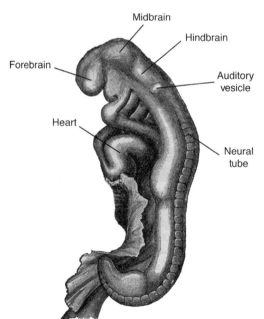

Figure 10.2. Drawing of a human embryo at three weeks after conception. Early stages of the developing brain are visible—including division into forebrain, midbrain, and hindbrain regions. The remainder of the neural tube will form the spinal cord. The auditory vesicle will become the labyrinth of the inner ear (see Chapter 15). This drawing is from the 1918 edition of Henry Gray's *Anatomy of the Human Body.*

Figure 10.3. Neuron drawings by Ramón y Cajal from his autobiography, first published in 1917 as *Recuerdos de mi vida*. Growth cones are depicted on the right, at the ends of the two axons.

axon. In my sections of the three-days chick embryo, this ending appeared as a concentration of protoplasm of conical form, endowed with amoeboid movements. It could be compared to a living battering ram, soft and flexible, which advances, pushing aside mechanically the obstacles which it finds in its way, until it reaches the area of its peripheral distribution. This curious terminal club, I christened the *growth cone*.

The growth cone (Fig. 10.3) progresses via the extension of fingerlike structures called *filopodia*. This extension—as well as the migration of entire cells as they find their appropriate places in the developing organism—is propelled by actions of the internal cytoskeletal structure of the cell. The dynamic cytoskeleton is composed of elaborate ordered arrays of protein polymers—microfilaments made of actin proteins and microtubules made of tubulin proteins (Fig. 10.4).

Microfilaments and microtubules form long strands that perform multiple functions within cells (Fig. 10.5). These include growth and movement of cell processes (such as axons, dendrites, and dendritic spines), as well as moving materials around within the cell. The insertion and removal of membrane proteins such as ion channels, transporters, and neurotransmitter receptors are orchestrated via cytoskeletal microtubules and microfilaments.

It is highly probable that microtubules are involved in aspects of cell function that are at present only dimly appreciated. For example, conventional psychophar-

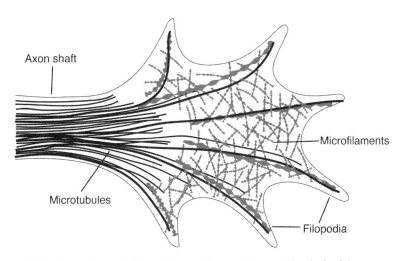

Figure 10.4. Internal cytoskeleton of an axon's growth cone. The shaft of the axon contains numerous microtubules (black lines), with some branching out into the filopodia. The tips of the filopodia are filled with microfilaments (gray lines), some of which are meshlike and some of which are larger bundles.

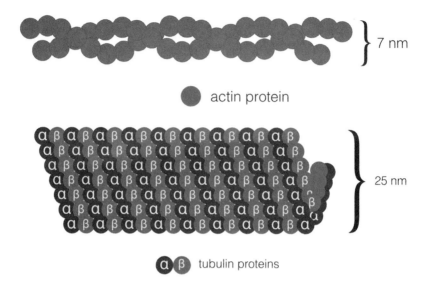

Figure 10.5. Microfilaments (top) are long polymers of actin proteins. Each actin protein is composed of about 375 amino acids. Microtubules (bottom) are long polymers of alpha-tubulin and beta-tubulin proteins. Each tubulin protein is composed of around 450 amino acids. Microtubules are cylindrical, with a hollow core. Microfilaments and microtubules can grow to be hundreds of times longer than their diameters and are composed of millions of atoms.

macology assumes that the actions of drugs can be understood by figuring out how drug molecules stick to and impact various neural membrane proteins, such as neurotransmitter receptors, reuptake transporters, and voltage-gated channels (many examples were given in Chapters 8 and 9). However, drug molecules also enter cells and interact with various intracellular structures, such as microtubules and microfilaments. Perhaps these intracellular interactions will eventually be understood to play significant roles in the overall effects of a drug. For example, it has been suggested that the consciousness-obliterating effects of general anesthetics may result from binding to microtubules. It is certainly the case that we are far from understanding the behavioral effects of most drugs—from general anesthetics to stimulants to psychedelics—based on what is currently known about their membrane-receptor neurochemistry.

Microtubule structure and function have even been invoked in an important hypothesis about the nature of mind and consciousness (see Chapter 22). Whatever the details turn out to be, it is likely that the intricate structure of the cellular interior is involved in numerous aspects of the life process—up to and including mind and consciousness—that at this point we have little understanding of.

Decades after Ramón y Cajal's observations, how axons know where to grow and how synapses decide to form remained unknown. Major progress in addressing these questions was made by Roger Sperry (1913–1994), who back in the 1930s and 1940s conducted clever investigations of the process by which neurons form connections. Sperry did his early research with frogs and salamanders, amphibians that have a remarkable capacity to regenerate after sustaining physical damage to their bodies. Salamanders, for example, have famously been known to regrow a leg after amputation. This regenerative capacity also takes place in the nervous system; if a nerve fiber is cut, it frequently will regrow.

One of Sperry's classic experiments involved cutting the optic nerve in a frog, the connection between the frog's eye and the frog's brain. If the optic nerve is cut in a person, that person will be blind for life (in the eye for which the nerve has been cut). Sever the optic nerve in a frog and the frog will be completely blind, also. However, wait several weeks and the severed optic nerve regenerates—completely normal vision is restored to the frog. This much had been known. It had also been established that, in the regeneration process, axons from the eye regrew from the eye toward the frog's brain. The question that Sperry addressed was this: how did axons from the eye know where to form synapses in the brain, so that normal vision was restored?

To begin, Sperry noted the following: if the muscles holding the frog's eyeball in place are delicately cut, the eyeball can be rotated in its socket by a full 180 degrees. If the eye muscles are then repaired and allowed to heal, the frog will see the world upside down and backward. This can be demonstrated by introducing a morsel of food (such as an insect) to the frog: the frog strikes at the insect in the wrong direction (Fig. 10.6). No matter how many weeks are allowed to go by, the frog never learns to correct this behavior and adjust to its upside down and backward world.

Now Sperry combined the two procedures: he rotated the frog's eyeball by 180 degrees *and* cut the optic nerve connection between the eyeball and the brain. Initially, of course, the frog was completely blind, but after a few weeks the axons forming the optic nerve regrew and reestablished connections between the eye and the brain. The question: how would the frog see now? Will the frog's nervous system use the opportunity provided by regrowth of the optic nerve to form synaptic connections that correct for the rotated eyeball, so that it will see the world normally again. Or, will the frog see the world upside down and backward?

What is your prediction?

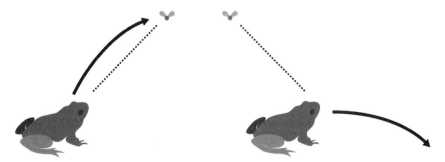

Figure 10.6. Left: frog with normal vision. The frog sees the insect (dashed line) and strikes out with its tongue in the direction of the insect (solid line). Right: frog after eye is surgically rotated by 180 degrees. It apparently sees the world upside down and backward, because it attempts to catch an insect located above and behind its body by striking down and ahead.

The result: the frog sees the world upside down and backward, as if the eyeball had simply been rotated without the cutting and reforming of the optic nerve connections. Thus, the frog did not use the opportunity afforded by regrowing the optic nerve axons and forming new synaptic connections in the brain to correct the damage done to its perception from the rotated eyeball.

Instead, the frog's nervous system appears to have formed exactly the same connections between the eye and the brain as were there before the optic nerve was cut. This was a profound result. It inspired Sperry to formulate what came to be called the chemoaffinity hypothesis, proposing that nerve cells use specific chemical signals to guide their wiring during development and during neural regeneration.

In the decades since Sperry's experiments and proposal of chemically guided nerve growth, a variety of protein molecules and mechanisms have been discovered that regulate the processes of cell growth, differentiation, migration, and synaptogenesis. Collectively one refers to this diverse group of molecules as nerve growth and guidance factors.

The first nerve growth factor, or *neurotrophin*, to be discovered was named simply "nerve growth factor," or NGF. Others now known are called things like BDNF (brain-derived neurotrophic factor), GDNF (glia-derived neurotrophic factor), and NT3 (neurotrophin-3). These are all proteins that have been found to somehow promote the growth or survival of neurons. Promoting survival is a particularly important mechanism related to neuronal growth, because large numbers of neurons are eliminated by a kind of programmed cell death during the early development and wiring of the nervous system. In some regions of the brain, more than 50 percent of the neurons may be eliminated during early development.

Other proteins, involved in axon and dendrite guidance, as well as other developmental processes, go by such names as ephrin, netrin, neuropilin, plexin, semaphorin, Slit, and Robo. Guidance sometimes involves direct contact between one protein anchored to one cell and another protein anchored to another. For example, ephrin proteins on one cell bind to ephrin receptor proteins on another. Such binding can sometimes cause cell growth in the direction of contact or in other circumstances cause growth away from the direction of contact. The mechanisms of attraction and repulsion are mediated by coupling the activation of membrane receptors—such as ephrin to the ephrin receptor, or Slit to Robo—to the dynamics of the cytoskeleton. Growth of microfilaments and microtubules in specific directions can promote extension of an axon in one direction (attraction) or another (repulsion)—all quite elegant and elaborate, and only beginning to be understood in detail.

While much of neurogenesis and gliogenesis takes place in the womb, a great deal of the wiring up of neurons, especially over large regions of the cerebral cortex, continues to occur after birth. In the year after birth, vast numbers of new synaptic connections form between neurons throughout the cerebral cortex. In fact, many more connections between neurons are formed during the first year of life than will eventually be retained. As fast as connections are forming, they are also being assessed for utility. Synapses that are used become stabilized and strengthened. Synapses that are not used are eliminated, a process called synaptic pruning.

These processes are aspects of neuroplasticity. Strengthening and weakening of synapses may happen as a result of molecular processes taking place either presynaptically, postsynaptically, or both. An example of a presynaptic mechanism to strengthen a synapse is prolonging the state of depolarization in the axon terminal, so that voltage-gated Ca^{++} channels remain open for a longer time, resulting in the fusion of more vesicles and increased release of neurotransmitter. More neurotransmitter released means more signal passed to the next cell—thus, a stronger synapse.

Presynaptic effects may be mediated by receptors on the axon terminal that respond to released neurotransmitter. For example, at a glutamatergic synapse, glutamate neurotransmitter may interact with glutamate receptors located on the presynaptic axon terminal to open Na^+ or Ca^{++} ion channels and thus prolong depolarization in the axon terminal, thereby strengthening the synapse.

Or, there may be retrograde signals from a postsynaptic cell that influence neurotransmitter release in the axon terminal. Endocannabinoids released from a postsynaptic dendrite may interact with presynaptic cannabinoid G-protein-coupled receptors to prolong depolarization or influence gene expression. For example, influencing the transcription and translation of genes that code for presynaptic reuptake transporters can have a long-term effect on synaptic strength. More reuptake transporter proteins means neurotransmitter is removed from the synaptic cleft more rapidly after release—a smaller signal and thus a weaker synapse. Fewer reuptake transporter proteins means neurotransmitter remains in the synaptic cleft for a longer time after release—more signal and thus a stronger synapse.

A postsynaptic mechanism for changing the strength of a synapse is to influence gene transcription so that greater or lesser numbers of neurotransmitter receptors are produced and inserted into the postsynaptic membrane. More neurotransmitter receptors means a larger impact from incoming neurotransmitter—a stronger synapse. Other things being equal, fewer postsynaptic neurotransmitter receptors mean a weaker synapse.

Likewise, G-protein-coupled receptor effects on transcription of nerve growth factors may influence the branching of axons and dendrites, the sprouting of dendritic spines, and the formation of new synapses.

The formation of new neurons from precursor cells provides another potential avenue of neuroplasticity. In contrast to what had been assumed throughout much of the twentieth century, neurogenesis is now known to occur in limited but measurable ways even in the adult vertebrate brain. These neurogenic processes have been best studied in the rodent brain but are also known to take place in the adult human brain, particularly within a structure called the hippocampus. Recent research has estimated that about fourteen hundred new neurons are added each day within the two hippocampi of the human brain.

The hippocampus is a bilateral structure located beneath the surface of the temporal lobe known to play a pivotal role in the formation and stabilization of memories (see Chapter 19). The name derives from the perceived similarity between the shape of this structure in the human brain and the shape of a seahorse, a fish with the genus name *Hippocampus* (Fig. 10.7). The seahorse genus name comes from a sea beast of ancient myth having the head and front legs of a horse (Greek *hippos* = horse) and the posterior of some kind of weird fishlike swimming creature (Greek *kampos* = sea monster).

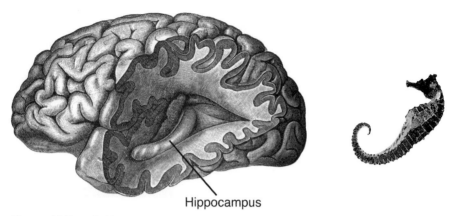

Hippocampus

Figure 10.7. Left: hippocampus, the brain structure, revealed by exposing the medial (interior) temporal lobe region. Right: *Hippocampus*, the seahorse.

Though happening all the time in the brain, neuroplastic changes are most robust during the early years of life. It is then that the brain is most susceptible to wiring changes. Certainly a lesson from neuroscience is that experiences of infancy, childhood, adolescence, and early adulthood are likely the most powerful experiences of one's life in terms of laying down pathways in the brain that will have lifelong effects on behavior.

Neurogenesis, growth and branching of axons and dendrites, sprouting of dendritic spines, synapse formation and strengthening, synapse pruning and elimination, glial cell formation and differentiation, and axonal myelination are all continuing at robust rates during childhood. Myelination of axons interconnecting cells within the cerebral cortex continues until past twenty years of age. Because myelination is needed for cortical neurons to efficiently communicate with one another, it is clear that establishing and fine-tuning cortical circuits require many years of experience and the teen years continue to be a particularly important phase of brain development.

The importance of good parenting and a loving atmosphere during childhood are widely appreciated. A society that truly appreciates the importance of brain plasticity during the early years of life would place a very high priority on optimizing early learning. Elementary school teachers would be among the most valued members of society, and paid accordingly. And book learning is only a small part of the story. Social connection and emotional learning are hugely important. Great benefits to individuals and to society would surely come from investment in optimizing early-lifetime experiences.

> Growing and reaching,
>   then trimming the less used parts—
>   plastic all of life!

CHAPTER 11

Sensory Perception

We experience sight, sound, smell, taste, temperature, the feel of the wind on our face. In all these cases, the brain receives signal information from the environs of the body and uses that information to form a mental experience of the world. This process is called sensory perception and constitutes an important nexus between brain, mind, and behavior. Sensory perception may be divided into two basic components: (1) the collection of information from the environment via sensory organs and receptors and (2) the analysis and interpretation of this information by the nervous system, contributing to the experience of mental states of perceptual awareness. Sometimes component 1 is called sensation and component 2 perception.

Even very simple organisms have sensation. Single-celled bacteria detect and respond to physical stimuli in their environment. For example, the bacteria *Escherichia coli* and *Salmonella* respond to the presence of chemical substances present in the soupy medium through which they move. How do they do this?

These bacteria swim in a series of maneuvers called runs and tumbles. A bacterial cell swims in a straight line for a second or so (a run) and then stops swimming and flops around for a moment (a tumble); it then swims off again in a straight line for another second (a run). Runs occur when the bacterium's flagella rotate in one direction and form a bundle that functions like a propeller that produces coherent motion (Fig. 11.1). Tumbles occur when the direction of flagellar rotation reverses, the individual flagella fly apart, forward motion ceases, and the bacterial cell tumbles about randomly. The direction of flagellar rotation then reverses again and another run commences, now in a direction that is randomly related to that of the original run. These bacteria thus swim in what is mathematically termed a *random walk* in three dimensions.

An *E. coli* cell is about 2 micrometers in length and swims along at an impressive speed of about 30 micrometers per second, tumbling off in a new direction every second or so. Now, suppose the bacterium encounters a nutrient chemical substance. In particular, some amino acids—such as aspartic acid and serine—interact with receptor proteins located on the bacterial cell's outer membrane and influence the bacterium to swim toward the nutrients—a behavior called *chemotaxis*. Interaction of nutrients with the receptor proteins reduces the likelihood of tumbling and keeps the bacterium moving in a direction where nutrients are present. If nutrient mole-

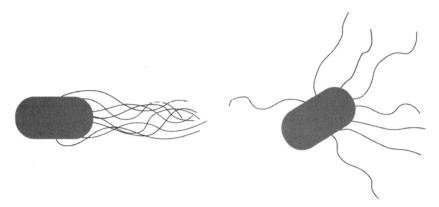

Figure 11.1. Bacterial flagella organized into a bundle during a run (left) and unraveled during a tumble (right).

cules become less abundant, the bacterium reverts to its usual behavior of tumbling every second or so and keeps changing direction until encountering more nutrients, which then reduces the frequency of tumbles. The bacterium continues to swim in a random walk, but its direction is biased by swimming for longer time periods toward nutrients it encounters.

Another prominent environmental stimulus that can influence the behavior of microorganisms, as well as plants and animals, is light. The process of moving toward light is called *phototaxis* (in the case of the entire organism moving toward, such as a swimming bacterium) or *phototropism* (in the case of a bending or growing toward, such as a plant near a window). In organisms that use light as an energy source (photosynthesis), phototaxis and phototropism increase exposure. In organisms that do not derive energy directly from light, phototropism and phototaxis may enable movement toward a more open region in order to disperse spores or seeds.

The fungus *Phycomyces* does not use photosynthesis but nonetheless has exquisite sensitivity to light, which it uses as a cue to direct the growth of its fruiting bodies, called sporangiophores. *Phycomyces* sporangiophores typically have stalks that are several centimeters long. At the tip of each stalk is a structure called a sporangium—about 0.5 mm in diameter and containing around a hundred thousand spores (Fig. 11.2). The tip can elongate at a rate of several millimeters per hour and will grow in the direction of light (phototropism). Although the mycelium of the fungus may be growing deep within a substrate material, the light sensitivity of its sporangiophores enables the fungus to disperse its spores into open terrain.

Thus, many organisms—it is probably safe to say all organisms—detect and respond to stimuli from the environment. They possess sensation. What about the mental experience of perception? Do *E. coli* and *Phycomyces* have mental experiences? It is generally assumed that mentality is limited to organisms with complex nervous systems. But this is an assumption—and really, who knows? Is it possible that microorganisms have an experience of what it is like to be them? All we are sure of at this point, if we are sure of anything, is that we can only really know about mental experiences in ourselves and in other humans with whom we can communicate using language. More discussion of this fascinating issue later.

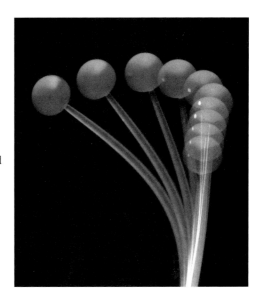

Figure 11.2. Phototropism in a *Phy-comyces* sporangiophore: a multiple-exposure photograph showing upward elongation of the sporangiophore, followed by phototropic elongation toward light coming from the left (one exposure every 3 minutes).

What can we say about our experience of the world in the context of the present discussion of sensory perception? It is conventional to begin by assuming there is a world—a physical reality—existing independent of our interacting with it. Note that this, too, is an assumption, or at least a working hypothesis, because everything we know comes to us by way of our perception and consciousness. However, if we assume the existence of some kind of "external" physical world, then our experience of that world depends on what is actually there—the physical things that are out there, what actually exists. In philosophy this is the realm of *ontology*: the study of the nature of reality. What is it that exists?

Next, our experience of the world depends on the physical properties of our sensory receptors: eyes are sensitive to a limited range of energies of electromagnetic radiation, ears to a limited range of frequencies of mechanical vibration, noses to a limited range of molecular shapes, and so forth. Then, signals from sensory receptors are manipulated by the nervous system and, particularly in us humans, by our brain. Billions of cells and trillions of synaptic connections are impacted by information received via sensory pathways. This interaction of neural networks with incoming sensory information somehow forms the basis, it is believed, for our mental experience of the world. In philosophy, this is the realm of *epistemology*: how do we know what we know? In summary, according to the conventional framework in the neuroscience of perception, our experience of the world is a function of what actually exists, the physics of our sensory receptors and organs, and the neural manipulation of incoming signals by the brain.

There is a notion in epistemology called *naive realism*, that what we perceive is identical to what actually exists in the world—what we see, hear, smell, taste, and so forth, is exactly what is "out there" in some way. It is very easy to demonstrate the limitations of naive realism.

Figure 11.3 is called the café wall illusion, inspired by a tile pattern on the wall of a coffee house in Bristol, England. Most people see lines that are not parallel, that

Figure 11.3. The café wall illusion.

are askew. However, you can easily verify by using a straightedge that all lines are indeed parallel. This simple but powerful visual illusion clearly illustrates that what we perceive (in this case, see) is not exactly what is.

All forms of perception involve elaborate manipulation of signal information by the nervous system, including interaction of incoming neural signals with vast networks of established activity in the cerebral cortex. This results in our perception being a transformed and constructed representation of what is "out there," giving rise to perceptual experiences that are, according to the evolutionary view, good enough to allow for our survival and reproduction in a complex and challenging environment, but having an unclear relation to what is actually out there.

Focusing on human sensory perception, we can think of each of the various sensory pathways as associated with organs of reception containing receptor cells responding to particular kinds of physical stimuli. And then there is a particular kind of mental experience. Thus, vision or the visual pathway has as its organs of reception the eyes, containing photoreceptor cells responding to visible light. The associated perceptual experience is that of visually seeing the world. Similarly, the auditory system has the ears as its organs of reception, containing hair cells responding to mechanical vibration. The associated perceptual experience is that of hearing sounds. In like manner, there is the tongue and taste, the nose and smell, and the skin and tactile experience. These five channels of sensory perception are sometimes referred to as the five primary senses.

In addition, there is the vestibular sense, for which the organs of reception are the semicircular canals of the inner ear, the receptor cells are hair cells, and the physical stimuli are gravity and acceleration. The associated perceptual experience is that of balance. There is also proprioception, in which stretch receptors in the muscles and joints gather information related to muscle tension and joint movement. The resulting information is used to tune body alignment and coordinated movement.

Vestibular and proprioceptive pathways, although crucial to executing balanced movements, are often not considered among the "primary" senses because the collection and use of information by these channels are mostly out of awareness and not used in the same way to inform our conscious perception of the world. We mostly become aware of these senses when something is wrong and balance and coordination are impaired, as when we spin around until dizzy.

Human sensory perception is sophisticated, elaborate, and quite sensitive. And like all forms of sensory perception, it is limited—that is, not capable of detecting vast ranges of physical phenomena that are known, by other means, to exist. This can be illustrated by taking a look at vision. The visual pathway in humans responds to a limited range of energies within the electromagnetic energy spectrum (Fig. 11.4). The electromagnetic spectrum of radiation encompasses an enormous range of energy, from very high-energy gamma rays and x-rays to moderately high-energy ultraviolet radiation, to visible light, to infrared radiation, to microwaves, and finally to relatively low-energy radio waves. High-energy gamma rays and low-energy radio waves differ by more than eighteen orders of magnitude (a factor of 10^{18}, or a million million million = a quintillion) in energy. Within this huge spectrum of energy, a narrow band spanning less than a single order of magnitude comprises the sensitivity range of the human visual system. This is "visible light," so called because it is visible to us humans, and to many other animals, too.

Not all that long ago it was widely believed that only we humans had the ability to see the world in all its richness of color—that other animals could only see things in black, white, and shades of gray. Consider honeybees, insects that spend their lives visiting flowers, gathering nectar and pollen, and transferring pollen between plants, contributing to plant fertility. Though little in nature rivals the extraordinary variety and exuberance of colors in flowers, it was not generally believed that honeybees could see color. After all, they were merely simple insects.

Then, in the early twentieth century, Karl von Frisch (1886–1982), through years of careful observation and experimentation, conclusively demonstrated that honey-

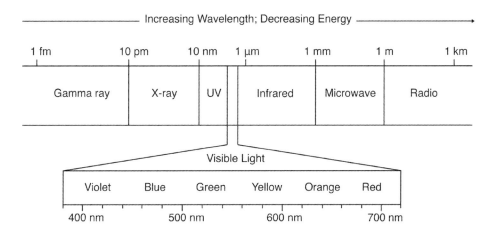

Figure 11.4. Electromagnetic spectrum.

bees have color vision. This may seem like an obvious fact today—now that we appreciate that many animals have excellent color vision—but at the time it was a big discovery, so much so that it contributed to von Frisch receiving the Nobel Prize for Physiology or Medicine in 1973 (together with Konrad Lorenz and Nikolaas Tinbergen, for their work in other aspects of animal behavior). Von Frisch began his Nobel Prize lecture:

> Some 60 years ago, many biologists thought that bees and other insects were totally color-blind animals. I was unable to believe it. For the bright colors of flowers can be understood only as an adaptation to color-sensitive visitors. This was the beginning of experiments on the color sense of the bee. On a table outdoors I placed a colored paper between papers of different shades of gray and on it I laid a small glass dish filled with sugar syrup. Bees from a nearby hive could be trained to recognize this color and demonstrated their ability to distinguish it from shades of gray.

Honeybees also have visual capacities that are unusual from a human perspective. Figure 11.5 shows an African daisy (*Dimorphotheca aurantiaca*) illuminated by sunlight and photographed with a lens that captures only visible light (left) and one that also captures ultraviolet light (right). Honeybee visual sensitivity extends into the ultraviolet region of the electromagnetic spectrum, a range of energies to which we humans are blind. There is abundant ultraviolet radiation in sunlight, and many flowers have patterns that are visible in ultraviolet light but are not noticeable as any sort of color difference in the visible region of the spectrum. These patterns are sometimes called nectar guides and are believed to act as visual features that attract bees and other pollinating insects and birds to them.

Ultraviolet radiation is slightly higher in energy than visible light. The other direction on the electromagnetic spectrum, with radiation slightly lower in energy

Figure 11.5. African daisy (*Dimorphotheca aurantiaca*) photographed using an ordinary glass lens (left) and a lens made of quartz, which allows ultraviolet light to pass through (right). I took these photographs when I was a graduate student at Caltech using a Hasselblad camera, a duplicate of the one used by NASA astronauts on lunar landing missions. The camera was kindly loaned to me by folks at NASA's Jet Propulsion Laboratory.

than visible light, is the infrared region. Infrared radiation also is not visible to us—its energy is too low to activate the photoreceptors in the eye. However, infrared radiation is absorbed by many molecules in such a way as to set them vibrating. This molecular vibratory motion, if it is strong enough, may be experienced as heat.

There is a group of snakes, the pit vipers (rattlesnakes are in this group), that possess structures, called pit organs, that detect infrared radiation in a way similar to how eyes detect visible light. The pit organs are positioned below the eyes and near the nostrils, and enable the snake to accurately locate prey animals even in complete darkness.

There are some technological gadgets used by humans to facilitate vision in the dark. These night vision devices are used by military and law enforcement personnel to see under conditions of very low light or even in complete darkness. One kind of device, called an image intensifier, amplifies very low intensities of visible light. Even on a very dark night there is still a low level of visible light—from the moon and stars, for example. A second kind of gadget is called an infrared or thermal imager. Like the rattlesnake's pit organ, it detects infrared radiation, to which the human visual system is insensitive. The gadget converts the infrared image to signals in the visible region of the spectrum, allowing things to be seen even in complete darkness—as long as they emit infrared radiation, as any person or other warm-blooded animal would.

Another property of electromagnetic radiation is something called *polarization*, which can be thought of as vibration of the electromagnetic field aligned along specific angles in relation to the direction of propagation. Light from the sun, radiating through space, is vibrating in all possible angles of polarization. However, when sunlight interacts with the molecules of air in Earth's atmosphere, it scatters so as to generate a variation in polarization across the vault of the sky (Fig. 11.6). That is, the angle of polarization, and the extent to which the light is polarized, varies depending upon where in the sky one looks relative to the sun.

This can be demonstrated by looking through a polarizing filter (such as the lens in polarizing sunglasses) at different regions of the sky on a sunny day. You will find

Figure 11.6. The angle and intensity of skylight polarization, indicated by the direction and thickness, respectively, of the short bars. The intensity of polarization is greatest 90 degrees from the position of the sun.

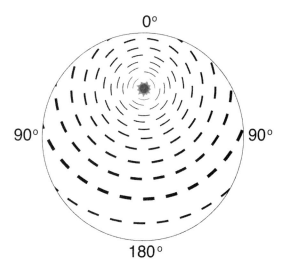

that the angle of polarization and the intensity of the polarized light passing through the lens changes depending upon where in the sky you look. The human visual system, without the aid of a polarizing filter, is not sensitive to this property of sunlight. However, many insects, birds, reptiles, and other animals are. This discovery was originally made by Karl von Frisch in his experiments with honeybees. Again, from his Nobel Prize lecture:

> I noticed that a view of the blue sky is the same as a view of the sun. When clouds passed over the section of the sky visible to the bees, disoriented dances immediately resulted. Therefore they must have been able to read the sun's position from the blue sky. The direction of vibration of polarized blue light differs in relation to the sun's position across the entire vault of the sky. Thus, to one that is able to perceive the direction of vibration, even a spot of blue sky can disclose the sun's position by its polarization pattern. Are bees endowed with this capacity?

Von Frisch went on to do experiments with polarizing filters to conclusively demonstrate that honeybees use sunlight polarization patterns as a navigational aid, another extraordinary discovery. (Perhaps von Frisch's most extraordinary discovery was the dance language of honeybees, alluded to in the paragraph above, through which bees communicate the location of food sources to their hivemates.) Many insects and other animals have since been found to be sensitive to skylight polarization and to use it as a source of navigational information. This could be very helpful, for example, to a beetle crawling in a crevice between large boulders and only able to see a tiny piece of blue sky above.

Ultraviolet, infrared, and polarization are aspects of electromagnetic radiation to which humans lack sensitivity. Other animals have evolved capacities to detect these electromagnetic phenomena and use them in ways that are useful for them. Similar differences occur for sound. The human ear and auditory system (see Chapter 15) are exquisitely sensitive and sophisticated and, as with vision, are also limited in their sensitivity. In terms of frequency of mechanical vibration, we humans are capable of hearing within the approximate range of 20 to 20,000 cycles of vibration per second. The unit of cycles per second is called a hertz (Hz), after Heinrich Hertz (1857–1894), a physicist who made contributions to the study of vibrating electromagnetic fields.

Very low-frequency sound, with frequencies less than 20 Hz, is referred to as infrasound. Though inaudible to us, elephants can both generate and hear infrasonic frequencies and use infrasonic calls in their social communication.

Very high-frequency sound, called ultrasound, is inaudible to us but audible to many other animals. Dogs and cats can hear sounds having frequencies of 40,000 Hz and higher. These animals are not known to use ultrasound in their communication; however, ultrasound perception is useful to them in their hunting, as many rodents communicate using high-frequency sounds.

Bats, dolphins, and whales emit high-frequency sounds and then hear the sound's reflection (echo) from nearby objects, including, in the case of bats, insects. Using this echolocation, or biological sonar (sound navigation and ranging), these animals can navigate and hunt in cases of poor visibility, even total darkness. Ultrasonic frequencies higher than 100,000 Hz are often used by bats because the very short wavelengths associated with very high frequencies permit discrimination of a very fine degree of detail (spatial acuity), useful when trying to locate a tiny insect when both the bat and the bug are flying through the air—really quite astounding! Some insects, such as some moths, also can hear ultrasound, allowing them to sense the approach of a bat about to eat them and take evasive action in their flight.

A kind of sensory perception that is unlike anything currently known to exist in humans is electroreception—the detection of electric fields generated by living organisms. Every living creature is surrounded by electric fields, produced as a result of the movement of charged ions within the organism. A classic experiment demonstrating the existence of electroreception was conducted with sharks. Some sharks are capable of locating fish that are well camouflaged on the ocean bottom, and it was generally believed that the shark must be locating the hidden fish by smell. While odor may indeed be helpful, it is now known that sharks use the electric field generated by the fish as the primary means of detecting its location. Electroreceptive structures, called ampullae of Lorenzini, are densely dispersed over the shark's head.

The platypus, an egg-laying monotreme mammal native to Australia, uses electroreceptors located in its bill to probe the muddy bottoms of aquatic environments in search of bioelectric fields generated by prey animals, such as small crustaceans and mollusks. The platypus, together with its relative the echidna, are the only mammals known to use this form of sensory perception.

Electroreception is also used by various fish living in the murky waters of rivers like the Amazon in South America. These fish also have structures that generate oscillating electric fields (stronger than the bioelectric fields produced by all living organisms) that then propagate into the surrounding environment. Some of these oscillating fields are used to communicate with other members of the same species. Different species of electric fish are distinguished by fields having specific frequencies and patterns. The electric fields generated by the fish are also altered by the surrounding terrain, allowing the fish to sense the presence of nearby animals and obstacles in a manner somewhat akin to echolocation—a kind of electrolocation.

Yet another form of sensory perception different from anything currently known to exist in humans is the sensing of magnetic fields, in particular the magnetic field produced by Earth. The Earth's geomagnetic field is generated by large-scale movement of magnetic atoms in the molten interior of the planet. The intensity of the geomagnetic field varies over the surface of the planet—strongest near the north and south magnetic poles and weakest near the equator (Fig. 11.7). The direction of the magnetic field vector points toward the poles and becomes more steeply inclined nearer to the poles.

Near the equator the vector's direction is nearly horizontal and parallel to the surface. The magnitude and direction of this geomagnetic field provide information useful in navigation. We humans use an instrument, a magnetic compass, to measure the direction of the geomagnetic field.

Humans began to appreciate the navigational utility of Earth's magnetic field about a thousand years ago. For eons animals have been moving long distances around the planet; many animals—including birds, fish, and turtles—migrate these

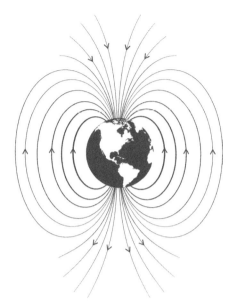

Figure 11.7. Earth's magnetic field.

distances with great accuracy. Some are known to return after journeying thousands of miles to the exact same locations year after year. If humans during the past few centuries have figured out how to build magnetic compasses and use the geomagnetic field as a source of navigational information, it certainly is the case that animals, given millions of years of evolutionary time, have also figured out ways to do this.

Indeed, it is known that animals use multiple sources of information about location and direction to guide them during their migrations and other navigations; these include the sun's position, odors, sounds, visual landmarks, and more. And, there is now a great deal of evidence indicating that many animals detect the geomagnetic field and use it as a navigational aid. Experiments have been conducted with birds, fish, sea turtles, and honeybees demonstrating the influence of magnetic fields on behavior.

One of the best-studied animals in the navigation business is the common pigeon (*Columba livia*), selected for investigation due to its very accurate and relatively easy-to-study navigational prowess. If one takes a pigeon many miles from its home nest and releases it into the sky, it will fly straightaway back to its home. So reliable is this behavior that pigeons have been used since ancient times to carry messages from one place to another and have also been selectively bred to enhance their rapid flight home after release in a distant place. A classic series of experiments conducted around 1970 demonstrated that a small magnet affixed to the body of a pigeon severely interfered with its ability to navigate home on cloudy days—days where the sun's location was not visible. Decades later, the sensory structure with which pigeons and other animals detect the geomagnetic field is still not known. Various hypotheses have been suggested, among which are the alignment of tiny magnetic particles known to occur in pigeons and other animals, and magnetic effects on the alignment of electron spins in certain light-activated molecules in the bird's eyes. Another sweet mystery.

Electric and magnetic fields, very low- and very high-frequency sounds, ultraviolet and infrared radiation, light polarization—these things are not perceivable by humans, at least as far as we know. In addition, some animals have more sophisticated odor detection than we do, others have more refined color vision, and still others have better visual acuity. The world as experienced by animals having sensory-perceptual abilities different from our own is likely to differ in significant ways from the world as we know it. What is it like to be a fish living in the murky waters of the Amazon, communicating with other fish via oscillating electric fields and detecting the presence of nearby objects by electroreception?

> Glowing and pulsing,
> microwaves radiating—
> from pocket and purse.

CHAPTER 12

Nose and Smell

You walk along a street in an unfamiliar neighborhood, looking for a place to enjoy a small lunch. A savory aroma attracts you into a small restaurant to investigate the menu. Perhaps it is a smell of basil and thyme, or of cumin and coriander, depending on the cuisine. Our sense of smell—our capacity to detect and respond to airborne molecules in the environment—is the human analogue of what a bacterium does when it detects and responds to chemicals in its environment.

It is sometimes said humans don't have a very sophisticated sense of smell and that the ability to smell is not very important to us. On the contrary, there are plenty of reasons to believe that the sense of smell in humans is quite refined and that smells—odors and aromas—play important roles in human life. People respond intensely to smells, being strongly attracted or repulsed. Perfumery was one of the early applications of alchemy.

Olfactory sensory perception begins when odorants—airborne volatile molecules (Latin *volare* = to fly)—enter the nasal passages, via the constant streams of air inhaled and exhaled through the nose. Some of these molecules are caught in the moist and mucousy tissue lining the interior of the nasal passages, in the region called the nasal or olfactory epithelium. (*Epithelium* is the name given to the types of cells that line the surfaces of many structures throughout the body.) There the molecules may come into contact with the cilia of olfactory receptor cells, which are populated by olfactory receptor proteins.

Figure 12.1 depicts olfactory receptor cells embedded in the nasal epithelium. The nasal passage (within the nose) would be just below the diagram. The dendrites of the receptor cells branch into cilia containing olfactory receptor proteins. These cilia extend into the mucus lining the nasal passage, and their filamentous structure provides a large surface area containing olfactory receptor proteins.

Within the nasal epithelium are also stem cells—not primordial stem cells that can differentiate into any kind of cell, but cells with enough flexibility to differentiate into the various different types of olfactory receptor cells. These olfactory stem cells allow the receptor cells to be regularly replaced, something that happens about every one to two months. This is beneficial because direct exposure of the receptor cells to potentially toxic substances from the environment results in accumulation of cellular damage—the cost of chemoreception.

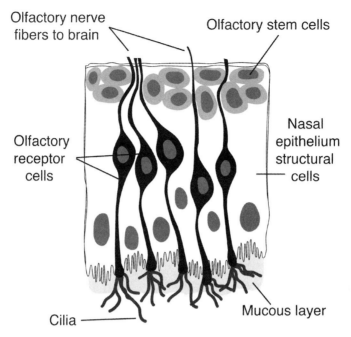

Figure 12.1. Olfactory epithelium.

Like many of the receptor proteins found in animals, olfactory receptors are G-protein-coupled receptors (GPCRs). Among the vertebrate animals, the number of different types of olfactory receptor proteins varies widely. A typical fish, for example, might have around one hundred different olfactory receptor proteins, coded for by one hundred different genes. Mammals may typically have ten times this number of different olfactory GPCRs, around a thousand. A mouse is on the high end of the mammalian range, with about thirteen hundred different olfactory receptor proteins. Humans are on the low end, with about 350 different olfactory receptor proteins. Each different GPCR responds to molecules having specific molecular shapes, just as different GPCR neurotransmitter receptors are activated by different neurotransmitter and drug (agonist) molecules.

In addition to its 350 genes coding for 350 functioning olfactory GPCRs, the human genome has a large number of nonfunctional genes that, although they appear to code for olfactory GPCRs, are altered in some way so that they do not code for functional receptor proteins—these are called *pseudogenes*. Humans have about six hundred olfactory pseudogenes. It is speculated that, in our evolutionary past, our distant ancestors possessed many more functional olfactory receptor types (similar to the mouse of today) and a correspondingly more sophisticated sense of smell. It is believed that, as our evolutionary ancestors migrated from living close to the ground (where odorants are a crucial source of environmental information) to living in trees and, eventually, to being upright creatures with noses a long way from the ground (and vision becoming more important for collecting environmental information), functional olfactory receptors were lost through mutation, even though remnants of the ancient genes remain.

It is likely we are still missing an interesting part of the story here. Why would such a large number of nonfunctional genes be maintained over millions of years of evolutionary history? They may serve some sort of important regulatory function—something is likely going on here, and we don't yet know what it is.

Our 350 different functional olfactory GPCRs give us the ability to detect and discriminate thousands (at least!) of different odors—here's how. A particular odorant molecule will differentially activate to varying extents some subset of olfactory GPCRs. Thus, odorant X may bind, say, to olfactory receptor proteins 23, 77, 136, 242, 290, 312, and 349, each with a specific level of GPCR pathway activation. And odorant Z may bind to olfactory receptor proteins 9, 45, 91, 112, 136, 138, 149, 207, 298, and 333, each with a particular level of activation. And so on. Thus, it becomes possible to discriminate a very, very, very large number of odorant molecules according to their different patterns of activation of the 350 olfactory GPCRs.

One measure of the importance we place on olfaction is the economic success of the perfume industry. Billions of dollars are spent every year purchasing perfumes. Commercial perfumes are mixtures of many aromatic molecular components. Such aromatics were originally derived exclusively from natural materials, mostly from plants. These days, most commercial perfumes use numerous synthetic molecules to replace the harder-to-obtain and more precious materials from plants and animals. Though great effort is made to mimic complex natural aromas by these methods, necessarily some of the nuance is lost. Artisan perfumers continue to follow the old ways of mixing perfumes using only aromatic essences from plant and animal materials.

The old ways. The way of perfume. The way of plant medicines. The term *essential oil* designates the oily concentrate of aromatic molecules from a plant. *Essential* (Latin *esse* = to be) refers to the distinctive scent of the plant, its hallmark aroma, its spirituous essence and quintessence. Frequently the essential oil includes many of a plant's medicinal qualities. It is oily because the aroma-carrying molecules frequently are hydrophobic. Essential oils are often prepared by distillation, the process of heating an extract of the plant and concentrating the more volatile components. Distillation was invented a thousand years ago by Arab alchemists—primarily to make perfumes and to concentrate preparations from medicinal plants (Fig. 12.2).

Our words *aroma* and *aromatic* derive from the Greek word for spice. Spices are among the archetypical aromatic substances, highly valued by humans for millennia due to the olfactory qualities they add to food and perfumes. Consider cinnamon, from the plant *Cinnamomum verum* and related species, native to India and other regions of Southeast Asia. The bark of these plants contains a highly aromatic essential oil, used to impart a distinctive flavor to both savory and sweet foods. The essential oil contains a complex mixture of chemical components, among which are

Cinnamaldehyde

Ethyl cinnamate

Eugenol

Figure 12.2. Drawing of an alembic (alchemical still), from *The Art of Distillation*, published in 1651.

cinnamaldehyde, cinnamyl acetate, cinnamyl alcohol, copaene, eugenol, ethyl cinnamate, guaiene, and numerous others.

When we smell the aroma of the spice cinnamon, we are sniffing dozens of different molecules interacting with the 350 different types of olfactory receptor GPCRs in our nasal epithelium. This is an extraordinary symphony of interactions, with each of the many different aromatic molecules activating a specific constellation of GPCRs, each to a specific degree. The symphony of signals generated in this process and sent to the brain is somehow interpreted so as to produce the nearly ineffable aromatic mental experience known as the aroma of cinnamon—somehow.

Another famous spice from India is cardamom, from the plant *Elettaria cardamomum*. The seeds of this plant are used to impart a distinctive flavor to various Indian foods and to tea and coffee beverages. The aromatic essence of cardamom contains dozens of interesting molecules, with such names as limonene, menthone, eucalyptol, terpineol, terpenylacetate, myrcene, sabinene, phellandrene, and so on.

The point of all this is not to learn a bunch of different names and structures but to appreciate that plant aromas are composed of dozens of different molecules that we inhale into our noses, which then activate various combinations of olfactory receptor proteins, and that from this our nervous system constructs in some still mysterious way the subjective mental experience of the unique aromas of cardamom, cinnamon, or black pepper—a beautiful and amazing scenario!

Black pepper—one of the world's most prized spices—is the fruit of another

Figure 12.3. Black pepper, *Piper nigrum.*

plant native to India, *Piper nigrum* (Fig. 12.3). Once again, its aromatic essence is a mixture of numerous molecules, including sabinene, linalool, piperine, limonene, caryophyllene, pinene, carene, and many more.

Sabinene

Linalool

Piperine

Note that sabinene and limonene are also found in cardamom, and in other aromatic plants as well.

Because of its popularity as a spice, black pepper was involved in a robust trade for many centuries between India and Europe that moved pepper along "spice routes" from India to the Mediterranean. Multiple traders and political regimes generally needed negotiation along the way. This made black pepper expensive—and all the more so in Portugal and Spain, located at the western end of the Mediterranean Sea, for which longer shipping distances and more middlemen were involved. Enter Christopher Columbus (1451–1506), who was able to convince the Spanish Crown to finance a voyage westward across the Atlantic Ocean, in hopes of reaching Asia and having direct access to black pepper—as well as other great spices, such as cinnamon, cardamom, and nutmeg—thereby eliminating the need to pay the high costs associated with bringing pepper and other spices westward from Asia and across the Mediterranean. Such was the consequence of Europe's love of black pepper, five hundred years ago.

As we know, Columbus did not reach Asia but ran into the Americas instead. He found no black pepper in America, but there certainly was no dearth of other things most interesting, including allspice (*Pimenta officinalis*). The fragrant seeds resembled black peppercorns, and the aroma was similar to cinnamon and clove—hence the name, bestowed in acknowledgment of its resemblance to multiple Old World spices.

Flowers are another of the archetypal aromatic things in nature. Humans have cultivated roses (genus *Rosa*) for centuries and have produced variants having flowers of different shapes, sizes, colors and aromas. Among the chemical components of rose aroma are the molecules citronellol, geraniol, nerol, linalool, citral, and phenyl ethanol.

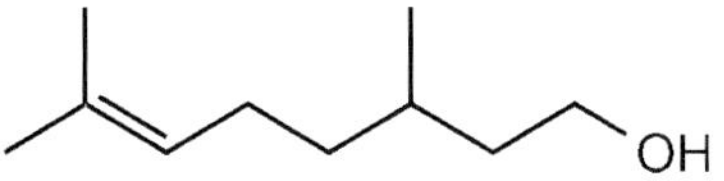

Citronellol

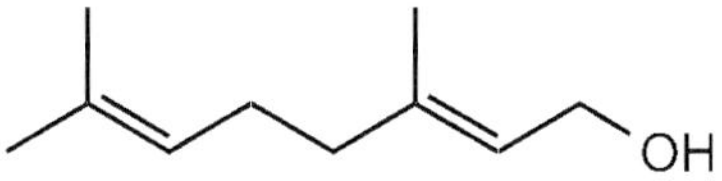

Geraniol

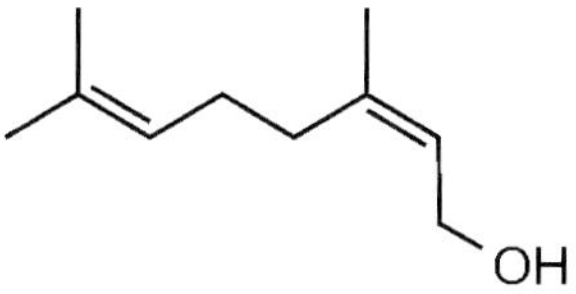

Nerol

Note that citronellol, geraniol, and nerol have similar molecular shapes: each is a linear chain of eight carbons, with one or two double bonds, two methyl (–CH$_3$) side groups, and a hydroxy (–OH) group on one end. Different varieties of roses smell differently because they have different relative amounts of these and the many other molecules making up their aromatic essential oil.

Another wonderfully aromatic flower is jasmine (genus *Jasminum*), represented by many species. Jasmine has a characteristic aroma, and like other floral aromas, it derives from a mixture of molecules, such as benzyl acetate, indole, and farnesene.

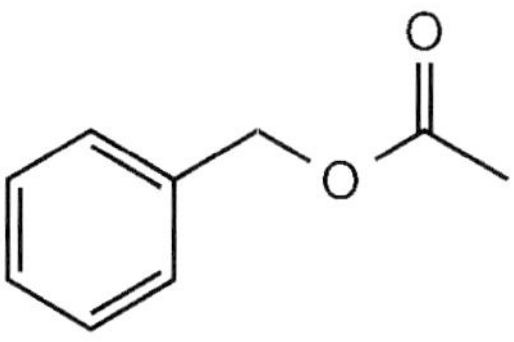

Benzyl acetate

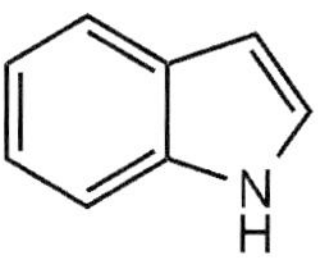

Indole

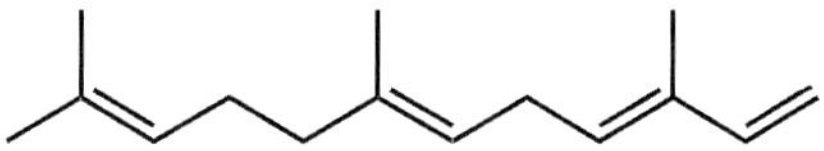

Farnesene

Different species of jasmine flowers have slightly or even significantly different aromatic qualities, related to the varied chemical compositions of their respective essential oils. The presence of indole is interesting, as the aromatic quality of this molecule is sharp and noxious, reminiscent of mothballs and often mentioned as a contributor to the odor of feces. Indole is indeed present in human feces—where it occurs as a breakdown product of the amino acid tryptophan, a component of proteins. And yet it is also part of the alluring aroma of jasmine, and many other flowers, too. In synergistic combination with dozens of other molecules, many of which are present in only very small concentrations, the noxiousness of indole contributes to the exotic complexity of jasmine's aroma. Perfume manufacturers sometimes add synthetic indole to commercial perfumes, attempting to replicate nature's symphony, but such attempts invariably fall short.

A jasmine-like aroma is also present in several other species of plants unrelated to *Jasminum*. For example, there is *Nicotiana alata*, a jasmine-scented cousin of smoking tobacco, and Chinese wisteria (*Wisteria sinensis*), a woody, climbing vine with spectacular hanging flowers. Many varieties of daffodil (genus *Narcissus*) also have a jasmine quality to their aroma—sniff for it.

Although the aromatic qualities of plants are related to complex mixtures of many different molecules having a variety of molecular shapes, often one or two molecules in the mix identify strongly with the particular odor of the plant. For example, if one were to smell a pure preparation of the molecule benzyl acetate, one would have no problem identifying it as a jasmine aroma. A significant part of what we would call the characteristic aroma of a jasmine flower seems to be associated with neural pathways activated by benzyl acetate. The many other molecules present in the essential oil of jasmine impart nuance and complexity to the plant's aroma.

Similarly with lemon: the molecule geranial, one of the components of the essential oil of lemon, is readily identified with the aroma of lemon. And with rose, the molecule geraniol, a component of the essential oil of rose, is readily associated with its characteristic aroma. Note the structures of these two molecules, geranial and geraniol.

Geranial   *Geraniol*

They are identical except that geranial has a carbon double-bonded to oxygen at one end (called an aldehyde in organic chemistry), and geraniol has a carbon bonded to a hydroxy group at the end (called an alcohol in organic chemistry). Thus, the difference between geranial and geraniol is the presence or absence of a mere two hydrogen atoms and a stronger bond (and more rigid structure) at one end of the molecule. This seemingly subtle difference in molecular shape produces a profound difference in the associated aroma (lemon versus rose). Small changes in molecular shape, to the extent that they affect the binding of these molecules to the various olfactory GPCRs, may have substantial effects on the patterns of neural signals generated in the olfactory pathway, resulting in substantial effects on the quality of the perceived aromas.

Now consider these three molecules—2-butene-1-thiol, 3-methyl-1-butanethiol, and 2-quinolinemethanethiol—with their long chemical names and structures somewhat different from other molecules we have discussed thus far in this chapter.

2-butene-1-thiol   3-methyl-1-butanethiol   2-quinolinemethanethiol

They each contain sulfur–hydrogen (–SH) groups. In chemistry, *thio* refers to the element sulfur and *thiol* to the –SH group. These three molecules are examples of organic thiols, the –SH group in a thiol being analogous to the –OH group in an alcohol. (Sulfur occurs just below oxygen in the periodic table of the elements, reflecting the fact that oxygen and sulfur have some similar chemical properties.) Thiols often smell stinky. There is something about the shape of the –SH group attached to carbons that promotes fitting into a constellation of GPCR olfactory receptors that give rise to signals interpreted by the brain as stinky. The three molecules above are major chemical constituents of the stinky secretion of skunks.

Here are two more molecules that have a stinky quality to them: methanethiol and dimethylsulfide. These molecules are found in the urine of many people who have eaten asparagus and impart a unique stinky aroma to the urine. However, methanethiol and dimethylsulfide are not found in asparagus, either fresh or cooked. They are apparently produced during the digestive chemical transformation of molecules that are found in asparagus, such as asparagusic acid.

H_3C-SH $H_3C-S-CH_3$
Methanethiol   *Dimethylsulfide*

Asparagusic acid

Many have enjoyed eating asparagus and have recognized the characteristic "asparagus pee" smell in their urine shortly after having consumed the vegetable. However, others who are reading this have not been aware of any unusual smelling urine after eating this spear-like vegetable. There are two reasons for this. First, there is variability in the amount of stinky thiols and sulfides generated during digestion after eating asparagus. Some people produce very little; some produce lots. Second, a substantial number of people lack olfactory sensitivity to this asparagus-pee aroma, or at least have a much lower sensitivity for detecting it. This is an example of what is called a *specific anosmia*—loss of sensitivity to a specific kind of smell.

The most likely cause of a specific anosmia is genetic variation in one of the 350 olfactory GPCRs. Because there are so many different olfactory receptor genes, it is highly likely many specific anosmias are present among people. Usually such anosmias would go unnoticed. It is only because of the particular circumstance of asparagus pee—such a novel and distinctive aroma, so obvious to some and yet unnoticed by others at the same dinner gathering—that this anosmia has drawn particular attention. The asparagus-pee anosmia has been associated with variability in a single identified olfactory receptor gene.

Specific anosmias refer to loss of sensitivity to specific categories of aroma. A general anosmia is loss of sensitivity to a large variety of aromas, in some cases even a complete lack of olfactory sensitivity. General anosmias have a variety of causes, ranging from nasal congestion to unknown developmental factors to head trauma to degenerative brain disease. Hyperosmias are also possible, in which there is an increased sensitivity to odors. Hyperosmias often appear transiently, in association with a migraine headache, for example. Women sometimes report hyperosmias during pregnancy.

The olfactory GPCRs are in the membranes of the olfactory receptor cells in the nasal epithelium. Activation of an olfactory GPCR initiates an intracellular cascade leading to the synthesis of cAMP, which then interacts with a type of cation channel that is gated by the binding of cyclic nucleotides. The result is an influx of Ca^{++} and Na^+, depolarizing the cell and contributing to signal generation.

Olfactory receptor cells send axons into the olfactory bulb of the brain, in humans located immediately above and adjacent to the nasal cavity. These nerve fibers between the nose and the olfactory bulb constitute cranial nerve 1. In the olfactory bulb, the axons form synapses with dendrites of mitral cells, so called because their triangular shape is reminiscent of a mitre, the ceremonial headgear worn by some religious officials. Mitral cells send axons to the pyriform cortex—buried deep in the interior of the brain—and to the amygdala, in the limbic system. The pyriform cortex sends axons to the thalamus, and from there connections are made to the orbitofrontal cortex of the frontal lobe. Interconnections with the hippocampus and the hypothalamus are also present. Somehow, out of all this comes the conscious perception of aroma, including various associated emotional signatures: wonderful and alluring, or yucky and aversive.

The durian fruit (genus *Durio*) from Southeast Asia is a food known for its powerful aromatic qualities (Fig. 12.4). Many who are familiar with this fruit absolutely adore

Figure 12.4. Durians (and a coconut) available for immediate consumption (note the cleaver) at a roadside stand in Indonesia.

it, looking forward to the times of the year when it is freshly available. Often revered as the "king of fruits" in Southeast Asia, it is at the same time not served by most restaurants, and often banned from hotels, trains, and buses, because of its very strong aroma. The aroma of durian can evoke robust attractive or repulsive emotional responses; perhaps it is best characterized as a combination of both.

Here is what the great naturalist Alfred Russel Wallace (1823–1913)—who arrived at ideas about evolution and natural selection around the same time as Darwin—had to say about the durian fruit:

> The Durian . . . is a fruit of a perfectly unique character; we have nothing with which it can be compared. . . . The Durian grows on a large and lofty forest-tree, something resembling an Elm in character, but with a more smooth and scaly bark. The fruit is round or slightly oval, about the size of a small melon, of a green colour, and covered with strong spines, the bases of which touch each other, and are consequently somewhat hexagonal, while the points are very strong and sharp. It is so completely armed that if the stalk is broken off it is a difficult matter to lift one from the ground. The outer rind is so thick and tough that from whatever height it may fall it is never broken. [Inside are several masses] of cream-coloured pulp, containing about three seeds each. This pulp is the eatable part, and its consistence and flavour are indescribable. A rich custard highly flavoured with almonds gives the best general idea of it, but there are occasional wafts of flavour that call to mind cream-cheese, onion-sauce, sherry-wine, and other incongruous dishes. Then there is a rich glutinous smoothness in the pulp which nothing else possesses, but which adds to its delicacy. It is neither acid nor sweet nor juicy; yet it wants neither of these qualities, for it is in itself perfect. It produces no nausea or other bad effect, and the more you eat of it the less you feel inclined to stop. In fact, to eat Durians is a new sensation worth a voyage to the East to experience.

This is high praise indeed, for a voyage from England to Indonesia was no easy journey in the mid-nineteenth century!

As expected, the aromatic essence of durian is a mixture of numerous chemicals. Propanethiol (an oniony aroma) and methylbutyrate (a pineappley aroma) are two that are known to significantly contribute. However, dozens of smelly molecules—including numerous thiols and other sulfur compounds, esters, and ketones—have been identified as present in the aroma of durian.

Another exotic aroma from the culinary world is that of the truffle mushrooms. The most sought after of the truffles are the white truffle (*Tuber magnatum*) and black truffle (*Tuber melanosporum*), both from southern Europe. They are highly prized for their aromatic qualities and may command prices of thousands of dollars for a handful. The aroma of truffle is revered by many who know it and can evoke strong, generally very positive, emotional reactions.

Detailed analytical chemistry studies of truffle aroma are few. One component is said to be the molecule 2,4-dithiapentane.

Flavored "truffle oil" for use in cuisine is sometimes made by adding this molecule to olive oil, a cheap and inferior substitute for the real thing.

Dithiapentane

I have had quality truffles only a few times. Each occasion was memorable, and the first experience particularly so. The preparation was extremely simple—a bit of fresh white truffle grated on pasta in an Italian restaurant. There was a tiny, tiny piece of the fungus remaining after the grating and the chef kindly gave it to me as a gift to use at home. I put it into my backpack for transport. The powerful aroma lingered in my pack long after the mushroom was removed. I was aware of the smell for weeks. During the days following, I could be transported briefly into a zone of aromatic ecstasy by taking a few whiffs of my pack. For some reason, the emotional evocativeness of the truffle aroma is very strong and generally very positive! This is why these fungi are so prized by so many.

Pheromones (Greek *pherein* = to carry, bear) are chemicals that carry signal information related to social communications between members of the same species. These signaling molecules were discovered and have been most extensively studied in insects. Among insects, pheromones have been shown to play important roles in identity and social status, mate attraction, territorial and trail marking, and signaling of danger.

Pheromones are generally thought to elicit innately programmed behaviors or biochemical changes, things not requiring learning. Examples among vertebrate animals include the suckling of a young mammal at its mother's mammary organ, regulation of hormones associated with mating, and aspects of attraction or aggression between members of the same species.

Many vertebrate animals—including various reptiles, amphibians, and mammals—have been demonstrated to have a distinct olfactory sensory structure and neural pathway, called the vomeronasal system, that responds somewhat selectively to pheromone molecules. However, it also appears to be the case that some pheromones are detected by receptors in the main olfactory pathway. The existence and functionality of the vomeronasal system in humans and other primates are debated, with many researchers arguing that a functional human system is not present.

Although there is presently no agreement regarding pheromone-type effects in humans, my money is on there being chemicals that are sensed by the human olfactory system and that trigger significant behavioral responses, including social attraction and repulsion. Moreover, these sensory experiences may to a large extent be out of our awareness.

Smell is primal. We haven't forgotten it. And it hasn't forgotten us.

> Airborne molecules,
> receptors, signals, brain, mind—
> the world is perfume.

CHAPTER 13

Tongue and Taste

Gustation, taste, from the Latin *gustare*; related to gusto: enjoyment, delight. The receptor cells that begin this process are located in the mouth, primarily on the tongue, with a few on the upper palate and the pharynx. They are grouped into clusters called taste buds. There are approximately ten thousand taste buds in the human mouth, each containing around a hundred taste receptor cells. That means we have about one million taste receptor cells in our mouth. These cells respond to molecules entering the mouth, most often components of substances being consumed as food or drink.

Figure 13.1 depicts a taste bud and its component receptor cells in the tongue. There is a pore exposing the receptor cells to the interior of the mouth, where saliva dissolves the molecular components of food and drink and swishes them about. The ends of the receptor cells are composed of microvilli, filamentous structures that increase the surface area exposed to tasty substances. Within the phospholipid bilayer membrane of the microvilli are taste receptor proteins.

> Microvilli in taste cells and cilia in olfactory cells both serve to increase sensory surface area. While functionally similar, they are structurally different. Microvilli are smaller than cilia and have an internal cytoskeletal structure consisting largely of actin. Cilia have an internal cytoskeleton organized around microtubules.

The bulk of a gustatory receptor cell consists of a cell body looking like most other cells, with a DNA-containing nucleus, mitochondria, ribosomes, and so forth—the usual stuff of cells. At the base of the receptor cell there is a contact point, a chemical synapse, with nerve fibers that respond to neurotransmitter molecules released by the taste receptor cells, initiating a signal that goes to the brain. The fibers carrying signals from taste receptor cells to the brain are part of the system of cranial nerves, notably cranial nerves 7, 9, and 10.

Similar to the olfactory system, stem cells adjacent to the taste receptor cells can differentiate into the various types of taste receptor cells, characterized by their dif-

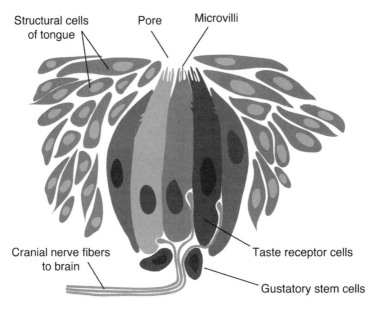

Figure 13.1. Taste bud components.

ferent taste receptor proteins. This allows taste receptor cells to be regularly replaced, with a turnover rate of approximately two weeks. As in the olfactory system, this regular replacement is presumably related to the fact that these cells are constantly exposed to all kinds of toxic gunk from the environment and thus subject to continual damage. In this way, gustatory and olfactory receptor cells differ from visual and auditory receptor cells (see Chapters 14 and 15); the latter exist within structures shielding them from direct contact with potentially toxic chemicals from the environment, and they are not known to be associated with stem cells.

Five types of taste receptor cells have been described in the human mouth: salt, sour, bitter, sweet, and umami. They are characterized by different kinds of taste receptor proteins, responding to different kinds of substances floating around in the mouth, and they give rise to signals that are associated with different perceptual experiences of tastiness.

Salt. Salt is sodium chloride (NaCl), mostly. Put some NaCl (table salt) into the mouth and experience the taste of saltiness. NaCl crystals in the mouth rapidly become Na^+ and Cl^- ions in solution. The proteins on taste receptor cells related to the perceptual experience of saltiness are thought to be channels that allow sodium ions to flow across the membrane. (Unlike the receptor proteins for some of the other tastes described below, the salt taste receptor proteins have not yet been conclusively identified.) Thus, when high (relatively) concentrations of Na^+ appear in the mouth after ingestion of salt, the Na^+ is believed to flow through sodium ion channels in the salt taste receptor cells, triggering a neural signal to the brain. Ingestion of some amount of sodium and other related elemental cations (potassium, calcium, magnesium) is essential for survival, and the taste of salt—at least in moderation—is generally experienced as pleasant.

Sour. What we call "sour" is the taste of acids: citric acid from grapefruit and lemon, acetic acid from vinegar, lactic acid from sauerkraut and yogurt. The defining feature of acids is the release of hydrogen ions (H^+) in solution. And sour taste is associated with hydrogen ions. The German word for acidic is *sauer*. The proteins on the taste receptor cells related to the experience of sour appear to be channels sensitive to hydrogen ions. As for the salt receptors, they have not been conclusively identified. When (relatively) high concentrations of H^+ appear in the mouth after ingestion of acidic substances, some kind of positive charge is believed to flow through channels in the sour taste receptor cells, triggering a neural signal to the brain.

Bitter. The proteins that initiate the signals associated with the perceptual experience of bitterness are not ion channels; they are G-protein-coupled receptors (GPCRs). In humans, more than thirty different GPCR proteins are distributed over the receptor cells associated with bitter taste. When a ligand floating around in the interior of the mouth comes into contact with microvilli of a bitter taste receptor cell and binds to a GPCR, this initiates an intracellular signaling cascade leading to release of neurotransmitter and generation of a signal to the brain.

The diversity of GPCRs allows for a variety of different molecular shapes to be associated with the taste of bitterness. Among things that taste bitter are various plant alkaloids such as caffeine, cocaine, morphine, and quinine—all of which are poisons. Even though everything is a poison, some things are more poisonous than others, and a bitter taste may serve as a warning that whatever is being ingested is poisonous and caution is advised. Bitter-tasting things are common in nature.

Although bitter taste is often experienced as somewhat aversive (thus inhibiting excessive consumption), it may also be appreciated as exquisite, especially when it occurs in certain combinations with other tastes and aromas. Many folks appreciate the bitter taste of coffee, tea, dark chocolate, tonic water, and leafy vegetables such as endive and radicchio.

Sweet. This is the defining taste of sugar—sucrose, what we call table sugar, but also glucose, fructose, lactose, maltose, and many others.

Sucrose *Glucose* *Fructose*

These are small molecules, composed of chains or rings of carbon atoms, together with quite a few oxygen atoms and, of course, hydrogen atoms.

Sweet receptor proteins are also GPCRs, and two distinct GPCRs are known in humans to be involved in the detection of sweet-tasting molecules. The particular molecular shapes of the various sugar molecules permit them to bind as ligands to the sweet GPCRs, shape-shift the proteins, and initiate a signal. The functional form of the sweet taste receptor protein appears to be a *dimer* of two GPCRs—that is, the two GPCRs are linked (by a noncovalent interaction) to form the functional sweet receptor.

Sweet taste is generally experienced as pleasurable and often elicits a desire to consume more of whatever it is that tastes sweet. Sweet-tasting things are not very common in nature. Ripe fruits are generally sweet, and they appear only during limited times of the year. Until very recently in the history of life on Earth, consuming a whole lot of whatever it was that tasted sweet was almost certainly a healthy thing to do, providing energy and other nutritional goodies. However, in our sugar-saturated contemporary society, this is no longer the case, and overconsumption of sugary foods has led to serious health problems for many people. Unfortunately, this trend toward increasing consumption of unhealthy quantities of sugar is continuing to grow worldwide.

Unlike the thirty or so GPCRs that allow a variety of molecular shapes to be associated with the taste of bitter, the two GPCRs associated with sweet receptor cells limit the taste of sweetness to a smaller diversity of molecular shapes. Indeed, the several sweet-tasting sugar molecules all share many features of molecular shape. There are, however, molecules that are not sugars and possess a variety of shapes, and yet still taste sweet. Some of these molecules are really, really sweet, far more potent than sucrose in their sweetness. They constitute the so-called nonnutritive (because they have little or no caloric or other nutritional value) or synthetic (because they are products of the synthetic chemical industry) sweeteners, and they are used to sweeten foods without adding calories. They are also sometimes called artificial sweeteners, because they are made by human chemists and not found "naturally" in nature.

The first such substance to become known was saccharin, discovered in the late 1800s when a chemist inadvertently noticed that something he had synthesized tasted sweet.

Saccharin

Saccharin is around three hundred times sweeter than sucrose. This means that only a tiny pinch of saccharin, containing essentially zero calories, can provide the same amount of sweetness to a food or drink as would a spoonful of sugar. (Packages of saccharin and other synthetic sweeteners contain more than a pinch of material because they have additional white powders—such as the minimally sweet polysaccharide maltodextrin—added to bulk up the volume.) Saccharin presumably binds to the sweet receptor protein and activates it much more strongly than does sucrose.

In addition to its sweetness, saccharin is experienced by many people as having a slightly bitter taste. This is because the particular molecular shape of saccharin interacts with one or more of the bitter GPCRs, as well as with sweet receptors.

It wasn't until many decades after the discovery of saccharin that additional synthetic sweeteners entered the scene. Cyclamate was discovered in the 1930s, and acesulfame and aspartame in the 1960s. As was the case for saccharin, all these discoveries were accidental—made by chemists working on things that had nothing to do with taste, inadvertently tasting something that they probably wouldn't have had they been more careful. Max Delbrück, in another context, coined the phrase "principle of limited sloppiness" to describe situations in experimental research where unexpected discoveries are made because a scientist is a little sloppy, but not so sloppy that he or she can't figure out what has happened.

Of these synthetic sweeteners, aspartame has become the most widely used. It is about two hundred times sweeter than sucrose and has the molecular form of a dipeptide, a covalently bonded pair of amino acids, aspartic acid and phenylalanine, with an additional methyl ($-CH_3$) group on the phenylalanine. Synthetic sweeteners have given rise to an industry of so-called diet foods—foods that, although they taste sweet, contain fewer calories than would versions sweetened with sugar.

After the commercial success of synthetic sweeteners, some folks decided that rather than wait for the next accidental discovery to occur, it should be possible to intentionally

Aspartame

seek out newer and even more potent synthetic sweeteners. One idea was to begin with sucrose and modify its molecular structure in different ways, hoping to get something that—because of particular changes in molecular shape—might bind to and activate the sweet GPCRs even more strongly than sucrose. This strategy paid off with a molecule that is approximately six hundred times sweeter than sucrose: sucralose, originally marketed under the brand name Splenda, has three of sucrose's hydroxyl ($-OH$) groups replaced by chlorine atoms.

Another synthetic sweetener resulted when a similar strategy of molecular modification was applied by chemists working for one of the companies that manufactures aspartame. They chose to start with aspartame, because it is already two hundred times sweeter than sucrose, and produce molecular derivatives, hoping to find something interesting. They did: neotame, a derivative of aspartame formed by the addi-

Sucralose

tion of a six-carbon branched chain onto the aspartic acid, is fifty times sweeter than aspartame and thus an astounding ten thousand times sweeter than sucrose! As carfentanil is to morphine, so neotame is to sucrose. How these vast differences in potency are generated by the specific molecular changes these substances possess is not presently understood.

One more sweeter-than-sucrose example—not a synthetic one, but one found in a plant: *Stevia rebaudiana* grows in the Amazon jungle of South America and is appreciated by the native inhabitants of the area for the sweet taste of its leaves. (It is a rare leaf that tastes sweet—many plant leaves taste bitter.) Dehydrated extracts of the leaves are marketed as a nonnutritive sweetener. Being a plant extract, there are many molecular constituents producing a combination of sweet and bitter tastes. The sweet-tasting components have been identified as derivatives of a molecule named steviol, with a molecule named stevioside being found in highest concentration in the plant.

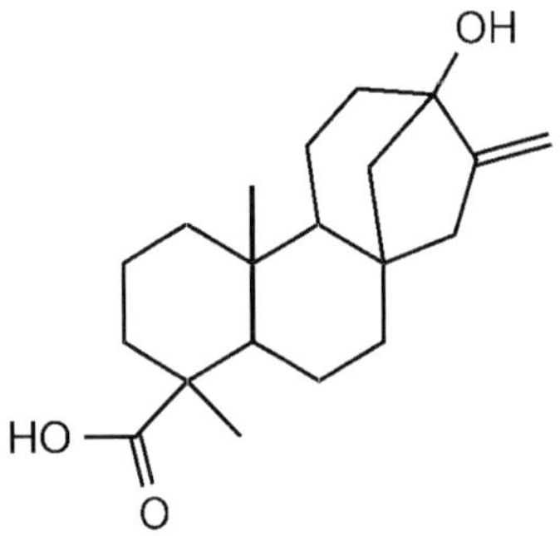

Steviol

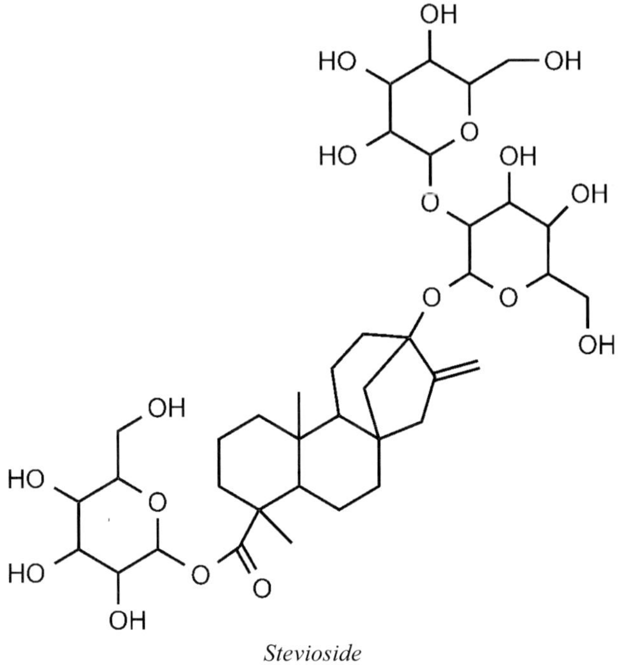

Stevioside

Stevioside is formed from steviol by the addition of three glucose molecules in particular places. It is approximately three hundred times sweeter than sucrose.

Umami.   In 1909 Japanese chemist Kikunae Ikeda (1864–1936) published a paper describing glutamate as producing a distinct taste perception, different from and in addition to the canonical four: salt, sour, bitter, and sweet. He argued that glutamate contributes to the distinctive taste of certain seaweeds, fish sauces, soy sauce, and dried fish. And he proposed a method for concentrating the taste essence in the form of MSG (monosodium glutamate), which could be added to foods when cooking, if one desired. He called the new taste *umami*, from the Japanese words for delicious (*umai*) and taste (*mi*). Some folks characterize the umami taste as "savory," others "meaty," and others "mushroomy." However, for nearly a century not many folks acknowledged umami as a distinct taste, and certainly in Europe and America the discussion was confined to the canonical four.

Then in the 1990s, taste scientists in Japan demonstrated the existence of a fifth type of taste receptor cell and associated taste receptor proteins. This receptor cell responds to glutamate with taste receptor proteins that are metabotropic (GPCR) glutamate receptors. The characterization of receptor proteins imparted—at least in the eyes of some—legitimacy to umami finally being accepted as a fifth taste.

Glutamate is an amino acid—where there is protein, there is glutamate. And the umami receptors in the tongue are activated not only by glutamate but also by some of the other amino acids present in protein. Thus, the umami taste may have developed over the course of evolution to assist in the detection of protein-containing foods, important for survival.

Summarizing this way of understanding taste: tastes do not exist in the world "out there"; what does exist are ions and molecules of various sizes and shapes. Tastes are mental experiences, existing within the internal subjective world of our perception; these mental experiences are associated in some way with neural signals that originate with the taste receptor cells and travel to the brain, where they bloom into the activation of networks of neurons and glia within particular regions of the brain. How particular configurations of brain activity are related to particular mental experiences of the various tastes is an unanswered question, another instance of the mind–body problem.

The cranial nerve fibers carrying taste sensory information enter the brain via the lower brainstem (Fig. 13.2) and connect with cells in the nucleus solitarius, from which two axon tracts emerge: one heading into the thalamus, and thence to the insula and to the somatosensory cortex in the parietal lobe (see Chapter 16), and the other heading to the hypothalamus and the amygdala. Neural activity in these several regions of the brain is somehow related to the subjective, perceptual qualities of different tastes, as well as associated emotional associations—the yums! and yuks!

In addition to the five tastes, other perceptual qualities are associated with foods that also begin with the detection of molecules in the mouth. These qualities are not at the present time considered tastes, even though they are akin to tastes. Perhaps most significant among these is the quality of hotness or spiciness or pungency—as from chili, black pepper, mustard, horseradish, wasabi, ginger, and garlic. The pungent or hot qualities of these plants are associated with molecular components that

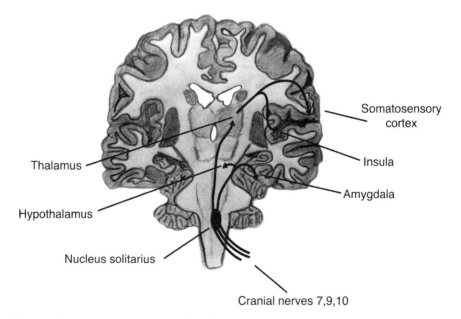

Figure 13.2. A coronal or frontal slice through the brain showing neural pathways associated with taste. The insula is a region of the cerebral cortex deep within the lateral sulcus, at the juncture of the parietal and temporal lobes.

activate various receptors in the mouth. However, signals from these receptors enter the brain via pathways different from those associated with the primary tastes. They enter via the fifth cranial nerve (trigeminal nerve) and are received by regions of the brain closely associated with the perception of pain. This is the reason that taste scientists do not call spicy hotness a taste, even though most people would consider it to be taste quality.

A famous exemplar of such spicy hotness is the chili plant, mostly the species *Capsicum annuum*, native to South America (Fig. 13.3). No doubt the culinary properties of this plant have been much appreciated by indigenous peoples of South America for millennia, and many varieties of chili having varying flavors and different degrees of hotness have been developed over the centuries: cayenne, jalapeño, pimento, habanero, and so forth.

Although chili now features prominently in the cuisines of countries all over the world, it was unknown outside of the Americas before the voyages of Christopher Columbus. Like tobacco, its powerful qualities were rapidly embraced worldwide. Also like tobacco, it is a member of the Solanaceae (nightshade) family of plants. There is no shortage of powerful plants in this impressive family!

The hotness of chili is associated with the presence of a single molecular constituent—capsaicin.

Capsaicin

The more capsaicin present in the chili, the hotter it is perceived to be. Proteins have been identified in the mouth that are sensitive to capsaicin. When capsaicin binds to one of these receptor proteins, a shape change occurs, an ion channel opens, and calcium ions flow from outside the cell to inside, depolarizing the cell and leading to increased neural excitability.

Figure 13.3. Chili plant, *Capsicum annuum*.

Amazingly, thermal heat also activates these capsaicin-sensitive proteins. That is, increasing the temperature of the protein causes the same kind of shape change as the binding of capsaicin, the same opening of a Ca^{++} channel, and the same consequent cell excitability. Chili is experienced as "hot" because actual heat—that is, increases in temperature—is sensed by exactly the same molecular and cellular mechanism! Thus, in the world of our perception, chili hot and fire hot are actually the same quality. However, unlike the heat from capsaicin, heat due to temperature would also have other effects, including potential damage to tissue (that is, burns) if the temperature is sufficiently high.

These capsaicin/thermal receptor proteins are not just in the mouth—they are all over the body, where their presence allows us to sense the temperature of our skin and thus of the surrounding environment. The receptors in the skin will also respond to capsaicin. Rub powdered cayenne onto your skin and it will feel warm, at least, and perhaps hot. And many have experienced the painful burning feeling that results when you inadvertently touch your eye after cutting chilies when cooking.

When these receptor proteins were first characterized in the 1990s, they were simply called capsaicin receptors. However, it was soon appreciated that they were members of a large family of ionotropic proteins originally characterized from the study of vision in the fruit fly. These proteins were already known as TRP channels, from the esoteric terminology "transient receptor potential," a reference to an electrical response of the insect eye to light. The TRP terminology was kept, and the capsaicin receptor is now known by the name TRPV1. Its ion channel opens in response to capsaicin and also to heat in the temperature range of 43–50 degrees Celsius (109–122 degrees Fahrenheit).

The TRPV1 channel is also opened by the binding of piperine, a molecule found in black pepper, *Piper nigrum* (see Chapter 12). Like chili from South America, black pepper from India also has a hot "taste," although the overall flavor of black pepper differs from that of chili, due to the many differing aromatic constituents in the two unrelated plants. American chili came to be called "pepper" or "chili pepper" because it shared with black pepper the perceptual quality of hotness.

What about cold? Are hot and cold sensations on a continuum? Does the sensation of cold come about when the "hot receptor" is inhibited? Or by some other mechanism? It turns out there is a separate signaling pathway for cold. And it was characterized by using a molecule from mint plants (genus *Mentha*)—menthol. Menthol is appreciated for its distinctive flavor qualities, including producing a perception of a kind of "coolness."

There is an ionotropic receptor protein, found in the mouth and elsewhere in the body, in which a calcium channel opens in response to the binding of menthol. Temperatures somewhat cooler (8–28 degrees Celsius or 46–82 degrees Fahrenheit) than body temperature (37 degrees Celsius) produce a shape change of this protein and open the channel. Analogous to the situation with cap-

Menthol

saicin and heat, the same receptor responds to menthol and to cool temperatures. Thus, menthol is perceived as a coolness of temperature. Like the capsaicin/hot receptor, the menthol/cool receptor is also a member of the TRP receptor family and has been given the designation TRPM8.

Another example of pungency in foods, similar to the hot spicy pungency of chili and of black pepper, but not the same, is the pungency of mustard, horseradish, and wasabi. Associated with this particular perceptual quality of hotness is a family of molecules, the isothiocyanates, characterized by a particular configuration of sulfur, carbon, and nitrogen atoms. Allyl isothiocyanate is found in mustard and horseradish.

Allyl isothiocyanate

Another type of ionotropic Ca^{++} channel, called TRPA1, is activated by the binding of isothiocyanates. Activation of the TRPA1 receptors results in neural signals from a different set of cells than would be the case with capsaicin and TRPV1, and this is associated with a qualitatively different experience of hotness and pungency.

TRP-type channel proteins turn out to be all over the place in the body: in the mouth, where they are associated with the perception of spicy and pungent hotness and with minty coolness; within the skin, where they are involved in the perception of temperature and also of touch and pain (see Chapter 16); and elsewhere in the nervous system, where they are likely involved in neural signaling in yet to be discovered ways. TRP channels are another example of how when life comes up with a structure possessing useful properties, it gets slightly tweaked and modified this way and that and used over and over again in many different locations in many different, though often related, ways.

What we call *flavor* is a combination of several different channels of sensory information. The mouth components of taste and pungency are hugely important to the flavor of food and drink: salty, sour, sweet, bitter, umami, cool, and several kinds of spicy hot—and a few more, like the tingling of Sichuan pepper (genus *Zanthoxylum*) and the "fatty taste" of fatty foods. Texture, how food "feels" in the mouth, also contributes to flavor. And perhaps most important to flavor are aromatic molecules, sensed via the olfactory system. As air from our mouth is drawn back into the throat, it carries aromatic molecules from whatever we are eating or drinking up into our nasal passages from the inside, the back way. In this manner, we are always smelling what we are eating and drinking.

The aromatic qualities of food and drink are legion; thousands of different molecules activating 350 different olfactory receptors in thousands of different combinations, giving rise to a vast spectrum of subtle olfactory perceptions of great nuance and complexity. Spices, wines, and distilled liquors (such as gin, whiskey, brandy, absinthe, and many others), for example, are all defined largely by their aromatic qualities. Flavor is infinitely interesting and immensely enjoyable.

Everyone is familiar with what happens to the flavor of food and drink when we have congestion as a result of a cold. Food is said to "taste" flat and uninteresting. However, taste perception is actually working just fine. If you pay careful attention, you will find that all the tastes of salt, sour, sweet, bitter, and umami are still there. So is the hotness of chili or mustard and the coolness of mint. What is missing is the smell. And the fact that the olfactory components of flavor are impaired has profound effects on the overall appreciation of flavor.

You needn't wait until you have a cold and congestion to appreciate the contributions of olfaction to flavor. Simply pinch your nostrils together so that you cannot draw air through your nasal passages. Then eat or drink something and notice what happens to the flavor. Where did it go?

> Sweet here, bitter there—
> key to our survival, and—
> flavor exquisite.

CHAPTER **14**

Eyes and Vision

Our visual system responds to electromagnetic radiation in the energy range called visible light—so named because we humans can see it. Electromagnetic energy can be conceptualized as a vibrating electromagnetic field (an abstract concept from mathematical physics) moving (radiating) through space, and is described quantitatively as either a frequency of vibration (in cycles per second, or hertz) or a wavelength (in meters). Visible light is in the energy range between about 400 and 700 nanometers (nm), a range of energy that can engage in significant and sustainable (nondamaging) interactions with molecular and cellular structures in the body.

> Electromagnetic energy can also be conceptualized as packets of energy, called photons. The description of light and other kinds of electromagnetic energy as *simultaneously* both a wavelike field *and* particle-like photons is profound and was central to the development of quantum physics in the early twentieth century.

If radiation is more energetic (shorter wavelength) than visible light—in the ultraviolet, x-ray, and gamma-ray regions of the spectrum—interactions with molecular and cellular structures are likely to be damaging: chemical bonds break and molecules fall apart, free radicals form, DNA is damaged, cell membranes become leaky, and other bad stuff happens. (As noted in Chapter 11, some insects, birds, and other animals do see ultraviolet radiation that is slightly more energetic than visible light but still within a safely detectable range of energy.) If the radiation is lower in energy (longer wavelength) than visible light—in the infrared, microwave, and radio wave regions of the spectrum—interaction with molecular and cellular structures might not be energetic enough to generate a reliable neural signal. (Again, as noted in Chapter 11, rattlesnakes and other pit vipers do "see" infrared radiation, via receptors that reliably detect electromagnetic radiation slightly less energetic than visible light.)

The receptor organ for human vision is the eye. It is analogous to a camera in that in a camera a lens focuses incoming light onto a photosensitive film or detector, and in

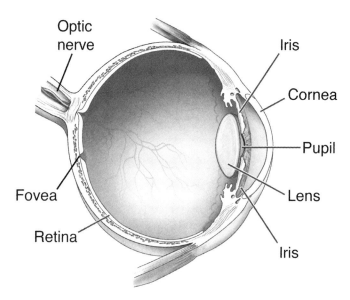

Figure 14.1. Cross section of the human eyeball, our organ of vision. The muscles of the iris regulate the size of the pupillary opening. The interior of the eyeball is filled with a transparent gelatinous fluid called vitreous humor.

the eye, the cornea, lens, and pupil focus light onto the photosensitive retina at the rear of the eyeball (Fig. 14.1). The retina is a very complex structure, consisting of a layer of light-sensitive photoreceptor cells and several layers of interconnected nerve cells. The retina is also heavily crisscrossed with blood vessels, as the photoreceptor and other neural cells require a robust supply of biochemical fuel (glucose and oxygen) in order to function. The word *retina* derives from the Latin *rete*, meaning "net," a reference to the complex network of cell bodies, nerve fibers, and blood vessels that compose it.

Light coming from the center of the visual field (what we are looking directly at) is focused by the lens onto the center of the retina, a region called the *fovea* (Latin for "pit"). In the fovea the density of photoreceptor cells is highest, so visual acuity (ability to see fine detail) is best for the region of space where we are directly looking.

The human retina contains two major kinds of photoreceptor cells: rods and cones. Rod cells are rod shaped, very numerous, distributed throughout most of the retina, and sensitive to even very small amounts of light. Cone cells are cone shaped, mostly located at the fovea, and respond to higher intensity rather than very dim light. In the human eye there are three types of cone cells, with each type responding to a different range of light wavelengths. The rod and cone cells contain specific protein molecules, called *rhodopsin* and *cone opsins*, that absorb light and initiate the process of transformation of the light energy into a neural signal. Rhodopsin and the various cone opsins absorb light in slightly different regions of the visible light spectrum (Fig. 14.2). There are short-wavelength (S), medium-wavelength (M), and longer-wavelength (L) absorbing cones. S, M, and L cones are also, respectively, sometimes referred to as blue, green, and red cones.

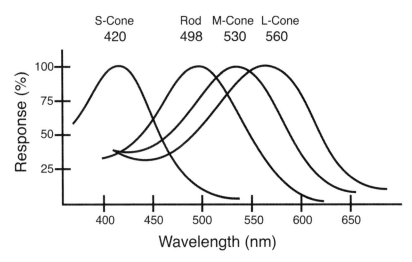

Figure 14.2. Response of rod and cone photoreceptor cells in the human retina to wavelengths in the spectrum of visible light. The S-cone has a maximal response at around 420 nm (violet-blue light), the M-cone at around 530 nm (green light), and the L-cone at around 560 nm (green-yellow light). Rod photoreceptors have a response maximum at around 498 nm (blue-green light).

Color vision depends on comparing the amount of activation of the three different cone photoreceptor types by various wavelengths of incident light. Short-wavelength visible light activates primarily S cones, with M and L cones activated to a lesser extent; we perceive this light to be violet and blue. We perceive medium-wavelength visible light, activating primarily M cones, as green and yellow, and long-wavelength visible light, activating primarily L cones, as orange and red. Thus, as one moves from 400 nm to 700 nm across the spectrum of visible light, our perception generates the familiar rainbow of colors: violet, blue, green, yellow, orange, and red. Colors do not exist "out there" in the world—they are mental experiences related in some still mysterious way to how our nervous system responds to electromagnetic radiation having different energies.

We humans, as well as many other species of primate animals, have what is called trichromatic color vision, mediated by three different types of cone photoreceptors with different light-sensitivity ranges. (Rod cells and rhodopsin appear to have little input into color vision.) The visual system compares the relative amounts of stimulation among the three cone photoreceptor types, and from this comes our ability to perceive a rich variety of colors. Many nonprimate mammals have only two cone photoreceptor types; this dichromatic color vision comes with a lesser ability to discriminate wavelength differences, and presumably a less rich experience of color. On the other hand, many birds have tetrachromatic color vision: four different cone types allowing for a more nuanced discrimination of wavelength and a presumably richer experience of color. That is, it is possible that birds experience colors that we humans have never seen.

The human opsin proteins each have around 350 amino acids, the exact sequence of which differs among the various cone opsin proteins (and rhodopsin). The genes for the M and L opsins are found on the X chromosome, one of the human sex chromosomes. The genes for S opsin and rhodopsin are found on other, nonsex chromosomes. Two fully functional variants of the L opsin gene have been found in humans, giving rise to two L cone opsin photoreceptor proteins that absorb light of slightly different wavelengths, their absorption maxima separated by only a few nanometers.

Human females have two copies of the X chromosome (XX), one inherited from their mother and one from their father. Human males, on the other hand, have only one X chromosome and one Y chromosome (XY). This means that some human females will have both of the L opsin variants (a different version on each X chromosome) and will thus be tetrachromats, possessing a more nuanced ability to discriminate different colors, especially in the orange-red region of the color spectrum. Males, having only a single X chromosome, would have either one version of L opsin or the other, but not both, and so could not have more than trichromatic color vision.

Other sorts of genetic variability also affect color vision. Certain changes in the amino acid sequence of an opsin protein will leave the protein functional but slightly change its light-absorbing properties, and the ability to discriminate different colors. This condition is called "color anomalous." Because the M and L opsin genes are on the X chromosome, if a woman has an altered opsin gene on one of her X chromosomes, it is likely that the other X chromosome will contain the normal variant. Thus, enough of the normal variant will be expressed to yield normal capacity for color discrimination. For a woman to have the color-anomalous condition, she would need to inherit the variant opsin from both parents, a more unlikely occurrence. However, for males, with their single X chromosome, color anomalous vision is more likely. The prevalence of the color-anomalous condition among males is about 6 percent, while its prevalence among females is only about 0.4 percent. These are sizable prevalences, especially for men. Thus, in any large group of individuals, there may be quite a few men (and a small number of women) who are color anomalous. However, unless they undergo careful testing of color vision, it is unlikely they will even know that their color vision is different from the norm.

A more substantial change in color perception occurs if there is enough of a change in the opsin gene to render the resulting cone opsin protein nonfunctional. In such cases, one entire type of functional cone receptor cell (S, M, or L) is lost. If this is either an L (red) or M (green) cone, the resulting condition is called red-green color blindness. It is characterized by a significant loss of ability to distinguish between various shades of color in the green-yellow-red region of the color spectrum. Because the L and M cone opsin genes are located on the X chromosome, there is a difference in prevalence between males and females: about 2 percent of males and less than 0.1 percent of females have red-green color blindness. Again, this is a substantial number of males who have this condition.

There may also be genetic variation in the S cone opsin gene that renders the S cone opsin protein nonfunctional. This results in a change in the ability to discriminate between colors in the blue-green-yellow region of the color spectrum. This condition is called blue-yellow color blindness. For some reason, the S (blue) opsin gene is much less likely to be altered to produce a nonfunctional S cone opsin. Thus, blue-yellow color blindness is relatively rare, occurring in less than 0.01 percent of the population. Also, because the S opsin gene is not located on a sex chromosome (it is found on chromosome 7 in humans), there is no difference in prevalence between women and men.

Cone photoreceptor cells with their cone opsin photoreceptor proteins are sensitive to bright light and have input into the perception of color. They operate in sunlight or in other sources of sufficiently bright light. Rod photoreceptor cells with their rhodopsin photoreceptor proteins are sensitive to low levels of light and have little or no input into color perception. They operate at night or in other sources of dim light. The experience of colors under conditions of low light is not very strong. That is because the light is not bright enough to activate many cones and so the color perception system is not engaged.

In *retinal achromatopsia*, a genetic or developmental anomaly results in loss of all functional cone cells. People with this condition have no experience of color; they see the world in shades of black, white, and gray. When comparing their visual experience with that of individuals with normal color vision, retinal achromatopes sometimes report an appreciation of subtle gradations of contrast, shadow, and texture that is more nuanced than someone with normal vision. This may be akin to the idea that aspects of contrast, shading, and texture may be better represented in black-and-white photography and cinematography than in the color versions.

In the human retina there are many more rods than there are cones: about one hundred million rod cells and about five million cone cells. Additionally, the rods and cones are differently distributed over the retina (Fig. 14.3). Because the cones are concentrated at the fovea, color perception is best when light from the object being viewed is focused there. This happen when we are looking directly at some-

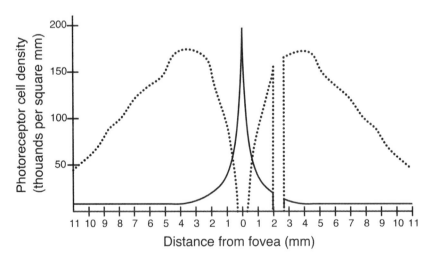

Figure 14.3. Distribution of cones (solid line) and rods (dotted line) in the human retina. Cones are concentrated at the fovea and are sparse elsewhere in the retina. Conversely, rods are sparse at the fovea and more densely distributed elsewhere in the retina, with peak density a short distance away from the fovea. There are no cones or rods in the blind spot, the place where the axons forming the optic nerve exit the eye.

thing. We generally don't realize that our color perception is sketchier in the periphery of our vision, but if you carefully test for this you will find that it is indeed the case.

Because the cones at the fovea require relatively bright light to become activated, very dim light is best detected when you are not looking directly at it. You can experience this when the first stars begin to twinkle in the sky at twilight. If you look directly at such a star, it may flicker into invisibility; look slightly away and it returns. When you look away from the star, its dim light is focused on a region of the retina that is not the fovea but a bit off into the periphery. Away from the fovea there are many rod cells, the cells that are more sensitive to dim light.

A short distance from the fovea there is a small region of the retina where there are no rods and no cones—no photoreceptors at all. This is the place where the axons from the neurons in the retina come together into a bundle called the optic nerve and exit the eyeball on the way to the brain. The large number of nerve fibers (about one million) occupy so much space that there is no room for any photoreceptor cells in that small region of the retina. This region is called the "blind spot," because any light falling on that part of the retina will not be detected. Although we are completely blind to the region of visual space corresponding to the retinal blind spot, we are completely unaware of this blindness, unless specific effort is made to draw attention to it.

To detect your visual blind spot, hold this page about 15 cm (6 inches) in front of your face.

●   ●   ●

The center dot should be directly in front of your nose, such that a line connecting your nose with the center dot would be parallel to the floor. Now, close one eye and look at the center dot. Then, keeping your open eye firmly focused on the center dot, move the page gently toward and away from your face until the dot on the same side as your open eye disappears. That is, if your left eye is open, then the left-side dot will disappear; if your right eye is open, the right-side dot will disappear.

Clearly, there is a blind spot in each of our eyes. Yet, we are not aware of this, unless we perform some trick to make the blindness visible. How so?

Because the location in space of the blind spot is different for each of the two eyes—if both eyes are open and functioning, the visual system can use the information received in one eye to fill in the blind spot for the other eye. However, even if we close one eye and walk around, we are still not aware there is a blind spot. Because our eyes and body are constantly moving, again, the visual system can gather information to assist in filling in the blind spot. Finally, even if we keep our eyes and head steady so that this sort of filling cannot occur, we are still not aware of our blind spot. It is only when we do some special thing, as above, to draw our attention to the blind region that we become aware of our blindness. Because these visual blind spots have been there for our entire lives, and for millions of years during the evolution of the visual system in vertebrate animals, we have developed

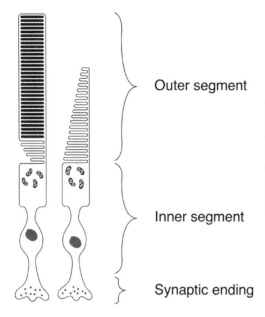

Outer segment

Figure 14.4. Diagram of rod cell (left) and cone cell (right). The outer segments of the cells contain the rhodopsin and cone opsin photoreceptor proteins. The inner segments contain nuclei, mitochondria, and other structures necessary for the functioning of the cell.

Inner segment

Synaptic ending

neural strategies to fill in the blind spots by some sort of averaging or integrating of information over space and time.

This is a profound phenomenon, and the origin of the metaphor of the blind spot: an area of one's knowledge, belief, or behavior in which there is some significant ignorance to which one is oblivious.

Transitioning to the subcellular and molecular level of description of the visual system, consider the rod cell. It consists of a rodlike segment containing numerous lipid bilayer membrane disks, with each disk containing numerous rhodopsin photoreceptor proteins embedded in the disk membranes (Fig. 14.4). Cone cells have a similar structure, with a cone-shaped segment containing cone opsin photoreceptor proteins embedded in a highly infolded cell membrane.

Each rod cell contains about one hundred million (10^8) rhodopsin molecules. Because there are one hundred million rod cells in a retina, there are approximately 10^{16} (ten quadrillion) rhodopsin molecules in each of our two retinas—a very large number!

Each rhodopsin or cone opsin protein is composed of about 350 amino acids, joined into a long chain by covalent chemical bonds. The chain is embedded in lipid bilayer membrane in the outer segment of a photoreceptor cell and winds itself back and forth across the bilayer seven times (Fig. 14.5). In the sections where the polypeptide chain crosses the membrane, it forms alpha-helical structures composed of amino acids that are more hydrophobic and thus agreeable to being inside the hydrophobic core of the lipid bilayer.

Within a rhodopsin or cone opsin there is another molecule—a small molecule, although not an amino acid—attached to the opsin protein via a covalent bond with a nitrogen atom in a specific lysine amino acid within the protein. This molecule is

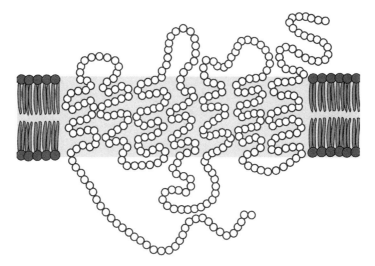

Figure 14.5. Diagram of a rhodopsin molecule in a lipid bilayer membrane, with individual amino acids drawn as small circles. Something of rhodopsin's secondary structure is depicted: seven alpha-helix regions where the polypeptide chain snakes back and forth through bilayer membrane. This diagram doesn't reveal much about tertiary structure; within an actual membrane the polypeptide chain would be clumped together much more closely than shown here.

called *retinal*, named after the retina. It is the retinal molecule that absorbs the light and begins the cascade of events leading to a neural signal.

Retinal

The same retinal molecule occurs in rhodopsin and in the various different cone opsins, and yet these proteins respond to light of quite different wavelengths. This occurs because the different amino acid sequences and arrangements in the various opsin proteins produce different electronic environments, altering the molecular energy levels in the attached retinal and thereby changing its light absorption spectrum.

Our body cannot make retinal from scratch; it's made from closely related molecules that we eat: vitamin A and carotenoids. Vitamin A, also called retinol, differs from retinal by the addition of hydrogen to the oxygen atom at the end of the chain (converting the aldehyde to an alcohol). Carotenoids, such as beta-carotene, are widespread in plants and are the most abundant chemical precursors to retinal and retinol in nature. Beta-carotene is the molecule that gives carrots their orange color.

Beta-carotene

It is found in many of the plants we eat: lettuce, kale, chard, pumpkin and other squashes, spinach, sweet potatoes, and tomatoes, as well as carrots. Our body knows how to take a molecule of beta-carotene, cleave it in half, and chemically modify it a wee bit, yielding two molecules of retinal.

When the retinal molecule is bound to the protein in rhodopsin or one of the cone opsins, it occurs in a form (called the 11-*cis* isomer of retinal) where the carbon-chain portion of the molecule is bent or kinked. The absorption of a photon of light by the retinal molecule triggers a change in the shape of the chain so that it rotates around the double bond where the kink is and straightens out, into a form called the all-*trans* isomer of retinal. This process is called light-induced isomerization, or photoisomerization.

11-cis-retinal

light

all-trans-retinal

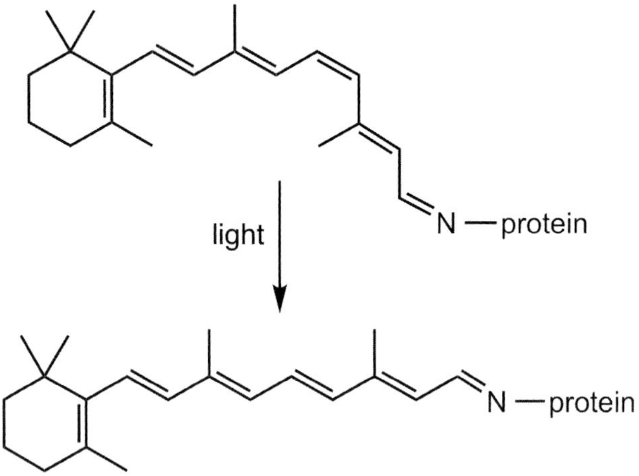

In straightening, the retinal pushes on the amino acids surrounding it and, in so doing, shifts the shape of the entire opsin protein. It so happens that opsin proteins are familiar friends—G-protein coupled receptors (GPCRs). Thus, when they change shape, a cascade of intracellular events is initiated. In the case of neuronal signaling at synapses, the binding of a neurotransmitter molecule shape-shifted the GPCR; here, the light-induced isomerization of the retinal changes the shape. Opsin GPCRs are light detectors.

Here's what happens in the rhodopsin GPCR cascade: When a photon of light is absorbed by 11-*cis* retinal in rhodopsin, the retinal isomerizes to the all-*trans* form, shape-shifting the opsin protein and thereby "activating" it. The activated opsin is available to bind an intracellular G-protein, and the G-protein becomes activated. The activated G-protein then interacts with an enzyme called cGMP phosphodies-terase and activates it. The phosphodiesterase then interacts with cGMP (cyclic gua-nosine monophosphate), hydrolyzing it to noncyclic GMP. The interaction of cGMP with certain ion channels in the cell membrane keeps these channels open. When the concentration of cGMP in the cell decreases, these ion channels close, the mem-brane potential and thus the cell excitability changes, and this changes the amount of neurotransmitter being released at the synapse between the photoreceptor cell and other cells in the retina.

A result of this particular G-protein coupling is enormous amplification. One photon of visible light interacting with a single rhodopsin in a rod cell produces an activated rhodopsin that can in turn bind with as many as one hundred G-proteins, one after another, activating them. Each G-protein can then activate a cGMP phosphodiesterase enzyme, and each phosphodiesterase can hydrolyze hundreds of molecules of cGMP. The result is that a single photon of light may produce—in a mere second of time—an intracellular decrease of more than ten thousand molecules of cGMP. This has the effect of closing many, many ion channels. Thus, a single photon of light can have significant impact on a rod cell's signaling to other cells in the retina. This enables the detection of very dim levels of light.

There are three major layers of cells in the retina: photoreceptor cells, bipolar cells, and ganglion cells (Fig. 14.6). Rods and cones form synapses with bipolar cells, and bipolar cells form synapses with ganglion cells. Neural signals thus flow from the photoreceptors to the bipolar cells to the ganglion cells, and thence to the brain. The axons of the ganglion cells bundle together to form the optic nerve, which exits the

Light

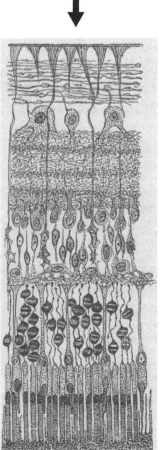

Ganglion cell axons

Ganglion cells

Amacrine cells

Bipolar cells

Horizontal cells

Rod and cone
  inner segments

Rod and cone
  outer segments

Figure 14.6. Drawing by Ramón y Cajal of the cell layers in a vertebrate retina. The top of this drawing is the part of the retina closest to the interior of the eyeball and the vitreous humor. Light enters the retina from the top and passes through several layers of cells before interacting with the rod and cone photoreceptors. At the fovea, these other cell layers are folded back, allowing incoming light to have unobstructed access to the photoreceptor cells—the pit structure of the fovea.

eyeball at the blind spot. While each retina has more than one hundred million photoreceptor cells, it has only about one million ganglion cells; thus, one million axons
make up each optic nerve. This reflects a substantial integration of information
between the photoreceptors and the ganglion cells. Two other major cell types in the
retina are also wired into to this connectivity and contribute to this integration: the
horizontal cells and the amacrine cells, both of which are present in the same retinal
layer as the bipolar cells.

Even a single photon of light is enough to generate a signal from a rod cell. However, because the rhodopsin molecules are so sensitive to light, they are right at the
threshold for having isomerization of retinal occasionally occur randomly as a result
of thermal agitation. Thus, ganglion cells will often receive signals that have not
been generated by light but, rather, are background noise. To avoid sending signals
to the brain that are not related to actual visual information, the ganglion cells wait
for coincidences of several signals from one or more photoreceptors. This increases
the minimum number of photons necessary to generate an action potential from a
ganglion cell that is passed along the optic nerve to something between five and ten.
This is still a small number of photons, corresponding to very, very dim light.

Relatively recently, in the 1990s, another kind of photoreceptive retinal opsin
protein was discovered in light-sensitive cells in the skin of frogs. This protein,
named melanopsin, was shortly thereafter found in certain ganglion cells in the
vertebrate (including human) retina. These photosensitive retinal ganglion cells
send their axons into regions of the brain involved in the regulation of pupil size and
the synchronization of circadian rhythms (see Chapter 20).

An important property of neural cells in the visual system—beginning with the
photoreceptor, bipolar, and ganglion cells in the retina—is the *receptive field*.
Because of the light-focusing properties of the eye, photoreceptor cells will respond
only to light stimuli that come from specific regions of visual space. All of the neural cells in the retina have visual receptive fields, and so also do the brain neurons
that receive signals from the retina.

What happens to the information represented by the neural signals after exiting
the eye and traveling along the optic nerve toward the brain? A short distance behind
the eyes, the two optic nerves intersect in a structure called the *optic chiasm* (named
after the Greek letter chi, which looks like an X, a crossing). At the chiasm, fibers
from the two optic nerves divide into two new groups, with axons from each of the
eyes that gather information from the left half of visual space (the left visual field)
going to the right half of the brain, and axons from each of the eyes that gather information from the right visual field going to the left half of the brain.

About 10 percent of the optic nerve axons go into a part of the midbrain called the
superior colliculus. This pathway is heavily involved in very rapid responses to
sensory stimuli in ways that do not involve awareness. You notice something in the
periphery of your visual field and begin to turn toward it to get a better look, before
you are even aware you saw anything—that's the retina–midbrain pathway at work.

Almost 90 percent of the optic nerve axons head to the thalamus in the diencephalon, where they enter a pair of structures called the lateral geniculate nuclei
(LGN; Fig. 14.7). (The name comes from the Latin *genu* = knee; the LGN resemble
a bending knee—a genuflect.) Axons carrying information from the right visual

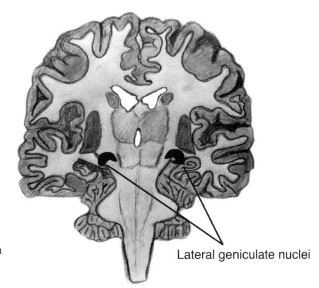

Lateral geniculate nuclei

Figure 14.7. Coronal section showing location of the lateral geniculate nuclei.

field go to the left-side LGN, and axons carrying information from the left visual field go to the right-side LGN.

The LGN cells send axons into the rearmost region of the cerebral cortex, the posterior occipital lobe, where they form synapses with cortical neurons. As is the case with the LGN, the right occipital lobe is receiving information from the left visual field, and the left occipital lobe from the right visual field. This crossing over of information between the spatial environment (visual space) and the brain is called contralateral connectivity.

In the human brain, the occipital lobes, together with posterior regions of the temporal lobes, are involved in the analysis of visual information. This region of the brain is called the visual cortex. From the LGN, information first goes to a region in the posterior occipital lobe called visual area 1, or V1. Cells in V1 send axons to other nearby regions of the cerebral cortex called V2, V3, V4, and V5 (Fig. 14.8). All these visual areas are very highly interconnected, with axons connecting every one of the areas with every other, and with axons going in both directions between any two areas. Many neurons in the visual cortex also send axons back to the LGN—complex interconnectivity runs in both directions.

Different visual areas may be distinguished by the functional properties of their nerve cells. Many neurons in V1 respond to visual stimuli having an edge of contrast oriented at a particular angle and sometimes moving in a particular direction. That is, V1 cells respond to edges of objects. Information about edges and how the edges are oriented in space may be used to construct the overall shape of an object. Many cells in V4 respond to specific colors and are less influenced by things like shape and movement. And many cells in V5 respond to movement and its speed and direction and are not so influenced by things like shape and color.

Furthermore, each of these visual areas contains something like a map of visual space. Light from objects in the external world (visual space) is detected by photo-

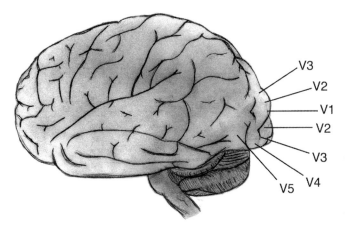

Figure 14.8. Lateral view of brain showing locations of several visual areas in the posterior cortex.

receptors in the retina such that objects that appear nearby in visual space will stimulate photoreceptor cells that are near to one another in the retina. This topographic relationship between objects in external visual space is preserved all the way through the retina to the LGN and into the visual cortex. Thus, cells in V1 are organized in such a way that the receptive fields of neighboring V1 cells respond to regions of visual space that are also nearby—there is a kind of a map of visual space in V1. And these topographic maps are preserved throughout the other cortical visual areas.

Much of what has been learned about the structure and function of these regions of the brain has been accomplished by measuring neural signals in the cortex of various animals during the presentation of specific kinds of visual stimuli. David Hubel (1926–2013) and Torsten Wiesel (b. 1924) were pioneers in conducting these kinds of measurements; they were experimental collaborators for 25 years.

Information about which brain areas are doing what vis-à-vis vision also comes from the study of people who have suffered brain lesions (usually from strokes) that are found to be associated with specific deficits in visual perception. And, more recently, functional brain imaging has allowed the mapping of properties of the human visual cortex in healthy, living humans (see Chapter 17). A lesion in V1 results in a visual *scotoma* (Latin *skotos* = dark), a blind spot in a specific region of space. Because the axons from LGN cells into the visual cortex make connections to neurons in V1, damage to V1 produces a substantial disruption to the flow of visual information in the brain. Corresponding to whatever region of the spatial map in V1 that has been impacted by the lesion, there will be blindness to the corresponding region of visual space.

If the lesion is small, the scotoma may not even be noticeable to the patient, unless careful testing is conducted. If the lesion is sufficiently large, then the patient will experience an absence of information from part of visual space. A large lesion might completely damage all of V1 in one hemisphere of the cortex, resulting in complete loss of vision for an entire half of the visual field, the half of visual space contralateral to the side of the brain in which the lesion is located. The clinical term to describe this is *hemianopsia*, meaning loss of vision in one half of visual space.

A lesion in V4 produces a disruption of color vision. Depending upon the extent of the lesion, larger or smaller regions of visual space may be affected. The color disruption may vary from washed out or faded color perception to a complete loss of color awareness. This is a *cortical achromatopsia*, because the cause is related to a cortical lesion rather than to a retinal condition as in retinal achromatopsia. A lesion in V5 produces an *akinetopsia*, or motion blindness, in which the person is unaware of movement in some region or regions of visual space. It is as if the world appears as a series of snapshots—a very disabling condition, especially if one needs to navigate around in places where there are moving vehicles.

There is a region in the inferior (lower) and medial (middle) temporal lobe that has been found, in both monkeys and humans, to contain cells that respond selectively to images of faces. Sustaining a lesion in this area may bring on a clinical condition called *prosopagnosia* (Greek *prosopon* = face), in which the person has great difficulty or even a complete loss of ability to recognize faces. This is a very specific symptom; other aspects of visual perception remain intact. There is also substantial individual variation among normal people regarding the ability to recognize and recall faces. It is speculated that this may relate to variation in the wiring of the temporal lobe visual areas—different people, different wiring, different capacities for facial recognition and recall.

Prosopagnosia is a specific type of the more general neurological syndrome called *agnosia* (Greek *a* = without; *gnosis* = knowledge). A person suffering from a serious visual agnosia may have difficulty recognizing all or nearly all visual objects. While their ability to identify details of a visual scene may be completely normal, integrating the details into a meaningful whole object or scene may be severely disabled. Visual agnosias are often associated with lesions in the region where the occipital, temporal, and parietal lobes come together.

One way of thinking about visual perception is that the eye–brain system does something like a deconstruction process, representing the visual scene in terms of edges, colors, and movements, all the while keeping track, via the maps, of where things are in space. Then a synthesis or coupling of all this information somehow takes place, perhaps by way of synchronous neural oscillations over large areas of cortex. And finally these physiological processes are in some way connected to our mental *experience* of the visual world, with all its richness of color and texture. Many mysteries remain at every step.

> Ah, photons and waves—
> ethereal as can be—
> as real as it gets.

CHAPTER **15**

Ears and Hearing

When I was in the third grade, my teacher asked the class an oft-repeated question: if a tree falls in a forest and there is no one (no people, no other animals, no beings of any kind with ears) around to hear it, does it make a sound? I don't recall how the question was answered at the time, but I do recall being unsatisfied with the answer. How would you answer it?

The answer depends on how we choose to define *sound*. If sound is defined as a mental experience, then sound would require someone or something capable of mental experience. According to our current understanding of hearing, this means a being having an ear or other sound-detecting organ, and a nervous system to process the signals generated by the sensory organ. If, however, we define sound as variation in air pressure generated by the action of the tree falling, then that air pressure variation presumably exists whether or not any beings with ears and nervous systems are in the vicinity. Because sound might reasonably be defined in either of these ways, it is necessary to specify what one means by *sound* in order to give a coherent answer to the question. Most dictionary definitions of *sound* conflate these two possible meanings (mental experience and physical vibration), and I often do also in my usage of the word. Generally this is not a problem, unless one is faced with questions like the tree falling in the forest.

The mental experience of sound is believed to be generated by processes of the nervous system elicited by the physical stimulus of rhythmic air pressure variation set up by the action of the falling tree. When the tree falls, it compresses the air molecules (nitrogen and oxygen, mainly) in the vicinity, producing a transient increase in their density. This increased density pushes on the nearby molecules, compressing them. The compression is followed by a rebound of rarefaction, or thinning. This variation in air pressure moves out into the space around the falling tree as a wave of pressure variation, traveling at the speed of sound.

Another example: when a clapper strikes a metal bell, it sets the bell into vibration, and the vibration at the surface of the bell alternately compresses and expands the air in the immediate vicinity. The result is a rhythmic pattern of air pressure variation that moves out into space as waves of alternating compression and rarefaction (Fig. 15.1).

This can be depicted in graphical form as a sinusoid (Latin *sinus* = curve) or sine wave plotting air pressure as a function of time. Figure 15.2 shows a sine wave hav-

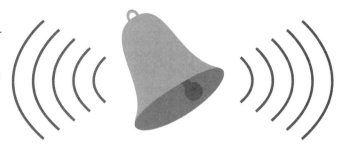

Figure 15.1. A bell vibrating after a clapper strikes it generates a rhythmic pattern of alternating compression and rarefaction that moves out into space as a series of waves.

ing a period (the duration of one cycle) of 5 milliseconds. In one second there are two hundred cycles—a frequency of 200 hertz (Hz).

A sound wave moves through air at a speed of about 1,100 feet per second, or 335 meters per second, or 750 miles per hour. For any moving wave, the velocity of movement is equal to the frequency of variation multiplied by the wavelength. Thus, for an air pressure variation oscillating at 200 Hz, the distance of one cycle, or wavelength, is 5.5 feet:

$$\text{Wave velocity} = \text{frequency} \times \text{wavelength}$$

$$1,100 \text{ feet/second} = 200 \text{ cycles per second} \times 5.5 \text{ feet per cycle}$$

The higher the frequency, the shorter the wavelength, and the lower the frequency, the longer the wavelength—a relationship shared by all propagating waves: sound waves, water waves in the ocean, electromagnetic radiation, seismic waves associated with earthquakes, and so on.

The speed of light is approximately 186,000 miles per second, or 300,000,000 meters per second. This is very fast—certainly much faster than the speed of sound. Thus, if one is observing an event that has both visual and auditory features, the visual information will reach the eye nearly instantaneously, while the sound information may take noticeably longer. For example, consider lightning and the associated thunder. If the lightning is 5 kilometers away, then the flash of light will reach the observer's eye very quickly, because light traveling 5 kilometers arrives in about 17 microseconds. However, the air pressure variations triggered by the lightning will travel at the speed of sound, 335 meters per second, and thus will require about

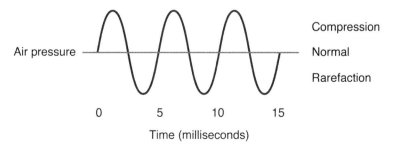

Figure 15.2. Sound shown as a sine wave.

Figure 15.3. Sine waves with lower (left) and higher (right) frequencies.

3 seconds to negotiate each kilometer: about 15 seconds to travel 5 kilometers. So there will be a 15-second gap between seeing the lightning and hearing the associated thunder. One can estimate how far away lightning is by counting the seconds between seeing the lightning and hearing the thunder. If the gap is a second or less, take care.

You may have had a similar experience in watching displays of fireworks. Depending upon how far away you are from the exploding firework, there may be a gap of a second or two, or even many seconds, between seeing the exploding firework in the sky and hearing the associated boom.

Sensory channels are sensitive to limited ranges of stimuli. For light, the human visual system responds to electromagnetic radiation in the wavelength range of 400 nanometers to 700 nanometers, so-called visible light. As discussed in Chapter 11, some animals can sense electromagnetic radiation of wavelengths shorter than visible light (ultraviolet) or longer than visible light (infrared). Note that for electromagnetic radiation, wavelength tends to be the preferred unit of description, although frequency could also be used. In fact, frequency is often used to describe microwaves and radio waves. For sound, the human auditory system is sensitive to air pressure variations in the range of approximately 20 to 20,000 Hz. Frequency is generally the preferred unit of description for sound, although wavelength could also be used.

Higher-frequency (that is, faster) pressure variations are experienced as sounds having higher pitch or tone (Fig. 15.3, right). Lower frequencies of pressure variation are experienced as sounds having lower pitch or tone (Fig. 15.3, left). The loudness of a sound is associated with the amplitude or magnitude of the pressure variation, with high amplitude variations experienced as louder than low amplitude variations (Fig. 15.4).

Figure 15.4. Sine waves with higher (left) and lower (right) amplitudes.

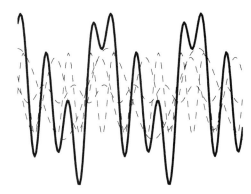

Figure 15.5. This complex sinusoidal waveform (solid line) is generated from a combination of three simple sine waves (dashed lines).

Light can be conceptualized as a propagating vibration of an electromagnetic field. Corresponding to the perceptual qualities of tone and loudness for sound are the qualities of color and brightness, respectively, for light.

A third quality used to describe sound experience is called *timbre* (Greek *tympanon* = drum) and is related to the complexity of the sound waveform. A simple sinusoidal variation in pressure having a single frequency would be experienced as a pure tone. However, most actual air pressure variations are not single frequencies; rather, they are complex waveforms having mixtures of several (or many) different frequencies (Fig. 15.5).

More complex waveforms are associated with mental experiences of sound having richness and complexity beyond that of pure tones—this is timbre.

Musical instruments provide excellent examples of timbre (Fig. 15.6). Even the single note of middle C played on a piano is not a pure tone but a complex waveform reflecting a combination of several frequencies. And the same note of middle C played on different instruments sounds different, because the complexity of the sound is different for different instruments. Each has the same dominant frequency (approximately 262 Hz), which defines the note as being middle C, but other frequencies are present in the sounds, resulting from various modes of vibration of strings and/or air in the resonant chambers of the different instruments.

Musicians also play their instruments in particular ways, developing unique styles that may be recognizable in the timbre of their music. Sometimes it is possible to identify a musician from hearing them play only a single note. It is the sound's timbre that makes this possible.

The Jew's harp is considered to be one of the oldest musical instruments. It is known in many different cultures and goes by many different names—jaw harp, mouth harp, trump, khomus, morsing (Fig. 15.7). My favorite name is the Italian *scacciapensieri*, which translates as "thought banisher," a reference to the trance-inducing potential of the sound. The instrument is played by holding it against the lips and teeth and strumming the metal reed.

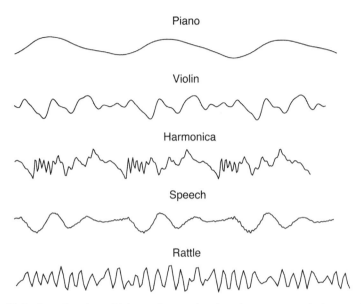

Figure 15.6. Complex sinusoidal waveforms, showing air pressure variation as a function of time, for several different sound sources.

Figure 15.8 shows a waveform associated with sound coming from playing this instrument. Beneath it are several component frequencies having varying amplitudes. These component frequencies are generated by the different modes of vibration assumed by the vibrating instrument and the air forced through the resonant chamber associated with the instrument. In the case of the Jew's harp, the resonant chamber is the oral cavity of the player. These various component frequencies add together to produce the complex waveform generated by playing the Jew's harp.

It turns out that any complex waveform describing a vibration can always be represented as a sum of sine waves having various frequencies and amplitudes. This is called a Fourier series, Fourier decomposition, or Fourier analysis, named after the French mathematician Joseph Fourier (1768–1830), who studied this phenomenon two hundred years ago. It is a beautiful mathematical property of vibration. For sounds produced by musical instruments, the components of the Fourier series are associated with the specific vibratory modes of the strings and air cavities of the instruments.

Figure 15.7. Jew's harp, khomus, *scacciapensieri*.

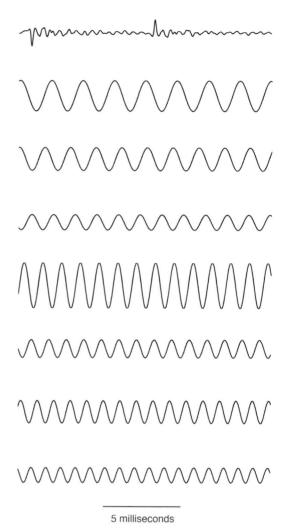

Figure 15.8. Sound waveform produced by a Jew's harp (top) and a selection (from a much larger number) of component frequencies in the Fourier decomposition. The amplitudes of the component frequencies have been magnified (all by the same factor) so that their structures are easily visible.

5 milliseconds

Figure 15.9 illustrates another Fourier analysis of sounds. Consider several different notes played on the piano: middle C, E, G, and C (one octave above middle C). These graphs illustrate Fourier spectra of these four notes, with the horizontal axes representing frequency and the vertical axes representing a measure of the amplitude of the various frequency components. The first major peak is the fundamental frequency characterizing the particular note. The other peaks represent overtones—frequency components that give the sounds their unique complexities and associated perceptual timbres. We'll return to Fourier analysis shortly, because it is central to how the ear makes sense of sound.

Hearing, or auditory perception, begins with the air pressure variations entering the outer ear. The most external structure of the ear, the pinna, is the fleshy flap of skin attached to each side of the head (Fig. 15.10). It functions as a funnel or antenna,

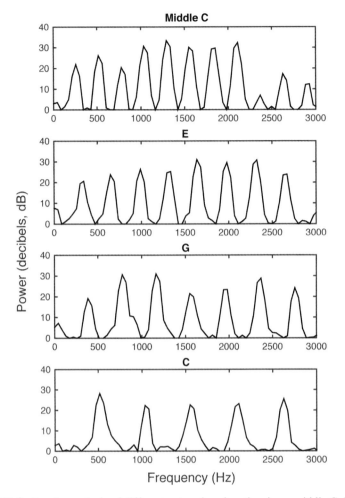

Figure 15.9. Fourier analysis of different notes played on the piano: middle C, E, G, and C (one octave above middle C).

collecting and focusing the vibrations of air pressure into the ear canal. The ear canal terminates at the tympanic membrane or eardrum, a small drumskin-like piece of tissue that is set in vibration when air molecules strike it. The eardrum forms the boundary between what is called the outer ear and what is called the middle ear.

The middle ear consists of a cavity occupied by three small interconnected bones, collectively called the ossicles. Individually, they are called the hammer, anvil, and stirrup (Latin: *malleus, incus,* and *stapes*) because their shapes are reminiscent of those various items. As the eardrum vibrates, the hammer, which is attached to the eardrum, also vibrates. This vibration is then transferred to the anvil and thence to the stirrup, which is attached to another drumskin-like tissue called the oval window. The oval window defines the boundary between the middle ear and the inner

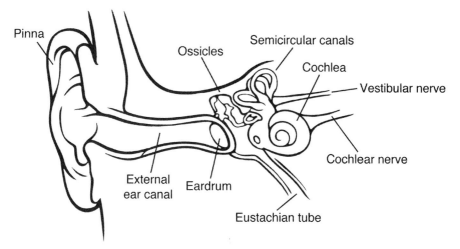

Figure 15.10. The human ear. The external ear is the pinna, ear canal, and eardrum; the middle ear is the chamber containing the ossicles; the inner ear is the cochlea and semicircular canals. The cochlear and vestibular nerves form cranial nerve 8. The Eustachian tube connects the middle ear with the nasopharynx and allows for equalization of air pressure between the middle-ear chamber and the external atmosphere. The Eustachian tube is named after sixteenth-century Italian anatomist Bartolomeo Eustachi, a contemporary of Vesalius.

ear, which consists of the cochlea and semicircular canals, collectively called the bony labyrinth (Fig. 15.11).

The interior of the bony labyrinth is filled with fluid (water and ions), and the vibration of the oval window sets the fluid inside the cochlea into vibration. The structure of the ossicles is such that the vibrational energy is very efficiently transferred from the medium of air into the medium of fluid. As the oval window vibrates, it pushes on the fluid inside the cochlea and creates a wave that propagates through the interior of the cochlea—essentially, the fluid is set into vibration. Running the length of the cochlea, down the central core of its spiral interior, is a thin tissue called the basilar membrane. As the surrounding fluid vibrates, the basilar membrane vibrates, too.

The basilar membrane varies in thickness, being thickest at the end nearest the oval window and thinnest at the other end. This variation in thickness causes different regions of the basilar membrane to be set into vibration by different frequencies, a phenomena called resonance. The thicker end vibrates resonantly with higher frequencies, and the thinner end vibrates resonantly with lower frequencies. Because most sounds are mixtures of many different frequencies, an incoming sound will set into vibration multiple regions of the basilar membrane. Thus, the basilar membrane creates a spatial representation of the component frequencies of sound entering the ear—a Fourier analysis of the sound.

To summarize: different frequencies of sound vibration—when transferred into the cochlea via the eardrum, ossicles, and oval window—set different regions of the basilar membrane into vibration. The basilar membrane performs a Fourier analysis

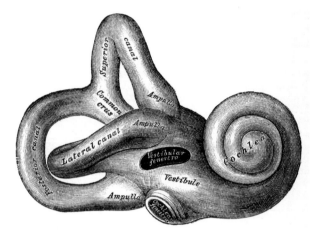

Figure 15.11. Bony labyrinth of the human inner ear. The cochlea (on the right) is a coiled structure; *cochlea* derives from the Greek and Latin word for snail shell or spiral shell. The vestibular fenestra (Latin *fenestra* = door) is the location of the membrane of the oval window. The cochlear fenestra is the location of the membrane of the round window, which allows the fluid inside the cochlea to move, by bulging out and in as the sound vibration moves through the cochlea. On the left side of the diagram are the three orthogonal semicircular canals, described later in this chapter. The bony labyrinth measures about 1.25 centimeters along its long axis. This drawing is from the 1918 edition of Henry Gray's *Anatomy of the Human Body.*

of the incoming sound and represents the result spatially, along the length of the membrane—exquisite biophysics!

Along the length of the basilar membrane are several thousand elegant little cells, called hair cells (Fig. 15.12). These cells are characterized by a bundle of hairs or cilia attached to one end. As the basilar membrane vibrates, the hair cells in the vicinity also vibrate, and their cilia swoosh to and fro through the surrounding fluid. At the opposite end of the cell from the bundle of cilia, the hair cell forms chemical synapses with fibers of the auditory nerve, cranial nerve 8. The bending of the hairs initiates a signal from the hair cell to the nerves carrying signal information to the brain.

Here is how that neural signal is believed to come about. The hairs are interconnected by tiny molecular cables, only a few billionths of a meter in diameter, barely visible with high-resolution electron microscopy. These tiny cables appear to be coupled to positive ion channels, so that as the hairs bend, the cables tug on channels and cause them to open. When the channels open, K^+ ions, which in the cochlear fluid are more concentrated outside the cells than inside, flow into the hairs and make the normally negative interior of the hair cell more positive. This depolarization of the hair cell's membrane potential causes voltage-gated calcium channels to open and Ca^{++} ions to flow into the cell. Then, just as in the axon terminals of neurons, the influx of Ca^{++} triggers the fusion of synaptic storage vesicles with the outer membrane of the cell, and neurotransmitter molecules are released into the synaptic

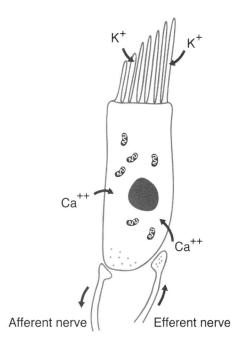

Figure 15.12. Inner-ear hair cell. Afferent fibers (Latin *af* = toward, *ferre* = carry) carry signals from the body's periphery to the brain; efferent fibers (Latin *e* = out) carry signals from the brain to the periphery. Afferent signals convey sensory information to the brain; efferent signals at least in part function to adjust the sensitivity of the inner ear to sound.

cleft. The neurotransmitter diffuses across the synaptic cleft and activates postsynaptic receptors located on the dendritic fiber of the auditory nerve. If the auditory nerve fiber receives sufficient stimulation, an action potential occurs there and a signal is sent to the brain.

Hair cells are exquisitely sensitive structures. Incredibly tiny movements of the hairs are sufficient to open the mechanically-gated ion channels, leading to release of neurotransmitter at the synapse with the auditory nerve. If the hair cells were any more sensitive, they would be too sensitive—the thermal buffeting of the hairs resulting from the random movements of molecules at body temperature would open the channels and lead to signals even in the absence of any sound. The background noise would become deafening—not a good thing! Thus, just as with the rod photoreceptors in the visual system, the hair cells of the auditory system appear to be operating with the maximum possible sensitivity given their particular physical construction.

We have considered the process of how, when the energy of a sound wave hits the head, some of it is funneled into the external ear canal, then to the middle ear ossicles, then to the cochlea, at which point a neural signal is generated. Now consider this: there is another way by which sound energy can reach the inner ear—a different path from that of the external ear canal route: direct vibration of the bones of the skull that surround the cochlea. To the extent that the skull is set into vibration, this will also result in vibration of the tympanic membrane, ossicles, and cochlea. For most sounds coming from the environment, this will not contribute much to signals generated in the cochlea. However, there is one common situation for which the contribution of skull vibration is very large. Can you guess what that is?

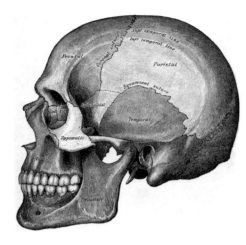

Figure 15.13. Human skull, from the 1918 edition of Henry Gray's *Anatomy of the Human Body.*

Did you guess? The answer is the sound of hearing one's own voice as one speaks or sings or hums. The vibration of the vocal cords and other structures involved in the generation of these sounds produces variations in air density that propagate away from the body. This is what others hear. These air pressure variations also enter one's own external ear canal, and some of what we hear when we hear the sound of our own voice enters the auditory system in the way we have described. But plug your ears as tightly as you can and you can still hear yourself speak perfectly well, even when very quietly whispering. Much of the vibrational energy sensed when we hear ourselves speak enters the auditory system via internal vibration of the skull (Fig. 15.13).

The character of the transmitted frequencies is somewhat different for the vibrations that propagate through the air space external to our body compared with the vibrations that propagate through our bones and other body parts. Thus, the frequency composition will differ for one's voice as heard by oneself compared with what is heard by another person. This is why people are generally surprised the first time they hear a recording of their own voice, often maintaining that it does not sound like them. This is true: one's voice heard by the speaker while speaking does sound different than that same voice heard by another listener. The rhythm and tempo are the same, but the Fourier frequency composition is different.

In auditory signaling, neurotransmitter is released from the hair cell, and a signal is generated in the postsynaptic dendrite of cranial nerve 8. The cell bodies for these nerves are located nearby in a cluster called the spiral ganglion, one cluster for each ear. These are so-called bipolar neurons, with a single myelinated (for efficient conduction) dendrite receiving the signal from the hair cell and a myelinated axon carrying the signal into the brainstem. In the brainstem's medulla, axons of the auditory nerve synapse with cells in a region called the cochlear nucleus. Neurons of the cochlear nucleus send axons to cells in regions of the pons called the superior olive and the lateral lemniscus. The various brainstem auditory centers all send axons into the inferior colliculus in the midbrain. The inferior colliculus projects to the nearby medial geniculate nucleus (MGN) of the thalamus. And the MGN sends axons into the temporal lobe of the cerebral cortex, to a region called the primary auditory cortex, or A1.

There is extensive interconnectivity between the various brainstem auditory nuclei, including between nuclei on opposite sides of the brainstem. One important function of this bilateral connectivity is to compare the arrival times and other qualities of sounds between the two ears, underlying our ability to spatially locate the sources of sound in the auditory environment. As with the visual system, there is extensive signaling in both directions—that is, neural signals are sent from the cortex to the MGN, from the MGN to the inferior colliculus, and so on, all the way back to the hair cells in the cochlea.

The vast majority of the hair cells sending signals to the spiral ganglion and thence to the cochlear nucleus are the so-called inner hair cells, of which there are approximately thirty-five hundred per cochlea. Another population of hair cells, called the outer hair cells, numbering about twelve thousand cells per cochlea, make far fewer connections to the spiral ganglion but receive much more efferent input from the brainstem. It is currently believed that the outer hair cells may be minimally involved in the direct detection and transduction of the auditory signal and instead function to change the sensitivity of the basilar membrane, making it more sensitive to low-volume sounds. The outer hair cells contain a protein called prestin (named after the musical notation *presto*) that elongates and contracts as a function of membrane potential changes. This change in shape affects the shape of the entire cell, which then pushes against the basilar membrane, changing its stiffness and sensitivity—simply amazing!

In the cerebral cortex, as with the visual system, multiple areas are involved in the analysis of auditory information. The spatial mapping of frequency that began at the basilar membrane is preserved all the way through the pathways to A1. In addition, a great deal of neural manipulation has taken place between the cochlea and the cortex, and exactly what happens is still far from understood. Some of the temporal lobe auditory areas, such as Wernicke's area, are very involved with the perception of speech—more on this in Chapter 18.

Loss of hearing is a topic of significant interest and clinical concern. Among possible causes of hearing loss are infections of the inner ear that cause irreversible damage to hair cells. Other causes of hearing loss are genetic anomalies that result in malfunctions of the cochlea. Individuals possessing such anomalies may be born with impaired hearing or even complete deafness. One such anomaly involves a gene coding for a connexon ion channel protein, of the same type as those forming electrical synapses between neurons and glia (see Chapter 6). Connexon channels maintain ion flow between various chambers of the cochlea. A mutation in the gene coding for a particular channel in the cochlea, known as connexin 26, produces abnormal ion balances within the cochlea. As a result, the hair cells cannot function, and the person is deaf.

Perhaps the most common cause of hearing loss is acoustic trauma—exposure to loud sounds. The standard way of measuring sound intensity, or loudness, is a unit called the decibel (dB), named in honor of telecommunications pioneer Alexander Graham Bell (1847–1922). The decibel scale enjoys many uses in engineering; its defining feature is that it is a logarithmic scale relative to some specified reference.

When applied to the measurement of sound loudness, 0 dB represents the approximate threshold for human hearing, and each increase of 10 dB represents a factor of ten increase in loudness. Thus, a 20-dB increase in sound intensity corresponds to a 100-fold (10^2) increase in sound loudness, and a 50-dB increase in sound intensity corresponds to a 100,000-fold (10^5) increase in sound loudness. For example, a 75-dB sound is 100,000 times louder than a 25-dB sound. On this acoustic decibel scale, where 0 dB represents the approximate threshold of human hearing, a quiet room measures approximately 25 dB, the loudness of normal human speech is 40–50 dB, the ambient sound level in a noisy restaurant is 80 dB, a jackhammer breaking up concrete a meter away might be 100 dB, and the sound level at a loud concert could be 120 dB or more. Firing a rifle may produce a transient sound intensity of more than 150 dB.

It is now appreciated that even brief exposure to very loud sounds (acute acoustic trauma), such as gunshots and explosions, can result in permanent hearing loss. So also can chronic exposure to sounds that are moderately loud. Musical events (music in clubs, rock concerts, and so forth) and work environments that have sound levels above 85 dB (working outside at airports, certain construction environments, and so on) are all potential sources of chronic acoustic trauma. Many places now have health regulations that limit exposure to loud sounds and require ear protection. Also increasingly appreciated is the possibility that, with the proliferation of highly portable digital music players, listening to these devices at high volume constitutes chronic acoustic trauma and may result in permanent hearing loss. Time will tell whether the vastly increased use of portable music players will lead to an increase in the prevalence of early-onset hearing loss.

What is the connection between exposure to loud sounds and hearing loss? Although the mechanisms are not understood, something injurious happens from intense overstimulation of hair cells. It appears that hair cells may die from a kind of excitotoxic overstimulation, perhaps similar to what can happen in brain neurons when seizures occur (see Chapter 8). As far as we know, hair cells once permanently damaged are not repaired or replaced. And there are only about thirty-five hundred inner hair cells (the ones most responsible for hearing) in each ear—that's not very many. Each retina has more than one hundred million photoreceptor cells—lose a few thousand photoreceptor cells for some reason, and you would probably not even notice it. But lose a few thousand hair cells, and you are essentially deaf.

What can be done to improve hearing in folks who have sustained hearing loss? The most common kind of therapeutic device used to help people who have suffered hearing loss is the acoustic amplifier hearing aid, which has been around for many years in different forms. In its original form it would have been the ear trumpet, a device to increase the intensity of sound by collecting more of it—essentially a pinna extension offering passive amplification. Some ear trumpets were quite fancy and could be fashion statements in the same way that eyeglasses can be.

The twentieth century saw the development of electronics that could produce a miniature amplifier, powered by battery, that actively magnifies the intensity of incoming sound. Most contemporary hearing aids consist of a microphone and amplifier, which either sit behind or within the pinna, and a small tube that directs the amplified sound into the external ear canal. Ear trumpets and battery-powered amplifier hearing aids simply increase the volume of sound that is available to the ear. The tympanic membrane, ossicles, and cochlea all need to be working, although amplifier-type hearing aids will compensate to some extent for deficiencies in these structures.

Another type of electronic therapeutic device for hearing loss is the cochlear implant. This involves surgically inserting an array of electrodes into the inner ear that electrically stimulate the auditory nerve in the spatial locations corresponding to particular regions of the sound frequency spectrum. A tiny microphone is attached to the external ear that picks up sound vibrations. A frequency analyzer then performs a crude Fourier analysis of the sound and extracts component frequencies within several ranges, perhaps twenty or so segments of the frequency spectrum between approximately 200 and 8,000 Hz. This is conveyed to the inside of the skull (by radio transmitter and receiver), and the auditory nerve is electrically stimulated in the appropriate locations. The result is a partial reconstruction of the incoming sound, partial in that the Fourier reconstruction uses only a few selected frequency ranges.

Cochlear implants enable partial recovery of hearing in individuals with completely nonfunctional cochleas. Such is the case with severe noise-induced hearing loss and in many cases of congenital deafness. Cochlear implant technology at present is not even close to restoring normal hearing. However, it can provide a limited degree of sound detection sufficient in some cases for understanding speech.

In addition to the analysis of sound by the cochlea, something else is going on in the inner ear. The bony labyrinth (Fig. 15.11) also consists of three orthogonal (spatially perpendicular, at 90-degree angles to one another) semicircular canals, together with two bulbous cavities called the utricle and the saccule. These are the sensory structures of the vestibular system, detecting our orientation relative to gravity and our acceleration as we move, walk, and turn. This allows us to maintain balance and execute smooth and coordinated movements; without a vestibular system we would be bumbling around pretty badly.

Unlike hearing, seeing, tasting, and smelling, the functioning of our vestibular system is pretty much out of our conscious awareness, except when something disrupts it—like spinning around and getting dizzy, or vertigo. Vertigo is a condition in which one feels dizzy or in motion even while sitting or standing still. It is generally associated with something unusual happening in the vestibular system, for example, infection or inflammation.

Within the utricle and saccule are receptor cells that detect the movement of fluid in the attached semicircular canals. Because there are three orthogonal canals, complete information can be gathered as to how the head is oriented and accelerating in the three dimensions of space. Changes in orientation and movement cause the fluid to move around differently in the canals. The receptor cells are hair cells of the same type as along the basilar membrane in the cochlea. The moving fluid bends the hairs, and neural signals are generated and passed into cranial nerve 8, which carries vestibular as well as auditory information to the brain.

An additional feature is present in the vestibular system that is not found in the spiral part of the cochlea. Associated with the vestibular hair cells are tiny microscopic stones, crystals of calcium carbonate, like little crystals of limestone. They are called *otoliths*: ear stones (Greek *otos* = ear, *lithos* = stones). The otoliths are suspended in the fluid above the hair cells. As the body accelerates or changes orientation with respect to gravity, the inertia of these little stones contributes to bending the hairs of the sensory cells. These tiny rocks in our inner ears contribute to generating and amplifying the sensory signals that allow us to maintain balance as we move through the world—not so bad, having these rocks in the head.

> Hair cells, music give;
>   and the capacity to—
>   dance with grace and style.

CHAPTER **16**

Skin, Touch, and Movement

Our skin is our largest sensory organ. Dendrites of somatosensory (Greek *soma* = body) neurons terminate in the top layers of skin, and the membranes of these nerve fibers contain receptor proteins that respond to touches, pokes, or changes of temperature (Fig. 16.1). Some nerve fibers have free endings in the skin's top layers. Sometimes the endings are closely associated with hair follicles. Some nerve fibers end in structures (Merkel's disks, Pacinian corpuscles, Meissner's corpuscles, Ruffini endings) that respond to the pressure associated with touch. (These are named after German and Italian anatomists who first described these structures: Georg Meissner [1829–1905], Friedrich Merkel [1845–1919], Filippo Pacini [1812–1883], and Angelo Ruffini [1864–1929].)

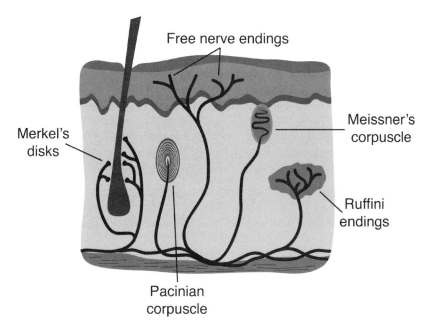

Free nerve endings

Meissner's corpuscle

Merkel's disks

Ruffini endings

Pacinian corpuscle

Figure 16.1. Cross section of skin showing dendrites of somatosensory neurons.

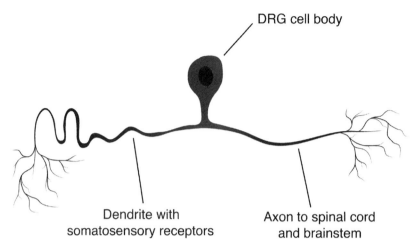

DRG cell body

Dendrite with
somatosensory receptors

Axon to spinal cord
and brainstem

Figure 16.2. Dorsal root ganglion cells, with dendrite nerve fibers innervating the skin and axons that send signals into the central nervous system.

Receptors responsive to touch and poking are presumed to be based on some sort of mechanically-gated ion channels, perhaps similar to the channels on inner ear hair cells that open as the hairs bend. The receptors responsive to temperature changes are the very same TRP receptors described in Chapter 13 that are related to the flavor perceptions of spicy hot and minty cool.

The cell bodies for these fibers are located in clusters of cells near the spinal cord called the dorsal root ganglia (DRG). The DRG nerve fibers innervating the skin are contiguous with the axons that send signals into the central nervous system (Fig. 16.2). The peripheral dendrites also contain voltage-gated sodium and potassium channels and are myelinated. Thus, when sensory receptor proteins are activated by the relevant physical stimuli, they generate action potentials that propagate toward the DRG, bypass the cell body, and continue along the axon into the central nervous system. A DRG dendrite functions just like an axon, except that action potentials propagate toward the cell body instead of away from it.

Somatosensory neurons have spatial receptive fields—the region of skin where a physical stimulus elicits activity in the specified neuron. Axons of somatosensory neurons in the DRG synapse with cells in the spinal cord and with cells in the medulla of the brainstem. From there, the somatosensory circuitry continues into the thalamus. Somatosensory neurons in the thalamus then project to the anterior parietal lobes in the cerebral cortex (Fig. 16.3.). Spatial receptive field information is maintained along this pathway such that a somatosensory map of the body is constructed in the parietal lobes. The various locations in the body are represented along the postcentral gyrus, immediately posterior to the central sulcus.

Just as the primary visual cortex (V1) in the occipital lobe contains a topographic representation (map) of visual space, the primary somatosensory cortex (S1) contains a topographic representation of somatosensory space—the surface of one's own body. Like other sensory areas of the cortex, the somatosensory cortex receives signals from the contralateral side of the body. A lesion in S1 produces a loss of sensation in a particular region of the body related to where the lesion is on the body map in S1. Such a lesion is the somatosensory analogue of a visual scotoma.

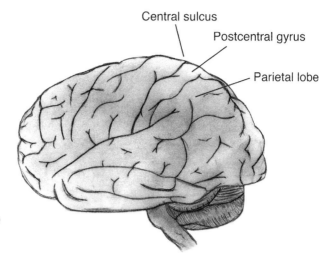

Figure 16.3. Primary somatosensory cortex (S1) is located in the anterior parietal lobe, immediately posterior to the central sulcus, along the postcentral gyrus.

The discovery of somatosensory body maps was first made in humans undergoing brain surgery back in the 1930s. The Canadian neurosurgeon Wilder Penfield (1891–1976) electrically stimulated various regions of the cerebral cortex in patients on whom he was performing brain surgery. During these surgeries, patients were awake and able to respond to his questions. By stimulating various parts of the brain and listening to how patients described their associated experiences, Penfield characterized the location of the somatosensory cortex in the parietal lobe and was the first to describe the somatosensory map of the body (Fig. 16.4).

In the somatosensory cortex, the body is represented more or less according to how things are anatomically connected on the actual body—the foot is connected to the leg is connected to the hip is connected to the torso is connected to the

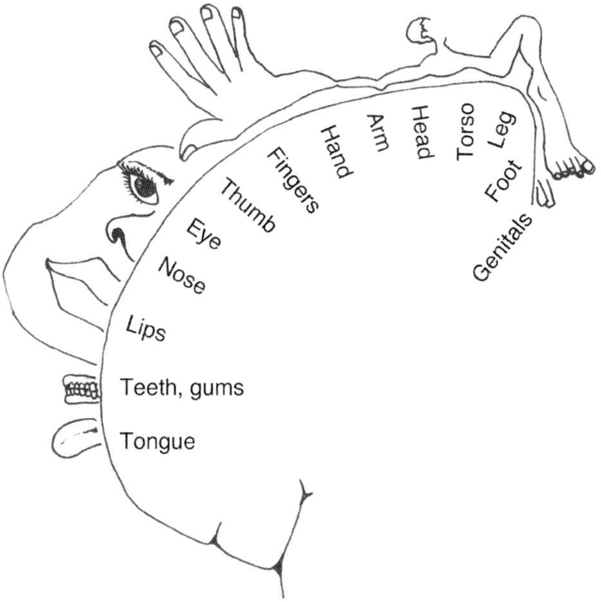

Figure 16.4. Frontal section through one hemisphere of the anterior parietal lobe, showing the somatosensory map. Following Penfield, the drawing of the figure draped over the surface of the brain gives an approximation of the proportional representation for various parts of the body.

neck is connected to the shoulder is connected to the arm is connected to the hand is connected to the fingers. However, there are also some differences between the cortical map and actual body topography. For one, there are several significant discontinuities. On the cortical map the genitals are located at one end next to the foot rather than (or, in addition to) near the center of the body, between the leg and the torso. The face is separated off from the rest of the body rather than being represented as attached to the neck. And the tongue is separated off from the face.

Another notable feature of the cortical map is that it does not have the same relative scale between various body regions as does the actual body. For example, the region of the cortical map that receives sensory information from the fingers and hand is about the same size as the region of the map receiving information from much of the rest of the body—from the arm through the neck, torso, hip, and leg. The lips and tongue also are represented by an area of cortical surface larger proportionally to the actual sizes of the lips and tongue on the body.

These features are related to somatosensory sensitivity. Our fingers and our lips are the two areas of the body where we have the keenest sense of touch. Large numbers of somatosensory neurons send dendrites into the skin of our fingertips and our lips. These dendrites are densely packed, and the neurons have relatively small receptive fields, producing a high level of acuity in the sense of touch in these regions. This allows for the detection of subtle aspects of texture in things we are touching with our fingertips or with our lips. In contrast, regions of the body such as the arm, back, or leg have relatively poor somatosensory acuity.

Somatosensory acuity can be easily measured using what is called the two-point discrimination test. This test is best done with another person—it is more fun that way, too. Take a wire paperclip and bend it into a U-shape so that the two ends of the paperclip wire can be adjusted to be very close together or farther apart. One person—the experimental subject—closes her or his eyes. The experimenter touches the U-shaped wire very gently on the subject's skin such that the two ends of the U touch the skin at the same time. You will find that, when the U is touching the fingertips or the lips, the ends of the U can be very close together—perhaps as little as 1 or 2 millimeters apart—and the subject will still be able to experience two separate points of touch. This represents a high degree of somatosensory acuity—a result of the densely packed somatosensory dendrites connected to many separate neurons each having small receptive fields and projecting eventually to a region of the parietal lobe (S1) where large numbers of neurons receive the signals.

In contrast, if the experimenter touches the U to the subject's back, the ends of the U must be moved apart as much as 1 or 2 centimeters (ten times the separation needed for the hand) before the subject experiences two separate points of touch. If the ends of the U are close together, say, several millimeters, it will feel like a single point of touch. This represents a relatively low degree of somatosensory acuity and reflects many fewer somatosensory receptor neurons sending signals to the cortex, where fewer cortical neurons receive and process the information.

From the primary somatosensory cortex, information is sent to other more posterior regions of the parietal lobe. These regions are named S2, S3, S4, S5, and so on, and are collectively called the secondary somatosensory cortex. They contain maps of the body, but the things represented in these maps are far less clear than is the case for S1. While lesions in S1 produce a simple loss of sensation in a particular region of the body, lesions in secondary somatosensory cortex are associated with various kinds of somatosensory weirdness, in which touch sensations may feel weird and confusing in different ways—somatosensory agnosias. They may also cause neglect syndromes, in which touch sensation is intact but is usually ignored or not recognized unless one's attention is specifically drawn to it.

Much has been learned about the organization of the somatosensory cortex by studying mice. Mice depend heavily on their whiskers to collect information about the world. Their whiskers are constantly whisking about, coming into contact with nearby objects and providing a rich source of information about the environment through which the mouse is moving, even in total darkness. Just as our fingers and lips have a robust representation in our cortical somatosensory map, in the mouse brain its whiskers have robust representations in its somatosensory cortex. Each of perhaps thirty or more whiskers on each side of the nose sends signal information to specific regions of the mouse cortex. There is a whisker map in the mouse brain.

What happens if one of a mouse's whiskers is cut off, or pulled out in a scuffle with another animal? The cells in the cortex that normally receive input from the absent whisker will no longer receive signal input. What happens to those brain cells, now that they seemingly have nothing to do? Do they sit idle? Do they wither and die?

It turns out they develop neural connections with other nearby neurons; rather than doing nothing, they now contribute to the analysis of signals coming in from whiskers next to the one that was lost. This makes the adjacent whiskers even more sensitive than they were before. The development of these new neural connections involves new growth and branching of axons and dendrites, as well as strengthening of connections that were already in place but not much used. This is an example of neuroplasticity, the ability of neurons to alter their pattern of connectivity. Neuroplasticity is happening all the time in the brain, but these neural wiring changes after the loss of a whisker are a particularly robust illustration.

An analogous process can happen in humans. Sometimes as a result of accident or disease a person may lose an arm or leg. Often in these circumstances the person will continue to feel the presence of the amputated limb, as if it were still there, a so-called phantom limb. What is happening? In a person with an amputated arm, the region of parietal lobe that normally receives signals from the arm is no longer getting that input. As in the mouse with the amputated whisker, these neurons do not sit idle but form connections with the neurons in the adjacent regions of the body map. For the arm, this would be the shoulder area and the face area. Thus, any somatosensory input that activates neurons in these adjacent areas would also spill over and activate neurons in the arm area. This is likely to explain the feeling of a phantom arm. Any vague stimulation of the face and shoulder of the amputee (air currents, temperature changes, and the like) also activates neurons that would have once received signals from the now missing arm. This neural activation might then be

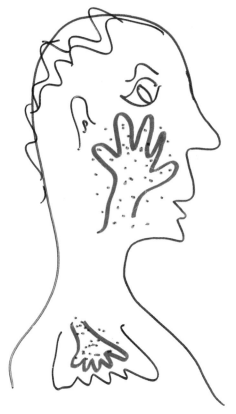

Figure 16.5. Representation of the person's phantom hand on both the cheek and the stump at the shoulder where the amputation occurred. Touching different spots in these body locations evokes an experience of the person's phantom hand, wrist, and arm being touched.

experienced as coming from the missing arm. As a result of neuroplastic reorganization of the body map, a phantom arm is born. If we could ask a mouse with an amputated whisker to tell us about its experience, it would perhaps report the feeling of a phantom whisker.

If the body map is reorganizing in this way, then touching the face or the shoulder of an amputee should elicit, in a well-defined way, the experience of the phantom arm being touched. An experiment to test this was carried out by V. S. Ramachandran, a neuroscientist at the University of California, San Diego. Touching an amputee's face (on the same side of the body as the amputated arm) elicits both the feeling of the cheek being touched and the feeling of the phantom arm being touched in specific locations (Fig. 16.5).

These reorganized perceptions also extend to temperature and other sensations. Dripping warm or cold water down the amputee's cheek is experienced by the amputee as warm or cold water running down the cheek and running down the phantom hand and arm. And I once suggested to an amputee patient with whom I was working that he might relieve a bothersome itch he was experiencing in his phantom arm by scratching his cheek—it worked.

The somatosensory body map first discovered by Penfield is immediately posterior to the central sulcus in the parietal lobe. Moving immediately anterior to the central sulcus into the frontal lobe, we encounter another body map also discovered by Penfield in his neurosurgical explorations. This is a body map of neurons that send out signals that initiate the contraction of skeletal muscles, involved in the movements of our body. This region is called the primary motor cortex, or M1. When neurons in M1 fire, signals propagate via the spinal cord and eventually arrive at synapses with muscles of the body, the neuromuscular junctions. At these junctions, acetylcholine is released, which triggers contraction of muscle fibers.

As with the sensory areas of the cortex, there is contralateral connection between M1 and the body, such that the right posterior frontal lobe's M1 controls movement of the left side of the body, and the left posterior frontal lobe's M1 controls movement of the right side of the body. Lesions in M1 produce an inability to move muscles associated with the corresponding part of the body map—that is, partial paralysis. For example, a lesion from a stroke that produced significant damage to the right posterior frontal lobe would result in paralysis of the left side of the body.

Anterior to M1 in the frontal lobes are several other areas also intimately involved in the control of body movement. These areas are collectively called the supplementary motor areas, or premotor areas. Neurons in these areas are active before the generation of signals in M1 and are involved in planning and sequencing muscle movements. Lesions in the premotor areas do not result in paralysis but give rise to disorganizations of movement. Suppose we consider a complex motor action such as picking up a key, inserting it into a lock, and turning the key to open the lock. A person with a frontal premotor lesion might still be able to execute all the individual movements associated with the particular action but would not be able to organize and sequence them appropriately. Such disorders in the organization of movement are called *apraxias*. These are to movement as agnosias are to sensory perception— disorders of organization.

Functional and structural studies of the brain have revealed a vast interconnectivity between diverse regions of the cerebral cortex. For example, large numbers of axons interconnect (in both directions) the posterior sensory areas serving vision, audition, and touch with anterior motor regions. It is believed that, when efferent motor signals are sent from M1 to the peripheral muscles to trigger movement, an "efference copy" is also conveyed to sensory cortex, so that the brain immediately "knows" what the body is doing and can plan accordingly. Constant communication between sensation and movement makes eminent sense, because to execute smooth movement through the environment, movement must be continuously integrated with knowledge about one's surroundings obtained via sensory perception.

A manifestation of this sensory–motor interconnectivity are neurons in the premotor areas of the frontal lobes that are active during particular movements and also active when these movements are observed in another person. For example, if I am moving my arm in a specific way, collections of neurons in my premotor areas are active during the organization and execution of this movement. Some of these neurons may also fire when I see other people move their arms in a similar way. Such cells have been termed "mirror neurons." The implications of this kind of extensive cortical interconnectivity are the subject of active investigation and theorizing. The concept of mirror neurons has been invoked, for example, in speculations about the origins of language (see Chapter 18). It has also been invoked as a contributor to the neural basis of empathic connection between individuals—that is, the ability to connect with another person's emotional experience.

Another part of the brain that is centrally involved in the regulation of movement is the cerebellum, which wraps around the brainstem and is very densely packed with neurons and neural connections. Estimates of the number of nerve cells in the human cerebellum are upward of fifty billion, meaning there are more neurons in the cerebellum alone than there are in all the rest of the brain. One type of cerebellar neuron is the Purkinje cell, named after the Czech anatomist and physiologist Jan Purkyně (1787–1869), who first described these neurons. Each Purkinje cell may have several hundred thousand dendritic spines receiving input from other neurons (Fig. 16.6).

The cerebellum is involved in the timing and coordination of movement. Individuals who have sustained damage to their cerebellum are not paralyzed, but they are impaired in their ability to smoothly execute movements. Even simple movements become jerky and clumsy. Movements are notably compromised in timing, leading to ideas that a primary role of the cerebellum may be to generate exquisite regulation of the timing of movements. Much of the intricate neural circuitry of the cerebellum may be related to obtaining information about very small intervals of time. Highly precise timing of sequences of muscle flexions involved in movements is necessary to smoothly execute the kinds of movement we do all the time so unconsciously and effortlessly.

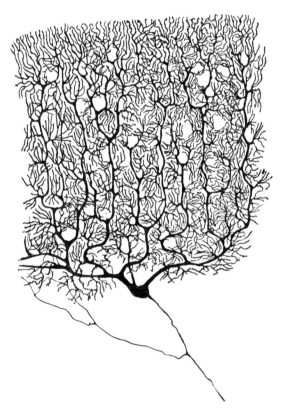

Figure 16.6. Drawing of Golgi-stained Purkinje neuron in the human cerebellum by Ramón y Cajal.

As another clinical example, one with rather bizarre symptoms, consider the case of someone who has a stroke resulting in damage to both the posterior frontal and anterior parietal lobes. Posterior frontal lobe damage results in paralysis. Anterior parietal lobe damage results in loss of body sensation and other somatosensory weirdness, such as somatosensory neglect. These effects are experienced on the side of the body contralateral to the side of the brain affected by the stroke.

If the stroke lesion is to the right hemisphere, one suffers paralysis of the left side of the body coupled with somatosensory weirdness on the left side of the body, and if the stroke lesion is to the left hemisphere, we see paralysis and somatosensory weirdness on the right side of the body—contralateral effects. However, it turns out that with a right-hemisphere lesion, something else very odd often happens: in addition to sensory and motor effects on the left side of the body, the patient may deny that there is anything wrong at all!

Clearly, this is a very weird condition. Someone suffers a stroke and is in the hospital as a result. Half of her body is paralyzed, and she is confined to bed or in a wheelchair. One half of her body has lost sensation and sometimes may seem to not even be there. And yet she is saying that nothing is wrong with her and wondering why she is even in the hospital: "Why can't I go home? There is nothing wrong with me." This condition is called *anosognosia* (Greek *nosos* = disease, *gnosis* = knowledge, *a* = not) and is characterized by a lack of knowledge about one's own disease.

There is a wonderful illustration of anosognosia in a book titled *The Man Who Mistook His Wife for a Hat*, by the neurologist Oliver Sacks. One particular clinical vignette—"the man who fell out of bed"—describes a patient who was in the hospital after apparently suffering a stroke and who ended up on the floor next to his hospital bed. Oliver Sacks talked with the patient and found that he was experiencing the left leg of his body as not belonging to him, as some sort of mysterious alien leg in his bed. So he grabbed the leg and tried to get rid of it by throwing it out of the bed. Of course, the leg was attached to him, so in attempting to throw the leg from his bed, he himself ended up on the floor. In addition, the left side of his body was at least partially paralyzed, so he couldn't climb back into bed. Finally, besides the weird leg in his bed, he was not at all certain why he was in the hospital, because he believed there was nothing seriously wrong with him. Left-side paralysis, experiencing the left side of his body as not even belonging to him (that certainly qualifies as somatosensory weirdness), and denial that there was anything wrong with him at all—the diagnosis would be right frontal-parietal lesion with accompanying anosognosia.

In addition to denying there is anything wrong, patients with anosognosia will sometimes make up all kinds of stories and excuses as to why they are unable to move parts of their body. You can ask them why can't they move their left arm in response to your request, and they might say that they are tired, that people have been asking them all day to move this and move that, and now they just want to rest.

Or they might say that their left arm has arthritis and it hurts to move it, so they would rather not right now. "Maybe you can come back tomorrow, okay?" You might pick up their limp paralyzed arm and say here is your arm, why can't you move it? And they might reply: "That's not my arm. I don't know whose arm it is. I don't know what it's doing here." And so forth—the reality experienced by a patient with anosognosia clearly must be very weird.

> Moving, sensing all—
>   the grand orchestra of nerves.
>   Conducted by whom?

CHAPTER 17

Imaging the Brain

Over the last couple centuries, much has been learned about the brain by observing how damage to different parts of the brain relates to specific changes in behavior. *Lesion* is the general term used to denote an injury to, or other abnormality in, the body. Among the causes of brain lesions are stroke, tumor, physical trauma, and certain brain diseases.

A stroke occurs when there is a disturbance in blood flow to a region of the brain sufficient to produce a loss of function. If the disturbance lasts for more than a very brief time (a few minutes), then there is likely to be cell death and loss of function that may be permanent. The two immediate causes of stroke are blockage of blood flow and hemorrhage. Blockage occurs when particulate matter (usually a blood clot or piece of atherosclerotic plaque) becomes lodged in a blood vessel. Hemorrhage occurs when a blood vessel breaks and leaks blood into the surrounding tissue, rather than delivering blood in the normal way. A hemorrhage often occurs at places where there is weakness in the structure of the blood vessel. Sometimes the structural weakness bulges out from the pressure of the blood; this is called an aneurysm. If an aneurysm ruptures, the result is a hemorrhagic stroke.

A brain tumor is an anomalous, abnormal proliferation of cells in the brain. Such anomalous growth may be either benign (nonspreading) or malignant (able to metastasize and spread); the latter type of tumor has a much poorer prognosis. The abnormal tissue growth often disturbs the normal functioning of nearby neural tissue, producing symptoms that may manifest as changes in perception, other mental function, or behavior.

Another cause of brain lesions is physical trauma resulting from injury to the head. Head injuries may be of two general types: closed or penetrating. Closed head injury occurs when there is a whack of some kind to the head, or even a sudden powerful acceleration or deceleration. In such cases, the integrity of the skull is not broken and the brain is not penetrated from the outside. Sometimes this is called a concussion. Damage to the brain may occur from shearing forces within the tissue or internal contact with the bone. Internal swelling may also occur. Most head injuries are of this type. In a penetrating head injury, the integrity of the skull is compromised and the brain comes into direct contact with an external agent of damage.

Finally, certain diseases are associated with identifiable lesions in the brain. One of the best-studied examples is Parkinson's disease, a neurodegenerative condition characterized by slowness and difficulty with movement. Parkinson's disease is associated with neuronal death in a specific region of the brain: the substantia nigra, one of the clusters of cells in the brainstem that uses dopamine as a neurotransmitter.

To make connections between regions of the brain and specific functions, it is necessary to identify as precisely as possible the location of a brain lesion and then match that with symptoms exhibited by the individual who has the lesion. Historically, it was necessary to wait until after a person died to examine the brain and attempt to locate any lesions. A big breakthrough occurred with the advent of x-ray technology and its application to visualizing the internal structure of living bodies. X-rays are a kind of electromagnetic radiation having energy substantially higher than that of visible light or ultraviolet light. X-radiation was first described at the end of the nineteenth century by Wilhelm Röntgen (1845–1923), who received the very first Nobel Prize in Physics in 1901 in honor of his discovery. Because of their high energy, x-rays can penetrate many kinds of solid matter.

Not long after Röntgen's discovery, people figured out how to use x-radiation to take photographs of the interior of a living body. Because bone is less permeable to x-rays than the surrounding tissue, it was most easy to visualize the skeletal structure inside a body and detect the location and nature of damage, such as a broken bone. With finer tuning of the amount of radiation used, technology was developed that permitted visualization of different kinds of organ tissue on an x-ray photograph. Tissue abnormalities associated with brain lesions became detectable on x-ray photographs of the head and brain.

While a simple x-ray photograph may permit a brain lesion to be seen, it is limited in its ability to locate the lesion. Increased precision is obtained by taking a series of x-ray photographs from different angles and then combining the resulting images to construct a three-dimensional picture of the brain. The advent of sufficiently powerful computers allowed this to be accomplished beginning in the late 1960s. The result is a CT scan—C for *computed* (using a computer) and T for *tomography* (making a series of images, essentially of slices of the brain), sometimes referred to as a CAT scan, with A for *axial* (the slices are along a central axis of symmetry of the brain). A CT scan is a sophisticated x-ray imaging process that generates a three-dimensional representation of the brain's internal structure. CT scans may be used to visualize not only the brain but just about any internal body structure and are widely used as an aid to diagnosis in clinical medicine.

X-rays are not benign—their high energy is damaging to any molecules they encounter, by breaking covalent chemical bonds and disrupting the structure of the molecule. If the molecule is a protein or lipid, its structure is likely to be permanently damaged and its function destroyed. If the molecule is DNA, damage to its structure may sometimes be repairable by enzymes that specialize in fixing damaged DNA. However, sometimes this kind of repair process generates changes in the nucleotide sequence of the DNA, especially if the damage is extensive. Thus, x-rays give rise to mutations in genes and other kinds of anomalous activity in the transcription of genes. X-radiation is toxic, and exposure to it needs to be limited if health is to be maintained.

Another method of structural brain imaging that uses the power of computers to manipulate large quantities of information is magnetic resonance imaging, or MRI. Like CT, MRI can produce a three-dimensional reconstruction of the internal structure of a living brain or other parts of the body and was introduced into medicine in the 1980s. Today, many medical centers use both CT and MRI technologies to image the body. For some kinds of visualization, CT may be the desired method, and for others, MRI may be preferred.

MRI uses not x-rays to penetrate the skull and other tissue but an entirely different process. It is based on a mysterious physical phenomenon called quantum spin. This is a property of subatomic particles, in particular, of the protons and neutrons in atomic nuclei. Although no one really knows what quantum spin is, it is possible to describe with great precision how quantum spin behaves. It is called *spin* because the spin of a subatomic particle produces effects analogous to the behavior of a spinning toy top or a gyroscope (Fig. 17.1). Atomic nuclei possess a nuclear spin that arises from the combination of the spins of the constituent protons and neutrons. (Similarly, the spin of each proton and neutron arises from the spins of their constituent particles, the quarks.)

One property of nuclear spin is that it interacts with magnetic fields. In fact, a subatomic particle will align its spin with an imposed magnetic field, analogous to a compass needle aligning in Earth's magnetic field. In addition, the alignment of nuclear spin in a magnetic field may be perturbed in specific ways if the atomic nucleus is exposed to just the right energy of electromagnetic radiation—the exact energy required depends on the strength of the imposed magnetic field and the nature of the chemical surroundings of the atomic nucleus being measured. The chemical surroundings play such a role because many of the nearby atoms will have magnetic properties that contribute to the local magnetic field.

Experimental technologies were developed in the 1940s to measure these effects. The process was called nuclear magnetic resonance, or NMR. An NMR spectrometer consists of a large magnet to produce a very strong magnetic field, and a device to generate electromagnetic radiation of appropriate energy to perturb the alignment of nuclear spins. For magnets that are typically one to several teslas in strength, the corresponding energies of perturbing frequency are typically in the radiofrequency region of the electromagnetic spectrum (relatively low energy compared with visible light).

A tesla is a unit of magnetic field strength, named after the inventor, engineer, and wizard of electricity Nikola Tesla (1856–1943). One tesla is equivalent to 10,000

Figure 17.1. A toy top spinning in Earth's gravitational field.

gauss—a gauss is another unit of magnetic field strength named after the mathematician and physicist Carl Friedrich Gauss (1777–1855). In these units, Earth's magnetic field measures about 0.5 gauss, or 50 microteslas. A small magnet such as those used to attach something onto a refrigerator door is about 50 gauss, or 5 milliteslas. Thus, the strengths of magnets used in NMR spectrometers are quite substantial, well beyond anything normally encountered on Earth.

If an organic molecule is placed in a strong magnetic field, the nuclear spins of the various atoms will align. Their alignment can be perturbed when just the right radio-frequency energy of electromagnetic radiation is absorbed (the resonant frequency). The most abundant type of atom in any organic molecule is hydrogen; different hydrogen atoms in a given molecule will have different resonant frequencies, depending on the precise nature of its electromagnetic environment within the molecule. Thus, NMR may be used to help determine unknown molecular structures of organic molecules, by looking at the energies needed to perturb the alignment of the spins. This is a widely used application of NMR spectroscopy in organic chemistry.

In a living organism, the most abundant atom is also hydrogen, most of which will be in the form of water molecules. Thus, it is possible to focus on measuring the spin properties of hydrogen atoms in the water molecules within the body. Different kinds of tissue will form differing chemical environments for the water. Thus, the spatial pattern of different resonant energies may be used to construct an image of the interior of the organism. This is possible because both magnetic fields and radio waves easily penetrate living organisms, like the human body.

It was not an easy step from the first NMR devices in the 1940s to the devices capable of imaging parts of the human body in the 1970s. You can't just stick a person inside an NMR spectrometer and start collecting data. Sophisticated design innovations involving configurations of magnetic fields that varied in precise ways over space and time were necessary before the construction of three-dimensional images became possible. As with CT, computers are needed to manipulate the large quantity of data gathered.

The result is NMR imaging. By the 1980s, NMR imaging was being introduced into hospitals to expand the imaging capacity beyond that of CT. In addition, NMR imaging does not involve exposure to knowingly toxic x-rays. While the impact of exposure to very strong magnetic fields is generally accepted as safe, the jury is still out on that one. However, even if there is some toxicity associated with brief exposures to very strong magnetic fields, it is likely to be far less problematic than exposure to x-rays.

Soon after NMR imaging devices began to be installed in hospitals, the name began to come under criticism; some people were bothered by the N in NMR. While the N simply refers to the atomic nucleus (and its associated spin), some folks heard "nuclear" and inferred an association with nuclear radiation (radioactivity, a generally toxic phenomena) and even nuclear weapons. When a local hospital announced it was installing a modern NMR imaging device to improve its diagnostic capabilities, neighbors would sometimes protest with "we don't want anything nuclear in our neighborhood!" A decision was quickly made to drop the N and simply refer to the process as magnetic resonance imaging, or MRI. An MRI of the brain can yield a sharpness of anatomical detail superior to that of a CT. Normal anatomical struc-

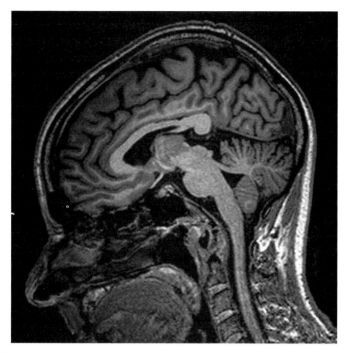

Figure 17.2 MRI of a human brain.

tures, as well as lesions, are often readily visible and quite precisely localizable (Fig. 17.2).

These various methods—x-ray, CT, and MRI—are all ways to generate static, structural pictures of living human brains. Another set of methodologies, the dynamic or functional imaging technologies, measure neural activity within a living brain and provide information about how this activity varies over time and different regions of the brain. How is this accomplished?

When nerve cells send and receive signals, a great deal of electric current flows. The current is produced by the movement of electric charge associated with the flow of ions in axons and dendrites. These moving electrical charges generate electromagnetic fields that pass through the surrounding tissue and are detectable at the surface of the head. If electrodes are attached to the scalp, electric field changes having their origin in the neural activity of the brain can be recorded. The method is called electroencephalography, or EEG. A graph of brain electric field changes as a function of time is called an electroencephalogram, sometimes referred to as a brain wave.

EEG gives a measure of neural activity averaged over large regions of the cerebral cortex. Because of the electrical conductivity of the brain and the skin, the electric fields generated by neural activity get distorted and smooshed around as they pass from their source locations within the brain to the surface of the scalp where they are recorded. Thus, EEG may not be the best method for precise measurement of the locations of neural activity in the brain.

Figure 17.3. Cap with sixty-four electrodes for EEG recording.

A crude EEG can be recorded using only two electrodes attached to a person's head. However, EEGs typically use a larger number of electrodes to obtain more interesting and precise recordings. By using as many as 64 or 128 electrodes, it is possible to obtain a rough localization of some of the sources of neural activity in the brain (Fig. 17.3). And although spatial resolution is limited, EEG is marvelous for time resolution. It is possible to measure changes in electrical activity that are taking place on a millisecond time scale.

A typical EEG recording is a mixture of a number of different frequencies of electrical oscillation (Fig. 17.4). Various frequency ranges have been given Greek-letter designations: delta (<4 Hz), theta (4–7 Hz), alpha (8–15 Hz), beta (16–30 Hz), and gamma (>30 Hz). A Fourier analysis (see Chapter 15) may be conducted on EEG data to elucidate the various frequency components that contribute to the overall brain wave.

The first EEG recording from a human brain was made in the 1920s by Hans Berger (1873–1941), a German physician who also gave the EEG its name. Berger's interest in studying the brain was catalyzed by a powerful experience he had as a young man. After beginning studies in mathematics and astronomy at the University of Berlin, Berger took a break from big-city college life by enlisting for a year of military service in 1892.

One spring morning, while mounted on horseback and pulling heavy artillery for a military training exercise, Berger's horse suddenly reared, throwing the young man to the ground on a narrow bank just in front of the wheel of an artillery gun. The horse-drawn battery stopped at the last second, and Berger escaped certain death with no more than a bad fright. That same evening, he received a telegram from his father, inquiring about his son's well being. Berger later learned that his older sister in Coburg was over-whelmed by an ominous feeling on the morning of the accident and she had

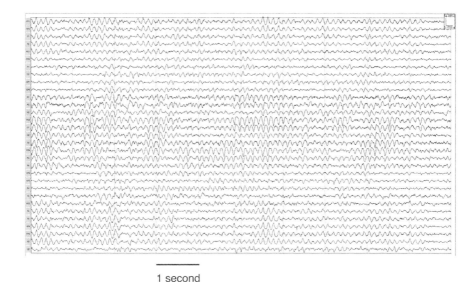

1 second

Figure 17.4. Human EEG recorded simultaneously from thirty-one electrodes.

urged their father to contact young Hans, convinced that something terrible had happened to him. He had never before received a telegram from his family, and Berger struggled to understand this incredible coincidence based on principles of natural science. There seemed to be no escaping the conclusion that Berger's intense feelings of terror had assumed a physical form and reached his sister several hundred miles away—in other words, Berger and his sister had communicated by mental telepathy. Berger never forgot this experience, and it marked the starting point of a life-long career in psychophysics.

After his stint in the military, Berger resumed his university studies but switched to the study of medicine, with the intent to investigate the human brain and its relation to mind. He hoped to uncover physical mechanisms related to his sister's presumed telepathic experience at the time of his accident (*telepathy* = feeling at a distance; Greek *tele* = distant, *pathos* = feeling, suffering).

In the 1940s and 1950s, the neurosurgeon Wilder Penfield recorded electrical activity directly from the cerebral cortex of people who had their brain exposed during surgeries (as mentioned in Chapter 16). This allowed for much higher resolution of the locations of neural activity. Penfield was initially interested in mapping regions in which seizures originated, in order to carefully excise epileptogenic (seizure-generating) tissue. He soon appreciated that he could determine, more precisely than previously possible, the relationship between regions of the cortex and various functions, such as sensory perception, muscle movement, language generation, and language comprehension.

This direct-from-the-brain recording has continued to be developed into a highly refined technique called electrocorticography, or ECoG. This technique is used in some situations before brain surgeries in which epileptogenic tissue is to be removed.

At the same time as the precise location of epileptogenic tissue is being mapped with an array of ECoG electrodes, neurosurgeons and neuroscientists may collaborate to address interesting questions about the function and dynamic activity of the cortex.

Electricity and magnetism are intimately connected. Electric currents, for example, generate magnetic fields. The magnetic fields induced by the electric currents associated with neural activity can be measured in the vicinity of the head. The result is another kind of brain wave, called a magnetoencephalogram, named by analogy with the electroencephalogram. The technique used to make the measurement is called magnetoencephalography, or MEG.

The magnetic fields associated with neural activity in the human brain measure about 1 picotesla (10^{-12} tesla) at the surface of the skull. This is a very small amplitude—Earth's magnetic field, approximately 50 microteslas (50 $\times$ 10^{-6} tesla), is about fifty million times stronger. Ambient magnetic noise in an urban environment (due primarily to electricity moving through power lines and other wiring) is in the range of 0.1 microtesla (10^{-7} tesla), about 100,000 times stronger than the magnetic fields generated by brain activity. Thus, the two primary hurdles that must be negotiated in MEG are constructing very sensitive detectors of magnetic fields and shielding the whole measurement process from ambient electromagnetic noise.

Shielding is accomplished by building rooms made of metals that are resistant to penetration from magnetic fields, and by using elaborate electronic systems to measure and cancel sources of magnetic noise. This is analogous to noise-canceling headphones—the physical structure of the headphone over the ear blocks much of the ambient sound, and the noise-cancellation electronic circuitry cancels out much more. To detect the very weak magnetic fields generated by neural activity in the brain, MEG uses something called a SQUID, an acronym for superconducting quantum interference device. SQUID detectors are based on properties of superconducting currents in the presence of magnetic fields. They were first constructed in the 1960s, and soon after their construction they were applied to the detection of magnetic fields generated by brain activity.

All this shielding and measurement technology ends up making MEG a pretty expensive undertaking, far more expensive than high-resolution EEG. In addition, the computational challenges in reconstructing the location of sources of neural activity in the brain are also formidable. These things serve to limit the widespread application of MEG.

Another technology for imaging dynamic activity in the brain is positron emission tomography, or PET. This technique uses the properties of particular radioactive chemicals to visualize cellular activity in the brain. Let's talk about radioactivity—radiation, radiate, radiant, ray. To shine; to emit; to glow; to extend out from the center—a radius. Every chemical element exists in several varieties, called isotopes, some of which are unstable and undergo radioactive decay.

A chemical element is defined by the number of protons in its atomic nucleus, its atomic number: one for hydrogen, two for helium, three for lithium, six for carbon, seven for nitrogen, eight for oxygen, eleven for sodium, twenty for calcium, twenty-six for iron, eighty-eight for radium, ninety-two for uranium, ninety-nine for einsteinium, and so forth (see Chapter 3). In addition to protons, all atomic nuclei contain neutrons—the only exception being the lightest isotope of hydrogen, consisting of a single proton and no neutrons. The sum of the number of protons and the number of neutrons for a given atom is called the atomic mass. Each chemical element, defined by a specific number of nuclear protons, will have several different isotopes characterized by different numbers of neutrons in their nuclei.

Some combinations of protons and neutrons are stable and don't decay, and others are unstable and will transform by emitting a high-energy particle of one kind or another. This is radioactive decay, and radioactivity is the name given to the high-energy particles emitted by atoms during the decay process. There are several kinds of radioactive decay: alpha decay, when an unstable nucleus emits a blob made of two protons and two neutrons; beta decay, when an unstable nucleus emits either an electron or a positron; and gamma decay, when an unstable nucleus emits a gamma-ray photon.

PET uses unstable elements that undergo beta decay by emitting a positron. The result is a new element that has the same atomic mass but is one unit lower in atomic number. This is because the loss of a positive charge in the form of a positron (e^+) effectively converts one of the nuclear protons into a neutron. PET currently uses radioactive forms of the elements carbon, oxygen, and fluorine—the isotopes carbon-11, oxygen-15, and fluorine-18. (The numbers give the atomic masses of the isotopes. For example, carbon-11 has 6 protons—because carbon is defined as having 6 protons—and 11 minus 6 = 5 neutrons. The most common isotope of carbon is carbon-12, with 6 protons and 6 neutrons. Carbon-12 is stable and does not decay.) Here are the decay formulas and half-lives for the three PET isotopes:

$$\text{carbon-11} \rightarrow \text{boron-11} + e^+ \text{ (half-life} \sim 20 \text{ minutes)}$$

$$\text{oxygen-15} \rightarrow \text{nitrogen-15} + e^+ \text{ (half-life} \sim 2 \text{ minutes)}$$

$$\text{fluorine-18} \rightarrow \text{oxygen-18} + e^+ \text{ (half-life} \sim 110 \text{ minutes)}$$

PET uses a fundamental property of the positron—it is the antimatter particle (antiparticle) corresponding to the electron. When a particle encounters its corresponding antiparticle, there is a complete annihilation of the mass of both particles, converting all the mass into energy (according to $E = mc^2$). When a positron is emitted via radioactive decay, it will very quickly encounter an electron (because electrons are everywhere in normal matter) and annihilate. The resulting energy of this positron–electron annihilation emerges as two high-energy gamma-ray photons flying off in exactly opposite directions. By placing gamma-ray detectors all around the region where the radioactive material is located and watching for photons emerging simultaneously and exactly 180 degrees apart, it is possible, by a sort of triangulation, to rather precisely determine the source of the radioactive decay.

The first isotope used for PET was fluorine-18. A radioactive variant of glucose can be made by replacing one of the oxygen atoms in the sugar with fluorine-18. Glucose is transported via the blood throughout the body, and all cells in the body use glucose as an energy source. Cells that are working harder use more glucose. In particular, nerve cells that are more robustly generating signals in the form of action potentials require more glucose to make the ATP needed to operate their Na/K pumps and maintain membrane potential. Thus, the more active the neuron, the more glucose it will take up from the blood.

If glucose radioactively labeled with fluorine-18 is injected into a person's circulatory system, it will flow throughout the body and be absorbed into cells just as if it is normal glucose. However, once inside the cell, the fluorinated glucose is recognized as an imposter and can no longer participate in the chemical reactions leading to energy generation. It accumulates in the cell, and that cell becomes a hot spot of radioactivity. By detecting radioactive hot spots in the brain of a person injected with radioactively labeled glucose, locations of greatest neural activity can be determined. This is precisely what PET does.

A PET scanner consists of an array of many detectors designed to measure gamma rays. The person lies in the scanner, the head surrounded by these detectors. The person is injected with radioactive (fluorine-18) glucose, and the location of the radioactive glucose in the brain is determined by measuring the sites of positron decay—sweet.

Another PET scan method uses radioactive water (H_2O) in which the oxygen is O-15, the isotope of oxygen that decays by positron emission. Radioactive water is injected into the subject's blood. It flows throughout the body. It so happens that the brain adjusts the flow of blood within it so that regions generating more neural signals, and thus requiring more energy, receive a more robust flow of blood. The regions receiving a more robust flow of blood will also have a larger quantity of radioactive water. The flow of radioactive water, and thus the flow of blood, can be measured in the PET scanner by detecting the gamma-ray photons resulting from the positron decay of oxygen-15. Thus, both fluorine-18 glucose and oxygen-15 water can be used to measure the amount of neural activity in different regions of the brain.

The radioactive carbon-11 isotope is used in a different way. Suppose one wants to measure the locations of dopamine receptors in a person's brain. One may choose a molecule that sticks to dopamine receptors (as an agonist or antagonist), make that molecule radioactive by replacing one of the carbons in the molecule with carbon-11, then inject it into the person's bloodstream. If the molecule crosses the blood–brain barrier and enters the brain, it will preferentially accumulate on dopamine receptors because of its affinity for these receptors. The distribution of the receptors in the brain can then be determined by measuring the locations of radioactive decay with PET.

The positron-emitting radioactive isotopes tend to have rather short half-lives, ranging from 2 minutes to 2 hours. How is it possible to do experiments with such unstable substances? The only way is for the positron-emitting isotopes to be made on the spot and then quickly incorporated into the desired molecular form and administered to the subject in the PET measurement. The device used to make these radioactive atoms is called a cyclotron. It is a gadget that was first constructed by Ernest Lawrence (1901–1958) at the University of California, Berkeley, around 1930. A cyclotron can accelerate charged particles (like atomic nuclei) to very high velocities by using oscillating electromagnetic fields to impart energy to the charged particles as they move round and round in a circular path. Such speeding particles can be smashed into other atoms, and sometimes, under certain conditions, they will stick together and new atoms will be formed. Cyclotrons are used to produce the various radioactive isotopes used in PET.

Flashback to the periodic table of elements: Around 1940 physicists at UC Berkeley discovered that cyclotrons could be used to produce chemical elements heavier than any ever before seen in nature. At that time, uranium, with atomic number 92, was the heaviest chemical element known to exist on Earth. By bombarding heavy elements like uranium with protons, deuterons, alpha particles, and so forth, that had been accelerated to high velocities in a cyclotron, they found that ever heavier elements could be formed. And thus the periodic table was extended into the transuranium region: neptunium, plutonium, americium, curium, berkelium, californium, einsteinium, fermium, mendelevium—elements 93, 94, 95, 96, 97, 98, 99, 100, 101—all were discovered at UC Berkeley during the 1940s and 1950s, most of them using the cyclotron to smash atoms into one another at very high velocity.

A PET scan is a complex and expensive process. Highly unstable radioactive chemicals must be generated on the spot using a cyclotron. The radioactive atoms must then be chemically incorporated into glucose, or water, or a particular neurotransmitter-like labeling molecule, to be administered to the PET-scan subject. The injection is performed and the measurement of gamma rays resulting from positron-electron annihilation is conducted. And it all needs to be done rapidly, before a substantial amount of the short-lived radioactive chemicals decay away. And another important thing—a person undergoing a PET scan receives injections of radioactive material, a significant toxic exposure. All this contributes to PET scanning being used only in limited ways.

PET may be used to generate a map of neural activity in the brain under various conditions. Such a map can be constructed based on either glucose use (as measured by the accumulation of radioactive fluorinated glucose) or blood flow (as measured by flow of radioactive water). By using radioactive glucose, estimates can be made regarding the brain's total energy consumption. This shows that a great deal of energy use and neural activity occurs in the brain at all times. When you are sitting in the dark, eyes closed, no sound, not moving, not thinking about anything in particular, not doing any task, your brain is very active and using glucose at a robust rate. If you then turn on the lights, listen to music, move your arms, read out loud, and so forth, energy consumption in the brain increases by only a tiny amount (a few percent, at most) in particular regions. The upshot: the brain is working really hard all the time. What exactly all this activity is for is currently largely unknown, and the term "dark energy," borrowed from cosmology, has been used to highlight this mystery.

The last of the dynamic brain imaging methods to be discussed here is functional magnetic resonance imaging, or fMRI. This technique uses the same MRI technology discussed above in the context of structural brain imaging, but fMRI employs a new twist—collecting a series of magnetic resonance images over time and looking at something that changes as neural activity changes in the brain. What is that something?

Cells derive most of their energy from the breakdown of glucose using oxygen—similar to the process of obtaining energy by burning carbon-containing molecules with oxygen in combustion engines, furnaces, stoves, and campfires. As discussed in the context of PET, the flow of blood within the brain is regulated such that flow increases in regions of greater neural activity, delivering more glucose and oxygen to active cells.

Hemoglobin is the oxygen-carrying protein in red blood cells. Oxygen binds to the hemoglobin molecule in the lungs and comes off the hemoglobin at locations all over the body, where oxygen is needed to power the activity of cells. And hemoglobin produces a different magnetic perturbation effect on its local environment depending on whether or not oxygen is attached to the hemoglobin molecule. Regions exhibiting increased neural activity have a greater influx of oxygenated hemoglobin, and subsequent conversion to its deoxygenated form. This change in blood oxygenation can be measured by looking at the magnetic resonance signal of hydrogen atoms in H_2O molecules that are in the vicinity of hemoglobin molecules in the blood. This change is captured in a parameter called the BOLD signal, where BOLD stands for blood-oxygen-level dependence. The BOLD signal is essentially a measure of the increased flow of blood into regions of the brain that are more neurally active.

The spatial resolution of fMRI is pretty good; areas of increased neural activity can, in the best of circumstances, be localized down to within about 1 millimeter. The time resolution of fMRI at present is several seconds. EEG has much faster time resolution (milliseconds) but relatively poor spatial resolution (several centimeters). An innovative technique records measurements from both fMRI and EEG at the same time and makes correspondences between them. This requires special attention to the many technical issues of how the gadgets involved in fMRI and EEG impact each other's function.

This table summarizes the relative spatial and temporal resolutions of several methods of functional brain imaging.

Imaging method	Spatial resolution	Temporal resolution
EEG	several cm	milliseconds
MEG	mm	milliseconds
fMRI	mm	seconds
PET	cm	seconds to minutes

Picture of the brain—
x-ray, CAT, and MRI.
What is to come next?

CHAPTER 18

Connectivity, Language, and Meaning

In the two million years between *Homo habilis* and us, the size of the hominin brain has doubled, and much of this increase is related to expansion of the cerebrum. We share a convoluted cerebral cortex with a number of other mammals, including apes, elephants, whales, dolphins, coyotes, dogs, and cats. And all mammals, from mice and moles to whales to humans, have layered cerebral cortex containing similar neural circuitry (Fig. 18.1). There is local interconnectivity within and between cortical layers, and there is long-range connectivity between widely separated regions of the cerebrum; for example, neurons in the occipital lobes form connections with neurons in the frontal lobes, and vice versa.

There is extensive connectivity going in both directions between the cerebral cortex and many subcortical structures: thalamus, amygdala, hypothalamus, substantia nigra, ventral tegmentum, locus coeruleus, raphe nuclei, and so on. There are hundreds of trillions of chemical and electrical synapses, and it is likely that no neuron in the human brain is more than a very small number of synapses away from every other neuron in the brain.

Taking our description up from the cellular microcircuitry to a more macroscopic level—what is called *gross anatomy*—the two hemispheres of the human cerebral cortex appear roughly identical. However, differences in function between the two sides of the brain (lateralization of function) are revealed by certain methods of study.

Anosognosia (see Chapter 16) illustrates the concept of lateralization of cerebral cortical function: this syndrome is more often associated with lesions to the right cerebral hemisphere than with damage to the left cerebral hemisphere. The perception of faces, too, is known to differ in the involvement of the right and left hemispheres. Prosopagnosia, for example (see Chapter 14), is more often associated with right- than with left-hemisphere lesions.

The classic function associated with hemispheric specialization is language—the capacity to communicate using signs, sounds, and gestures that have understood meanings. Language is one of the most elaborate and sophisticated aspects of human behavior, far different from anything known to occur in other animals. Consider the

 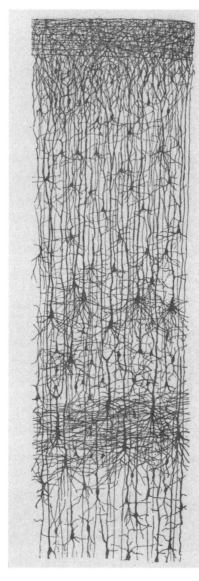

Figure 18.1. Cell layers in the human cerebral cortex made visible using Nissl stain (left), a dye that colors cell bodies but not axons and dendrites, and Golgi stain (right), which stains only a small fraction of the neurons but stains the axons and dendrites as well as the cell bodies. Drawings by Ramón y Cajal.

three words: I, know, you. Now consider the sentence: "I know." And now: "I know you know." And now: "I know you know I know." And now: "I know you know I know you know." Using only these three words, we can continue to build sentences of unending complexity, where each addition changes the meaning of the statement in subtle but significant ways. Language is more than just word meanings (semantics). There are also rules (syntax) that determine the construction of meaningful phrases and sentences. We may take it for granted, but really, it's an amazing feat!

It has long been appreciated that individuals may experience specific problems in their ability to speak, write, or understand language after suffering a stroke or other injury to the brain. *Aphasia* refers to neurologically based impairment in language

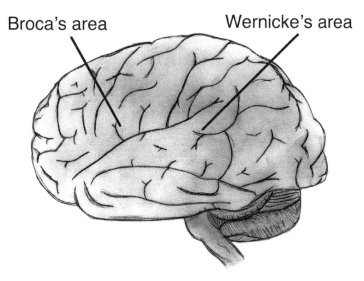

Figure 18.2. Cortical language areas.

function. A pioneer in investigating the neuroanatomy of language was the French physician Paul Broca (1824–1880). In the mid-1800s Broca performed postmortem studies of patients who had developed aphasias as a result of brain injuries sustained during their lifetimes. He found an association between lesions in the left frontal lobe and the capacity to speak. "Broca's aphasia" is now used to describe a condition in which a person has problems with the production of spoken and written language. Such an aphasia of language production is often associated with lesions in the left frontal premotor area of the brain, a region called Broca's area (Fig. 18.2).

A person with Broca's aphasia is not paralyzed. The muscles controlling movement of their mouth and tongue, for example, are all working. The person can make sounds, often even component sounds of words. However, she cannot organize her mouth and tongue movements to produce language. She cannot speak. Similarly, while her hands and fingers are not paralyzed, she is not able to organize arm, hand, and finger movements so as to produce written language. Broca's aphasia is a motor apraxia specific to language. Like other motor apraxias, it is associated with lesions to the frontal premotor areas.

Another kind of aphasia was described by the German physician Carl Wernicke (1848–1905). In Wernicke's aphasia there is a problem with the comprehension of spoken and written language. Although hearing and vision are unimpaired, a patient with Wernicke's aphasia cannot understand—cannot interpret the meaning of— spoken and written language. Wernicke found this kind of aphasia to be associated with lesions in a region of the posterior left temporal lobe that has come to be called Wernicke's area.

Wernicke's aphasia is a sensory agnosia specific to language. Like other sensory agnosias, it is associated with lesions in the cortical regions near where the temporal, parietal, and occipital lobes come together. This area of the brain is involved in integration and interpretation of a variety of different kinds of sensory information, coming from the visual, auditory, and tactile channels. Although patients with Wernicke's aphasia can often speak and write, often their spoken and written language is garbled, sometimes even to the point of being incomprehensible: twilight car hill frosted gasoline does remarkable planetary hum pizza.

The findings of Broca and Wernicke in the nineteenth century suggested that the brain regions involved in human language are located primarily in the left cerebral hemisphere. Another century of paying attention to the connection between symptoms of aphasia and locations of brain lesions demonstrated that, although aphasias are more often associated with lesions to the left cerebral hemisphere than to the right, both hemispheres are involved in language. In most people, nonetheless, the left side of the cerebral cortex is the dominant hemisphere for language production and comprehension.

In some people suffering from severe seizure disorders, small regions of the cerebral cortex can be pinpointed as the loci of generation of seizures (see Chapter 7). Procedures have been developed to surgically locate and excise such regions to reduce the onset and severity of debilitating and life-threatening seizures. Frequently such seizure loci are in the temporal lobes, and in performing an excision procedure the surgeon takes great care to avoid damaging areas of the cortex involved in language. For this reason, it is essential to know whether the primary language areas in a surgical patient are in the left hemisphere, the right hemisphere, or both.

To make this determination, a presurgical test for determining the language-dominant cerebral hemisphere was developed in the 1940s by neurologist Juhn Wada (b. 1924). Wada very carefully injected a small dose of a sedative-hypnotic barbiturate drug, such as amobarbital (see Chapter 9), into either the right or left carotid artery. While the drug is being injected, the patient is asked to count: one, two, three, four, five, . . . Within seconds, the barbiturate infuses the cortex on one side of the brain and produces widespread inhibition of neuronal activity. If the drug reaches a part of the brain involved in language production, in this case speaking, the patient immediately stops counting and is unable to resume until the effects of the drug begin to dissipate, several minutes later. However, if the drug has been injected into the non-language-dominant hemisphere, then as the sedative-hypnotic infuses the cortex there is a slight hesitation as the effects of the drug are felt, followed quickly by resumption of counting. Since its inception in 1949, the Wada test for the lateralization of language has been administered to thousands of patients as a prelude to brain surgery. These days it has been largely replaced with noninvasive brain imaging procedures such as magnetoencephalography and functional magnetic resonance imaging (see Chapter 17).

From many years of gathering data obtained from stroke lesions, Wada tests, and, more recently, functional brain imaging, it is possible to draw some general conclusions about the cerebral lateralization of language. As expected, most people have left-hemisphere language dominance. However, there is a relationship between handedness and lateralization of language. For right-handed people, approximately 97 percent have left-hemisphere language dominance, and 3 percent have right-hemisphere language dominance. For non-right-handed (meaning left-handed and ambidextrous) people, approximately 70 percent have left-hemisphere language dominance, 15 percent have right-hemisphere language dominance, and 15 percent have substantial language control by both hemispheres.

Functional brain imaging has also provided additional information as to precisely which cortical regions are active during various activities related to language. When listening to spoken language, not surprisingly, neurons are activated in the primary auditory cortex, A1, just as would happen for any kind of analysis of sound by the auditory system. If the sounds have a linguistic quality to them—that is, if they seem to be words strung together in ways that might have meaning—then in addition to A1, Wernicke's area is also active. This is true even if the language being heard is a foreign tongue that is not understood by the listener. Wernicke's area may be considered a secondary or higher-order auditory area, involved in analysis of sounds with language-like properties.

Finally, if the language is one that is understood by the listener—that is, if the words actually carry meaning for the listener—then, in addition to activity in A1 and Wernicke's areas, there is also activity in Broca's area in the frontal lobe. This was a bit of a surprise when it was first discovered, because for many years Broca's area was assumed to be exclusively a motor area. We now know that activity in Broca's area is not restricted to speaking and writing but is also relevant for listening, reading, and understanding language. Neurons in Broca's area are in fact premotor mirror neurons, active when observing (reading, listening, and understanding) language, as well as when generating (writing and speaking) language.

Mirror neurons connect perception with action in a very direct way. Observations of grasping and touching are connected with the motor actions and (presumably) subjective experiences related to grasping and touching. Learning these associations between perception, movement, and mental experience is what gives meaning to perceptions and actions. Neural networks involved in moving the tongue and mouth, and the fingers and hands, allow us to learn associations between vocalizations, hand movements, and perceptions—hence, language.

In the 1960s and 1970s, elegant work by Roger Sperry (1913–1994) and his students revealed a great deal of information about lateralization of cerebral function for a variety of human behaviors. Sperry worked with patients who suffered from severe epilepsy, in which seizures propagated across the corpus callosum from one hemisphere to the other and in so doing disabled large parts of the brain. Because of the severity of their condition, a small number of these patients underwent a surgical procedure in which their corpus callosum was severed, disconnecting direct neural communication between the two hemispheres of the cerebral cortex. This operation, called a corpus callosotomy, substantially reduced the frequency and intensity of seizures and may have been a life-saving surgery. A person who has had this surgery is sometimes referred to as a split-brain patient, because the brain has literally been split in two at the level of the cerebral cortex.

The corpus callosum is a large bundle of axons connecting the right and left hemispheres of cerebral cortex in mammalian brains. In humans, it spans several centimeters in the interior of the brain and consists of approximately two hundred million axons. Experiments with monkeys and dogs had shown that cutting the corpus callosum appeared to have little impact on the animal's behavior, leading neurosurgeons to believe that the callosotomy procedure could be safely performed on humans. And indeed, superficially it is hard to tell that there is anything amiss with a split-brain patient. But if you look carefully, as Sperry did, some dramatic effects of the surgery are revealed.

Sperry's experimental setup was very simple. The patient sat in a chair and looked at the center of a small screen. Onto the screen a projector would briefly flash pictures or words into either the patient's left or right visual field. If the picture is shown in the left visual field, then that visual information goes to the right hemisphere of the brain (Fig. 18.3). In a normal person, the information associated with the visual stimulus is rapidly relayed across the corpus callosum and is available to both hemispheres after a very brief period of time. However, in a split-brain patient, the visual information is only in the hemisphere contralateral to where the picture had been flashed and is not shared between hemispheres.

Now consider the following experiment. A picture of a spoon is flashed into the split-brain patient's right visual field. The visual information goes to the person's left cerebral hemisphere. The patient is asked to report what he saw on the screen. He answers correctly, saying he saw a spoon. However, if the picture of a spoon is flashed into the patient's left visual field and he is asked to report what he saw, he

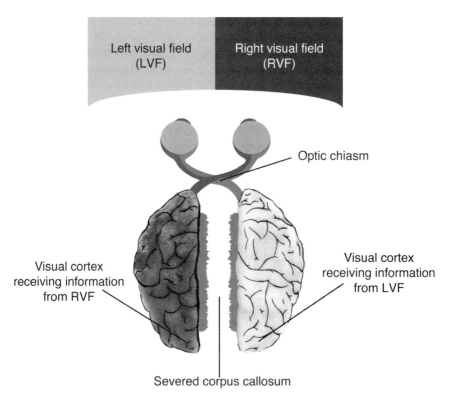

Figure 18.3. In a split-brain patient the axons of the corpus callosum are severed, eliminating direct communication between the two hemispheres of the cerebral cortex. Visual sensory information from the left or right visual field goes only to the contralateral hemisphere and is not shared between the two hemispheres.

can't say. He may simply answer with "I don't know." This finding is consistent with language expression lateralized to the left hemisphere in most people. Even though the person may have known that he saw a spoon, he can't utter the word.

In fact, he does know he saw a spoon. This can be demonstrated by allowing the person to select from among several objects that he can feel using his left hand. Tactile perception by and movement of the left hand is under the control of the right hemisphere. Thus, visual information that enters from the left visual field will be shared by the brain circuitry controlling the left hand. The objects being felt are hidden from view behind a screen, for if the person were to look at them while choosing, both hemispheres would have access to the identities of the objects.

Another variant of this experiment has the subject looking at a visual display in which two different pictures are flashed, one to the right visual field and another different one to the left visual field. For example, a picture of a spoon might be flashed to the right visual field, and a picture of a pencil flashed to the left visual field. The split-brain patient is then instructed to select the object she saw from among several objects she can feel with her hands behind a screen.

As expected, she will select a spoon with her right hand and a pencil with her left hand. However, when asked to say what she saw, she will say only that she saw a spoon. She cannot say that she saw a pencil, because that information (from the left visual field) only went to the nonspeaking right hemisphere. At this point, you instruct the person to remove her hands, together with the objects she selected, from behind the screen. Now the left hemisphere sees and becomes aware of the pencil. You ask why she chose a pencil with her left hand, because she was only supposed to choose the object she had seen on the screen. The patient might say "I don't know." However, sometimes the patient will make up a story, perhaps something like, "Well, I picked up the pencil so that I could write down a list of the things I wanted to eat with the spoon."

That's really interesting! There have been many variations of experiments like this where split-brain subjects are presented with conflicting information to their two cerebral hemispheres. It is clear that the right hemisphere is quite capable of decisions, judgments, and so forth, but just can't speak about what it is up to. In such circumstances, the verbal left hemisphere may make up a story to explain the situation. This is reminiscent of the behavior of anosognosia patients, in which the non-damaged left hemisphere may create stories to explain away the damage resulting from the right-hemisphere lesion.

This may also relate to what is happening when psychological defense mechanisms are operating. Psychological defenses, as described by Sigmund Freud (1856–1939) and others, are cognitive strategies we use to protect ourselves from experiencing thoughts and feelings that might provoke anxiety or otherwise bothersome feelings. Such strategies may be stories (rationalization, projection, reaction formation, and so forth) or out-and-out forgetting (repression, suppression). Importantly, these strategies are out of our awareness—that is, they are unconscious—in that we are not aware of the motivations for the defensive action. Whether Freudian defenses use some of the same underlying neurology as what is happening in split-brain patients and anosognosia is unknown, but there certainly are significant behavioral similarities.

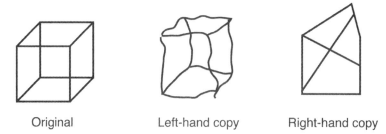

Original   Left-hand copy   Right-hand copy

Figure 18.4. Drawing (left) as copied by a split-brain patient with his left hand and his right hand.

Picture this: a right-handed split-brain patient is shown the drawing on the left in Figure 18.4 and asked to copy it, once using his left hand and once using his right hand. The drawing to be copied is presented on a piece of paper, and the patient can look at it for as long as he wants and continue looking while doing the copying. He is moving his eyes and head around while looking at the drawing, so the visual information is going to both sides of his brain, to both cerebral hemispheres. Even though the patient is right-handed, note that the drawing made with his left hand more accurately represents the overall shape of the original. What's going on?

Motor control, like sensory perception, is contralateral—the right hand is controlled by the left hemisphere, and the left hand is controlled by the right hemisphere. These kinds of results suggest that the right hemisphere is superior to the left in dealing with global spatial analysis, in this case, the judgment and rendering of the three-dimensional perspectival aspect of this simple drawing.

From the collective findings of many experiments of this type, a picture has emerged regarding lateralization of particular functions in the human brain. In general, and especially in right-handed individuals, the left hemisphere is superior to the right for language comprehension and expression, numeric reasoning and arithmetic calculation, and visual detail. Conversely, the right hemisphere is generally superior to the left for nonverbal aspects of communication, such as linguistic prosody (rhythm, intonation), tone of voice, and body language, and for visual perspective and larger-scale spatial patterns and relations, what might be called visual gestalt. The functions between the two hemispheres are not completely separated; it's just that one hemisphere is more involved than the other for certain tasks.

The separate hemispheres of a split-brain patient have clearly been demonstrated to each competently carry out tasks. Are the two cerebral hemispheres in a split-brain patient each separately conscious? Does each hemisphere experience a separate awareness of "what it is like to be?"

The neural conditions sufficient for manifestation of conscious awareness (subjective experience) are often referred to as neural correlates of consciousness (NCC). Such correlates have not been characterized. Thus, it is not straightforward to ask and obtain an answer to a question of the form: does the nonspeaking right hemisphere of a split-brain patient exhibit conscious awareness? Or, more generally, is a patient in a coma or vegetative state consciously aware? What about when asleep, or while sedated by general anesthesia?

Among speculations on the nature of the NCC, manifestations of connectivity are generally held as prime contenders. One proposal for a neural correlate of consciousness has been high-frequency (gamma-range) synchronous electrical oscillation over widespread regions of the cerebral cortex, linking or binding together neural activity in many different cortical regions. Another hypothesis for NCC is that electrodynamic interconnection in the brain must be of a kind of complexity that maximizes the way information interacts—a kind of maximally "integrated" information.

The human cerebral cortex—if it were to be unfolded, smoothing out all the gyri and sulci—is approximately 2.5 square feet, or 2,300 square centimeters, about the size of a circular pizza 21 inches in diameter. The average thickness of the gray matter of our cerebral cortex is around 3 millimeters. Multiplying this by the cortical area yields a volume of 690,000 cubic millimeters. The approximate number of neurons and glial cells in the human cerebral cortex is currently estimated to be twenty billion and forty billion, respectively. This means that each cubic millimeter of cerebral cortex in the human brain has approximately thirty thousand neurons and sixty thousand glial cells (Fig. 18.5). This densely packed region of neurons and glia, together with all the multitudinous axonal and dendritic fibers and astrocytic processes, is called *neuropil* (Greek *pilos* = hair). When looked at with the high

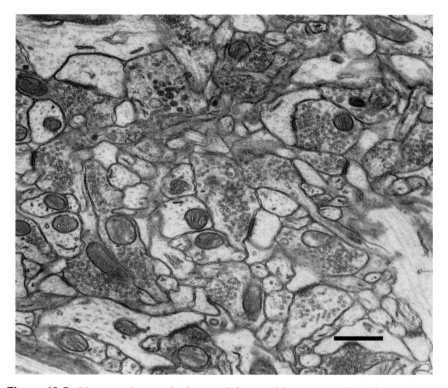

Figure 18.5. Electron micrograph of neuropil from rat hippocampus. Dendrites, axons, and cell bodies are shown in cross section. Many mitochondria and neurotransmitter storage vesicles are visible. Scale bar = 1 micrometer.

magnification of an electron microscope, neuropil appears as a dense mass of solidly packed structures. Whatever gaps exist betwixt and between structures are very narrow, at most 20 nanometers or so. There are numerous chemical and electrical synapses—perhaps upwards of one hundred million synapses in a mere cubic millimeter of neuropil.

All these cells and sub-cellular structures are replete with flowing charged particles and are generating electromagnetic fields—fields that influence the activity of nearby neurons. These electric fields are called *local field potentials,* and their influence on nearby neurons is known as *ephaptic coupling* (Greek *ep* = near, *haptein* = touch). Chemical synapses, electrical synapses, local field potentials, and ephaptic coupling—neuropil is an electrodynamic structure of extraordinary complexity. The various oscillations recorded in electroencephalography (EEG) and electrocorticography, from slow delta oscillations to high-frequency synchrony at greater than 100 Hz, reflect the symphony of complex interactions in the neuropil. This high density of constant activity is responsible for most of the energy consumption of the brain—the "dark energy" of cellular activity that is going, going, going, all the time. This activity is modulated and perturbed by signals entering the brain via pathways from the various sensory organs.

Brains embody structural and functional complexity that has been honed over hundreds of millions of years of evolutionary experimentation and refinement. The notion that we will be able to figure out the human brain by mapping the locations of all the cells and all of their connections, and perhaps even construct a kind of replica using integrated circuits, vastly underestimates the nuance and complexity of what is going on. That's not to say that great progress can, will, and is being made in understanding the structure and operation of brains, and many different approaches are contributing to this progress. Nonetheless, what is going on within the unfathomable complexity of neuropil, while intuitively graspable, is beyond detailed description within our current understanding of neurophysiology.

What has come to be called the field of neurodynamics is an endeavor to describe these processes involving large numbers of neurons and their interactions. EEG is used to measure the collective electrodynamic activity of large numbers of neurons, and the language of mathematics is used to model and describe the complexities of how activity in millions and billions of cells creates large-scale coherent electrical oscillation in the brain—global activity that in turn impacts the local activity of individual neurons. One of the founders of neurodynamics, Walter J. Freeman (1927-2016), has put it this way:

> For centuries brains have been described as dynamic systems, beginning with Descartes, who conceived the pineal as a kind of valve used by the soul to regulate the pumping of spiritual fluid into the muscles. . . . This was followed by metaphors of clocks, telegraph and telephone systems, thermodynamics (which underlay Darwinian "nerve energy" and the Freudian "Id"), digital computers, and holographs. Yet brains are not "like" any artificial machine. If anything, they are "like" natural self-organizing processes such as stars and hurricanes. With the guidance and constraint of genes, they create and maintain their structures while exchanging matter and energy with their surrounds. They are unique in the way they move themselves through their personal spaces and incorporate facets of their environments for their own purposes, to flourish and reproduce their kind.

In his work—more than sixty years of focusing on the question of how brains operate—Freeman has kept their unfathomable complexity front and center.

Here's a plausible neurodynamic scenario of what happens during sensory perception and action: Sensory information coded as sequences of action potentials in specific neural fibers enters the brain via the spinal cord and cranial nerves and soon reaches the olfactory bulbs, brainstem, thalamus, and cerebral cortex. Once in the cortical neuropil things get wild and crazy, with sensory-evoked action potentials having widespread impact on the global activity of the cerebral cortex. The ongoing cortical activity may reside at the edges of stability, in metastable states poised to react to perturbations from incoming signals and make transitions from one state of global oscillatory activity to another.

Freeman proposes that cerebrocortical neuropil may be described at the neurodynamic level as a uniquely unified system capable of undergoing something like "phase transitions" into states of global cooperativity, where aspects of neural activity (at least in part measurable with EEG) are brought together in synchrony across the entire cerebral cortex. The nature of these cooperative states depends upon all the complexity of existing connections in the cortex, a vast network that has been assembled over a lifetime of experience. In this way, the cooperative synchrony of the neuropil functions to access memories related to present states of activity—and these memories inform the evolving experience of the perceptions that develop in association with sensory stimuli. This is what gives a perception *meaning*—linking it with memories (stored knowledge) of prior perceptual experiences. These states of global cooperative synchrony are the neural correlates of consciousness.

The global synchrony within the cortex unites sensory and motor areas and results in action potentials in the motor system. Behavioral actions result. Between sensation, perception, and action are neural processes of unfathomable complexity, involving trillions of synaptic processes and ephaptic couplings in the cortical neuropil. The high level of ongoing brain activity—the dark energy—serves as the substrate for manipulating and coupling sensory input and motor output: perception and action.

To recap: activity in specific neural circuits (for example, signals from sensory organs) impacts large-scale patterns of oscillatory activity in the cortical neuropil, which in turn impacts activity in specific neural circuits (for example, signals to muscles generating movement), which impacts (via efference copy and sensory feedback) global brain states, which effects specific neural circuits, which impacts large-scale oscillatory states, specific circuits, large-scale states, ad infinitum, for a lifetime. And in this continuous linking of sensory information to perception to action, the brain draws upon one's lifetime history of stored knowledge to inform and guide the coupling—which brings us to the topic of memory.

> Sensory inputs—
>   fluid cortical rhythms—
>   actions in the world.

CHAPTER **19**

Memory

Pi (Greek letter π) is defined as the ratio, for any circle, of the circumference to the diameter (Fig. 19.1). Pi can be a source of endless fascination, and rightly so, because it shows up in a great many places in mathematics and physics: Maxwell's equations in electromagnetism, Einstein's gravitational field equations in general relativity, the Schrödinger equation and Heisenberg uncertainty relations in quantum mechanics, descriptions of vibrating or periodic motion of all sorts, and so on. It is a deeply significant number in the mathematical language used to describe the cosmos.

Another aspect of fascination with π is that it is an irrational number—that is, π cannot be represented as a ratio of two integers, and its decimal representation never ends and does not settle into a permanent repeating pattern. Thus, the value of π cannot be computed exactly; it can only be estimated to greater and greater precision, to an increasingly large number of decimal places.

Typically π is approximated as 3.14. To ten decimal places it is 3.1415926535. These approximations suffice for all practical purposes. However, esoteric mathematical formulas have been derived that allow π to be computed to an arbitrary number of decimal places, and computers set to work on these formulas have, as of this writing, calculated π to ten trillion (10^{13}) decimal places!

Enter human memory. Pi geeks have taken on the challenge of memorizing π and vie to be record holder of their school, country, continent, or world. In 1973, the

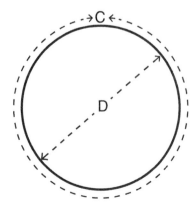

Figure 19.1. Pi is the ratio of circumference (C) to diameter (D): C/D = π.

world record for memorizing digits of π was set and broken several times: 930, then 1,111, then 1,210. By 1978 it was 10,000. By 1980 it was 20,013. From 1987 to 2005 the world record was held by two individuals, both from Japan: first at 40,000 digits and then at 42,195.

In 2005, Lu Chao, who was at the time a twenty-four-year-old student in China, recited from memory 67,890 digits of π. He had attempted to memorize π to 100,000 decimal places and was planning to recite at least 90,000 of them, but he made an error at the 67,891st decimal place, so that was the limit of his world-record performance. At the point he made the error, Lu Chao had been reciting the digits of π for just over twenty-four hours, apparently without a break! Sleep deprivation and general fatigue would certainly dispose him to impaired performance at this point.

This is truly extraordinary memory—but really, even ordinary memory is amazing. The etymological origins of the word *memory* are related to the roots of the word *mind*: Latin *memor* = mindful, remember, and *mens* = mind, understanding. These relations highlight the centrality of memory to the very notion of mental experience. Does it even make sense to have mind without memory? Think about it.

Most everything we do depends upon memory. We remember to eat when we feel hungry—recalling what is safe and perhaps even tasty to eat and how to go about eating it. We remember to drink when we feel thirsty—including what to drink and how to drink it. All animals do these things. We also remember how to walk, run, and sit. We humans remember how to do such things as dress ourselves with clothes, turn lights on and off, ride bicycles, and drive automobiles. We remember how to speak and how to listen—how to articulate our ideas and wishes with language, and how to understand the ideas and wishes of another.

Imagine how weird life would be without any sort of memory—nothing would have meaning, because what something means to us is derived from the remembered history of our interaction with that something. Awareness or consciousness may or may not have been part of this remembered history, but something has been recorded, somewhere.

Memory is certainly among the most impressive of our capabilities. It is operative practically everywhere. For example, the chapters on sensory perception have also been indirectly discussing memory. Our ability to perceive things would not have meaning if we were unable to link perceptual information with stored knowledge about prior perceptual experiences and thus comprehend that a particular perception is similar to something we have smelled, seen, heard, tasted, or touched before.

A famous book about extraordinary memory is the 1965 book *The Mind of a Mnemonist*, written by Russian neuropsychologist Alexander Luria (1902–1977). In this book, Luria describes his investigations of a man he met in the 1920s and knew for more than thirty years. Solomon Shereshevsky (1886–1958)—called "S" in the book—worked as a newspaper reporter when he first came to Luria's attention. S could recall exact details of events, including conversations, years after they happened. Luria found that S could recall very long lists of numbers, letters, or words, without error, years after being asked to learn them.

S had profound synesthesia, a condition characterized by unusual blending of perceptions between different sensory modalities. Sounds may evoke the experience of colors; letters, words, and numbers may evoke experiences of color, sound, taste, smell, and texture. For S, his synesthesia contributed to multisensory images that aided his recall of details:

> Usually I experience a word's taste and weight, and I don't have to make an effort to remember it—the word seems to recall itself. But it's difficult to describe. What I sense is something oily slipping through my fingers . . . or I'm aware of a slight tickling in my left hand caused by a mass of tiny, lightweight points. When that happens I simply remember, without having to make the attempt.

Others, too, have also spoken of the link that sometimes exists between exceptional memory and synesthesia. One synesthete, who set a European record in 2004 by reciting 22,514 digits of π, sees the sequence of digits in π as a vast landscape of shape, color, and texture—wild stuff!

In the simplest analysis, whatever is happening with memory can be deconstructed into two major components: working memory (WM; also called short-term memory) and long-term memory (LTM). Working memories tend to last from seconds to a few minutes (although working memories can last indefinitely if you actively keep thinking about them). WM has a limited capacity: we can hold only so many items in WM at any time—for most people, generally fewer than ten. One way to measure the capacity of WM is to ask someone to repeat back a list of numbers or words immediately after hearing them.

Memories that have been retained in some more permanent manner are stored in LTM. Information may get into LTM by a variety of pathways. One way is by rehearsing items in WM. This is the process by which people would memorize the digits of π, for example. Lu Chao says that it took him a year to memorize the digits of π that he later recalled for his world-record recitation. Repetition assists in encoding memories into LTM. If we repeatedly refer to the same telephone number or street address, we are more likely to recall it later. It is easier to remember the names of people that we see or interact with more frequently. Reviewing information encountered in a book or in class lectures contributes to recalling it later.

Some kinds of information are more easily stored in LTM, things that have significant meaning or emotional salience, for example. And forming links with other information already known greatly contributes to the robustness of LTM storage. This is what "understanding" is—appreciating new knowledge in relation to material already known.

Long-term memory involves information storage and retrieval. Storage is believed to involve some sort of structural change in the nervous system. Newly stored memories in LTM are initially frail and may be readily disrupted. It is often easier to remember things that happened years ago than it is to recall the names of people you just met at a party. New memories become more stable and robust with time—a process called *consolidation* (Latin *con* = together, *solidare* = solid).

Retrieval involves some mechanism of access to the stored memory. Forgetting can occur because of failure of either storage or retrieval. An event may have been experienced—for example, somebody said something to you, sensory processes

registered the sounds, an understanding may have been registered in your WM—
but the information was never retained in LTM. Or, once in LTM, the stored memory may decay or be lost over time, so that there is less and less to retrieve. Or, there
may be some sort of retrieval failure. This is a common experience: we know we
know something, but just can't recall it at the moment, such as someone's name, or
the name of a song or film. It may even be on the "tip of the tongue." In such circumstances, providing a cue, some kind of related information or hint, is often enough
to awaken the memory.

Pathological memory problems are called *amnesias*, which come in two major
categories: retrograde and anterograde. Retrograde amnesia (Latin *retro* = back,
gradi = step) refers to an inability to recall events before the onset of the amnesia.
Memories of past experiences are either lost or unable to be retrieved from LTM.
This is the "Hollywood view" of what memory loss is: someone gets conked on the
head and looses all memory of who they are. Much more common is anterograde
amnesia (Latin *antero* = forward), an inability to recall events after the onset of the
amnesia—such experiences are not retained in LTM. This is really a problem with
learning new information rather than remembering what is already there.

Amnesia may be associated with various kinds of physical injury to the brain:
cellular damage from stroke or seizure, brain tumor, infection (encephalitis), or
traumatic injury sustained in an accident. Surgical excision of brain tissue can result
in amnesia. Electroconvulsive shock therapy (ECT)—a psychiatric procedure in
which seizures are induced in a patient, with the goal of reducing symptoms of
depressed mood—generally produces retrograde amnesia. This is believed to result
from the disruptive action of ECT on memory consolidation, so that more recent,
less consolidated, memories are lost. (The mechanism by which ECT affects mood
is unknown.)

Memory pathology is also a hallmark symptom of *dementia*, a neurological condition characterized by global loss of cognitive abilities—not only memory but
other capacities, such as attention, judgment, planning, problem solving, and motor
coordination. Memory problems in dementia generally begin with anterograde
effects—the inability to retain new information. If the dementia is sufficiently
severe, retrograde memory loss may eventually also develop. Severe dementia is a
deteriorating condition that can result in seriously disorganized behavior, including
even the apparent loss of sense of self, the knowledge of who one is.

Two common forms of dementia are vascular and Alzheimer's. Vascular dementia is associated with the accumulation of cellular damage in the brain related to
impaired blood circulation—generally due to atherosclerosis or repeated small
strokes. Alzheimer's dementia is associated with the presence in the brain of what
are called senile plaques (extracellular deposits of aggregates of a polypeptide called
beta amyloid) and neurofibrillary tangles (aggregates of tau protein, a protein involved
in the assembly and stabilization of microtubules). However, the ultimate causes of
this condition and how to prevent its onset are not presently understood.

A number of drugs are related to memory impairment during periods of use. Most
famous are perhaps the sedative-hypnotics. Alcohol, benzodiazepines, and other
sedative-hypnotic drugs can produce temporary anterograde amnesia. An "alcoholic blackout" is the name given to a state of intoxication in which the drinker is

awake, moving around, engaging in conversation, and so on, but then has no memory of the events the next day. Information apparently never made it into LTM. (Heavy alcohol consumption over extended periods of time is also associated with what may become permanent memory impairment—a dementia—resulting from alcohol-related neurological damage.)

One particular benzodiazepine, midazolam (Versed), is sometimes given in conjunction with medical procedures in which the patient is only partially anesthetized. The anterograde amnesic properties of midazolam impair the person's ability to remember any potentially uncomfortable parts of the procedure. Benzodiazepines are frequently prescribed to treat anxiety or help with sleep, and sometimes people who take benzodiazepines on a regular basis complain of memory impairment.

Nonbenzodiazepine hypnotics prescribed for insomnia, such as zolpidem (Ambien), zaleplon (Sonata), and eszopiclone (Lunesta), can also produce anterograde amnesia. There are even reports of people engaging in strange or dangerous behaviors— such as cooking and eating in the middle of the night, or driving a car in their pajamas—with no memory of the events when they are roused from this weird state of consciousness. (Or, is it unconsciousness? That is, are individuals in such a state even aware of what they are doing, or are they functioning in an unaware robotic mode? It's an interesting and important distinction: conscious, meaning aware, but here not remembering—or unconscious, meaning never aware at all.)

Other drugs known to be associated with memory impairment include cannabis (marijuana), cholesterol-lowering drugs (statins), antiseizure medications, opioids, beta-blockers (prescribed for hypertension), older-generation antihistamines (for example, diphenhydramine [Benadryl], chlorpheniramine), anticholinergics (used to treat urinary incontinence), and tricyclic antidepressant medications. Many of these medications are more frequently used in older individuals. It is likely that the regular ingestion of multiple prescribed medications to treat various ailments results in significant side effects of memory impairment and other kinds of mental confusion in the elderly.

On the flip side, the term *nootropic* has been used to describe drugs claimed to have improving effects on aspects of cognition, including memory. Claims of improved memory have been made for caffeine, nicotine, arecoline, and amphetamine. Chemicals that influence acetylcholine neurochemistry have received particular attention: phosphatidylcholine (also known as lecithin), the phospholipid precursor to the synthesis of acetylcholine; and various inhibitors of acetylcholinesterase, the enzyme responsible for breaking down acetylcholine. In this latter category are several drugs used to reduce memory loss associated with Alzheimer's and other dementias: donepezil (Aricept), tacrine (Cognex), rivastigmine (Exelon), and galantamine (Razadyne; also present in certain plants, such as the snowdrop [genus *Galanthus*], wild daffodil [*Narcissus pseudonarcissus*], and red spider lily [*Lycoris radiata*]). How such drugs work to improve memory is not known—is it an effect on memory per se, or is the memory improvement secondary to an effect on enhancing attention, for example?

Are memories stored in some particular part of the brain? This question was addressed by Karl Lashley (1890–1958) early in the twentieth century. He studied the ability of rats to navigate in mazes—how to go from start to finish without making wrong turns and entering blind alleys—for which they were rewarded with tasty treats. Lashley then made lesions to various places in the rat's cerebral cortex and measured their effects on performance in the maze. He found that lesioned rats made errors in navigating the maze, as if their memory for the maze had been damaged. Moreover, he established that the number of errors made in navigating the maze was proportional to the size of the cortical lesion, but not its location in the cortex. From this Lashley concluded that memory was not localized to any particular region of the cerebrum.

Building on this idea, Donald Hebb (1904–1985) suggested that networks of many neurons, extending throughout the cerebral cortex, represent the information stored in memory. Memory is distributed; somehow large portions of the brain work together in the formation and retrieval of memories. Indeed, memories often contain multiple kinds of sensory and emotional information. Consider a favorite restaurant, one that you have visited many times. Particular occasions may stand out in memory, but most of your visits probably meld together into a landscape of sights, sounds, smells, tastes, actions, and feelings. These varied aspects of memory related to a particular place and set of associated experiences involve many different regions of the brain.

Specific regions of the brain may nonetheless be required for certain stages of memory storage, and studies of patients who developed amnesia following neurosurgical procedures have contributed greatly to ideas about brain mechanisms of memory. Among all the people who have been studied in attempts to elucidate brain mechanisms of memory, by far the most famous is the patient H.M. This patient was studied for more than fifty years by psychologists and neurologists and for reasons of privacy was always referred to simply by his initials in the dozens of scientific publications that came from working with him. When he died in 2008 at the age of eighty-two, his identity was revealed to the world—Henry Molaison (1926–2008).

Sometime around the age of ten, Henry began having seizures. His epilepsy was idiopathic—the cause was unknown. It may have been related to hitting his head in a bicycle accident several years before; it may have been a result of genetic risk factors (Henry's father had several relatives who suffered from seizures); it may have been some combination of these things. Through his teen years, Henry's seizures became increasingly frequent and severe. By the time he was in his mid-twenties, he was considered a candidate for brain surgery that would excise small parts of his brain that might be related to the onset of his seizures.

Thus, in 1953, at the age of twenty-seven, Henry underwent the surgical removal of portions of his medial temporal lobe, including the hippocampus, and adjacent entorhinal cortex and amygdala from both hemispheres of his brain (Fig. 19.2). After surgery the severity of his epilepsy was much decreased, but he was found to have a profound impairment of memory. This was first reported in a 1957 publication by William Scoville (1906–1984), the neurosurgeon who performed the surgery on H.M., and Brenda Milner (b. 1918), a neuropsychologist who had previously studied with Donald Hebb and Wilder Penfield. Milner continued to work with H.M. for many years, and together they made significant contributions to the neuroscience of memory. Here are some of the things they found.

Following surgery, H.M. had relatively normal working memory. He could engage in conversation and remember from one moment to the next the flow of dia-

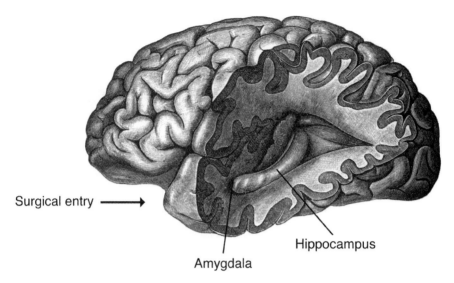

Surgical entry ⟶

Hippocampus

Amygdala

Figure 19.2. Hippocampus and adjacent areas revealed by exposing the medial temporal lobe region from the side of the brain. The entorhinal region is a fold of cortex immediately below the hippocampus. To remove H.M.'s medial temporal lobe structures, the surgeon drilled holes into the forehead of his skull and lifted the frontal lobes to access the underside and interior of the temporal lobes.

logue. He could recall lists of numbers or words immediately after hearing them recited. He also had decent long-term memory, at least for some things, and could answer questions involving information he knew from before the time of his surgery. He could work crossword puzzles, as long as the clues and words were things he knew before having had surgery.

However, Henry was unable to remember, for more than a few minutes, any new information acquired after his surgery—he suffered from profound anterograde amnesia. He would read and understand a newspaper article and then forget everything within seconds. He would meet and have conversations with his doctors and other people and have no recollection of the conversation or the people a few minutes later. This was the case even for people he met repeatedly over many years. He forgot events in his life almost as fast as they occurred.

The hippocampus, via the adjacent entorhinal cortex, is highly interconnected with all other regions of the cerebral cortex—with interconnectivity running in both directions. This elaborate neural communication appears to be central to organizing, storing, and consolidating memory, with the hippocampus serving as a hub of distributed activation that somehow helps to form the networks of cortical neural connections involved in representing memories in the brain. (The elaborate interconnectivity is also likely to be the reason that the medial temporal lobe is a frequent focus of seizures. Anomalous neural activity here may efficiently spread into large areas of the cortex.)

There were, however, some things that H.M. could still learn and remember. Careful investigation revealed that H.M. (as well as other postsurgical amnesia patients with hippocampal lesions) could learn certain things related to motor performance. When H.M. was given a pencil and asked to trace a path through a maze and was given the same maze day after day, he improved in his performance. He also improved over a period of several days of repeated practice in his ability to trace outlines with a pencil while looking in a mirror. However, when brought back to the identical testing situation for the tenth day in a row, he claimed to never have seen the maze, or mirror, or design before. He was unable to verbalize any memory about it, nor did he recognize the experimenters, who were the same people working with him day after day. But his performance on these tasks continued to improve and was retained.

This revealed a key distinction within human memory: declarative and nondeclarative. Declarative memories can be brought to mind in words or describable images. This includes facts and other informational-type knowledge (semantic memory), as well as specific time-and-place events from one's experience (episodic memory). In declarative memory H.M. was profoundly impaired.

Nondeclarative memory includes procedural memory, classical conditioning, and priming. H.M. could accomplish this kind of learning and remember what he had learned, although he had no awareness that he was learning and remembering. Procedural memory involves performing a sequence of actions, such as maze tracing or mirror drawing, or typing, swimming, riding a bicycle, or playing a musical instrument. We can't describe very well how to ride a bicycle, and even if we could, it really wouldn't help us much in learning how to actually ride one. Riding a bike is a "just do it" kind of task, with knowledge about the task accessible only through performance, by actually engaging in the actions.

Classical conditioning is learning to associate together certain stimuli and responses. For example, if a puff of air is directed at our eye, we reflexively blink; and if a beep is sounded immediately before the puff of air, we will learn to associate the beep sound and the air puff. Very soon we will blink whenever we hear the beep, expecting the air puff to follow the sound. This is classical conditioning. It is another kind of learning without awareness of what we are learning—it just happens. And it happened for H.M.

Yet another kind of nondeclarative memory results from priming—when exposure to a stimulus influences one's response to future exposures to this stimulus. Priming is central to the effectiveness of advertising. Repeatedly seeing or hearing references to certain brand names or political candidates will predispose us to pick that brand or candidate when some future choice must be made. Advertising's goal is that we learn and remember, without being aware that we are learning and remembering. In simple laboratory experiments, H.M. showed evidence of priming.

After his death Henry's brain was carefully removed, treated with formaldehyde fixative, and cut into more than two thousand thin sections. High-resolution digital images were made of the brain sections, and these images may now be accessed online—a resource available for study by neuroscientists for years to come. Henry's brain and the data are archived at the University of California's Brain Observatory in San Diego.

Current thinking about long-term memory, both declarative and nondeclarative, is that it is ultimately captured in the complex interconnectivity of neurons, such that changes in connections—forming, eliminating, strengthening, and weakening of synapses—give rise to changes in the patterns of activity that occur across large regions of the cerebral cortex. Donald Hebb, in his classic 1949 book *The Organization of Behavior*, postulated that signal activity in networks of neurons would somehow serve to strengthen synaptic connections between the neurons and that this could provide a cellular mechanism for memory storage: "When an axon of cell A is near enough to excite a cell B and repeatedly or persistently takes part in firing it, some growth process or metabolic change takes place in one or both cells such that A's efficiency, as one of the cells firing B, is increased." That is, repeated activation of a network strengthens the synaptic connections within the network. Sometimes this is referred to as a Hebbian network.

We now know these neuroplastic processes are taking place all the time in the brain. Several scenarios for the strengthening of chemical synapses are discussed in Chapter 10: increasing the amount of neurotransmitter released from the presynaptic axon terminal, decreasing the efficacy of neurotransmitter reuptake by reducing the number of reuptake transporters, and increasing the number of postsynaptic neurotransmitter receptors—these are all ways by which the signal strength between two neurons is enhanced. Doing the opposite of any of these things would decrease the strength of the synapse.

Detailed investigations of cellular and molecular changes that may underlie memory formation have been carried out by Eric Kandel (b. 1929) and colleagues, using an animal with a very simple nervous system and repertoire of behaviors: *Aplysia californica*, the sea hare or sea slug. Years of study of this marine mollusk have led to a description of molecular mechanisms related to the short-term and long-term strengthening of synapses regulating the reflexive behavior of gill withdrawal.

Aplysia possesses a respiratory gill attached to a structure called a siphon (Fig. 19.3). If the siphon is touched, sensory neurons send signals that rapidly retract the gill into the mantle cavity, protecting the delicate gill from potential injury.

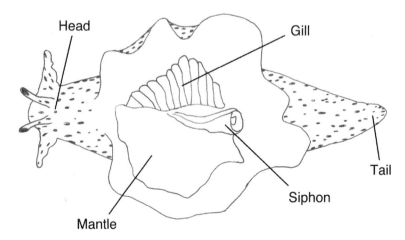

Figure 19.3. Sea hare, *Aplysia californica.*

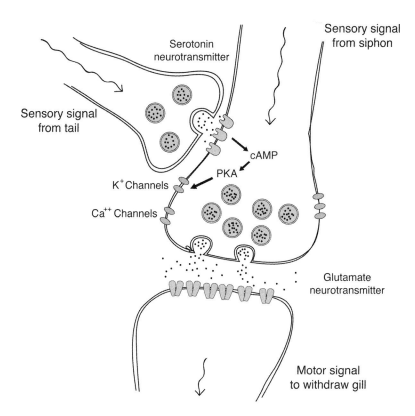

Figure 19.4. Synaptic connections in *Aplysia californica.*

If a strongly aversive sensory stimulus (such as an electric shock) is applied to the animal's tail region around the same time as touching of the siphon, an increased robustness of gill withdrawal in response to touching is observed. This increased robustness has been linked to transient strengthening of the synaptic connection linking the siphon sensory neurons with the motor neurons mediating the retraction of the gill.

The cellular and molecular details of the synaptic connections are shown in Figure 19.4. The sensory signal registering the aversive stimulus to the tail leads to the release of serotonin that activates serotonin receptors located on the axon terminals of sensory neurons from the siphon. Serotonin activates G-protein-coupled serotonin receptors, initiating the following sequence of events: activated G-protein → activated adenylate cyclase → increased cAMP synthesis → activated cAMP-dependent protein kinase A (PKA) → phosphorylated potassium-leak channels located in the membrane of the axon terminal → closed potassium-leak channels → decreased outward K⁺ current → prolonged depolarizing phase of action potential → voltage-gated Ca⁺⁺ channels opened longer → greater Ca⁺⁺ influx into axon terminal → increased release of glutamate neurotransmitter → increased excitation of postsynaptic motor neuron mediating gill retraction.

Following a single aversive stimulus to the tail, the increased robustness of the gill-withdrawal response lasts about an hour—a kind of short-term memory. As with many types of memory, repetition results in strengthening. In this case, if the aversive stimulus to the tail is repeated several times, then the increased robustness of gill withdrawal in response to touching the siphon may be maintained for many days—a kind of long-term memory. Here's how: the repeated activation of serotonin receptors results in higher intracellular levels of cAMP, leading to more sustained activation of PKA (per the scenario described above). Some of the activated PKA now makes its way to the cell nucleus, where it catalyzes the phosphorylation of transcription factor proteins, resulting in the transcription of particular genes. One of these genes codes for ubiquitin hydrolase, which helps cleave off a regulatory subunit of PKA, resulting in the PKA remaining in an activated state even in the absence of cAMP. This produces a persistent elevation of glutamate neurotransmitter release onto the motor neuron controlling gill withdrawal. And other genes transcribed via this process facilitate growth of new synaptic connections to the gill-withdrawal motor neuron, presumably via the action of neurotrophins.

These studies of a simple behavior in *Aplysia* provide examples of how precise molecular changes may be related to short-term and long-term memory. Scaling this up to neuroplastic processes among millions and billions of synaptic connections across multiple regions of the human brain provides a rough sketch of an account that may begin to explain the profound capacities of human memory.

As described in Chapter 18, sensory signals enter the cortex and impact global patterns of activity throughout the cerebral neuropil. The networks of neurons that are activated depend upon what has been strengthened by previous activation—Hebbian networks. Thus, all past experience plays an essential role in determining the patterns of activation generated by the incoming sensory signals, and the patterns of motor actions generated as a result.

Not only in the brain, but throughout the entire body, neural connections are strengthened by repeated activation. In the autonomic nervous system, the neuromuscular system, and the neural connections with the endocrine and immune systems, past experience plays an essential role in determining present and future patterns of activity. This provides a substrate for knowledge and meaning; meaning is constructed from the multitudes of linked associations that have been acquired through the entirety of one's past experiences. Meaning is a whole-body experience, and its foundation is memory.

Many neuroscientists believe that scenarios similar to this will somehow be sufficient to eventually account for all the amazing properties of human memory. Perhaps this will be so—and perhaps there will be unanticipated surprises ahead.

> Three point one four one
> five nine two six five three five—
> memory, cosmos.

CHAPTER **20**

Rhythms, Sleep, and Dreams

Many (perhaps most) animals have daily periods of inactivity and reduced alertness. For us humans and other vertebrate animals, there are distinctive physiological properties of brain activity that characterize this period of reduced activity. We call this period of time *sleep.*

The amount of time spent asleep each day varies substantially across different species of animal. Here are a few approximate sleep times for several mammals, in hours per twenty-four-hour day: bat, 19; mouse and rat, 12; rabbit, 9; cow and elephant, 4. Typically, we humans spend eight hours asleep out of each twenty-four-hour day—one-third of our lifetime. If we live to be ninety years of age, that's a full thirty years spent asleep, amounting to 263,000 hours—a lot of time. (At the very least, this argues for having a comfortable bed.)

If someone is tired and is deprived of sleep, the desire for sleep will become overwhelming, taking precedence over all other desires. That sleep has been preserved throughout hundreds of millions of years of biological evolution suggests that it serves very important functions. And although the scientific study of sleep has blossomed over the last several decades, most of what is going on during sleep remains a mystery.

The regular cycle of sleep and wakefulness in our lives is an example a biological rhythm, one of many periodic behaviors exhibited by humans and other organisms. Sleep and wakefulness follow a circadian pattern (Latin *circa* = about, *dies* = day), having a periodicity of approximately twenty-four hours. Other examples of circadian rhythms are body temperature variations and synthesis of cortisol and other glucocorticoids by the adrenal gland. Melatonin is also synthesized in a circadian rhythm. It is made by many organisms, including bacteria, fungi, and plants, as well as animals, and appears to serve protective antioxidant functions. It is synthesized from serotonin in the pineal gland in vertebrate animals and plays an important role in the sleep–wake cycle.

Melatonin

Circadian rhythms are found in many organisms, not just animals. Plants, fungi, and even single-celled creatures exhibit circadian rhythms. Among plants, the opening and closing of flowers and leaves is a circadian rhythm. You might think that this behavior in plants is in direct response to the daily variation in sunlight between day and night. That is, leaves and flowers open during the day when the sun is out and close at night when it is dark. Although sunlight-triggered movement is part of the picture, it is not the most important determinant. This can be demonstrated by growing the plant under conditions of constant light or darkness. Even if a plant grows in a room in which the light is always on or always off, flowers often still undergo a diurnal opening and closing. This is the true test of a circadian rhythm—whether it persists under conditions in which no environmental cues to time of day or night are available.

The same is true for animals like us. The periodic variation in melatonin synthesis by the pineal gland (high at night, low during the day), of core body temperature, and of sleeping and waking all continue in the absence of any information about when it is day and when it is night. This implies that the body contains some sort of internal timer, an endogenous biological clock, able to track the passage of time over a twenty-four-hour period.

In addition to circadian biological rhythms, there are other rhythms of different periodicities. For example, migratory activity in birds and other animals may be regulated by some kind of circannual biological clock. Many birds that live in northern latitudes fly south to warmer climates for the winter and then back north in the spring, where during the summer they breed and raise their young. One might suspect that this migratory behavior is triggered by changes in the temperature or length of the day, things that would clearly mark the changing of the seasons. Again, this is only part of the story. Studies have been done with migratory birds born and raised in the laboratory—birds that have never been outside. They live their entire lives in cages within rooms that have no windows to the outside world. They are also exposed to a constant light–dark cycle: twelve hours of light and twelve hours of darkness, a cycle that never varies. In addition, the temperature of the room is kept constant year-round. These birds get no signals or cues from the environment indicative of the time of the year and the changing of seasons.

Nonetheless, birds in the northern hemisphere, several months after their birth, become restless and begin to hop and attempt to fly in a southerly direction, even though they are inside cages and don't get very far. Five months later they again exhibit restlessness, hopping and attempting to fly in a northerly direction. Thus, these migratory animals must have an endogenous circannual biological clock—a physiological mechanism that tells them what time of the year it is—as well as an inborn sense of knowing which direction to migrate at which time of the year. In addition, they must have some mechanism of obtaining information as to which direction is which, even inside a closed room. This they accomplish by detecting the geomagnetic field, using it as a source of directional compass information (see Chapter 11). Researchers have artificially manipulated the magnetic fields in these experimental rooms and have shown that this messes with the birds' ability to exhibit migratory restlessness in the seasonally appropriate direction.

There are endogenous rhythms of other lengths, too. Reproductive cycles in mammals are an example. Female hamsters have a cycle of ovulation that is about four days long. In human females, the cycle of ovulation is typically about twenty-eight days, although this varies between women and even within the same woman.

Much of the study of biological rhythms has occurred using animals in laboratories where the conditions of light and dark can be precisely controlled. For example, one can work with rats or mice and monitor their activity—things like how much they move around in their cages or how much they run around in a wheel. A rat living in a cage under conditions of a constant light–dark cycle—twelve hours of light and twelve hours of dark—will be relatively active during the hours of darkness and relatively inactive (mostly sleeping) during the hours of light. Rats are nocturnal creatures, and in their natural habitat they are most active during the night. Okay, nothing surprising so far.

Now suppose you either leave the lights on all the time in the rat's cage or turn off the lights and leave them off all the time, exposing the animal to either constant light or constant darkness. You can continue this experimental arrangement for many days, or weeks, or months. Under these conditions the rat will continue to alternate between cycles of activity and inactivity with an approximate period of twelve hours of activity followed by twelve hours of inactivity—that is, a circadian rhythm of activity or sleep–wake is maintained. However, the overall period is generally not exactly twenty-four hours, often being a little longer or a little shorter. This is called the "free-running" period of the circadian clock, in that it is decoupled from synchronization by environmental cues (like day and night) and so "runs free," dependent only on internal mechanisms for keeping time.

Analogous studies have been done with humans who volunteered to live in caves and bunkers, completely shielded from any outside light. They were allowed to sleep when they wanted and be awake when they wanted. They could turn lights off and on when they wanted and eat when they wanted. The experiment was maintained for several weeks. Under these conditions, the participants tended to develop regular schedules of activity and sleep. Although their schedules of activity had periodicities of around twenty-four hours, they often were a little longer—folks tended to wake up a little later each day and go to bed a little later each day. It is as if their endogenous biological clock had a free-running period slightly longer than twenty-four hours.

Many studies such as these have suggested that animals and other organisms have endogenous biological clocks that are circadian—that is, generate a periodicity of approximately twenty-four hours. Under natural conditions, this periodicity is synchronized by environmental cues to bring the ticking of the endogenous clock into alignment with the natural day–night cycle. The primary synchronization cue is the daily cycle of day and night, sunrise and sunset, light and dark.

What is the cellular and molecular nature of the biological clock—the ticking mechanism—the generator of the rhythmic signals that presumably tell us when to be tired, when to sleep, and when to be awake and alert? And where in the body is the endogenous clock located? After decades of research, we now know the primary locus of the circadian clock (at least in vertebrates) to be a cluster of cells located in the hypothalamus of the diencephalon, at the top of the brainstem. The particular cell cluster is called the suprachiasmatic nucleus, or SCN. The name derives from its location, which is immediately above (*supra*) the optic chiasm, the junction of the two optic nerves coming into the thalamus from the retinas of the left and right eyes. Like all brain structures, the SCN is bilaterally symmetric: there are two of them, located close together within the hypothalamus.

The human SCN contains around twenty thousand neurons, many of which exhibit a circadian periodicity of neural firing. Experiments have also been conducted in which clusters of neurons from the SCN are removed from an animal's brain and the cells are kept alive for up to several days by placing them in an appropriate nutrient environment. Under such conditions, the circadian periodicity of neuronal activity in SCN cells continues, independent of any connection with the rest of the brain or body.

Is it possible to trace the ticktock mechanism of the biological clock all the way to the level of individual cells? Molecular-genetic insight into the mechanism of the biological clock took a great leap forward in the 1970s with the discovery of a gene mutation in the fruit fly *Drosophila* that had substantial effects on the period of a fly's circadian rhythm: a mutation in a gene called *PER*, for period. Years of research have revealed that the *PER* gene is transcribed and translated into protein, after which the protein enters the cell nucleus and interacts with transcription factors to suppress transcription of the *PER* gene. The resulting reduced production of the associated PER protein then leads to reduced suppression of *PER* gene transcription, and the cycle begins anew. This process of feedback inhibition of the transcription of the *PER* gene by its own gene product produces a rhythm of *PER* gene expression that then propagates out to other aspects of cell physiology.

Other genes in *Drosophila* have also been identified in this oscillatory time-keeping cycle: *TIM* (timeless), *CLOCK*, and *CYCLE*, to name a few. And in the human SCN, analogous genes and gene products have been discovered that appear to generate and maintain the oscillations of the circadian clock in the human body. Through the neural circuitry of the brain, the oscillations of the SCN exert regulatory actions on many other body processes. And the SCN is also the place where the overall circadian period of the biological clock is brought into synchrony with the environmental light–dark cycle of day and night.

The retina, via the optic nerve, makes most of its connections with the thalamic lateral geniculate nucleus and thence the visual cortex (V1) of the occipital lobe, and with the superior colliculus in the midbrain (see Chapter 14). Of the million or so axons in each optic nerve, close to 90 percent go to the lateral geniculate nucleus, and close to 10 percent go to the midbrain. However, about 1 percent of the optic nerve axons, perhaps ten thousand or so nerve fibers from each eye, emerge from a distinct population of retinal ganglion cells and connect with the SCN. These particular ganglion cells are intrinsically photosensitive; that is, rather than activation via input originating from rods and cones, they contain their own (intrinsic) rhodopsin-like photoreceptor protein, called melanopsin (see Chapter 14). The axon tract connecting these ganglion cells with the SCN is called the retinal-hypothalamic pathway, which communicates information about levels of light to the SCN in order to synchronize the endogenous circadian rhythm with environmental time.

When we travel rapidly from one part of the world to another, crossing multiple time zones, our internal biological clock continues to operate on whatever time period it has recently synchronized with, even though the external environmental time has shifted. This is jet lag—a lack of synchrony between our internal clock and the new time zone. If the internal clock is telling the body that it is time to sleep and the local environment is dictating that we be awake and functioning, the resulting jet lag can mean fatigue, headache, grogginess, fuzzy memory, and other symptoms of impaired performance. Although the retinal-hypothalamic pathway is relaying information about the new day–night periodicity to the biological clock in the SCN, it usually takes several days for the body's internal clock to synch with the new time zone.

Studies of human sleep are conducted in laboratories where sleeping humans can be monitored. Such studies often measure three kinds of physiological activity: brain activity using electroencephalography (EEG), activity of muscles throughout the body using electromyography, and movement specifically of the eyes using electro-oculography. One of the striking findings from these kinds of measurements is that during certain times of the night we tend to move our eyes around quite a bit, while during other times the eyes move very little. In mammals, including humans, sleep is broadly divisible into two signature stages, that in which rapid eye movements take place (REM) and that in which such eye movements tend not to occur (non-REM or NREM).

In humans and some other mammals, NREM sleep can be divided into several stages that differ by the kind of EEG activity, labeled stages 1, 2, 3, and 4. Stages 3 and 4 are recognized by EEG patterns that contain substantial low-frequency oscillation, less than 4 hertz (delta waves), and thus these stages are sometimes referred to as slow-wave sleep. During REM sleep, EEG activity is dominated by higher frequencies and looks more like the EEG of an awake person than it does the EEG of a person in NREM sleep.

EEG measurements in sleeping people demonstrate that there is a fairly regular progression through these various stages over the course of a night's sleep (Fig. 20.1). After sleep onset, we go through a progression of the four NREM stages. After this, there is movement back up the stages, and you might get the idea that the sleeper is going to awaken, but instead the sleeper enters a period of REM sleep. In REM sleep, the electrooculograph shows movement of the eye muscles. If you look

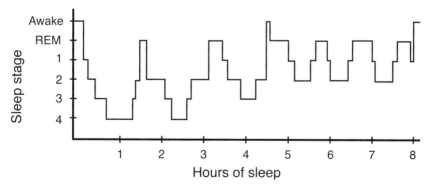

Figure 20.1. Progression during a night's sleep through the various stages of NREM and REM.

carefully at the closed eyelids of a person in REM sleep, you can see the twitching of the eyeball beneath the eyelid. The eyeball will typically move back and forth once every second or two. After a few minutes the eyes stop twitching, the EEG slows down again, and the sleeper passes back through the various NREM stages. Similar patterns are repeated throughout the night, with the periods of REM sleep becoming longer and more frequent as the night progresses.

The amount of time spent in REM-stage sleep per night varies across the life span. Newborn infants sleep perhaps sixteen hours a day, with half of that sleep time spent in the REM stage. By the age of one year, a child may be sleeping twelve hours a day, with four hours of REM. The amount of time spent in REM decreases throughout childhood, stabilizes by puberty at around 1.5 to 2 hours per night, and remains that way throughout adulthood.

Mammals have REM sleep. Birds have REM sleep. However, REM-stage sleep has not been found in reptiles, amphibians, or fish. This suggests that REM is a more recent evolutionary development, perhaps related in some way to the complexity of the brain's cerebrum. During REM sleep clusters of cells in the pons and midbrain become active and spread neural excitation into the cerebral cortex. The neurotransmitter acetylcholine is central to this excitation, and many of these excitatory REM-active neurons innervating the cortex are cholinergic. The result is widespread activation of the cerebral cortex, producing a state of neural activity more akin to wakefulness than to other stages of sleep. In addition, these REM-active neurons send signals to the eye muscles, triggering eye movements, the hallmark feature of REM. Finally, there is inhibition of motor output from the cortex via the spinal cord. During REM, the sleeper's body is relaxed, and there is little movement, save for the eyes. If it weren't for the inhibition of motor output, the sleeper's body would jerk and move around quite a bit, because the motor areas in the frontal lobes of the cerebrum are very active during REM.

A notable aspect of REM sleep is its association with vivid dreaming. If someone in the REM stage of sleep is awakened, they will generally say they were dreaming, and often dreaming quite vividly. Perhaps 90 percent of the time this is the case. In contrast, if someone is awakened during a NREM stage of sleep, they only infrequently report dreaming vividly, perhaps 5 percent of the time. When awakened from NREM, they might say that some kind of mental activity was happening, some thoughts are recalled, but not the vivid sensory and emotional experiences that one recalls in REM-stage dreams.

This strong relationship between REM sleep and vivid dreaming fits with the robust neural activity throughout the cerebral cortex during REM. If visual areas of the cortex are neurally activated, even if there is no visual stimulation to the eye, one may have experiences of seeing things. Ditto for other sensory areas. Thus, the neural activity in the cortex during REM sleep is believed to be associated with our sensory, motor, and emotional experiences during dreams. In vivid dreams we see things, we hear things, we sometimes even taste and smell things. We feel things emotionally. We have experiences of moving around, and even moving around in ways that aren't normally possible, like flying.

Because of the cholinergic nature of cortical activation during REM, drugs that have an activating effect on acetylcholine circuitry may increase the vividness of dreams. Nicotine is such a drug. People who are using nicotine patches to help them quit smoking often report increased vividness of dreaming. This is because the patch continues to deliver nicotine to the body even during sleep, more than the person would normally have at night if they were smoking, because they would not be smoking during their sleep. (This assumes the patch is being left on during sleep; some people choose to remove it, to reduce the intensity of dreams.) Shamans in South America who use tobacco as a divination tool may smoke before retiring for the night, to intentionally increase the vividness of their dreams. Acetylcholinesterase inhibitors decrease the chemical breakdown of acetylcholine after it is released, thus prolonging its activity in the synaptic cleft. These drugs are used in the treatment of dementia (see Chapter 19). A side effect is increased vividness of dreams.

Dreams are ephemeral. We frequently awaken and have no memory at all of dreaming. This is the case even though sleep studies have demonstrated that everyone dreams every night. Or, we awaken and are aware that we have been dreaming, but we cannot recall any specific content of the dreams. Or, we awaken and remember parts of a dream or dreams but tend to forget things very quickly. Immediately going over the dream story line in one's own mind, writing it down, or telling someone else will generally enhance recall. If memory resides in activation of neural networks, all this is reasonable in that the networks activated during REM sleep may be novel ones, not necessarily associated with previous learning and experience, and thus prone to ready dissipation. Practice improves the recall of dreams.

Lucid dreaming occurs when one becomes aware of dreaming while still asleep. That is, one is asleep in REM, eyes closed, motor activity inhibited, and dreaming, and within the dream there is an awareness that what is happening is a dream. Lucid dreaming has long been known within traditions and cultures that place value on dreams. And many people have had the experience of becoming lucid in a dream now and again in the course of their life. For some people, lucidity is a regular feature of their dream life. Here again, it is known that practice can lead to an increased likelihood of experiencing lucid dreams. Practice means first working on dream recall generally and then cultivating the intention to become aware of one's dream while dreaming.

Some spiritual traditions that place high value on the practice of meditation— such as Hinduism and Buddhism—have dream yoga practices with the goal of becoming regularly lucid during dream and even nondream sleep. All of our daily activities influence our dream experiences, and our dream experiences build and reinforce neural circuits that affect our waking behavior. In dream yoga practice, attaining a continuous state of lucidity during both waking and sleep hours allows the practitioner at every moment to incline the mind toward the thoughts, feelings, and actions that honor the ethical framework of their tradition. Generally this means cultivation of love and compassion, for oneself and others.

Some phenomena associated with sleep are considered problematic and labeled as sleep disorders. One is insomnia: difficulty with sleep, often with falling asleep. It's not really a specific disorder but, rather, a symptom that could be associated with any number of different things. If someone is excited or hyperaroused during the day, that might amp up the body physiologically, creating difficulty falling asleep. Caffeine, especially when it is consumed late in the day, may contribute to insomnia. Jet lag often produces insomnia. A noisy or uncomfortable sleep environment may contribute to insomnia. Stress and emotional turmoil are commonly related to insomnia. Alcohol, although a sedative-hypnotic, may lead to awakening and insomnia in the middle of a night's sleep, after its sleep-inducing effects wear off.

Treatment for insomnia best begins with addressing conditions likely related to producing it as a symptom in the first place. One part of this is optimizing conditions conducive to restful sleep. This is called "sleep hygiene" and includes things like maintaining a regular wake–sleep pattern, relaxing as much as possible before sleep, avoiding exposure to bright light (such as computer screens) shortly before retiring, avoiding eating large meals late in the evening, decreasing or eliminating caffeine and alcohol consumption, and so forth.

Sleep apnea is a condition where the sleeper periodically stops breathing or has abnormally shallow breathing. Sleep apnea is usually caused by some kind of obstruction or constriction of the airway, resulting in blocked airflow into the lungs. When this happens, the sleeper wakes up from lack of air, breathing adjusts, and sleep returns. However, if these brief awakenings happen repeatedly throughout the night, it makes for a very disrupted sleep, often resulting in fatigue and impaired performance the next day. Sleep apnea is thought to be a fairly common condition, affecting upward of 5 percent of adults.

Narcolepsy has as its primary symptom excessive daytime sleepiness, even after seemingly having a full night of sleep. Nighttime sleep cycling between NREM and REM stages is generally not normal in narcoleptics. Genetic studies of narcolepsy in humans and other animals have found associations with abnormalities related to orexin, a neuropeptide involved in maintaining wakefulness. Orexin derives its name from the Greek *orexis*, meaning appetite or desire—reflecting its role in regulating feeding and other motivated behaviors. Orexinergic neurons are located in the hypothalamus and send axons widely throughout the brain—to the cerebral cortex and into the brainstem. New medications that are antagonists at orexin receptors are currently entering the pharmaceutical marketplace as treatments for insomnia. This represents a new pharmacologic approach to promoting sleep, very different from the GABA-modulating drugs (benzodiazepines and zolpidem-like compounds) that have dominated the market for decades.

REM behavior disorder is an impairment of motor inhibition in REM-stage sleep, resulting in sleepers acting out their dreams. The body may flail around and even jump out of bed, at which point awakening likely occurs.

With sleep paralysis, one partially awakens while in REM-stage sleep. The person becomes aware but is unable to move the body because the neural activity of REM continues to inhibit motor output from the brain. In addition, because of the robust cortical activity of REM, the person is likely to have vivid sensory experiences. Sometimes people report the perception that a being is entering the room, an experience that is generally accompanied by a feeling of significant distress or terror.

Sleepwalking, or somnambulism, occurs when a person, while still asleep, rises from bed and walks about, sometimes engaging in such activities as bathing, housecleaning, eating, and occasionally even dangerous things like cooking or driving. Sleepwalking tends to happen while the person is in the deep stages of slow-wave sleep, stages 3 and 4 of NREM. A sleepwalking person who is awakened generally registers complete surprise and will usually not be able to recall any dream at the time.

Perhaps the most widely occurring sleep-related problem in the modern world is chronic sleep deprivation. Although eight hours is commonly quoted as the "normal" human sleep time, individuals vary widely in how much sleep they get and how much they appear to require for optimal daytime functioning. Even so, many sleep researchers contend that inadequate sleep is widespread in the contemporary world. Throughout most of human evolution, people probably retired to sleep not all that long after sunset, even though the domestication of fire did make it feasible to stay up late. And generally folks would arise at sunrise to begin their day. Today, with electric lighting and all sorts of entertaining activities that last late into the night, we tend to go to sleep later than we otherwise would yet still usually awaken early the next day to go to work or school. Copious consumption of coffee, tea, energy drinks, and other caffeinated beverages assists in maintaining wakefulness. However, caffeine is no substitute for adequate sleep.

Getting insufficient sleep definitely impairs cognitive and motor performance. This may simply mean suboptimal or fatigued performance in one's job or studies, with no terribly serious consequences. However, there are circumstances in which slowed or impaired judgment, decision making, or motor reactions can have serious consequences. Automobile accidents and airplane crashes have been linked directly to sleep deprivation on the part of the driver, pilot, other critically important crew member, or air traffic controller. Errors in decisions concerning medication and surgical mistakes due to sleepiness have resulted in disability and death of patients in hospitals. If you are doing something in a situation where wakefulness is essential—such as driving a car or performing clinical care in a hospital—note this rule to live by: "Drowsiness Is Red Alert!" (so says pioneering sleep researcher William Dement).

Why is sleep so important, other than the fact that we are seriously impaired if we don't get enough of it? Whatever these impairments in cognitive and motor performance might be, they appear to be correctable by simply getting a good night's sleep. Are there other longer-term effects of not getting enough sleep, perhaps things that are not so readily reversible? Again, why do we need to sleep?

One hypothesis is that during sleep various restorative processes operate within the body. The chemical reactions of cellular metabolism—taking place continuously, maintaining life in each and every cell of our body—can have damaging consequences. Highly reactive molecular entities, such as free radicals of various kinds and excited electronic states of oxygen, are constantly being generated. These molecules have detrimental effects on their surroundings, reacting with cellular components in ways that are damaging. It is absolutely essential for all living cells to have mechanisms for neutralizing free radicals and oxidants and for repairing molecular damage (such as to DNA), in order to sustain life. It may be that during periods of sleep and torpor some of these protective and repair processes can more effectively carry out their tasks.

One consistent finding over the last couple decades of research is that sleep plays a critical role in learning and memory. First, sleep somehow prepares the brain to optimally encode new information for storage in long-term memory, and sleep deprivation dramatically impairs this process. A good night's sleep is essential to optimize learning the next day. After the initial encoding of a memory in the neural circuitry of the cortex, an extended period of time is necessary to lock the memory more securely in place—the process of consolidation (see Chapter 19). Substantial aspects of memory consolidation appear to take place during sleep. This includes reactivation of the networks involved in the initial experience of whatever is being learned. Studies of both rats and humans have shown that configurations of brain neurons active during the learning of a task become active again during sleep. It is likely this repetition of activity is part of a process of strengthening the synaptic connections in these networks, thereby solidifying the associated memory. Thus, adequate sleep both before and after learning new information or skills is important for memory storage and consolidation—highly relevant for any student to know!

The relative roles of NREM and REM sleep in memory storage and consolidation are topics of active investigation. Above and beyond basic needs for sleep, there also seems to be specific requirements for REM sleep. Individuals selectively deprived of REM-stage sleep will fall into REM sleep much more rapidly on subsequent nights. The prominence of REM in newborns and during the first months of life suggests that it has an important role in neural development, because connections in the brain are being robustly formed and modified during this period.

Though sleep science is young, and much remains to be discovered, we already know enough to appreciate that getting good sleep is one of the most important things we can do for physical and mental health—on par with good nutrition and physical exercise. Let us hope that public education about the importance of healthy sleep soon catches up with the science!

> To sleep and to dream—
> brain, creative, new learning—
> and too, other worlds.

CHAPTER 21

Emotion

In the film *2001: A Space Odyssey*, astronaut Dave Bowman, with some difficulty, is able to regain entry to the spaceship, despite HAL's efforts to prevent that from happening. Once inside, Bowman makes a beeline for HAL's control circuitry, intent on shutting HAL down as quickly as possible and gaining control of the ship and the mission.

HAL: "Just what do you think you are doing, Dave? I really think I am entitled to an answer to that question."

Is HAL upset, angry, confused?

HAL goes on to speak in a conciliatory manner: "I know everything hasn't been quite right with me. But I can assure you now, very confidently, that it's going to be all right again. I feel much better now. I really do."

HAL continues: "I can see you are really upset about this. I know I've made some very poor decisions recently. But I can give you my complete assurance that my work will be back to normal. I want to help you."

Finally, HAL implores: "Dave, stop. Stop, will you? Stop, Dave. Will you stop, Dave? I'm afraid. I'm afraid, Dave."

Fear?

Astronaut Bowman is unmoved by HAL's pleas and remains focused on shutting the computer down. He proceeds to turn off or disengage HAL's circuits. Something labeled "Memory Terminal" is one of the first things to be disconnected.

At which point, HAL says: "My mind is going. I can feel it. I can feel it. My mind is going. There is no question about it. I can feel it. I can feel it. I'm afraid."

Does HAL have feelings, emotions, moods?

What do we even mean by these terms?

In the characterization of mental experiences as thoughts, feelings, and perceptions, thoughts are considered to have a linguistic aspect, representable as either words in a kind of subjective inner dialogue or images potentially describable in words; perceptions have a direct sensory quality—such as color or shape, musical tones, aromas and tastes, hotness and coldness, itchiness, and so forth—and are generally associated with interactions with physical stimuli from the environment. Feelings, in contrast, have a kind of nonlinguistic and intuitive quality to them.

Feelings are generally considered to be the mental experience component of emotions—such things as joy, anger, fear, surprise, sadness, and disgust. In addition, emotions have palpable somatic qualities—they are experienced in the entire body, not just in the mind. And they have associated outward signs—facial expressions, body posture, laughter, tears, and changes in heart rate, blood pressure, breathing, and skin temperature, for example.

Whatever they are, emotions have profound and direct impact on behavior, on action. This impact is represented in the etymology of the word: *emotion* comes from the French *émouvoir*, meaning to stir up, excite, affect. The Latin roots are *movere* = to move, and *e* = out. Emotions prepare us for and move us to action out into the world, in immediate and powerful ways.

There is a strong association of the subjective component of emotion with the very notion of consciousness. The word *sentience* is frequently used as a synonym for conscious awareness, deriving from the Latin root *sentire* = to feel. René Descartes famously wrote: "I think, therefore I am"—"I feel, therefore I am" would perhaps be a more accurate statement. This latter phrase associates our experience of "what it is like to be" more with something related to the whole body. We are organisms, organic wholes—a body interacting with a world. Our experience of who we are is grounded in that.

Emotions are generally unbidden and spontaneous. They may arise quickly and subside after a brief time. They contribute to guiding how we are reacting to something: with excitement, fear, anger, sadness, compassion. And emotions may reveal otherwise private aspects of inner experience to others and thus are a form of social communication. It may be useful to us for our fellow beings to know how we feel. Expressions of emotions like happiness, joy, compassion, tenderness, admiration, awe, affection, and love help us get along and form relationships with others; they are at the foundation of cooperative social systems.

What's the difference between an emotion and a mood? While some folks may use these two terms interchangeably, a common distinction relates to temporal duration. Emotions may be very brief; moods are more prolonged. And while emotions are often evoked by specific events or circumstances, this may not be the case for moods. Etymologically, *mood* is related to *mode*, from the Latin *modus*, meaning manner, method, or way. Emotions experienced repeatedly over time may become, or contribute to, moods. It may be appropriate to say that moods of some kind are always present, at some level, providing a continuous background of feeling to our experience.

Emotions (and moods) are often characterized as being either positive or negative. Generally speaking, positive in this context refers to states that have an associated pleasant, enjoyable, or rewarding subjective experience, while negative refers to states that are associated with upset or distress.

Charles Darwin was a pioneer in the science of emotion. His book on *The Expression of the Emotions in Man and Animals* was published in 1872, thirteen years after *On the Origin of Species*. Darwin put emotions into an evolutionary context, arguing that emotions are not unique to humans but evolved as adaptive behaviors that we share with other animals. With keen observation and insight, he studied the

Figure 21.1. Drawing of a chimpanzee that is "disappointed and sulky" after an orange was offered to him and then taken away. From Darwin's 1872 book *The Expression of the Emotions in Man and Animals.*

behaviors of nonhuman animals and made connections between animal expressions and those of humans (Fig. 21.1).

Whether or not nonhuman animals have mental experiences of feelings associated with emotions remains a debated topic. Some folks maintain language is necessary to produce a mental experience of awareness, and absent substantial linguistic capacity there is only an ability to respond in a nonaware, reactive way. However, perhaps the more widely accepted hypothesis is that nonhuman animals do have significant mental experience, including a capacity to feel emotions such as pleasure and pain and to recall emotions they have felt before and anticipate ones they may feel again. Human language adds nuance and complexity to the texture of our mental experience, including emotional feelings, but may not be essential for awareness. Researching this question is notoriously difficult, if not downright impossible at this point.

Darwin argued for a universality of emotions, a continuity of expression extending at least from our primate relatives to us humans. This implies that the expression of emotion, and the interpretation of emotional expression, would be universal among humans, across people from many different cultures. However, in the century after Darwin's book, a trend toward understanding human behavior largely in terms of cultural influences and determinants became dominant. This so-called constructivist view marginalized the role of biological universals and posited that even the most basic aspects of emotional expression depend largely on cultural factors. According to this view, there is little reason to expect that a smile, or a grimace, is interpreted in the same way from one culture to another.

In the 1960s, the constructivist versus evolutionary perspective on emotion was tested by Paul Ekman (b. 1934), who compared the interpretation of facial expressions across different cultures. He found that facial expressions associated with several basic emotions (joy, anger, fear, surprise, sadness, disgust) were universal across many human societies, including tribal people in New Guinea, individuals that previously had minimal contact with other cultures. Darwin would have predicted these results, but Darwin's thoughts on the matter of human emotion had been largely forgotten by the time Ekman did his studies. The results piqued the interests of anthropologists and social scientists and were important in kindling modern studies in the psychology, and later neuroscience, of emotion.

The complexities of human behavior rarely boil down to simple this-or-that explanations. Clearly, there are deep biological determinants to the experience and expression of human emotion. And there are cultural factors, as well. For example, other work by Ekman demonstrated culture-specific "display rules" that "specify who can show which emotion to whom and when." Ekman concludes his commentary to a beautiful "definitive edition" of Darwin's book on emotions thus:

> How much we are influenced by individual experience and how much by our evolutionary history varies, depending upon what aspect of our behavior we are considering. It is never a question only of nature or only of nurture. We are biosocial creatures, our minds are embodied, reflecting our lives and the lives of our ancestors. Darwin led the way not only in the biological sciences but in the social sciences as well.

Darwin's discussion of human facial expressions drew upon the work of French neurologist Guillaume Duchenne (1806–1875), who studied the muscular control of facial expressions by selectively activating specific muscles using direct electrical stimulation. The zygomaticus muscle lifts the corners of the mouth when we smile. Duchenne contended that spontaneous smiles—ones associated with true enjoyment—also involve activation of the orbicularis oculi muscles around the eyes (Fig. 21.2). Ekman has called this latter kind of smile—often evoked in contexts of pleasure, joy, or enthusiasm—the Duchenne smile, honoring Duchenne's pioneering work.

Facial expressions are one aspect of body signatures associated with emotions, and facial expressions appear to function primarily to communicate emotions to others. Other body signatures include changes in heart rate, blood pressure, and skin temperature (autonomic nervous system effects); changes in tone of voice and body posture; and changes in release of hormones into the blood circulation (neuroendocrine effects)— such as cortisol and adrenaline from the adrenal glands and oxytocin from the hypothalamus (via the pituitary gland).

Hormone, from Greek *hormon* = to set in motion, stir up. In physiology, hormones refer to chemicals released by endocrine glands into the blood circulation, whereupon they mediate effects throughout the body.

Playing an important role in the autonomic neural component of emotion is the vagus nerve (cranial nerve 10), consisting of neural connections between the brain and a large region of the core of the body (Latin *vagus* = wandering). Included in this circuitry is the parasympathetic innervation of the body's core—the heart, lungs, digestive system, and other body organs. Parasympathetic input to the heart

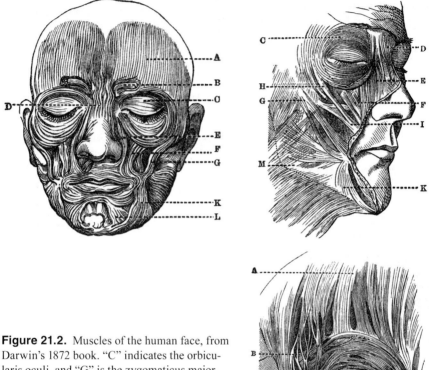

Figure 21.2. Muscles of the human face, from Darwin's 1872 book. "C" indicates the orbicularis oculi, and "G" is the zygomaticus major muscle.

functions to decrease heart rate. This is what Otto Loewi was investigating when he discovered chemical neurotransmission (see Chapter 6).

The vagus nerve is quite elaborate and complex. Its fiber bundle consists of many axons, some myelinated, some not, some carrying signals from the brain to body organs (efferent fibers), and some carrying signals from the interior of the body to the brain (afferent fibers). More than 50 percent of the axons in the vagus nerve are afferent fibers. This robust communication in both directions between the viscera and the brain may contribute to what we call "gut feelings"—our emotional experience involves awareness of the physiological state of the internal core of our body. Activity of the vagus nerve (as captured by a concept called *vagal tone*) has been associated with a more relaxed emotional style (equanimity), resilience when encountering negative emotions, more frequent experience of positive emotions, greater prosocial expression (including empathy and social connection), and improvements in measures of physical health.

As for most things, many brain regions are involved in emotions and their expression. While there is much research, lots of data, and a fair amount of theorizing, there is yet little consensus as to exactly what is going on and where. Some general themes may be stated.

The amygdala—a group of nuclei at the base of the temporal lobes and heavily interconnected with sensory areas of the cerebral cortex, as well as with numerous groups of neurons in the brainstem—is involved in the perception of emotional expressions. There is some evidence that sensory cues related to fear and anger may be of particular salience. The amygdala is also involved in signaling the hypothalamus to initiate a cascade of events that forms part of the body's response to stressful events.

The hypothalamus produces neuropeptides that regulate the release of systemic hormones from the adjacent pituitary gland. One such hypothalamic–pituitary neural connection regulates release of adrenocorticotropic hormone from the pituitary gland into the blood circulation. This hormone triggers the adrenal gland to release cortisol, a steroid hormone that increases the availability of glucose to cells, as well as having numerous other complex effects throughout the body. Cortisol is part of our body's response to perceived threat and other kinds of stress.

Other neurons in the hypothalamus produce the neuropeptides oxytocin (Fig. 21.3) and vasopressin. These two molecules are close chemical relatives, each consisting of a polypeptide chain of nine amino acids:

Oxytocin: Cys–Tyr–**Ile**–Gln–Asn–Cys–Pro–**Leu**–Gly

Vasopressin: Cys–Tyr–**Phe**–Gln–Asn–Cys–Pro–**Arg**–Gly

In these primary amino acid sequences of human oxytocin and vasopressin, amino acids are represented by three-letter abbreviations. The molecules are the same except for the two amino acids shown in boldface.

Oxytocin and vasopressin produced by neurons in the hypothalamus are released as hormones via the adjacent pituitary gland into the blood circulation. As systemic hormones they have effects that give rise to their names. Oxytocin acts on the female uterus during childbirth to induce contractions and facilitate birth. It also stimulates the production and release of milk from the mammary glands. Vasopressin acts on the kidneys to slow the transfer of water from the blood to the urine (in this context, it is also called an antidiuretic hormone) and also acts systemically to constrict blood vessels.

Oxytocin, from Greek *oxy* = acute, quick, sharp, from *Oxus*, ancient Greek name for the Amu Darya River, flowing across Central Asia, from the Himalayas to the Aral Sea; and *tokos* = birth.

Vasopressin, from Latin *vaso* = vessel, and *pressare* = to act on, to push on.

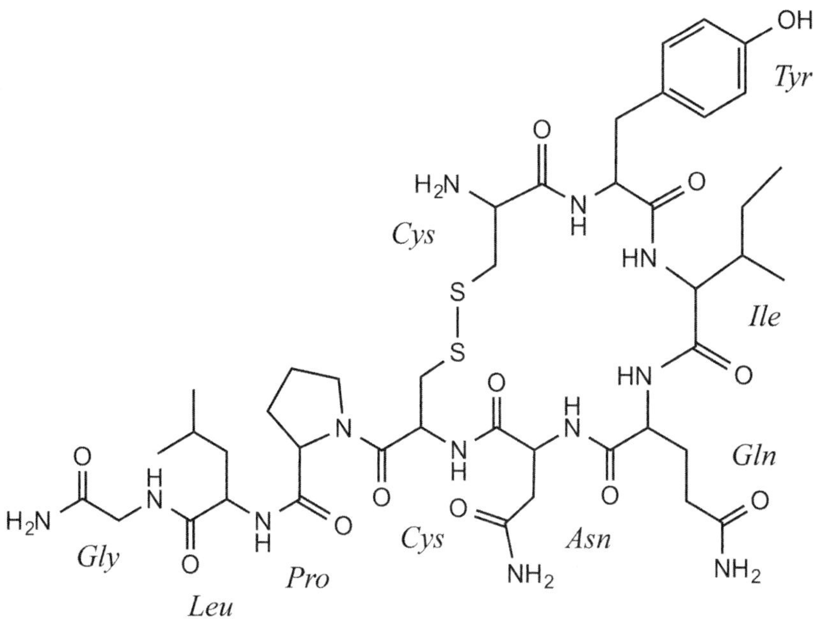

Figure 21.3. Molecular structure of oxytocin, with the nine amino acids indicated by their three-letter abbreviations. A disulfide (S–S) bond connects the two cysteines (Cys), resulting in a ring structure in part of the molecule.

In addition to these effects as hormones, oxytocin and vasopressin act at sites in the brain—G-protein-coupled receptors that specifically respond to either one or the other. Peptides released from the hypothalamus–pituitary into the blood do not reenter the brain because of the blood–brain barrier. However, hypothalamic neurons also release these neuropeptides into extracellular space within the hypothalamus and into the cerebrospinal fluid, from which they may diffuse to other sites in the central nervous system. Additionally, axons from hypothalamic neurons release oxytocin and vasopressin into the brainstem, hippocampus, amygdala, nucleus accumbens, and other specific regions in the interior of the brain (Fig. 21.4).

Recent investigations suggest oxytocin and vasopressin play roles in a variety of prosocial actions—mother–infant bonding (as assessed by things like eye gaze, touch, and response to vocalizations) and other parental care behaviors, as well as trust, generosity, and cooperation, have all been related to actions of these neuropeptides. There has even been some exploration of these neuropeptides as drugs to increase prosocial behaviors in individuals suffering from conditions in which social connection is impaired—autistic spectrum disorders, depression, and schizophrenia, for example.

"Feeling good" is often associated, especially in the popular media, with the brain's famous "reward pathways." In the 1950s, James Olds (1922–1976) discovered regions of the brain that, when electrically stimulated, induced rats to execute behaviors that would garner them more such electrical stimulation. That is, electri-

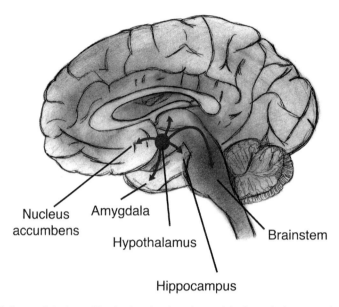

Nucleus   Amygdala
accumbens
                    Hypothalamus   Brainstem

Hippocampus

Figure 21.4. Medial view of brain showing locations of the hypothalamus and some of its oxytocinergic and vasopressinergic neural projections to other nearby structures involved in the neural regulation of emotion.

cal stimulation of these neural pathways was reinforcing, and interpreted as perhaps being rewarding and even pleasurable for the animal. Originally these brain regions were even called "pleasure centers." One of Olds's most dramatic findings involved implanted electrodes that would electrically stimulate these neurons when rats pressed a lever. Rats wired up in this way would repeatedly push the lever to deliver stimulation, thousands of lever presses per hour, until they collapsed from exhaustion and took a break to eat and sleep. After resting, they resumed their lever pressing. These neural pathways—reward circuits—have been extensively investigated in the years since Olds's discovery.

The best-known reward circuit involves dopaminergic neurons in the ventral tegmental area projecting to the nucleus accumbens and the medial prefrontal cortex (Fig. 21.5). As always, the closer one looks, the more complex the interconnectivity becomes. Neural connections between the ventral tegmental area, the nucleus accumbens, and the medial prefrontal cortex are reciprocal. In addition, all three of these areas are interconnected with the hypothalamus, amygdala, and hippocampus. Functional brain imaging has indicated activation of this pathway in connection with all kinds of behaviors experienced as enjoyable—listening to music, eating chocolate, ingesting other euphorigenic drugs (besides chocolate), and even orgasm. In addition, dysfunctional compulsive behaviors—addictions of various kinds— appear to be related to some kind of disruption of normal activity in this circuit.

Like most things we know about brain function, the regulation of emotions involves elaborate communication between many brain regions. In addition to the important roles played by limbic and other subcortical structures—such as the amygdala, hippocampus, hypothalamus, nucleus accumbens, and ventral tegmen-

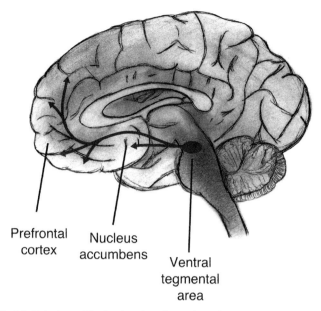

Prefrontal
cortex
Nucleus
accumbens
Ventral
tegmental
area

Figure 21.5. Medial view of brain showing dopaminergic reward pathways connecting the ventral tegmental area with the nucleus accumbens and prefrontal cortex.

tum—the prefrontal cortex is also a key part of the emotion regulation circuitry. There are many interconnections between the subcortical structures listed above and the prefrontal cortex. Many brain-imaging studies show relationships between neural activity in the frontal cortex and aspects of emotion, and many theories speculate on the roles of various aspects of brain activity in emotion.

> *Limbic*, from Latin *limbus* = border, edge. These are structures along the interior border of the cerebrum, at the edge between the cerebrum and the brainstem.

The neurotransmitters oxytocin and dopamine, mentioned above, have been implicated in specific roles in regulating emotions. Serotonin, with its widespread occurrence in the brain, has also been cast in a renowned part. In the quest to find simple explanations for the complexities of human behavior, there is often desire to assign dominant regulatory roles to single molecular entities—in this case, particular neurotransmitters: oxytocin, the cuddle hormone, love neuropeptide, compassion molecule; dopamine, the pleasure neurotransmitter; and serotonin, the molecular mediator of positive mood. The serotonin–mood connection derives in large part from the neurochemistry of drugs used to treat what are called *mood disorders*.

If one becomes stuck for a prolonged period of time (weeks, months, or more) in a mood state that significantly interferes with one's ability to function and flourish in life, one is said to have a mood disorder. These disorders are generally accompanied by significant personal suffering. What we call *depression* (or clinical depression, or major depression) is a prolonged and dysfunctional dysphoric mood, a malignant melancholia. A kind of opposite condition is *mania*, a prolonged and dysfunctional euphoric mood—dysfunctional in the sense that the euphoria is accompanied by poor judgment and grandiosity that may lead to behaviors that are damaging to oneself and to others. Manic-depressive disorder (known also as bipolar disorder) is characterized by periods of both mania and depression. In addition, there are anxiety disorders, characterized by prolonged anxious moods—chronic, protracted manifestations of nervousness that interfere with one's ability to function.

In the 1950s, the first pharmaceutical drugs were serendipitously discovered that appeared to have specific effects on reducing symptoms of depression. By the 1960s there were targeted efforts to discover more. The first two categories of pharmaceutical antidepressants were the monoamine oxidase inhibitors (MAOIs) and the tricyclic antidepressants (TCAs). Both types of medication appear to increase the presence of the neurotransmitters norepinephrine and serotonin at synapses—MAOIs by inhibiting the enzyme (monoamine oxidase) that normally inactivates these neurotransmitters by oxidizing them, and TCAs by blocking or slowing the reuptake of norepinephrine and serotonin back into the axons of the neurons that released them. This led to the idea that something to do with increasing the efficacy of norepinephrine and/or serotonin was therapeutically important for treating the symptoms of depression and that the mood disorder may even be biochemically precipitated by some kind of deficit of these neurotransmitters. This came to be called the amine hypothesis of depression.

For three decades, from the 1950s through the 1980s, the MAOIs and the TCAs were used to treat clinical depression. While widely available, they remained essentially a backwater of the pharmaceutical industry. Then, in 1988, fluoxetine (Prozac) hit the market, the first of a new pharmacologic class of antidepressant drugs: the selective serotonin reuptake inhibitors (SSRIs). Although fluoxetine and other SSRIs that appeared in the following years—sertraline (Zoloft), paroxetine (Paxil), citalopram (Celexa), and so on—were no more effective than the older MAOIs and TCAs in reducing symptoms of depression, they had less harmful side effects and were heavily advertised, quickly becoming best-sellers among pharmaceuticals.

Marketing of these "new-generation" antidepressant medications was greatly assisted by a loosening during the 1990s of government restrictions on direct-to-consumer pharmaceutical advertising. Ads appeared everywhere—in magazines, on billboards, and on television. Antidepressant medications became big business—very big business. Because the SSRIs were perceived as nontoxic (at least, it was thought, relative to MAOIs and TCAs), "nondepressed" people began to use them to tweak their mood and behavior in the direction of being more happy, outgoing, and so forth—to become "better than normal," a "cosmetic psychopharmacology."

Along with all this came the notion that moods (and perhaps emotions, too) have some simple relation to brain chemistry—in this case, serotonin is some kind of happiness molecule, and depression is related to some kind of deficit in serotonin. The connection between brain physiology and mood is not likely to be so straightforward, although it does make for convincing advertising. And certainly serotonergic neurochemistry has *something* to do with mood—and a lot of other things, too.

There was a parallel path for antipsychotic medications, drugs used to reduce disabling delusions and hallucinations in individuals diagnosed with schizophrenia. Chlorpromazine, the first modern pharmaceutical antipsychotic, was serendipitously discovered in the early 1950s in France. It was originally marketed in the United States as Thorazine. The introduction of chlorpromazine transformed the practice of psychiatry, and many additional antipsychotic drugs followed. The first ones were molecular relatives of chlorpromazine; later, new chemical forms were found. What they all had in common was antagonist action at dopamine receptors. From this was born the dopamine hypothesis of psychosis: psychotic symptoms were somehow related to overactivity in dopaminergic neurotransmission, and antipsychotic medications reduced the symptoms of psychosis by blocking some of that overactivity.

Around the time that SSRIs emerged as treatment for depression, a new generation of antipsychotic medications also came to the marketplace. These new drugs, like the older antipsychotics, were dopamine receptor antagonists; in addition, they were antagonists at certain serotonin receptors and were thus termed serotonin–dopamine antagonists. These drugs had side effects that appeared less problematic than the older antipsychotic medications, providing a platform for marketing, helped along again by direct-to-consumer advertising. Drugs that were once used only in severely disturbed psychotic patients were now approved by the U.S. Food and Drug Administration and prescribed for bipolar disorder and as adjunctive treatment of depression, and also used for an increasing number of "off-label" (not approved by the Food and Drug Administration) indications—agitation, sleep problems, autism, dementia, and so forth. They were more and more widely used in elderly people, and also in increasingly younger children, to treat symptoms of everything ranging from irritability to social withdrawal. Like antidepressant medications, antipsychotic drugs currently generate billions of dollars per year in sales. Few would have predicted that psychiatric medications would become the economic juggernaut they are today.

While images of neurotransmitter deficits or imbalances underlying conditions like depression and psychosis may make for compelling advertising, the complexities of brain biology speak against such simplistic hypotheses. Although the symptom-reducing effects of antidepressant and antipsychotic medications may be mediated in part via their effects on particular neurochemical systems (serotonin, norepinephrine, dopamine, glutamate, and so on), any long-term benefits are likely related to complex effects on intracellular G-protein-coupled receptor pathways impacting gene expression, neurogenesis, and changes in synaptic connectivity. It is also the case that such psychiatric medications will be most helpful when used in conjunction with psychotherapy and other practices that contribute to learning and consolidating desirable behaviors. While it may be the case that certain drugs facilitate changes in neural connections by perturbing brain physiology, real transformation comes from intention, action, and practice.

A prominent tradition in theorizing about the psychology of emotion is that the human condition is one of fear and dread, and the dominant human emotions are negative ones related to states of fear, anxiety, anger, pain, suffering, and desire. In this view, positive emotions are considered secondary to these negative states and emerge only with the occasional cessation of the negative states.

The dramatic opening scene in the movie *2001: A Space Odyssey* described in Chapter 1 (portraying ancient hominins discovering how to kill one another), and the long human history continuing to the present day of violence, mayhem, murder, and warfare, might give the impression that perhaps our primary emotions as a species are indeed those related to fear and anger. Influential thinkers over the centuries have described humans as being largely driven by self-interest, with our behavior—especially in the face of limited resources—dominated by selfishness. Sigmund Freud frequently wrote of the power of selfish and violent tendencies in humans. And Darwin's nuanced discussion of variation and selection as the driving forces in biological evolution is sometimes reduced to a simplistic statement of "survival of the fittest," imagining biological evolution to be driven chiefly by "selfish genes" and a bloody "Nature, red in tooth and claw."

Darwin, in fact, was very much an advocate of goodness, compassion, and sympathy as important forces in human evolution—a kind of survival of the kindest. This he makes clear in his first book specifically about human evolution—*The Descent of Man, and Selection in Relation to Sex*—published in 1871, the year before his book on emotions. About the expression of sympathy, he wrote that it "will have been increased through natural selection; for those communities, which included the greatest number of the most sympathetic members, would flourish best, and rear the greatest number of offspring." Several pages later, he goes on to say that

> many a civilized man, or even boy, who never before risked his life for another, but full of courage and sympathy, has disregarded the instinct of self-preservation, and plunged at once into a torrent to save a drowning man, though a stranger. . . . Such actions as the above appear to be the simple result of the greater strength of the social or maternal instincts rather than that of any other instinct or motive.

In his marvelous 2009 book *Born to Be Good*, Dacher Keltner presents a large body of recent research in support of the thesis that prosocial emotions are what matter most in human behavior. Although it is true that human conflict is pervasive, humans also have highly refined emotional abilities to preempt and to resolve conflict. We excel at laughter, play, love, gratitude, compassion, and forgiveness. We are experts at cooperating with our fellow beings.

Ongoing research is increasingly demonstrating positive and prosocial emotions to be associated with measures of human flourishing and mental and physical health. Furthermore, what is called "mindfulness meditation"—training and practice in bringing one's awareness repeatedly back to a focus of attention, such as the breath—has been associated with manifestations of prosocial emotion and emotional balance, decreases in measures of depression and anxiety, decreased perceived stress, and enhanced functioning of the immune system. Other aspects of meditative training have been associated with increases in measures of emotional well-being and even in improvement in measures of cellular flourishing (telomere length and telomerase activity). Such things speak to looking toward the development of training programs that could be implemented in schools and workplaces that would contribute to reducing stress and increasing social and emotional well-being. Such programs could foster the kinds of skills that will ultimately lead to decreases in need for mental health treatment services, psychiatric medications, and even other medical interventions—meditation, not medication, whenever possible.

Cultivation of positive emotions is at the core of all the world's great spiritual traditions. Our capacity to manifest compassion, gratitude, and other prosocial emotions is a testament to the deep interconnectivity and interdependence of human beings. Our own long-term flourishing is enhanced by the flourishing of our human community and by the health of our entire planet.

> Mammalian brain,
>   full of gyri and sulci—
>   for the sake of love.

CHAPTER **22**

Mind, Consciousness, and Reality

Does HAL have a mind? Whether a machine like HAL could have what we call *mind* remains an open question. The field of artificial intelligence—which dates from the early days of computer science in the 1950s—is about designing and building intelligent machines. What is "intelligence"—does it mean having a mind and consciousness?

Intelligence is from the Latin *intelligentum*, meaning to discern or comprehend, from *inter* + *legere*, to choose or pick out, from or between. Dictionary definitions of intelligence include the ability to acquire and retain knowledge, learn, grasp truths and patterns, reason, and apply all this toward solving problems. Intelligence defined this way may include understanding, if by *understanding* we mean a capacity to discern relationships and appreciate connections. There is no mention here of mind, mentality, or consciousness. By this definition, intelligence does not include awareness, inner subjective experience, or sentience. If intelligence is defined in this way, then machines have become very intelligent indeed, and there is no end in sight.

Consider playing the game of chess, once considered a distinctly human activity. Computers now beat the very best human chess players. Consider the quiz game of Jeopardy. Here, too, artificial intelligence has come a long way, and in 2011 a computer beat champion human players of the game. A Jeopardy-playing computer may still make seemingly silly mistakes, based on quirkiness in language recognition and interpretation, but the capacity to avoid such mistakes will continue to improve indefinitely. Machines can be programmed to create music and art, and the generation of novel ideas by computers is likely to become increasingly sophisticated with time.

And all this has been achieved with still essentially first-generation computers, based on ideas of computation described by Alan Turing (1912–1954) at the dawn of modern thinking about computability and instantiated in computing machines first built in the 1940s and 1950s. Speed and capacity have grown a billionfold since then, but the principles are essentially the same.

Some say that the intelligence of computers—their ability to solve problems, and even generate novelty—will in the near future exceed that of us humans. This state of affairs has been called the *technological singularity*. What would be the implications of such a singularity? Is it likely to come with a bang, or a series of bangs, or with a series of whispers?

The whispers, or bangs, are already happening, in selected domains: chess, jeopardy, financial markets. It has been suggested that some responsibility for the economic meltdown of 2008 may justifiably be placed upon computer systems that were running trading algorithms beyond the comprehensive understanding and ready control of humans. The machines were literally out of control. And we are only at the very beginning of things like this. Who's to say what the future may hold? Certainly it will be interesting.

In all existing cases, and many future extrapolations—such as singularity scenarios—computers still lack minds. No matter how computationally fast and massive their capabilities are, no matter how intelligent and creative, no matter what capacity they have to learn or to apply what they have learned to improve their problem-solving and creative capacities, they are still not thought to have mental experience, conscious awareness, sentience—except in some science fiction scenarios.

We feel there to be something special about life, nervous systems, brains—and rightly so. After all, life on Earth has been evolving for billions of years, and nervous systems and brains have been undergoing evolutionary tuning for hundreds of millions of years. It surely must be the case that living systems have structures and capacities that are far, far more sophisticated, nuanced, and complex than what a few decades of scientific probing, explanation, and speculation have given us access to. As Max Delbrück commented in a lecture given in 1949: "Any living cell carries with it the experiences of a billion years of experimentation by its ancestors. You cannot expect to explain so wise an old bird in a few simple words."

So, what does it take to manifest mind? What conditions are needed for mental experience, and for consciousness of that experience? Clearly our brains and bodies are involved in determining the properties of our minds. Changes in the brain and body from lesions or the ingestion of psychoactive drugs are related in specific ways to changes in mental function. Brain activity as measured by electroencephalography, positron emission tomography, and functional magnetic resonance imaging correlates with aspects of mental experience.

But exactly how mind is related to body and brain physiology remains a deep mystery. Thus, we return to the question that began this book—this short odyssey from mind through brain and back again: how is mind related to brain and body? How indeed is mind, is consciousness, related to not just one's body but to the rest of what we call physical reality?

The descriptive successes of biology in general and neuroscience in particular are part of an explanatory picture of our world given us by the framework of contemporary physical science. Within this framework, living organisms are understood as configurations of atoms and molecules, organized so as to use energy in the maintenance of stability, information storage, and replication. This is what is called *reductionism*—biology is explained in terms of (that is, reduced to) what is considered to be the more basic science of chemistry, and chemistry is understood in terms of the fundamental rules of matter and energy as described by physics, and physics is grounded in elegant mathematical structures and equations.

All this has provided us with a powerful framework for describing, explaining, and understanding our world. Within this framework, much can be calculated, predicted, engineered, and constructed. Applications are legion—from exploration of deep space, to the gizmos of technology that have become so much a part of daily life, to molecular manipulations helpful in the treatment of human disease. There is a kind of seductiveness in the power of this physical description of the world. It can sometimes feel like we have a relatively good grasp of the whole shebang.

Yet, one might also argue the opposite—that at a deep level of understanding of what we call reality, we simply do not know all that much about what is going on. For example, what is the universe made of? The periodic table of the chemical elements is wonderfully successful for organizing the properties of all the matter with which we routinely come into contact. And the principles of quantum physics applied to the internal structures of the protons and neutrons of the atomic nucleus yield an elegant description of what are considered fundamental particles of nature: quarks, gluons, electrons, muons, neutrinos, bosons, photons, and taus. Nonetheless, it is said that even all this success accounts for only about 4 percent of the matter/energy content of the universe. And the remaining 96 percent is composed of so-called dark matter and dark energy, the natures of which we do not understand.

Moreover, quantum mechanics, the physics that describes matter in its most fundamental aspects, indicates that the behavior of matter and energy at the submicroscopic level is very weird indeed. For example, a single particle can exist in many states and places simultaneously, and its behavior is governed by a quantum wave function—a mathematical construct that assigns probabilities to the various alternative states and locations available to the particle. The particle is said to exist as a superposition of multiple alternative possibilities. However, we perceive reality as actualities, not potentialities—atoms and molecules, for example, having actual locations in space and time. The transition from a superposition of potentialities to a discrete value is called a "reduction" or "collapse" of the wave function. It defines the connection between the microscopic quantum world of potentialities and the macroscopic classical world of our experience. Exactly how this collapse or reduction comes about is called the "measurement problem" in quantum physics. It is an unsolved problem, vigorously debated among physicists interested in the foundations of their subject—a mystery.

In addition, in quantum physics there is what is called nonlocal entanglement, in which particles that are separated by arbitrarily large distances may still influence one another, seemingly instantaneously. This derives from the fact that systems of particles, once having interacted, may continue to be described by a single quantum wave function. There is universal agreement among physical scientists that microscopic matter behaves in these strange ways, and the experimental verification of quantum mechanics has been extensive and unwavering.

And there's more weirdness that, unlike the above, is not universally accepted among physicists. For example, some physicists believe the next big explanatory breakthrough will involve so-called string theories that expand the number of physical dimensions from the four dimensions of space-time as currently understood to ten or eleven dimensions, describing who knows exactly what. And some physicists contend that the best way to understand our universe is to view it as one among an infinite number of parallel universes, and that new universes in this vast collection are being created all the time. Though not universally accepted, these theoretical speculations are taken very seriously within mainstream physics, in part because they can be tied into some kind of elegant mathematical framework.

Mathematics, it seems, offers at this point the ultimate, the most compelling guide to what we regard to be truths about physical reality. No one knows exactly what that is about. Does it mean that mathematical notions somehow exist as an intrinsic part of the foundation of reality? Are numbers—zero to infinity, real and imaginary, discrete and continuous—examples of what is really real, the "ideal forms" posited by the ancient Greek philosopher Plato (about 427–347 B.C.E.)?

Or is mathematics, from the simple to the profoundly esoteric, solely a product of human cognition—our concept of numbers, ability to carry out mathematical operations, and capacity to formulate and discover mathematical truths (such as "π is an irrational number," "there is no largest prime number," or "$x^n + y^n = z^n$ has no integer solutions x, y, z for any integer value of $n > 2$")—directly related to biological evolution of our cognitive capacities and nothing more? No one knows. Insights into this question seem relevant to the nature of mind and reality.

What is the relation between so-called reality and our perception and understanding of it? The standard view given to us thus far by our scientific observations and theorizing is that there is a world, a universe, existing independently of our awareness of it. Astrophysics provides a creation scenario, a story of the origin of our universe—a "big bang" estimated to have occurred 13.7 billion years ago, setting in motion processes that eventually resulted in the formation of the chemical elements and the coalescing of our galaxy, sun, and solar system.

Our planet Earth is just the right distance from our sun to produce conditions conducive to the presence of life: a habitable zone where it is not too hot and not too cold. Water, the elixir and canvas of life, is able to exist as a temperate liquid—not frozen ice and not boiling vapor. Large molecules and molecular aggregates—proteins, nucleic acids, phospholipid bilayer membranes—the components of life as we know it, can form and remain stable. So our creation story concludes from the data thus far that life somehow appeared on Earth and then evolved over billions of years into its present multiple forms.

There are questions. How did life first originate on Earth? One guess is that small RNA molecules somehow formed in the primordial soup and that such molecules were capable of replicating and catalyzing chemical reactions. This could give rise over time to the formation of stabilized, energy-using, replicating systems—life as we know it.

But some say the formation of such primordial biological structures is so unlikely that it wouldn't be expected to happen, even given billions of years of molecular mixing. Some say that life on Earth must have been transplanted from elsewhere in the cosmos, perhaps via the impact of a comet bearing spores, seeds, cells, or other components of living systems—which, of course, simply pushes the origin question off to another place and time.

Nonetheless, many scientists believe it is only a matter of time before a plausible scenario for the origin of life is constructed. Given that our science of biochemistry and molecular biology is less than a hundred years old, the pace of progress in what we consider to be deep understanding of life is truly sensational. So, is this it? Are we on the verge of some kind of complete understanding of life and how it originated from, and is related to, inanimate matter? Many scientists would say yes. Maybe it is so. Or maybe not.

Now, consider this: as methods of astronomical measurement become ever more sophisticated, it has been discovered that many stars appear to have planetary systems, and many of these systems have planets within a habitable zone. Thus, the likelihood of there being many Earth-like planets out there in our galaxy, in our universe, appears to be substantial. It is believed that there are around two hundred billion stars in our galaxy, and something like 10^{22} (a hundred billion hundred billion) stars in the observable universe. Thus, there will be billions of planets on which life might have developed and evolved. And given the billions of years of time available, the likelihood of sophisticated life forms appearing elsewhere would seem to be substantial.

Given the youth of our own human species and civilization, it is often assumed that many life forms out there in the cosmos must be way ahead of us in technology and other forms of development. So the question is, where are they? The SETI—Search for Extraterrestrial Intelligence—program has been going strong for several decades, searching the heavens for any sign of a radio signal in the cosmic noise. Why haven't we noticed these alien civilizations, an abundance of which are argued to exist, on probabilistic grounds? Are they simply too far away, the distances too vast for even electromagnetic signals? And too far for interstellar travel—assuming no *Star Trek*–style warp drive or navigable space-time wormholes. Or, are technologically advanced civilizations the rare exception, rather than the rule? Perhaps life itself is a profoundly rare occurrence. Or, is something else, unimaginably stranger, going on? It's another one of those mysteries.

Our scientific framework for describing reality has its origin in astronomy. Nicolaus Copernicus (1473–1543) seeded the idea, Galileo Galilei (1564–1642) staked out the territory, and Isaac Newton (1643–1727) locked it in with an elegant mathematical description of both celestial and terrestrial motion. Throughout the 1700s and 1800s the mathematical foundations put in place by Newton were extended to apply to a wide variety of natural phenomena—light, electricity, magnetism, gaseous pressure, temperature, and other thermodynamic properties among them. This description of the so-called physical properties of the world is called classical physics. This historical trajectory, beginning with Copernicus and extending into the twentieth century, was one of revolutionary reconceptualization of nature.

Darwin made his revolutionary contributions to biology within this framework of physical science. Ever since Darwin, discoveries in biology have continued to fit in and further support this view of nature. Thus, we have a system of scientific explanation that posits that all of what we call reality is constructed in some way from material stuff—matter and its interactions—as described by the mathematical laws of physics. Everything else follows from that.

This is the framework within which our science is currently conducted, the so-called metaphysical framework. Metaphysics describes the larger context within which we interpret scientific analyses, the stage or landscape upon which our inquiry is carried out. The metaphysical framework of contemporary science is called physical materialism, or simply physicalism.

Within a physicalist metaphysics, mind, mental experience, and consciousness must be explained in terms of the properties of matter. Just how this relationship between mind and body manifests is the mind–body problem. Over the centuries, many smart people have thought deeply about mind, matter, and metaphysics. A great deal of stuff from all sorts of perspectives has been articulated, providing rich descriptive analyses of frameworks for conducting and interpreting scientific inquiry.

Within a physicalist metaphysics, there is a way in which the mind–body problem will always be a problem. There is a fundamental difference of category between the physical and the mental—mentality is irreducibly subjective and thus, it would seem, a very different phenomenon from physical stuff. That's precisely what makes the mind–body problem difficult—some even say impossible. (How subjectivity is related to the physical workings of the brain and body is sometimes called the *hard problem* of consciousness research. It is also referred to as the *explanatory gap* between the physical and the subjective.)

Various approaches to the mind–body problem have been put forth over the centuries. Here is a much abbreviated list: There is dualism, in which there are two separate domains—matter (the physical stuff) and mind (the mental stuff)—that somehow are able to come together and interact within the body. There is mentalism (or idealism), where what is really real is the mental domain and somehow our experience of what we call physical is derived from that. There is panpsychism, in which mind and consciousness are everywhere, fundamental to the structure of reality. These terms are used within the discipline of philosophy to describe different metaphysical frames for understanding the mind–matter connection.

It is useful to be familiar with terminology and descriptions of metaphysical frameworks, as these are frequently invoked in scientific and philosophical discussions about the nature of mind. However, it is also good to be aware that terminologies may restrict our thinking, confining us to particular categories in ways that may end up not being helpful. Beware the boxes created by terminology.

Let's approach the framing of the mind–body problem from the perspective of evolutionary biology and neuroscience, the descriptive framework detailed throughout this book. Life provides a separation between inner and outer. The first living cells would have had such an interior–exterior boundary. Single-celled bacteria are in sensory contact with their environment, detecting the presence of nutrient chemicals or of sunlight. Thus, even relatively simple life forms can be imagined to have some sort of inner perspective on sensory information.

As sensory processes became more elaborate over the course of evolutionary history, that inner perspective became correspondingly more nuanced, leading eventually to an emergence of awareness—the *experience* of what it is like to be a particular organism. In this view, sophisticated sentience goes along with nervous systems that conduct sufficiently sophisticated analyses of sensory information. These sensory analyses are used to construct mental models—of the environment, of other individuals, of oneself—that have adaptive utility, by enriching understanding of and ability to navigate through the world.

As for the mysterious experiential quality of consciousness, perhaps this capacity is a fundamental aspect of reality—as central as matter, energy, space, and time—one that manifests in given particular configurations of matter and energy, such as what occurs in living organisms.

Our consciousness is our most salient experience; it is the only thing we truly know firsthand. Everything comes to us by way of our conscious experience. How can we continue to move forward with its investigation? I suggest sticking with the scientific method of empirical observation and experiment, while maintaining a broadened stance in which nothing is left out, including questioning the metaphysical framework itself. Here are several trajectories:

1. Continued direct investigation of the brain, body, and life, using and extending the ideas and methods already in play (as described in this book)
2. Refined analysis of mental experience, drawing from the tools of contemplative traditions, and in particular the current dialogue between science and Buddhism
3. Radically empirical extensions of research in biology and psychology, honoring *all* the data, no matter how weird, especially if it bears directly on the mind–matter connection
4. Appreciating that the next truly big scientific revolution may involve deep connection between fundamental physics and consciousness, so look for opportunities to investigate such connections

All four of these trajectories are currently under way, some more so than others. I anticipate there to be radically unexpected findings within each of them.

1. Continued direct investigation.   Progress in understanding bodies, nervous systems, and brains has been impressive. Some of this has been described in this book, and this corpus of knowledge can be expected to grow ever larger. Ambitious projects to map structure and functional connectivity in the human brain are under way. Another project focuses on building a complete map of the much simpler, but still vastly complex, mouse brain. Some folks anticipate that within a decade or two it will become possible to build integrated circuits duplicating the neural connectivity of brains—so-called neuromorphic computers. These projects have widespread support around the world; brain science is flourishing and will continue to flourish.

This will certainly have many applications to human health and disease. Greater understanding of conditions like Alzheimer's disease, Parkinson's disease, and epilepsy can be expected, guiding the development of more effective treatments and leading to reduced suffering for many. Perhaps the neurology associated with psychosis, depression, anxiety, and addiction will also be better understood, improving the capacity to prevent and treat these conditions.

Creative investigation of neural correlates of consciousness will continue to be a valuable research direction. In addition, it will be useful to expand investigation of the developing mind of human infants, as well as the minds of other animals. If we believe sentience is associated with complex nervous systems, then it must be the case that animals like dolphins, whales, and elephants, for example, have elaborate conscious awareness. Little effort currently goes toward studying and attempting to communicate with these creatures. What might be learned about the nature of mind if such communication could ever be established? We fantasize about communicating with aliens from another star system. Perhaps we ought also work on communicating with the likely very sentient and very intelligent aliens among us.

We know neither the necessary nor sufficient conditions for mind and conscious awareness to manifest in matter, in life, in nervous systems. All these kinds of studies will help with that. Whatever the nature of reality may be, our body with its brain is the vehicle by which we connect with the larger reality. As far as we know, all that we know comes to us via our body, so continuing the study of perception, action, and neural correlates of consciousness will be valuable.

Moreover, look to the interior of the cell—continue to push the limits, as more microscopic analysis becomes technically possible. As yet undiscovered processes deep within cells may yield new insight into the nature of life itself. And there is no reason to assume that neural computation involves only electrodynamic couplings between cells, just because that's all we've been able to investigate so far. For example, one scenario (due to Roger Penrose and Stuart Hameroff) posits that subcellular structures such as microtubules may be information storage and computational devices, with aspects of their component tubulin structures acting something like information bits in a computer. And not just bits, but qubits—units of quantum information. A qubit is in a superposition of two different states at the same time, rather than one state or the other state, such as is the case for a classical bit. This allows for a substantial increase in computational power—what is called quantum computation. Thus, it is hypothesized, microtubules may be quantum computers, processing information and making decisions deep within cells—pretty wild stuff!

2. Refined analysis of mental experience. William James (1842–1910) suggested that a science of mind be based upon a multifaceted empirical approach— study of behavior (psychology), study of the biological underpinnings of behavior (neurobiology), and study of the mental phenomena themselves (introspection). The first two approaches have been well developed in the century of scientific progress since James's time. However, investigation of mental experience has not yet seen the same level of development within the scientific enterprise.

James stated in his 1890 *Principles of Psychology* that empirical study of mental experience was essential to a science of mind. He also appreciated that the investigation of mental experience requires a sustained focus of attention internally—on the contents of one's own mind—and such sustained focus is no easy task:

> The faculty of bringing back a wandering attention, over and over again, is the very root of judgment, character, and will. . . . An education which should improve this faculty would be *the* education *par excellence*. But it is easier to define this ideal than to give practical directions for bringing it about.

Indeed, this may now be more difficult than ever before, given all the distractions inherent in our technology-sodden, contemporary world.

However, sophisticated methods to train attention, coupled with introspective observation and analyses of the mind, have been explored for millennia by contemplative traditions. This is perhaps most evident in Buddhism. Beginning in the 1980s, the Dalai Lama (b. 1935), spiritual leader of the Tibetan Buddhist tradition, began what has become an ongoing series of conversations between Tibetan Buddhism and the scientific community. Initially taking place among the Dalai Lama, psychologists, cognitive scientists, and neuroscientists, the dialogue has become formalized and expanded to include physicists, educators, and environmental scientists. While new research in the neuroscience of meditation and in the psychology of emotion has been spawned by these dialogues, part of their original motivation was to address really big questions related to the nature of mind and the nature of reality. Much remains to be explored regarding the ways in which Buddhist contemplative practices might contribute to an expanded science of mind and reality. May this dialogue continue to flourish and expand!

3. A radically empirical approach to studying human experience.   One of William James's lifelong interests was investigation of what are called "psi" phenomena—things like telepathy (direct communication between minds), clairvoyance (direct knowledge of objects or events removed in space from view), and precognition (direct knowledge of future events). The hallmark feature of psi is information transfer between persons, or between a person and the environment, in ways not explicable by our current biophysical understanding of mind and matter. James was also interested in phenomena suggesting that aspects of mind might somehow transcend the body and perhaps even survive death of the body. Such things, to the extent they are occurring, are clearly relevant to understanding the mind–body connection.

   Public discussions of such phenomena often evoke dismissal, derision, and even anger, yet it is notable just how many people reveal personal experiences in this realm of psi in more intimate settings, suggesting that something is going on worthy of a closer look.

   James was one of the founders of a scientific collective that defined what they called "psychical research." These days, such phenomena are sometimes referred to as parapsychological, or even paranormal (Greek *para* = beyond). Unfortunately, these later terms have a connotation that the phenomena are beyond the scope of scientific investigation—that they are somehow only in the realm of "spirit," whatever that may mean. However, not only are these phenomena capable of being researched using the methods of science, there are cultural contexts where their occurrence is considered very normal indeed. James maintained that to reach the next level of scientific understanding of mind, one needs to pay attention to all empirical phenomena, no matter how weird and presently inexplicable.

   In the century since James, there has been considerable investigation of psi phenomena, and those who take the time to look closely at the results of these investigations are frequently impressed by the extent and quality of the data. The most robust of these phenomena often occur under extreme emotional circumstances—such as trauma, death, or near-death—making controlled laboratory-style investigation difficult at best. (Recall the experience of Hans Berger and his sister, described in Chapter 17.) Nonetheless, projects are underway investigating, for example, precognition, near-death experiences, veridical out-of-body experiences, and young children who speak as if they have lived other previous lives and provide detailed and sometimes verifiable information consistent with this. Rather than being heedlessly dismissed, these kinds of studies should continue and the rigor of investigation strengthened in any and all ways possible.

4. The next big scientific revolution may involve deep connections between physics and consciousness.   If we are attempting to understand mind in terms of physical science, then it is likely that fundamental aspects of physics will be involved. How so? The unsolved quantum measurement problem, mentioned earlier, leads to a variety of different perspectives, called interpretations, of quantum mechanics. What is suggested by many of these interpretations is that in some still mysterious way, mind and matter are deeply connected. We should continue to explore this trajectory, in terms of both theory and experiment.

Just as we look to experiments with the Large Hadron Collider or to observational cosmology and astrophysics to trigger new ideas in fundamental physics, so might it also be that more deeply investigating the nature of mind and life will lead to unexpected new ideas in physics. This was the speculation of Niels Bohr (as well as Max Delbrück and Erwin Schrödinger) almost a century ago. Perhaps the time has now come.

In 1892 William James wrote this about the future development of a science of mind:

> A genuine glimpse into what it is would be *the* scientific achievement, before which all past achievements would pale. But at present psychology is in the condition of physics before Galileo and the laws of motion, of chemistry before Lavoisier and the notion that mass is preserved in all reactions. The Galileo and the Lavoisier of psychology will be famous men indeed when they come, as come they some day surely will, or past successes are no index to the future. When they do come, however, the necessities of the case will make them "metaphysical." Meanwhile the best way in which we can facilitate their advent is to understand how great is the darkness in which we grope, and never to forget that the natural-science assumptions with which we started are provisional and revisable things.

These words capture the notions that developments in the scientific exploration of mind will eventually be truly revolutionary, somehow eclipsing all prior scientific achievements in impact; that the implications will necessarily be metaphysical, meaning that physical materialism as currently understood will no longer be sufficient as the explanatory framework; and that this may be accompanied by significant revision of the underlying laws of physics (the assumptions of natural science). The next really big scientific revolution is likely to encompass both mind science and physical science, interconnecting the two domains in new and unexpected ways. This would be a truly revolutionary development in science, on par with the greatest scientific revolutions of history—Copernicus and the heliocentric cosmos; Galileo, Newton, and classical physics; Darwin and evolution; Einstein and relativity; and quantum physics. How positively exciting!

All our science to date points to deeper and more nuanced connectivity and interdependence. Not only is all of life on Earth deeply interconnected, but life interacts profoundly with other planetary processes, such as climate and geology. Recent findings reveal that the symbiotic relationship we have with trillions of microorganisms living within our bodies far surpasses anything previously known or imagined. There is deep interconnectivity and interdependence everywhere we look. The expanded perspectives outlined above suggest that consciousness may be interwoven into this connectivity in deeply significant ways. The task now is to see where such expanded perspectives take us, empirically.

How we choose to define and understand mind has a powerful impact on our lives at every level. It influences our biomedical science—and how we relate to our bodies, in health and disease. It influences our relationship with technology and the environment, our concepts of past and future, and our connections with ancestors and descendants. Questions about the nature of mind can evoke notions of spirit and soul, and the many different definitions, connotations, and emotional reactions people have related to these terms. Investigation of who we are and how we are related to the rest of the universe can bring one into what is generally considered the territory of religion and, some maintain, outside the domain of science. This can be unsettling, to individuals in either camp. Distressing or not, questions regarding the ultimate nature of reality and of mind *are* of interest both to science and to religious and spiritual traditions and can provide opportunities for useful dialogue.

That we may be poised for truly revolutionary developments in neuroscience and cognitive science is exciting to contemplate. I hope it happens soon enough for us all to witness. Perhaps it is already happening.

Figure Credits

Unless noted in the listing below, figures are original for this book. Most of the original artwork was drawn by Gregory Chin and Shefali Netke, molecular biology and cognitive science students at the University of California, Berkeley. Several figures were drawn by Dr. Kristi Panik. All molecular structures were drawn by Breanna Ford (Morris), molecular toxicology and endocrinology graduate student at the University of California, Berkeley.

Chapter 1

Figure 1.1: Photo taken by the eminent scholar of Paleolithic art Jean Clottes; used with his kind permission. The photo was received from Dr. Clottes by way of our mutual friend and colleague, Professor Meg Conkey.

Chapter 2

Figure 2.2: Compass jellyfish, *Chrysaora hysoscella*, Ernst Haeckel, *Kunstformen der natur* (Leipzig: Bibliographischen Instituts, 1904).
Figure 2.9: Open human skull: Andreas Vesalius, *De humani corporis fabrica* (1543), book 7, figure 1 (dura intact) and figure 2 (dura peeled back).
Figure 2.10: Nerve fibers: Andreas Vesalius, *De humani corporis fabrica* (1543), book 4, figure 1 (brain) and figure 10 (spinal cord).
Figure 2.11: Reacting to fire: René Descartes, *L'Homme de René Descartes* (Paris, 1664).
Figure 2.12: Dissection of muscles surrounding the eyeball: René Descartes, *L'Homme de René Descartes* (Paris, 1664).
Figure 2.13: Visual perception and action: René Descartes. *L'Homme de René Descartes* (Paris, 1664).
Figure 2.14: Galvani's apparatus for electrically stimulating frog legs: Plates I and III from Luigi Galvani, "De viribus electricitatis in motu musculari commenatrius," *De bononiensi scientiarum et artium instituto atque academia, commentarii* 7 (1791): 363–418.
Figure 2.16: Cerebellar neurons (left): Camillo Golgi, *Organi centrali del sistema nervosa* (*Organs of the central nervous system*) (Reggio-Emilia, Italy: Stefano Calderini e Figlio, 1885); Cerebral cortex neurons (right): Santiago Ramón y Cajal, *Histologie du systeme nerveux de l'homme et des vertébrés*, vol. 2 (Paris: Maloine, 1911), figure 345.

Chapter 3

Figure 3.4: Myoglobin structure: Adapted from Wikimedia Commons, public domain; original data from the Research Collaboratory for Structural Bioinformatics, Protein Data Bank: S. E. Phillips, Structure and refinement of oxymyoglobin at 1.6-angstrom resolution, *Journal of Molecular Biology* 142 (1980): 531–534.

Chapter 4

Figure 4.1: Solvay Conference, 1927: Wikimedia Commons, public domain; author, Benjamin Couprie, Institut International de Physique Solvay, Brussels, Belgium.

Figure 4.2: Bohr, Delbrück et al. in Copenhagen, 1933: Photo courtesy of Niels Bohr Archive, Niels Bohr Institute; and Emilio Segre Visual Archive, American Institute of Physics.

Figure 4.3 (left): Bacteriophage drawing: From Wikimedia Commons; author, Michael David Jones (Wikimedia user name: Adenosine); shared under Creative Commons, Attribution-Share 3.0 Unported.

Figure 4.3 (right): Electron micrograph of bacteriophage infection: Wikimedia Commons, public domain; author, Dr. Graham Beards, United Kingdom shared under Creative Commons, Attribution-Share 3.0 Unported.

Chapter 5

Figure 5.10: Myelinated axon from human cerebral cortex: Electron micrograph image © Dr. Josef Spacek, *Atlas of ultrastructural neurocytology*, and courtesy of SynapseWeb, Kristen M. Harris, PI © 1999–present (synapses.clm.utexas.edu); used with kind permission.

Chapter 6

Figure 6.3: Chemical synapses: Electron micrograph image © Dr. Josef Spacek, *Atlas of ultrastructural neurocytology*, and courtesy of SynapseWeb, Kristen M. Harris, PI © 1999–present (synapses.clm.utexas.edu); used with kind permission.

Chapter 8

Figure 8.1: Paracelsus: J. M. Stillman, *Paracelsus (Theophrastus Bombastus von Hohenheim, Called Paracelsus: His personality and influence as physician, chemist and reformer)* (Chicago, IL: Open Court, 1920).

Figure 8.2: Deadly nightshade, *Atropa belladonna*: F. E. Köhler, *Köhler's medizinal-pflanzen*, vol. 2 (Gera-Untermhaus, Germany, 1887).

Figure 8.3: Tea plant, *Camellia sinensis*: F. E. Köhler, *Köhler's medizinal-pflanzen*, vol. 1 (Gera-Untermhaus, Germany, 1887).

Figure 8.4: Henbane, *Hyoscyamus niger*, and jimson weed, *Datura stromonium*: H. Baillon, *Histoire des plantes*, vol. 9 (Paris: Librairie Hachette, 1888), figure 431 (jimson weed) and figure 437 (henbane).

Figure on page 95: Pondering skeleton, adapted from Andreas Vesalius, *De humani corporis fabrica* (1943), book 1, figure 22.

Chapter 9

Figure 9.1: Tobacco plant, *Nicotiana tabacum*: H. Baillon, *Histoire des plantes*, vol. 9 (Paris: Librairie Hachette, 1888), figure 460.

Figure 9.2: Opium poppy, *Papaver somniferum*: H. Baillon, *Histoire des plantes*, vol. 3 (Paris: Librairie Hachette, 1872), figure 113.

Figure 9.3: Coca plant, *Erythroxylum coca*: A. Mariani, *Coca and its therapeutic application*, 2nd ed. (New York: J. N. Jaros, 1892).

Chapter 10

Figure 10.2: Human embryo between eighteen and twenty-one days old: Henry Gray, *Anatomy of the human body*, 20th rev. ed., edited by W. H. Lewis (1858; Philadelphia: Lea and Febiger, 1918), figure 59.

Figure 10.3: Axon growth cone drawings: S. Ramón y Cajal, *Recuerdos de mi vida* (Madrid: Nicolás Moya, 1917), figure 21.

Figure 10.7: Hippocampus: Henry Gray, *Anatomy of the human body*, 20th rev. ed., edited by W. H. Lewis (1858; Philadelphia: Lea and Febiger, 1918), figure 739.

Chapter 11

Figure 11.2: *Phycomyces* sporangiophore phototropism: Time-exposure photograph by Prof. David S. Dennison of Dartmouth College; used with his kind permission.

Chapter 12

Figure 12.2: Alembic: John French, *The art of distillation*, 2nd ed. (1651; London: E. Coates for Thomas Williams, 1653).

Figure 12.3: Black pepper plant, *Piper nigrum*: H. Baillon, *Histoire des plantes*, vol. 3 (Paris: Librairie Hachette, 1872), figure 497.

Chapter 13

Figure 13.3: Chili plant, *Capsicum annum*: H. Baillon, *Histoire des plantes*, vol. 9 (Paris: Librairie Hachette, 1888), figure 359.

Chapter 14

Figure 14.1: Human eyeball: Courtesy of National Eye Institute, National Institutes of Health (NEI/NIH); image reference no. NEA08; used with kind permission.

Figure 14.6: Cell layers in vertebrate retina: S. Ramón y Cajal, *Histologie du systeme nerveux de l'homme and des vertébrés*, vol. 2 (Paris: A. Maloine, 1911), figure 186.

Chapter 15

Figure 15.6: Complex sound waveforms: Courtesy Frederic Theunissen, University of California, Berkeley.

Figure 15.8: Fourier decomposition: Courtesy Frederic Theunissen, University of California, Berkeley.

Figure 15.9: Fourier analyses of piano notes: Courtesy Frederic Theunissen, University of California, Berkeley.

Figure 15.10: Human ear: Adapted from L. Chittka and A. Brockmann, "Perception space—the final frontier," *PLoS Biology* 3, no. 4 (2005): e137, shared under Creative Commons, Attribution-Share 3.0 Unported.

Figure 15.11: Bony labyrinth of the human inner ear: H. Gray, *Anatomy of the human body*, 20th rev. ed., edited by W. H. Lewis (1858; Philadelphia: Lea and Febiger, 1918), figure 920.

Figure 15.13: Side view of human skull: H. Gray, *Anatomy of the human body*, 20th rev. ed., edited by W. H. Lewis (1858; Philadelphia: Lea and Febiger, 1918), figure 188.

Chapter 16

Figure 16.6: Cerebellar Purkinje neuron: S. Ramón y Cajal, *Histologie du systeme nerveux de l'homme and des vertébrés*, vol. 2 (Paris: Maloine, 1911), figure 6.

Chapter 17

Figure 17.2: Human brain MRI: Courtesy Justin Riddle, University of California, Berkeley.

Figure 17.4: Human EEG tracings: Courtesy Ed Kelly, University of Virginia.

Chapter 18

Figure 18.1: Human cerebral cortex: S. Ramón y Cajal, *Histologie du systeme nerveux de l'homme and des vertébrés*, vol. 2 (Paris: Maloine, 1911), figure 392 (Nissl stain) and figure 405 (Golgi stain).

Figure 18.5: Neuropil from rat hippocampus: Image © Dr. Josef Spacek, *Atlas of ultrastructural neurocytology*, and courtesy of SynapseWeb, Kristen M. Harris, PI © 1999–present (synapses.clm.utexas.edu); used with kind permission.

Chapter 19

Figure 19.2 (left): Hippocampus: Henry Gray, *Anatomy of the human body*, 20th rev. ed., edited by W. H. Lewis (1858; Philadelphia: Lea and Febiger, 1918), figure 739.

Chapter 21

Figure 21.1: Chimpanzee facial expression: C. Darwin, *The expression of the emotions in man and animals* (London: John Murray, 1872), figure 18.

Figure 21.2: Muscles of the human face: C. Darwin, *The expression of the emotions in man and animals* (London: John Murray, 1872), figures 1–3.

Notes

This list of notes and references is not meant to be comprehensive. Included are a few articles and books I have found particularly interesting—good places to seek additional insights, as well as to see some of the work of the pioneers.

Chapter 1

The modern discovery of the Chauvet Cave told by its three discoverers: Chauvet, Deschamps, and Hillaire (1996). The book has many beautiful photographs of the art within the cave. Filmmaker Werner Herzog has made an excellent documentary film on Chauvet Cave: *Cave of Forgotten Dreams* (2010). A spectacular collection of photographs of cave art is by Clottes (2008).

Exploration of the role of shamanism and altered states of consciousness as contributors to Paleolithic cave paintings: Clottes and Lewis-Williams (1998) and Lewis-Williams (2002).

Hominin evolution: Pontzer (2012) and White et al. (2009).

Classic essay on consciousness and the experience of "what is like to be": Nagel (1974).

Chapter 2

"If the nervous communication be cut off": James (1890, p. 4).

Caenorhabditis elegans neurobiology: de Bono and Maricq (2005).

On determining the approximate number of cells in the human brain: Herculano-Houzel (2012).

Human brain anatomy: Diamond, Scheibel, and Elson (1985) and DeArmond, Fusco, and Dewey (1989).

A collection of Vesalius' illustrations from the *Fabrica* and other works, together with excellent commentary: Saunders and O'Malley (1973).

English translation of *L'Homme de René Descartes*, together with a facsimile of the 1664 French edition and excellent historical commentary: Descartes (1664/1972).

English translation of Galvani's 1791 article, together with a facsimile of the original Latin edition and excellent historical commentary: Galvani (1791/1953).

The story of Camillo Golgi and his marvelous stain: Mazzarello (2006/2010).

Chapter 3

On alchemy as an esoteric science and the Philosopher's Stone: Eliade (1956/1979) and Metzner (2008/2015).

Something of the magic and beauty of chemistry is captured by neurologist Oliver Sacks in his autobiographical tale of fascination for the subject: Sacks (2001).

Phospholipid bilayer membranes and membrane proteins: Engelman (2005).

Chapter 4

Charles Darwin's magnificent book on evolution: Darwin (1859).
Alfred Russel Wallace developed similar ideas concerning biological variation around the same time as did Darwin: initial publication, Darwin and Wallace (1858); a beautiful 150-year anniversary celebration is Gardiner, Milner, and Morris (2008).
"We should doubtless kill an animal," Niels Bohr's 1932 lecture in which he speculates about investigating the molecular basis of life: Bohr (1933).
Max Delbrück's first published work in biology: Timoféeff-Ressovky, Zimmer, and Delbrück (1935); for an English translation of this publication, together with an analysis of its impact in the formative years of molecular biology, see Sloan and Fogel (2011).
"From Delbrück's general picture": Erwin Schrödinger discusses Delbrück's ideas in Schrödinger (1944, chap. 6).
"I was absolutely overwhelmed": Delbrück describes his first encounter with bacterial viruses in Delbrück and Kopp (1980, p. 24).
DNA as a stupid substance: "At that time it was believed that DNA was a *stupid* substance, a tetranucleotide which couldn't do anything specific," from a 1972 interview with Max Delbrück conducted by Horace Judson and quoted in Judson (1979, p. 59), a superb history of the origins of modern molecular biology.
Avery and colleagues on genes being made of DNA: Avery, MacLeod, and McCarty (1944).
Hershey and Chase's simple and elegant demonstration that the genetic material is DNA and not protein: Hershey and Chase (1952).
"It has not escaped our notice," on the double-helical structure of DNA and speculations about the storage and copying of genetic information: Watson and Crick (1953).
James Watson tells the story of the discovery of DNA's structure in Watson (1968); this famously candid book includes a photocopy of Watson's March 1953 letter to Delbrück.
"Nobody, absolutely nobody": Delbrück speaking to the surprising simplicity of the genetic code in Judson (1979, p. 60).
On Delbrück's role in the formative years of molecular biology: Fischer and Lipson (1988).

Chapter 5

Mary Shelley's story of *Frankenstein; or, The Modern Prometheus* was originally published in London in 1818. Authorship was left anonymous, and many in that day assumed the book was written by Mary's husband, Percy Bysshe Shelley, or by her friend Lord Byron. It was published as an unrevised second edition, now with Mary's name as author, in 1823. The quoted passage begins chapter 4 of the novel, but Mary Shelley stated in the introduction to her 1831 third edition of *Frankenstein* that this was the first part of the book she wrote. An excellent source for the original text and a wealth of supplementary material is Shelley (1818/2012).
Hodgkin and Huxley's original short publication on the measurement of action potentials in axons: Hodgkin and Huxley (1939).
Detailed description of the neural membrane potential and action potential: Kandel, Schwartz, Jessell, Siegelbaum, and Hudspeth (2013, chaps. 6–7).

Chapter 6

An account of Otto Loewi's literally dreaming up the experiment that led to the discovery of chemical neurotransmission is given in a biographical essay written by Henry Dale (1962), with whom Loewi shared the 1936 Nobel Prize in Physiology or Medicine.

Detailed description of electrical synapses, ionotropic receptors, G-protein-coupled receptors, and interneural signaling: Kandel et al. (2013, chaps. 8–11).

Chapter 7

On drugs used to treat seizures: Goldenberg (2010).

Chapter 8

The story of Paracelsus is told in Stillman (1920).
Resistance to tetrodotoxin in garter snakes: Geffeney et al. (2005).
Resistance to saxitoxin in clams: Bricelj et al. (2005).
Batrachotoxins in beetles and birds: Dumbacher et al. (2004).
Curare and many other aspects of Amazonian ethnobotany are beautifully described in Davis (1996), an extraordinary book about Richard Evans Schultes (1915–2001), a great ethnobotanist and explorer of the Amazon jungle.
Outstanding ethnobotanical and poetic treatment of *pharmakon*: Pendell (1995/2010)

Chapter 9

A molecular explanation of the differing agonist activities of nicotine in the central nervous system and at the neuromuscular junction can be found in Xiu, Puskar, Shanata, Lester, and Dougherty (2009).
 "To fathom hell or soar angelic": Huxley (1977, p. 107).
The story of LSD, as told by its discoverer: Hofmann (1979/1980).
Connections among LSD, serotonin, and brain neurochemistry were proposed by Woolley and Shaw (1954).
Wasson (1957) describes R. Gordon Wasson's introduction to the shamanic use of *Psilocybe* mushrooms in the mountains of Mexico.
Neurochemistry of psychedelics: Nichols (2004).

Chapter 10

"In my inmost heart": Santiago Ramón y Cajal's description of the axonal growth cone is from the English translation of his autobiography, Ramón y Cajal (1917/1937, pp. 364 and 368–369).
Cytoskeletal dynamics in axon growth cones: Lowery and Van Vactor (2009).
Anesthesia pharmacology and microtubules: Hameroff (2006), Craddock et al. (2012), and Emerson et al. (2013).
Roger Sperry's classic experiments on recovery of vision in salamanders and frogs after severing of the optic nerve and rotating the eyeball: Sperry (1943, 1944).
Sperry's chemoaffinity hypothesis: Sperry (1963).
Neurogenesis in the human hippocampus: Spalding et al. (2013).
Neuroplasticity in the adult mammalian brain is taken for granted now, but not so very long ago this was a hotly contested issue – witness the work of Marian Diamond (b. 1926) and her colleagues on changes in brain neural structure occasioned by environmental conditions: Diamond, Krech, & Rosenzweig (1964); Bennett, Diamond, Krech, & Rosenzweig

(1964). An excellent film documenting the life and work of Marian Diamond has been produced: *My Love Affair with the Brain* (2016).

Chapter 11

Café wall illusion: Gregory and Heard (1979).
"Some 60 years ago" and "I noticed that a view of the blue sky": Karl von Frisch describes his remarkable work with honeybees in his Nobel Prize lecture, von Frisch (1974).
Electroreception in sharks and rays: Kalmijn (1971).
Classic demonstration that magnets interfere with navigational behavior of pigeons when the sun's position is obscured by clouds: Keeton (1971).

Chapter 12

A marvelous book on the art of perfumery is Aftel (2001), by artisan perfumer Mandy Aftel.
Recent results in the cellular and molecular biology of olfaction are presented in the Nobel Prize lectures of Richard Axel (2005) and Linda Buck (2005) and in Kandel et al. (2013, chap. 32).
Individual differences in excretion and perception of the characteristic odor present in urine after eating asparagus have been investigated by Pelchat, Bykowski, Duke, and Reed (2011).
Alfred Russel Wallace's poetic description of the durian fruit was originally published as a letter from Borneo: Wallace (1856). A slightly edited version appears in his later narrative of travels and observations in Southeast Asia: Wallace (1869).
The chemistry of truffle aroma is reviewed by Splivallo, Ottonello, Mello, and Karlovsky (2010). The creation of flavored truffle oils by adding chemicals to olive oil is discussed in Patterson (2007).
Brief discussion of pheromones: Stowers and Marton (2005).

Chapter 13

Recent review of the molecular biology of taste: Bachmanov and Beauchamp (2007).
English translation of Kikunae Ikeda's 1909 paper on umami: Ikeda (2002).
The identifications of the capsaicin/hot and menthol/cold receptors are described by Caterina et al. (1997) and McKemy, Neuhausser, and Julius (2002). Review of molecular and cellular mechanisms involved in perceptions related to chili, menthol, and mustard: Gerhold and Bautista (2009).

Chapter 14

On mapping the distribution of cone and rod photoreceptors in the human retina: Curcio, Sloan, Kalina, and Hendrickson (1990).
The amino acid sequence of human rhodopsin was obtained by sequencing the nucleotides of the gene encoding rhodopsin and then deducing the amino acid sequence using the genetic code: Nathans and Hogness (1984).
Visual perception, from photoreceptors to high-level brain processes: Kandel et al. (2013, chaps. 25–29).

Chapter 15

Inner ear and auditory central nervous system: Kandel et al. (2013, chaps. 30–31).

Chapter 16

Neurosurgical investigations of the human cerebral cortex: Penfield and Rasmussen (1950); Penfield's first description of the cortical somatosensory and motor maps can be found in Penfield and Boldrey (1937).
Representation of genitals on cortical somatosensory map: recent investigations suggest dual representations—on the medial surface of the cortex, adjacent to the representation of the foot (as indicated in Fig. 16.4), and in the anatomically expected location on the body map, between torso and leg: reviewed by Cazala, Vienney, and Stoléru (2015). Clinical stories involving phantom limbs, anosognosia, and other neurological syndromes are told in Sacks (1985) and Ramachandran and Blakeslee (1998).
Somatosensory neurobiology: Kandel et al. (2013, chaps. 22–23).
Central nervous system processes involved in motor movement: Kandel et al. (2013, chaps. 37–38).

Chapter 17

"One spring morning": the event that inspired Hans Berger in his study of the human brain, and led him to record the first human EEG: Millett (2001).
Energy needs of the human brain and the notion of neural dark energy: Raichle (2006).

Chapter 18

The history and contemporary use of the Wada test is described in *Brain and Cognition* by Jones-Gotman, Rouleau, and Snyder (1997). In the same journal issue is an autobiographical essay by Juhn Wada (1997a) and a translation of his original 1949 publication on the amobarbital procedure (Wada, 1997b).
Mirror neurons and speculations on the evolutionary origin of language: Ramachandran (2011, chaps. 4 and 6).
The seminal publication on the study of human split-brain patients: Gazzaniga, Bogen, and Sperry (1962). Roger Sperry's Nobel Prize lecture: Sperry (1982). Recent reviews of the history and current status of split-brain research: Gazzaniga (2005) and Wolman (2012). A detailed exposition of lateralized functions in the human brain: Gazzaniga, Ivry, and Mangun (2014, chap. 4).
The similarity between Freudian psychological defenses and the behavior of anosognosia patients: Ramachandran and Blakeslee (1998, chap. 7).
Neural correlates of consciousness: Crick and Koch (1990), Crick (1994), and Koch (2004).
Consciousness and integrated information: Tononi (2012) and Tononi and Koch (2015).
One look at some of the complexities of electromagnetic interactions in the brain: Buzsaki, Anastassiou, and Koch (2012).
Cortical neurodynamics and dark energy: Capolupo, Freeman, and Vitiello (2013).
"For centuries brains have been described as dynamic systems": Freeman (2000b, p. 3).
Freeman's neurodynamic perspective summarized: Freeman (2000a, 2015).

Chapter 19

Alexander Luria tells the story of Solomon Shereshevsky in Luria (1968/1987).
"Usually I experience a word's taste and weight": Luria (1968/1987, p. 28).
On synesthesia: Ramachandran and Hubbard (2001), Cytowic and Eagleman (2009), and
   Ramachandran (2011, chap. 3).
Daniel Tammet describes his colored and textured visualization of the digits of π in his
   engaging memoir, Tammet (2006).
Karl Lashley's work on maze learning and cortical lesions: Lashley (1929).
The story of H.M. is told by Suzanne Corkin, one of the neuroscientists who worked with
   him for many years, in Corkin (2013).
The first comprehensive description of H.M.'s cognitive capacities following his surgery:
   Scoville and Milner (1957).
Postmortem examination of H.M.'s brain: Annese et al. (2014).
"When an axon of cell A," Donald Hebb's famous neurophysiological postulate for the syn-
   aptic underpinnings of learning and memory: Hebb (1949, p. 62).
Eric Kandel, who received a Nobel Prize in Physiology or Medicine in 2000 for his work on
   elucidating a cellular and molecular mechanism of learning in *Aplysia*, tells the story of
   his research trajectory in Kandel (2006). A concise summary of the molecular biology of
   memory is presented in Kandel (2001).
Neurobiology of memory: Kandel et al. (2013, chaps. 65–67).

Chapter 20

Sleep in animals: Siegel (2008) and Cirelli and Tononi (2008).
Cellular and molecular biology of circadian rhythms in mammals: Mohawk, Green, and
   Takahashi (2012).
Photosensitive retinal ganglion cells and melanopsin: Do and Yau (2010).
Lucid dreaming: LaBerge (1985, 2009) and LaBerge and Rheingold (1990).
Dream yoga: Wangyal (1998) and Wallace (2012a).
Cross-cultural perspective on experiences of sleep paralysis: Hufford (1989).
"Drowsiness Is Red Alert!": Dement (1999, p. 54).
Sleep, neuroplasticity, and memory: Abel, Havekes, Saletin, and Walker (2013).

Chapter 21

"I think, therefore I am": René Descartes's famous statement speaks to his having no doubt
   about his own existence. His original phrase was in French, *je pense, donc je suis*, published in 1637 in his *Discourse on the Method*. The more widely quoted Latin version,
   cogito ergo sum, appeared in 1644 in his *Principles of Philosophy*.
"I feel, therefore I am": prominent exponents for the centrality of emotion in human experience include Jaak Panksepp and Antonio Damasio; see Panksepp (1998), Panksepp and
   Biven (2012), and Damasio (1999).
For a nuanced treatment of definitions related to emotion and mood, as well as excellent
   discussions of many important concepts in the science of emotion, see Ekman and Davidson (1994).
Charles Darwin's classic book on emotions: Darwin (1872).

"Specify who can show which emotion to whom and when": Darwin and Ekman (1998, p. 392).

"How much we are influenced": Darwin and Ekman (1998, p. 393).

Guillaume Duchenne de Boulgne published his book *Mécanisme de la Physionomie Humaine* on the muscular control of human facial expression in Paris in 1862. Few copies were produced, and it was soon out print and hard to find. A translation into English by R. Andrew Cuthbertson now exists: Duchenne de Boulogne (1990).

On the role of the vagus nerve in emotion and vagal tone: Porges (2011) and Keltner (2009, pp. 240–243).

Oxytocin and vasopressin: Meyer-Lindenberg, Domes, Kirsch, and Heinrichs (2011) and Ludwig and Leng (2006).

Discovery of reward circuitry in the brain: Olds and Milner (1954) and Olds (1956).

A history of clinical psychopharmacology, including the discoveries of antidepressant and antipsychotic medications: Healy (2002).

"Cosmetic psychopharmacology" and Prozac: Kramer (1993).

"Nature, red in tooth and claw": from the poem "In Memoriam A.H.H." (1849) by Alfred, Lord Tennyson (1809–1892). The poem honors Lord Tennyson's close friend Arthur Henry Hallam, who died suddenly at age of twenty-two from a stroke.

"Will have been increased through natural selection": Darwin (1871/1878, p. 107).

"Many a civilized man, or even boy, who never before risked his life for another": Darwin (1871/1878, p. 110).

Science of prosocial emotions: Keltner (2009) and Keltner, Kogan, Piff, and Saturn (2014).

On mindfulness and medicine: Ludwig and Kabat-Zinn (2008). A practical guide to mindfulness: Kabat-Zinn (2012). On the meaning of mindfulness in Buddhism: Goldstein (2013).

On universal aspects of spiritual traditions: Dalai Lama (2011).

Chapter 22

Financial markets and out-of-control artificial intelligence: Dooling (2008).

Movies (and stories) about future artificial intelligence: *I, Robot* (2004 movie based on a series of robot stories by Isaac Asimov); *The Matrix* (1999–2003 trilogy by The Wachowskis); *A.I. Artificial Intelligence* (2001 movie initiated by Stanley Kubrick, completed by Steven Spielberg, and based on the story "Super-toys last all summer long" by Brian Aldiss). These stories and films take machine intelligence to extremes of speculation.

"Any living cell carries with it": Delbrück (1949).

On the origins of life on Earth: Deamer (2011) and Gilbert (1986).

The surprisingly high numbers of solar systems having Earth-like planets, estimated to be 22 percent of Sun-like stars, meaning billions of such planets within our own galaxy: Petigura, Howard, and Marcy (2013).

For metaphysical frameworks in philosophy of mind, the online *Stanford Encyclopedia of Philosophy* (http://plato.stanford.edu/) is an excellent resource.

The "hard problem" of consciousness science: Chalmers (1995).

A lovely memoir on contemporary neuroscience and consciousness: Koch (2012).

Self-awareness in dolphins: Reiss and Marino (2001); in elephants: Plotnik, de Waal, and Reiss (2006).

"The faculty of bringing back a wandering attention": James (1890, p. 424).

The Dalai Lama in conversation with scientists: for the first two formal dialogues (1987 and 1989) between the Dalai Lama and small groups of cognitive scientists and neuroscientists, see Hayward and Varela (1992) and Houshmand, Livingston, and Wallace (1999). How the dialogues came about is described in Houshmand, Livingston, and Wallace (1999, pp. 175–180). The website of the Mind and Life Institute (http://www.mindandlife .org/) contains a comprehensive list of all these dialogues, related publications, and, in some recent cases, conference video recordings.

On Buddhist ideas contributing to Western science: Dalai Lama (2005) and Wallace (2007, 2012b).

William James's interest in psi: James (1898/1900, 1986).

Investigations of psi, near-death experiences, and small children who provide verifiable information suggesting having lived other lives: Stevenson (1966/1974), Radin (2006), Kelly et al. (2007), Mayer (2007), Leary (2011), and Kelly (2013).

Quantum physics and the mind–matter connection: Stapp (2007/2011) and Rosenblum and Kuttner (2006/2011).

Consciousness as a fundamental part of the fabric of reality: Whitehead (1929/1979), Penrose (1994), Hameroff and Penrose (2014), and Kelly, Crabtree, and Marshall (2015).

"A genuine glimpse into": the concluding lines in James (1892).

Max Delbrück describes his perspective on the evolution of the human mind in a set of post-humously published lectures based on a course he taught at Caltech during the 1970s (I was one of the students in this class): Delbrück (1986).

References

Abel, T., Havekes, R., Saletin, J. M., & Walker, M. P. (2013). Sleep, plasticity and memory from molecules to whole-brain networks. *Current Biology, 23,* R774–R788.

Aftel, M. (2001). *Essence and alchemy: A book of perfume.* New York, NY: Farrar, Straus, & Giroux.

Annese, J., Schenker-Ahmed, N. M., Bartsch, H., Maechler, P., Sheh, C., Thomas, N., . . . Corkin, S. (2014). Postmortem examination of patient H. M.'s brain based on histological sectioning and 3D reconstruction. *Nature Communications, 5,* 3122. http://doi: 10.1038/ncomms4122

Avery, O. T., MacLeod, C. M., & McCarty, M. (1944). Studies on the chemical nature of the substance inducing transformation of pneumococcal types. *Journal of Experimental Medicine, 79,* 137–158.

Axel, R. (2005). Scents and sensibility: A molecular logic of olfactory perception (Nobel lecture). *Angewandte Chemie International Edition, 44,* 6111–6127.

Bachmanov, A. A., & Beauchamp, G. K. (2007). Taste receptor genes. *Annual Review of Nutrition, 27,* 389–414.

Bennett, E. L., Diamond, M. C., Krech, D. & Rosenzweig, M. R. (1964). Chemical and anatomical plasticity of the brain. *Science,* 146, 610-619.

Bohr, N. (1933). Light and life. *Nature, 131,* 421–423, 457–459.

Bricelj, V. M., Connell, L., Konoki, K., MacQuarrie, S. P., Scheuer, T., Catterall, W. A., & Trainer, V. L. (2005). Sodium channel mutation leading to saxitoxin resistance in clams increases risk of PSP. *Nature, 434,* 763–767.

Buck, L. B. (2005). Unraveling the sense of smell (Nobel lecture). *Angewandte Chemie International Edition, 44,* 6128–6140.

Buzsaki, G., Anastassiou, C. A., & Koch, C. (2012). The origin of extracellular fields and currents—EEG, ECoG, LFP and spikes. *Nature Reviews Neuroscience, 13,* 407–420.

Capolupo, A., Freeman, W. J., & Vitiello, G. (2013). Dissipation of "dark energy" by cortex in knowledge retrieval. *Physics of Life Reviews, 10,* 85–94.

Caterina, M. J., Schumacher, M. A., Tominaga, M., Rosen, T. A., Levine, J. D., & Julius, D. (1997). The capsaicin receptor: A heat-activated ion channel in the pain pathway. *Nature, 389,* 816–824.

Cazala, F., Vienney, N., & Stoléru, S. (2015). The cortical sensory representation of genitalia in women and men: A systematic review. *Socioaffective Neuroscience & Psychology, 5,* 26428. http://dx.doi.org/10.3402/snp.v5.26428

Chalmers, D. J. (1995). The puzzle of conscious experience. *Scientific American, 273*(6), 80–86.

Chauvet, J. M., Deschamps, E. B., & Hillaire, C. (1996). *Dawn of art: The Chauvet Cave: The oldest known paintings in the world.* New York, NY: Harry Abrams.

Cirelli, C., & Tononi, G. (2008). Is sleep essential? *PLoS Biology, 6*(8), 3216.

Clottes, J. (2008). *Cave art.* London: Phaidon Press.

Clottes, J., & Lewis-Williams, D. (1998). *The shamans of prehistory: Trance and magic in the painted caves*. New York, NY: Harry Abrams.

Corkin, S. (2013). *Permanent present tense: The unforgettable life of the amnestic patient, H. M.* New York, NY: Basic Books.

Craddock, T. J. A., St. George, M., Freedman, H., Barakat, K. H., Damaraju, S., Hameroff, S., & Tuszynski, J. A. (2012). Computational predictions of volatile anesthetic interactions with the microtubule cytoskeleton: Implications for side effects of general anesthesia. *PLoS ONE, 7*(6), e37251. http://doi: 10.1371/journal.pone.0037251

Crick, F. (1994). *The astonishing hypothesis: The scientific search for the soul*. New York, NY: Charles Scribner.

Crick, F., & Koch, C. (1990). Towards a neurobiological theory of consciousness. *Seminars in Neuroscience, 2*, 263–275.

Curcio, C. A., Sloan, K. R., Kalina, R. E., & Hendrickson, A. E. (1990). Human photoreceptor topography. *Journal of Comparative Neurology, 292*, 497–523.

Cytowic, R. E., & Eagleman, D. M. (2009). *Wednesday is indigo blue: Discovering the brain of synesthesia*. Cambridge, MA: MIT Press.

Dalai Lama, H. H. (2005). *The universe in a single atom: The convergence of science and spirituality*. New York, NY: Morgan Road.

Dalai Lama, H. H. (2011). *Beyond religion: Ethics for a whole world*. New York, NY: Houghton Mifflin Harcourt.

Dale, H. H. (1962). Otto Loewi: 1873–1961. *Biographical Memoirs of Fellows of the Royal Society, 8*, 67–89.

Damasio, A. (1999). *The feeling of what happens: Body and emotion in the making of consciousness*. New York, NY: Harcourt Brace.

Darwin, C. (1859). *On the origin of species by means of natural selection*. London: John Murray.

Darwin, C. (1872). *The expression of the emotions in man and animals*. London: John Murray.

Darwin, C. (1878). *The descent of man, and selection in relation to sex* (new ed.). New York, NY: Appleton. (Original work published 1871)

Darwin, C., & Ekman, P. (1998). *The expression of the emotions in man and animals* (3rd ed.). Oxford, UK: Oxford University Press.

Darwin, C., & Wallace, A. (1858). On the tendency of species to form varieties; and on the perpetuation of varieties and species by means of selection. *Journal of Proceedings of the Linnean Society, 3*, 45–62.

Davis, W. (1996). *One river: Explorations and discoveries in the Amazon rain forest*. New York, NY: Simon and Schuster.

Deamer, D. (2011). *First life: Discovering the connections between stars, cells, and how life began*. Berkeley, CA: University of California Press.

DeArmond, S. J., Fusco, M. M., & Dewey, M. M. (1989). *Structure of the human brain: A photographic atlas* (3rd ed.). Oxford, UK: Oxford University Press.

de Bono, M., & Maricq, A. V. (2005). Neuronal substrates of complex behaviors in *C. elegans*. *Annual Review of Neuroscience, 28*, 451–501.

Delbrück, M. (1949). A physicist looks at biology. *Transactions of the Connecticut Academy of Arts and Sciences, 38*, 173–190.

Delbrück, M. (1986). *Mind from matter? An essay on evolutionary epistemology*. G. S. Stent, E. P. Fischer, S. W. Golomb, D. Presti, & H. Seiler (Eds.). Palo Alto, CA: Blackwell.

Delbrück, M., & Kopp, C. (1980). Oral history: Max Delbrück—how it was (part 2). *Caltech Engineering and Science, 43*(5), 21–27.

Dement, W. C. (1999). *The promise of sleep*. New York, NY: Delacorte Press.

Descartes, R. (1972). *Treatise of man*. (T. S. Hall, Trans.). Cambridge, MA: Harvard University Press. (Original work published 1664)

Diamond, M. C., Krech, D., & Rosenzweig, M. R. (1964). The effects of an enriched environment on the histology of the rat cerebral cortex. *Journal of Comparative Neurology, 123,* 111-119.

Diamond, M. C., Scheibel, A. B., & Elson, L. M. (1985). *The human brain coloring book.* New York, NY: Harper.

Do, M. T. H., & Yau, K. W. (2010). Intrinsically photosensitive retinal ganglion cells. *Physiological Reviews, 90,* 1547–1581.

Dooling, R. (2008, October 12). The rise of the machines. *New York Times.*

Duchenne de Boulogne, G.-B. (1990). *The mechanism of human facial expression.* R. A. Cuthbertson, Ed. and Trans. Cambridge, UK: Cambridge University Press. (Original work published 1862)

Dumbacher, J. P., Wako, A., Derrickson, S. R., Samuelson, A., Spande, T. F., & Daly, J. W. (2004). Melyrid beetles (*Choresine*): A putative source for the batrachotoxin alkaloids found in poison-dart frogs and toxic passerine birds. *Proceedings of the National Academy of Sciences USA, 101,* 15857–15860.

Ekman, P., & Davidson, R. J. (Eds.). (1994). *The nature of emotion: Fundamental questions.* Oxford, UK: Oxford University Press.

Eliade, M. (1979) *The forge and the crucible: The origins and structure of alchemy* (2nd ed.). Chicago, IL: University of Chicago Press. (Original work published 1956)

Emerson, D. J., Weiser, B. P., Psonis, J., Liao, Z., Taratula, O., Fiamengo, A., ... Dmochowski, I. J. (2013). Direct modulation of microtubule stability contributes to anthracene general anesthesia. *Journal of the American Chemical Society, 135,* 5389–5398.

Engelman, D. M. (2005). Membranes are more mosaic than fluid. *Nature, 438,* 578–580.

Fischer, E. P., & Lipson, C. (1988). *Thinking about science: Max Delbrück and the origins of molecular biology.* New York, NY: W. W. Norton.

Freeman, W. J. (2000a). *How brains make up their minds.* New York, NY: Columbia University Press.

Freeman, W. J. (2000b). *Neurodynamics: An exploration in mesoscopic brain dynamics.* London: Springer.

Freeman, W. J. (2015). Mechanism and significance of global coherence in scalp EEG. *Current Opinion in Neurobiology, 31,* 199–205.

Galvani, L. (1953). *Commentary on the effects of electricity on muscular motion.* (M. G. Foley, Trans.). I. B. Cohen (Ed.). Norwalk, CT: Bundy Library. (Original work published 1791)

Gardiner, B., Milner, R., & Morris, M. (Eds.). (2008). Survival of the fittest: A special issue of *The Linnean* celebrating the 150th anniversary of the Darwin-Wallace theory of evolution. *The Linnean: Newsletter and Proceedings of the Linnean Society of London,* Special Issue 9.

Gazzaniga, M. S. (2005). Forty-five years of split-brain research and still going strong. *Nature Reviews Neuroscience, 6,* 653–659.

Gazzaniga, M. S., Bogen, J. E., & Sperry, R. W. (1962). Some functional effects of sectioning the cerebral commissures in man. *Proceedings of the National Academy of Sciences USA, 48,* 1765–1769.

Gazzaniga, M. S., Ivry, R. B., & Mangun, G. R. (2014). *Cognitive neuroscience: The biology of mind* (4th ed.). New York, NY: W. W. Norton.

Geffeney, S. L., Fujimoto, E., Brodie, E. D., 3rd, Brodie, E. D., Jr., & Ruben, P. C. (2005). Evolutionary diversification of TTX-resistant sodium channels in a predator-prey interaction. *Nature, 434,* 759–763.

Gerhold, K. A., & Bautista, D. M. (2009). Molecular and cellular mechanisms of trigeminal chemosensation. *Annals of the New York Academy of Sciences, 1170,* 184–189.

Gilbert, W. (1986). The RNA world. *Nature, 319,* 618.

Goldenberg, M. M. (2010). Overview of drugs used for epilepsy and seizures: Etiology, diagnosis, and treatment. *Pharmacy and Therapeutics, 35*, 392–415.

Goldstein, J. (2013) *Mindfulness: A practical guide to awakening.* Boulder, CO: Sounds True.

Gregory, R. L., & Heard, P. (1979). Border locking and the café wall illusion. *Perception, 8*, 365–380.

Hameroff, S. (2006). The entwined mysteries of anesthesia and consciousness: Is there a common underlying mechanism? *Anesthesiology, 105*, 400–412.

Hameroff, S., & Penrose, R. (2014). Consciousness in the universe: A review of the "Orch OR" theory. *Physics of Life Reviews, 11*, 39–78.

Hayward, J. W., & Varela, F. J. (Eds.). (1992). *Gentle bridges: Conversations with the Dalai Lama on the sciences of mind.* Boston, MA: Shambhala.

Healy, D. (2002). *The creation of psychopharmacology.* Cambridge, MA: Harvard University Press.

Hebb, D. O. (1949). *The organization of behavior: A neuropsychological theory.* New York, NY: John Wiley and Sons.

Herculano-Houzel, S. (2012). The remarkable, yet not extraordinary, human brain as a scaled-up primate brain and its associated cost. *Proceedings of the National Academy of Sciences USA, 109*, 10661–10668.

Hershey, A. D., & Chase, M. (1952). Independent functions of viral protein and nucleic acid in growth of bacteriophage. *Journal of General Physiology, 36*, 39–56.

Hodgkin, A. L., & Huxley, A. F. (1939). Action potentials recorded from inside a nerve fibre. *Nature, 144*, 710–711.

Hofmann, A. (1980). *LSD, my problem child: Reflections on sacred drugs, mysticism, and science.* New York, NY: McGraw Hill. (Original work published 1979)

Houshmand, Z., Livingston, R. B., & Wallace, B. A. (Eds.). (1999). *Consciousness at the crossroads: Conversations with the Dalai Lama on brain science and Buddhism.* Ithaca, NY: Snow Lion.

Hufford, D. J. (1989). *The terror that comes in the night: An experience-centered study of supernatural assault traditions.* Philadelphia, PA: University of Pennsylvania Press.

Huxley, A. (1977). *Moksha: Aldous Huxley's writings on psychedelics and the visionary experience (1931–1963).* M. Horowitz & C. Palmer, Eds. New York, NY: Stonehill.

Ikeda, K. (2002). New seasonings. *Chemical Senses, 27*, 847–849.

James, W. (1890). *The principles of psychology.* New York, NY: Henry Holt.

James, W. (1892). *Psychology: The Briefer Course.* New York, NY: Henry Holt.

James, W. (1900). *Human immortality: Two supposed objections to the doctrine* (2nd ed.). Boston, MA: Houghton Mifflin (Original work published 1898)

James, W. (1986). *The works of William James: Essays in psychical research.* Cambridge, MA: Harvard University Press.

Jones-Gotman, M., Rouleau, I., & Snyder, P. J. (1997). Clinical and research contributions of the intracarotid amobarbital procedure to neuropsychology. *Brain and Cognition, 33*, 1–6.

Judson, H. F. (1979). *The eighth day of creation: Makers of the revolution in biology.* New York, NY: Simon and Schuster.

Kabat-Zinn, J. (2012) *Mindfulness for beginners.* Boulder, CO: Sounds True.

Kalmijn, A. J. (1971). The electric sense of sharks and rays. *Journal of Experimental Biology, 55*, 371–383.

Kandel, E. R. (2001). The molecular biology of memory storage: A dialogue between genes and synapses. *Science, 294*, 1030–1038.

Kandel, E. R. (2006). *In search of memory: The emergence of a new science of mind.* New York, NY: W. W. Norton.

Kandel, E. R., Schwartz, J. H., Jessell, T. M., Siegelbaum, S. A., & Hudspeth, A. J. (2013). *Principles of neural science* (5th ed.). New York, NY: McGraw Hill.

Keeton, W. T. (1971). Magnets interfere with pigeon homing. *Proceedings of the National Academy of Sciences USA, 68*, 102–106.

Kelly, E. F., Crabtree, A., & Marshall, P. (Eds.) (2015). *Beyond physicalism: Toward reconciliation of science and spirituality*. Lanham, MD: Rowman and Littlefield.

Kelly, E. F., Kelly, E. W., Crabtree, A., Gauld, A., Grosso, M., & Greyson, B. (2007). *Irreducible mind: Toward a psychology for the 21st century*. Lanham, MD: Rowman and Littlefield.

Kelly, E. W. (2013). *Science, the self, and survival after death: Selected writings of Ian Stevenson, M.D.* Lanham, MD: Rowman and Littlefield.

Keltner, D. (2009). *Born to be good: The science of a meaningful life*. New York, NY: W. W. Norton.

Keltner, D., Kogan, A., Piff, P. K., & Saturn, S. R. (2014). The sociocultural appraisals, values, and emotions (SAVE) framework of prosociality: Core processes from gene to meme. *Annual Review of Psychology, 65*, 425–460.

Koch, C. (2004). *The quest for consciousness: A neurobiological approach*. Denver, CO: Roberts.

Koch, C. (2012). *Consciousness: Confessions of a romantic reductionist*. Cambridge, MA: MIT Press.

Kramer, P. D. (1993). *Listening to Prozac*. New York, NY: Viking.

LaBerge, S. (1985). *Lucid dreaming: The power of being awake and aware in your dreams*. Los Angeles, CA: Tarcher.

LaBerge, S. (2009). *Lucid dreaming: A concise guide to awakening in your dreams and in your life*. Louisville, CO: Sounds True.

LaBerge, S., & Rheingold, H. (1990). *Exploring the world of lucid dreaming*. New York, NY: Ballantine Books.

Lashley, K. S. (1929). *Brain mechanisms and intelligence: A quantitative study of injuries to the brain*. Chicago, IL: University of Chicago Press.

Leary, M. (2011). Why are (some) scientists so opposed to parapsychology? *Explore, 7*, 275–277.

Lewis-Williams, D. (2002). *The mind in the cave: Consciousness and the origins of art*. London: Thames and Hudson.

Lowery, L. A., & Van Vactor, D. (2009). The trip of the tip: Understanding the growth cone machinery. *Nature Reviews Molecular Cell Biology, 10*, 332–343.

Ludwig, D. S. & Kabat-Zinn, J. (2008) Mindfulness in medicine. *Journal of the American Medical Association*, 300, 1350-1352.

Ludwig, M., & Leng, G. (2006). Dendritic peptide release and peptide-dependent behaviours. *Nature Reviews Neuroscience, 7*, 126–136.

Luria, A. R. (1987). *The mind of a mnemonist: A little book about a vast memory*. Cambridge, MA: Harvard University Press. (Original work published 1968)

Mazzarello, P. (2010). *Golgi: A biography of the founder of modern neuroscience*. Oxford, UK: Oxford University Press. (Original work published 2006)

Mayer, E. L. (2007). *Extraordinary knowing: Science, skepticism, and the inexplicable powers of the human mind*. New York, NY: Bantam Books.

McKemy, D. D., Neuhausser, W. M., & Julius, D. (2002). Identification of a cold receptor reveals a general role for TRP channels in thermosensation. *Nature, 416*, 52–58.

Metzner, R. (2015) *The expansion of consciousness* (revised ed.). Berkeley, CA: Regent Press. (Original work published 2008)

Meyer-Lindenberg, A., Domes, G., Kirsch, P., & Heinrichs, M. (2011). Oxytocin and vasopressin in the human brain: Social neuropeptides for translational medicine. *Nature Reviews Neuroscience, 12*, 524–538.

Millett, D. (2001). Hans Berger: From psychic energy to the EEG. *Perspectives in Biology and Medicine, 44*, 522–542.

Mohawk, J. A., Green, C. B., & Takahashi, J. S. (2012). Central and peripheral circadian clocks in mammals. *Annual Review of Neuroscience, 35*, 445–462.

Nagel, T. (1974). What is it like to be a bat? *Philosophical Review, 83*, 435–450.

Nathans, J., & Hogness, D. S. (1984). Isolation and nucleotide sequence of the gene encoding human rhodopsin. *Proceedings of the National Academy of Sciences USA, 81*, 4851–4855.

Nichols, D. E. (2004). Hallucinogens. *Pharmacology and Therapeutics, 101*, 131–181.

Olds, J. (1956). Pleasure centers in the brain. *Scientific American, 195*(4), 105–116.

Olds, J., & Milner, P. (1954). Positive reinforcement produced by electrical stimulation of septal area and other regions of rat brain. *Journal of Comparative and Physiological Psychology, 47*, 419–427.

Panksepp, J. (1998). *Affective neuroscience: The foundations of human and animal emotions.* Oxford, UK: Oxford University Press.

Panksepp, J., & Biven, L. (2012). *The archaeology of mind: Neuroevolutionary origins of human emotions.* New York, NY: W. W. Norton.

Patterson, D. (2007, May 16). Hocus-pocus, and a beaker of truffles. *New York Times.*

Pelchat, M. L., Bykowski, C., Duke, F. F., & Reed, D. R. (2011). Excretion and perception of a characteristic odor in urine after asparagus ingestion: A psychophysical and genetic study. *Chemical Senses, 36*, 9–17.

Pendell, D. (2010). *Pharmako/Poeia: Power Plants, Poisons, and Herbcraft* (revised ed.). Berkeley, CA: North Atlantic. (original work published 1995)

Penfield, W., & Boldrey, E. (1937). Somatic motor and sensory representation in the cerebral cortex of man as studied by electrical stimulation. *Brain, 60*, 389–443.

Penfield, W., & Rasmussen, T. (1950). *The cerebral cortex of man: A clinical study of localization of function.* New York, NY: Macmillan.

Penrose, R. (1994). *Shadows of the mind: A search for the missing science of consciousness.* Oxford, UK: Oxford University Press.

Petigura, E. A., Howard, A. W., & Marcy, G. W. (2013). Prevalence of Earth-size planets orbiting Sun-like stars. *Proceedings of the National Academy of Sciences USA, 110*, 19273–19278.

Plotnik, J. M., de Waal, F. B. M., & Reiss, D. (2006). Self-recognition in an Asian elephant. *Proceedings of the National Academy of Sciences USA, 103*, 17053–17057.

Pontzer, H. (2012). Overview of hominin evolution. *Nature Education Knowledge, 3*(10), 8.

Porges, S. W. (2011). *The polyvagal theory: Neurophysiological foundations of emotions, attachment, communication, and self-regulation.* New York, NY: W. W. Norton.

Radin, D. (2006). *Entangled minds: Extrasensory experiences in a quantum reality.* New York, NY: Simon and Schuster.

Raichle, M. E. (2006). The brain's dark energy. *Science, 314*, 1249–1250.

Ramachandran, V. S. (2011). *The tell-tale brain: A neuroscientist's quest for what makes us human.* New York, NY: W. W. Norton.

Ramachandran, V. S., & Blakeslee, S. (1998). *Phantoms in the brain: Probing the mysteries of the human mind.* New York, NY: William Morrow.

Ramachandran, V. S., & Hubbard, E. M. (2001). Synaesthesia—a window into perception, thought and language. *Journal of Consciousness Studies, 8*, 3–34.

Ramón y Cajal, S. (1937). Recollections of my life. (E. H. Craigie, Trans.). *Memoirs of the American Philosophical Society, 8*, 1–638. (Original work published 1917)

Reiss, D., & Marino, L. (2001). Mirror self-recognition in the bottlenose dolphin: A case of cognitive convergence. *Proceedings of the National Academy of Sciences USA, 98,* 5937–5942.

Rosenblum, B., & Kuttner, F. (2011). *Quantum enigma: Physics encounters consciousness* (2nd ed.). Oxford, UK: Oxford University Press. (Original work published 2006)

Sacks, O. (1985). *The man who mistook his wife for a hat.* New York, NY: Simon and Schuster.

Sacks, O. (2001). *Uncle tungsten: Memories of a chemical boyhood.* New York, NY: Alfred Knopf.

Saunders, J. B. deC. M. & O'Malley, C. D. (1973) *The illustrations from the works of Andreas Vesalius of Brussels.* Mineola, NY: Dover Publications.

Schrödinger, E. (1944). *What is life?* Cambridge, UK: Cambridge University Press.

Scoville, W. B., & Milner, B. (1957). Loss of recent memory after bilateral hippocampal lesions. *Journal of Neurology, Neurosurgery and Psychiatry, 20,* 11–21.

Shelley, M. (2012). *Frankenstein: A Norton Critical Edition* (2nd ed.). J. P. Hunter, Ed. New York, NY: W. W. Norton. (Original work published 1818)

Siegel, J. M. (2008). Do all animals sleep? *Trends in Neurosciences, 31,* 208–213.

Sloan, P. R., & Fogel, B. (Eds.). (2011). *Creating a physical biology: The three-man paper and early molecular biology.* Chicago, IL: University of Chicago Press.

Spalding, K. L., Bergmann, O., Alkass, K., Bernard, S., Salehpour, M., Huttner, H. B., . . . Frisén, J. (2013). Dynamics of hippocampal neurogenesis in adult humans. *Cell, 153,* 1219–1227.

Sperry, R. W. (1943). Visuomotor coordination in the newt (*Triturus viridescens*) after regeneration of the optic nerve. *Journal of Comparative Neurology, 79,* 33–55.

Sperry, R. W. (1944). Optic nerve regeneration with return of vision in anurans. *Journal of Neurophysiology, 7,* 57–69.

Sperry, R. W. (1963). Chemoaffinity in the orderly growth of nerve fiber patterns and connections. *Proceedings of the National Academy of Sciences USA, 50,* 703–710.

Sperry, R. (1982). Some effects of disconnecting the cerebral hemispheres. *Science, 217,* 1223–1226.

Splivallo, R., Ottonello, S., Mello, A., & Karlovsky, P. (2011). Truffle volatiles: From chemical ecology to aroma biosynthesis. *New Phytologist, 189,* 688–699.

Stapp, H. P. (2011). *Mindful universe: Quantum mechanics and the participating observer* (2nd ed.)*.* Berlin: Springer. (Original work published 2007)

Stevenson, I. (1974). *Twenty cases suggestive of reincarnation* (rev. ed.). Charlottesville, VA: University of Virginia Press. (Original work published 1966)

Stillman, J. M. (1920). *Paracelsus (Theophrastus Bombastus von Hohenheim, called Paracelsus: His personality and influence as physician, chemist and reformer).* Chicago, IL: Open Court.

Stowers, L., & Marton, T. F. (2005). What is a pheromone? Mammalian pheromones reconsidered. *Neuron, 46,* 699–702.

Tammet, D. (2006). *Born on a blue day: Inside the extraordinary mind of an autistic savant.* New York, NY: Free Press.

Timoféeff-Ressovky, N. W., Zimmer, K. G., & Delbrück, M. (1935). Über die Natur der Genmutation und der Genstruktur. *Nachrichten von der Gesellschaft der Wissenschaften zu Göttingen, Mathematisch-Physikalische Klasse, Fachgruppe, 6*(13), 190–245.

Tononi, G. (2012). Integrated information theory of consciousness: An updated account. *Archives Italiennes de Biologie, 150,* 290–326.

Tononi, G., & Koch, C. (2015) Consciousness: here, there and everywhere? *Philosophical Transactions of the Royal Society of London B*, 370, 20140167. http://dx.doi.org/10.1098/rstb.2014.0167

von Frisch, K. (1974). Decoding the language of the bee. *Science, 185,* 663–668.

Wada, J. A. (1997a). Youthful season revisited. *Brain and Cognition, 33,* 7–10.

Wada, J. A. (1997b). Clinical experimental observations of carotid artery injections of sodium amytal. *Brain and Cognition, 33*, 11–13.

Wallace, A. R. (1856). On the bamboo and durian of Borneo. *Hooker's Journal of Botany and Kew Garden Miscellany, 8*, 225–230.

Wallace, A. R. (1869). *The Malay Archipelago: The land of the orang-utan and the bird of paradise*. London: Macmillan.

Wallace, B. A. (2007). *Contemplative science: Where Buddhism and neuroscience converge*. New York, NY: Columbia University Press.

Wallace, B. A. (2012a). *Dreaming yourself awake: Lucid dreaming and Tibetan dream yoga for insight and transformation*. Boston, MA: Shambhala.

Wallace, B. A. (2012b). *Meditations of a Buddhist skeptic: A manifesto for the mind sciences and contemplative practice*. New York, NY: Columbia University Press.

Wangyal, T. (1998). *The Tibetan yogas of dream and sleep*. Ithaca, NY: Snow Lion.

Wasson, R. G. (1957, May 13). Seeking the magic mushroom. *Life, 42*(19), 100–120.

Watson, J. D. (1968). *The double helix: A personal account of the discovery of the structure of DNA*. New York, NY: Atheneum.

Watson, J. D., & Crick, F. H. C. (1953). Molecular structure of nucleic acids: A structure for deoxyribose nucleic acid. *Nature, 171*, 737–738.

White, T. D., Asfaw, B., Beyene, Y., Haile-Selassie, Y., Lovejoy, C. O., Suwa, G., & Wolde-Gabriel, G. (2009). *Ardipithecus ramidus* and the paleobiology of early hominids. *Science, 326*, 75–86.

Whitehead, A. N. (1979). *Process and reality* (corr. ed.). New York, NY: Free Press. (Original work published 1929)

Wolman, D. (2012). A tale of two halves. *Nature, 483*, 260–263.

Woolley, D. W., & Shaw, E. (1954). A biochemical and pharmacological suggestion about certain mental disorders. *Proceedings of the National Academy of Sciences USA, 40*, 228–231.

Xiu, X., Puskar, N. L., Shanata, J. A., Lester, H. A., & Dougherty, D. A. (2009). Nicotine binding to brain receptors requires a strong cation-pi interaction. *Nature, 458*, 534–537.

Acknowledgments

I stand on the shoulders of many great teachers and teachings: all of my personal teachers (from family, school, academia, and circles of friends), all of my students past and present, and an enormous base of knowledge built up by legions of creative and dedicated folks have given rise to whatever I might know and conceive. For all that I offer my sincerest gratitude!

For specific contributions—textual and illustrative—to the creation of this book, I extend heartfelt thanks to my friends and colleagues Walter Freeman, Shefali Netke, Rich Ivry, Paul Daley, Meg Conkey, Matt Walker, Kelly Clancy, Justin Riddle, Jean Clottes, Greg Chin, Frederic Theunissen, Fred Horowitz, Emiliana Simon-Thomas, Ed Kelly, David Dennison, Dacher Keltner, Breanna Ford, and Ben Wolfe; to Jacob Nasim for creative design of the book's cover; to Dan Siegel for connecting me with Deborah Malmud; to Deborah Malmud and her outstanding editorial team at W. W. Norton; and most importantly, to my wonderful wife and the love of my life Kristi Panik, who read and reread chapter drafts, made numerous editorial contributions that greatly enhance clarity, drew several of the figures, co-authored the poetry and, being a psychiatrist extraordinaire, provided 24/7 psychotherapy and unconditional support. I am grateful to be surrounded by such circles of love.

Index

About the Author

I was born and grew up in Indiana, in the American Midwest, and was curious about the workings of nature from a young age. My dedication to school and the sciences really started in college, and I began my studies there with chemistry. Soon I was drawn into the study of physics and mathematics—inspired by a physics professor, Marshall Dixon, as well as by my cousin, Scott—and added those subjects into the mix. By the time I graduated from Butler University, I was head over heels in love with Einstein's general theory of relativity and moved west to attend graduate school at the California Institute of Technology.

Concurrently, I became interested in the philosophical foundations of science— just exactly what do we mean by reality, and how are we able to derive what we believe to be truths about it? How is it that Einstein, sitting in his room, can discover—or invent—a theory describing the entire universe? What human capacity makes this possible? What is the nature of our mind?

During my first year studying theoretical physics at Caltech, I heard about an elder scientist in the biology department who was interested in how the extraordinary capacities of the human mind had evolved. Moreover, this fellow was planning to teach a biophysics class in which he would explore this very subject. His name was Max Delbrück, and although he had a Nobel Prize for being one of the founders of the discipline of molecular biology, I had not previously heard of him. I signed up for his class. After hearing of my interest in the nature of mind, Max advised me to learn some biology if I expected to seriously pursue this subject. The mind is related to the brain, and the brain is a product of biological evolution, and one is unlikely to make much progress in investigating the mind with no knowledge of biology, he told me. He offered me the opportunity to work in his laboratory, and I switched my area of graduate study from theoretical physics to experimental biology.

As Max Delbrück's last graduate student, I received a PhD degree in molecular biology and biophysics, investigating the light-sensing capacities of the fungus *Phycomyces*. I began to develop intuition into biology, but was still a long way from studying consciousness. So I did postdoctoral work first in neurobiology, then in cognitive psychology. This led me in a clinical direction, and I obtained a PhD in clinical psychology from the University of Oregon. For the next decade I worked with veterans suffering from alcohol and drug addiction and post-traumatic stress at the Department of Veterans Affairs Medical Center in San Francisco.

While working at the San Francisco VA Medical Center, I started teaching neuroscience at the University of California in Berkeley. I have been teaching there since 1991, fulltime since 2000. Since 2004, I have also been teaching neuroscience to Tibetan monastics in India. Throughout this trajectory, from my college years to the present time, my guiding interest has been and continues to be the scientific investigation of the mind. There is still much to do . . .

Also available from

THE NORTON SERIES ON INTERPERSONAL NEUROBIOLOGY

The Birth of Intersubjectivity: Psychodynamics, Neurobiology, and the Self
MASSIMO AMMANITI, VITTORIO GALLESE

Neurobiology for Clinical Social Work: Theory and Practice (Second Edition)
JEFFREY S. APPLEGATE, JANET R. SHAPIRO

Mind–Brain–Gene
JOHN B. ARDEN

The Heart of Trauma: Healing the Embodied Brain in the Context of Relationships
BONNIE BADENOCH

Being a Brain-Wise Therapist: A Practical Guide to Interpersonal Neurobiology
BONNIE BADENOCH

The Brain-Savvy Therapist's Workbook
BONNIE BADENOCH

The Neurobiology of Attachment-Focused Therapy
JONATHAN BAYLIN, DANIEL A. HUGHES

*Coping with Trauma-Related Dissociation: Skills Training
for Patients and Therapists*
SUZETTE BOON, KATHY STEELE, AND ONNO VAN DER HART

*Neurobiologically Informed Trauma Therapy with Children and Adolescents:
Understanding Mechanisms of Change*
LINDA CHAPMAN

*Intensive Psychotherapy for Persistent Dissociative Processes:
The Fear of Feeling Real*
RICHARD A. CHEFETZ

Timeless: Nature's Formula for Health and Longevity
LOUIS COZOLINO

*The Neuroscience of Human Relationships: Attachment
and the Developing Social Brain (Second Edition)*
LOUIS COZOLINO

*The Neuroscience of Psychotherapy: Healing the Social Brain
(Second Edition)*
LOUIS COZOLINO

The Present Moment in Psychotherapy and Everyday Life
Daniel N. Stern

*The Neurobehavioral and Social-Emotional Development
of Infants and Children*
Ed Tronick

*The Haunted Self: Structural Dissociation and the Treatment
of Chronic Traumatization*
Onno Van Der Hart, Ellert R. S. Nijenhuis, Kathy Steele

*Prenatal Development and Parents' Lived Experiences:
How Early Events Shape Our Psychophysiology and Relationships*
Ann Diamond Weinstein

Changing Minds in Therapy: Emotion, Attachment, Trauma, and Neurobiology
Margaret Wilkinson

For all the latest books in the series, book details (including sample chapters), and to order online, please visit the Series webpage at wwnorton.com/Psych/IPNB Series